Communications in Computer and Information Science 1098

Commenced Publication in 2007
Founding and Former Series Editors:
Phoebe Chen, Alfredo Cuzzocrea, Xiaoyong Du, Orhun Kara, Ting Liu,
Krishna M. Sivalingam, Dominik Ślęzak, Takashi Washio, Xiaokang Yang,
and Junsong Yuan

More information about this series at http://www.springer.com/series/7899

Auhood Alfaries · Hanan Mengash ·
Ansar Yasar · Elhadi Shakshuki (Eds.)

Advances in Data Science, Cyber Security and IT Applications

First International Conference on Computing, ICC 2019
Riyadh, Saudi Arabia, December 10–12, 2019
Proceedings, Part II

 Springer

Editors
Auhood Alfaries
Princess Nourah Bint Abdul
Rahman University
Riyadh, Saudi Arabia

Ansar Yasar (iD)
Hasselt University
Hasselt, Belgium

Hanan Mengash
Princess Nourah Bint Abdul
Rahman University
Riyadh, Saudi Arabia

Elhadi Shakshuki
Acadia University
Wolfville, NS, Canada

ISSN 1865-0929   ISSN 1865-0937 (electronic)
Communications in Computer and Information Science
ISBN 978-3-030-36367-3   ISBN 978-3-030-36368-0 (eBook)
https://doi.org/10.1007/978-3-030-36368-0

This Springer imprint is published by the registered company Springer Nature Switzerland AG
The registered company address is: Gewerbestrasse 11, 6330 Cham, Switzerland

Preface

A very warm welcome to the proceedings of ICC 2019. In light of the Saudi Arabia vision 2030, Princess Nourah Bint Abdulrahman University (PNU) held the International Conference on Computing on-campus, during December 10–12, 2019, in Riyadh, Saudi Arabia. At our conference, we brought executives, professionals, educators, researchers, and practitioners from across the world to one hub. In this hub, we spoke of tomorrow's challenges, suggested solutions, shared trading ideas, and analyzed and discussed current developments in information technology within data science, cybersecurity, network and IoT, as well as information technology and its applications.

ICC 2019 had five keynote speakers from all corners of the world and four technical tracks dealing with the aspects of data science, cybersecurity, networks and IoT, information technology and its applications. All submitted papers underwent a rigorous peer-review process by a Technical Program Committee (TPC) consisting of an international group of interdisciplinary scientists and engineers. The accepted papers were then revised according to the referees' comments for camera-ready submission to the conference. These papers covered a broad range of topics within the field of: big data and analytics, bioinformatics, distributed systems, AI, network security, access control, ubiquitous computing, IoT networks, software engineering, and computer-aided design. ICC 2019 received 174 paper submissions. Each paper received a minimum of 3 reviews, and we accepted 53 papers (an acceptance rate of 38%).

One of the goals of ICC 2019 was to foster collaboration among the scientists and the practitioners developing the concepts to solve various real-world problems. It was our wish and hope that the people participating in the conference would find common ground on which they could learn from each other, and that the conference would engender future fruitful scientific activities. Such collaborative endeavours are necessary for the development of the cutting-edge solutions embodied within our society and its fabrics.

We wish to thank the general chairs, the local arrangements chairs, the publicity chairs, the TPC and reviewers, the participants, and, most importantly, the researchers who submitted the articles to make this event a success. Furthermore, we would like to extend our gratitude to PNU who supported the organization of this conference at every stage.

November 2019

Auhood Alfaries
Hanan Mengash
Ansar Yasar
Elhadi Shakshuki

Organization

General Chairs

Auhood Abd. Al Faries   Princess Nourah Bint Abdulrahman University,
Saudi Arabia

Hanan Almengash   Princess Nourah Bint Abdulrahman University,
Saudi Arabia

Ansar Yasar   Hasselt University, Belgium

Hend Al-Khalifa   King Saud University, Saudi Arabia

Local Arrangements Chairs

Dua Nassar   Princess Nourah Bint Abdulrahman University,
Saudi Arabia

Evon Abu-Taieh   Jordan University, Jordan

Ghadah Aldehim   Princess Nourah Bint Abdulrahman University,
Saudi Arabia

Hanan Aljuaid   Princess Nourah Bint Abdulrahman University,
Saudi Arabia

Hanen Karamti   Princess Nourah Bint Abdulrahman University,
Saudi Arabia

Heba A. Kurdi   King Saud University, Saudi Arabia

Hessah Aleisa   Princess Nourah Bint Abdulrahman University,
Saudi Arabia

Mada Alaskar   Princess Nourah Bint Abdulrahman University,
Saudi Arabia

Manel Ayadi   Princess Nourah Bint Abdulrahman University,
Saudi Arabia

Myriam Hadjouni   Princess Nourah Bint Abdulrahman University,
Saudi Arabia

Samiah Chelloug   Princess Nourah Bint Abdulrahman University,
Saudi Arabi

Steering Committee

Hadil Ahmed Shaiba   Princess Nourah Bint Abdulrahman University,
Saudi Arabia

Heba A. Kurdi   King Saud University, Saudi Arabia

Mai Alduailij   Princess Nourah Bint Abdulrahman University,
Saudi Arabia

| Maali Alabdulhafith | Princess Nourah Bint Abdulrahman University, Saudi Arabia |
| Shiroq Al-Megren | Massachusetts Institute of Technology (MIT), USA |

Technical Program Committee Members

Safia Abbas	Ain Shames University, Egypt
Nagwan Abdulsamie	Princess Nourah Bint Abdulrahman University, Saudi Arabia
Mohammad Syuhaimi Abrahman	The National University of Malaysia, Malaysia
Maysoon Abulkhair	King Abdulaziz University, Saudi Arabia
Hanan Adlan	Princess Nourah Bint Abdulrahman University, Saudi Arabia
Shaimaa Ahmad	Princess Nourah Bint Abdulrahman University, Saudi Arabia
Muna Ahmed	Princess Nourah Bint Abdulrahman University, Saudi Arabia
Issam Al Hadid	The University of Jordan, Jordan
Hassanin Al-Barhamtoshy	King Abdulaziz University, Saudi Arabia
Fahad Al-Zahrani	UQU, Saudi Arabia
Heyam Albaity	King Saud University, Saudi Arabia
Lamia Albraheem	King Saud University, Saudi Arabia
Hend Alkhalifa	King Saud University, Saudi Arabia
Abdulhadi Alqarni	Jubail University College, Saudi Arabia
Elsayed Alrabie	Menoufia University, Egypt
Nazek Alturki	Princess Nourah Bint Abdulrahman University, Saudi Arabia
Sarra Ali. Ayouni	Princess Nourah Bint Abdulrahman University, Saudi Arabia
Romana Aziz	Princess Nourah Bint Abdulrahman University, Saudi Arabia
Ammar Belatreche	Northumbria University, UK
Jawad Berri	Sonatrach - Algerian Petroleum and Gas Corporation, Saudi Arabia
Dalila Boughaci	INCA/LSIS, LRIA/USTHB, Algeria
Omar Boussaid	ERIC Laboratory, France
Hsing-Lung Chen	National Taiwan University of Science and Technology, Taiwan
Salim Chikhi	MISC laboratory, University of Constantine 2, Algeria
Amer Draa	Mentouri University, Algeria
Ridha Ejbali	National School of Engineers (ENIG), Tunisia
Tamer El-Batt	Nile University, Egypt
Ali El-Zaart	Beirut Arab University, Lebanon
Dalia Elkamchouchi	Princess Nourah Bint Abdulrahman University, Saudi Arabia

Nazik Turki	Princess Nourah Bint Abdulrahman University, Saudi Arabia
Brent Wilson	George Fox University, USA
Ansar Yasar	Universiteit Hasselt - IMOB, Belgium
Ali Zolait	University of Bahrain, Bahrain

Contents – Part II

Information Technology and Applications

EMD for Technical Analysis 3
  Jürgen Abel

Enhancement of the Segmentation Framework for Rotated Iris Images...... 16
  Fati Oiza Salami and Mohd Shafry Mohd Rahim

Domain and Schema Independent Ontology Verbalizing 30
  Kaneeka Vidanagea, Noor Maizura Mohamad Noora,
  Rosmayati Mohemada, and Zuriana Abu Bakara

The Effect of User Experience on the Quality of User Interface Design
in Healthcare 40
  Hanaa Alzahrani and Reem Alnanih

Saudi Arabia Market Basket Analysis 52
  Monerah Alawadh, Israa Al-turaiki, Mohammed Alawadh,
  and Shahad Tallab

Determining the Best Prediction Accuracy of Software Maintainability
Models Using Auto-WEKA 60
  Hadeel Alsolai and Marc Roper

Shark Smell Optimization (SSO) Algorithm for Cloud Jobs Scheduling 71
  Yusra Mohamed Suliman, Adil Yousif, and Mohammed Bakri Bashir

A Visual Decision Making Support System for the Diabetes Prevention..... 81
  Fatima Zohra Benhacine, Baghdad Atmani, Mohamed Benamina,
  and Sofia Benbelkacem

Sensor-Based Business Process Model for Appliance Repair............ 93
  Mayada Elsaid, Ayah Alhamdan, and Sara Altuwaijri

A Multi-labels Text Categorization Framework for Cerebral
Lesion's Identification 103
  Hichem Benfriha, Baghdad Atmani, Belarbi Khemliche,
  Nabil Tabet Aoul, and Ali Douah

Fuzzy Adaptation of Surveillance Plans of Patients with Diabetes 115
  Mohamed Benamina, Baghdad Atmani, Sofia Benbelkacem,
  and Abdelhak Mansoul

Arabic Real-Time License Plate Recognition System   126
  Shaimaa Ahmed Elsaid, Haifa Alharthi, Reem Alrubaia, Sarah Abutile,
  Rawan Aljres, Amal Alanazi, and Alanoud Albrikan

Exploring Barriers Mobile Payments Adoption: A Case Study
of Majmaah University in Saudi Arabia   144
  Rana Alabdan

A Method for 3D-Metric Reconstruction Using Zoom Cameras   161
  Boubakeur Boufama, Tarik Elamsy, and Mohamed Batouche

Bellman-Ford Algorithm Under Trapezoidal Interval Valued
Neutrosophic Environment   174
  Said Broumi, Deivanayagampillai Nagarajan,
  Malayalan Lathamaheswari, Mohamed Talea, Assia Bakali,
  and Florentin Smarandache

Design and Implementation of Secured E-Business Structure
with LTL Patterns for User Behavior Prediction   185
  Ayman Mohamed Mostafa

Association Rules for Detecting Lost of View in the Expanded
Program on Immunization   201
  Fawzia Zohra Abdelouhab, Baghdad Atmani,
  and Fatima Zohra Benhacine

Hybrid Model Architectures for Enhancing Data Classification
Performance in E-commerce Applications   214
  Ayman Mohamed Mostafa, Mohamed Maher, and M. M. Hassan

Performance Dashboards for Project Management   228
  Samiha Brahimi, Aseel Aljulaud, Anwar Alsaiah, Norah AlGuraibi,
  Mariam Alrubei, and Haneen Aljamaan

Neural Iris Signature Recognition (NISR).   241
  Ali Mehdi, Safaa Ahmad, Rawand Abu Roza, Mohammed Alawairdhi,
  and Mousa Al-Akhras

Healthcare Information System Assessment Case Study
Riyadh's Hospitals-KSA   252
  Muna Elsadig, Dua' A. Nassar, and Leila Jamel Menzli

Network and IoT

OpenCache: Distributed SDN/NFV Based in-Network Caching
as a Service   265
  Shiyam Alalmaei, Matthew Broadbent, Nicholas Race,
  and Samia Chelloug

Comparative Study of the Internet of Things Recommender System   278
Halima Bouazza, Laallam Fatima Zohra, and Bachir Said

High DC-Gain Two-Stage OTA Using Positive Feedback
and Split-Length Transistor Techniques   286
*Jamel Nebhen, Mohamed Masmoudi, Wenceslas Rahajandraibe,
and Khalifa Aguir*

Automated Detection for Student Cheating During Written Exams:
An Updated Algorithm Supported by Biometric of Intent.   303
*Fatimah A. Alrubaish, Ghadah A. Humaid, Rasha M. Alamri,
and Mariam A. Elhussain*

Integration of Internet of Things and Social Network: Social IoT
General Review   312
Halima Bouazza, Laallam Fatima Zohra, and Bachir Said

Enhanced Priority-Based Routing Protocol (EPRP)
for Inter-vehicular Communication   325
Amaliya Princy Mohan and Maher Elshakankiri

Author Index   339

Contents – Part I

Cyber Security

A Comparative Study of Three Blockchain Emerging Technologies:
Bitcoin, Ethereum and Hyperledger 3
   Dalila Boughaci and Omar Boughaci

Comparison of Supervised and Unsupervised Fraud Detection 8
   Ashay Walke

Cybersecurity: Design and Implementation of an Intrusion Detection
and Prevention System. 15
   Shaimaa Ahmed Elsaid, Samerah Maeeny, Azhar Alenazi,
   Tahani Alenazi, Wafa Alzaid, Ghada Algahtani, and Amjad Aldossari

Detailed Quantum Cryptographic Service and Data Security
in Cloud Computing 43
   Omer K. Jasim Mohammad and Safia Abbas

The Effects of the Property of Access Possibilities and Cybersecurity
Awareness on Social Media Application 57
   Bedour F. Alrashidi, Aljawharah M. Almuhana,
   and Alanoud M. Aljedaie

A Blockchain Review: A Comparative Study Between Public Key
Infrastructure and Identity Based Encryption. 69
   Lujain Alharbi and Dania Aljeaid

Data Science

ɛrbeng:- Android Live Voice and Text Chat Translator 85
   Abanoub Nasser, Ibram Makram,
   and Rania Ahmed Abdel Azeem Abul Seoud

Improving Accuracy of Imbalanced Clinical Data Classification Using
Synthetic Minority Over-Sampling Technique. 99
   Fatihah Mohd, Masita Abdul Jalil, Noor Maizura Mohamad Noora,
   Suryani Ismail, Wan Fatin Fatihah Yahya, and Mumtazimah Mohamad

Learning Case-Based Reasoning Solutions by Association
Rules Approach 111
   Abdelhak Mansoul, Baghdad Atmani, Mohamed Benamina,
   and Sofia Benbelkacem

Stochastic Local Search Based Feature Selection Combined
with K-means for Clients' Segmentation in Credit Scoring   119
  Dalila Boughaci and Abdullah A. K. Alkhawaldeh

Real Time Search Technique for Distributed Massive Data Using
Grid Computing   132
  Mohammed Bakri Bashir, Adil Yousif, and Muhammad Shafie Abd Latiff

Analytical Experiments on the Utilization of Data Visualizations.   148
  Sara M. Shaheen, Sawsan Alhalawani, Nuha Alnabet,
  and Dana Alhenaki

A Tweet-Ranking System Using Sentiment Scores
and Popularity Measures   162
  Sumaya Aleidi, Dalia Alsuhaibani, Nora Alrajebah, and Heba Kurdi

Event-Based Driving Style Analysis   170
  Zubaydh Kenkar and Sawsan AlHalawani

Swarm Intelligence and ICA for Blind Source Separation.   183
  Monia Hamdi, Hela ElMannai, and Abeer AlGarni

Shiny Framework Based Visualization and Analytics Tool
for Middle East Respiratory Syndrome   193
  Maya John and Hadil Shaiba

Ensemble Learning Sentiment Classification for Un-labeled Arabic Text   203
  Amal Alkabkabi and Mounira Taileb

Predicting No-show Medical Appointments Using Machine Learning   211
  Sara Alshaya, Andrew McCarren, and Amal Al-Rasheed

Cancer Incidence Prediction Using a Hybrid Model of Wavelet Transform
and LSTM Networks.   224
  Amani Alrobai and Musfira Jilani

Enhanced Support Vector Machine Applied to Land-Use Classification   236
  Hela ElMannai, Monia Hamdi, and Abeer AlGarni

Predicting Students' Academic Performance and Main Behavioral
Features Using Data Mining Techniques   245
  Suad Almutairi, Hadil Shaiba, and Marija Bezbradica

Crime Types Prediction   260
  Hanan AL Mansour and Michele Lundy

Intensive Survey About Road Traffic Signs Preprocessing, Detection
and Recognition   275
  Mrouj Almuhajri and Ching Suen

Machine Learning for Automobile Driver Identification Using
Telematics Data   290
    Hanadi Alhamdan and Musfira Jilani

Employee Turnover Prediction Using Machine Learning   301
    Lama Alaskar, Martin Crane, and Mai Alduailij

Predicting Saudi Stock Market Index by Incorporating GDELT Using
Multivariate Time Series Modelling.   317
    Rawan Alamro, Andrew McCarren, and Amal Al-Rasheed

Author Index   329

Information Technology and Applications

EMD for Technical Analysis

Jürgen Abel[(✉)]

Ingenieurbüro Dr. Abel GmbH, Lechstrasse 1, 41469 Neuss, Germany
juergen@mve.info

Abstract. The decomposing of stock market prices into a set of sub waves with different frequencies by the discrete Fourier transform provides unstable and unsatisfying results. The Empirical Mode Decomposition (EMD) is a decomposing algorithm which uses sub waves with amplitude modulation and frequency modulation, leading to better adapted analyze results. As a non causal algorithm the EMD bears challenges for the technical analysis. Nevertheless, the EMD provides valuable information about market data. This paper presents the EMD algorithm and its features within the context of technical analysis.

Keywords: EMD · Technical analysis · Spectral analysis · Price sequence

1 Introduction

Stock market prices are time discrete signals which are nonlinear and non stationary. One of the most important models in technical analysis is the wave model of the market [1]. The wave model assumes that the final market price is the sum of several sub oscillating waves and a final trend component, which is not oscillating. The sub waves are also price sequences which oscillate with different period lengths. This model can be exactly calculated by using digital signal processing techniques [1, 2].

The decomposing of the price sequence into a set of sub waves with different frequencies by the discrete Fourier transform, which is the most common spectral analysis transform, e.g. by the Goertzel algorithm [3], provides only unsatisfying results. The main problem is that the discrete Fourier transform uses sine waves with constant frequencies, which are not optimal in modeling the price waves of the market, as the frequencies of the sub waves are not constant but change permanently, leading to harmonic waves which disappear within less than a period in the output of the Fourier transform. Furthermore, the Fourier transform assumes that the input signal is linear and stationary [4], but stock price sequences are neither linear nor stationary. The Empirical mode decomposition (EMD) is an algorithm which operates on the local time scale of the data and can handle nonlinear and non stationary data [5]. Their components consist of oscillating waves with slightly changing frequencies and changing amplitudes, which are more applicative in modeling the price waves. Unfortunately, the EMD is a non causal algorithm, which causes problems when used for technical analysis. Subsequently the algorithm of the EMD is explained, afterwards the properties, advantages and disadvantages of the EMD within the context of technical analysis are unveiled.

© Springer Nature Switzerland AG 2019
A. Alfaries et al. (Eds.): ICC 2019, CCIS 1098, pp. 3–15, 2019.
https://doi.org/10.1007/978-3-030-36368-0_1

2 The EMD Algorithm

The empirical mode decomposition (EMD) is an algorithm, which dissects a price sequence $x(t)$ into a number of sub waves plus a final residuum between the start of the price sequence t_s and the end of the price sequence at t_e. The sub waves are called Intrinsic Mode Functions (*IMF*), which have slightly changing frequencies and changing amplitudes. The final residuum *FR* is non oscillating.

Therefore, the price sequence $x(t)$ can be constructed by the sum of the IMF_i plus *FR*:

$$x(t) = \sum_{i=0}^{n-1} IMF_i(t) + FR \qquad (1)$$

The EMD algorithm is described in detail in several publications [5–9], therefore here a brief description from a programmer's perspective is given. The algorithm works top/down, and has an outer and an inner loop. It starts the outer loop with the input signal as the starting signal. From this signal the first *IMF*, called IMF_0, is calculated. Then the algorithm continues with the difference of the former signal minus IMF_0 as the new signal. This outer loop is continued until the difference is not oscillating any more, i.e. the number of maxima or the number of minima is smaller than 2.

The inner loop calculates the *IMF*, which is called sifting process. The sifting process calculates the local maxima and the local minima of the signal. Next, a cubic spline which uses the local maxima as its knots is calculated and used as the upper part of an envelope. Then a cubic spline which uses the local minima as its knots is calculated and used as the lower part of the envelope. The middle of the envelope is defined as the mean signal. The boundary conditions at the beginning of the price sequence t_s and at the end of the price sequence t_e need a special treatment. At the border the cubic spline is not restricted by any more knots so it tends to raise or decrease quite strongly. In order to achieve a better alignment, the last two knots at each border of the spline are mirrored behind the border. This way, the route of the spline shows a more realistic behavior. Finally the difference between the signal and the mean is used as the new signal and the inner loop is repeated until the number of maxima plus the number of minima is smaller or equal than the number of zero crossings of the signal. This condition ensures that between two zero crossings are only one maximum or one minimum respectively, which is important as the *IMF* should be an orthogonal signal [5]. The second condition of the inner loop requests that the average mean of the signal is zero, i.e. the signal has no non zero trend part left, which is also important for an orthogonal signal [5]. Figure 1 lists the simplified algorithm as a structured program. Note that the variables Input_Signal, Signal, Mean, Local_Maxima etc. are series, i.e. arrays of numbers and not single numbers. Figure 2 displays the first mean (red line) together with the envelopes (blue lines) and the original price sequence $x(t)$ (black line). Figure 2 until 7 are all calculated for the same time interval on the x-axis on a daily price frame. In Fig. 3 IMF_0 is drawn as a green line. Note that this IMF has a short period as it is the first IMF. IMF_1 (red), IMF_2 (green) and IMF_3 (blue) are shown in Fig. 4. The higher $IMFs$ have longer periods and get smoother than lower $IMFs$. For all $IMFs$ the amplitude is not constant (amplitude modulation) and the period length is changing slightly (frequency

```
{ Initializing }
Signal := Input_Signal;

{ Calculate until final residuum is reached }
I := 0;
While (Signal is oscillating) do
 Begin { While }
  { Save old signal }
  Temp_Signal := Signal;

  { Sifting loop }
  While (Signal is oscillating) and
  (Number_of_Maxima (Signal) + Number_of_Maxima (Signal) >
  Number_of_Zero_Crossings (Signal) + 1) and
  (Sum (Signal) > Threshold) do
   Begin { While }
    Local_Maxima := Calculate_Local_Maxima (Signal);
    Local_Minima := Calculate_Local_Minima (Signal);

    Maxima_Signal := Calculate_Cubic_Splines (Local_Maxima);
    Minima_Signal := Calculate_Cubic_Splines (Local_Minima);

    Mean := (Maxima_Signal - Minima_Signal) / 2;

    Signal := Signal - Mean;
   End; { While }

  { Save IMF }
  IMF (I) := Signal;

  Signal := Temp_Signal - Signal;
  I := I + 1;
 End; { While }

{ Save FR }
FR := Signal;
```

Fig. 1. EMD algorithm

modulation). In Fig. 5 *mean₁* (red), *mean₂* (green) and *mean₃* (blue) are displayed. All means render the peak in May 2015 very well, which is an effect of the approximation process, by taking all prices into account, and not only prices before May 2015.

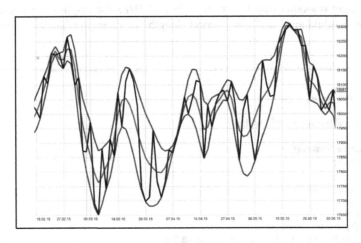

Fig. 2. First mean with envelope based on DOW-JONES (signal: black, envelope: blue, mean: red) (Color figure online)

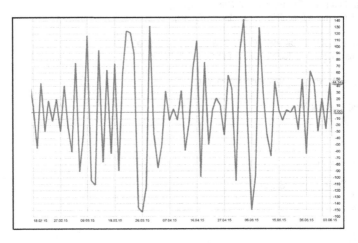

Fig. 3. *IMF₀* based on DOW-JONES (Color figure online)

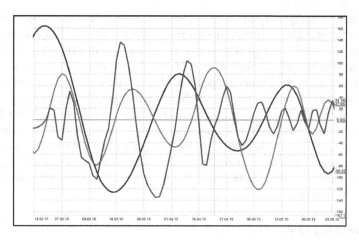

Fig. 4. *IMF₁* (red), *IMF₂* (green) and *IMF₃* (blue) based on DOW-JONES between 18.02.2015 and 03.06.2015 (Color figure online)

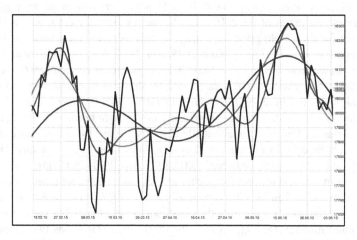

Fig. 5. *Mean₁* (red), *Mean₂* (green) and *Mean₃* (blue) based on DOW-JONES between 18.02.2015 and 03.06.2015 (Color figure online)

3 Properties of EMD in the Context of Technical Analysis

3.1 Computational Complexity

Most indicators of the technical analysis [10] have a computational time complexity of $O(n)$, with n equal to the number of values of the price sequence; examples are:

- standard (arithmetic) moving average,
- the exponential moving average,
- low, high and band-pass filters,
- MACD (Moving Average Convergence/Diverg.).

Some have a complexity of $O(n * m)$ with m equals the span of an interval for example for the standard deviation like Bollinger Bands [10]. The EMD algorithm has a complexity of $O(n^2 * p * q)$ with p equals the number of *IMFs* (outer loop) and q equals the number of iterations of the sifting process (inner loop). The quadratic factor n^2 is a result of the spline interpolation [11]. This complexity has consequences for the trading, as depending on the number of prices inside the price sequence the calculation of the EMD might need several seconds to be calculated. If the EMD is used for real time trading, where several price signals can occur within a second, the system might hang as the calculation for one new price tick need to calculate all *IMFs* again and this might take longer than the left over time until the next price tick arrives. If the EMD is used for longer time frames like days or weeks, the time for calculation is usually not a problem.

3.2   Consistency of Results

The basis of the EMD is an approximation procedure. Since all prices of the sequence are taken into account for the approximation and since the mirrored prices at the right boundary, which is moving one point to the right with every new price, are replaced by the new prices, the graph of the *IMFs* can change not only for the points at the right boundary but for the whole price sequence. Figure 6 presents the change of *IMF₃* for three consecutive prices between 20.05.2018 and 22.05.2015. At Fig. 6(a) the price sequence is drawn from February to May 2015. Figure 6(b) contains *IMF₃* calculated on 20.05.2015. The graph of *IMF₃* calculated on the next day is shown in Fig. 6(c). There is only a small difference in the shape of *IMF₃*. One day later, on 21.05.2015 in Fig. 6(d), the graph of *IMF₃* changes noticeably on the right border. Note that not only the values of the last few days but about all values for the last two month have changed. Figure 7(a)–(d) reveals an even more drastic example for *IMF₂* and *IMF₃* between 28.04.2015 and 30.04.2015. Between 28.04.2015 and 29.04.2015 *IMF₃* changes its values for about one month and *IMF₂* changes its values for about two months. The next day on 30.04.2015 in Fig. 7(d) about all values of *IMF₂* and *IMF₃* have changed for the last four months. But not only the amplitudes have changed but also the number of maxima and minima. On Fig. 7(c) for the 29.04.2015, *IMF₃* has two maxima and one minima. One day later on Fig. 7(d), *IMF₃* has three maxima and two minima, which means that the frequency of *IMF₃* has changed. If entry and exit signals are calculated based on the graph of *IMF₂* and *IMF₃*, this signals would have changed vigorously too. Therefore, the consistency of *IMFs* signals calculated between two consecutive points of time is not ensured, the graph of the *IMFs* can be much different calculated on two consecutive points of time.

3.3   Frequencies

Table 1 shows the period length, the reciprocal value of the frequency, for different *IMFs* and for different price series. In technical analysis the period length is more widely used than the frequency value. The second column displays the period lengths for the Dow Jones Industrial Average (DOW-JONES) for daily time frames between 01.01.2014 and 31.12.2017. The next column contains the period values for the German DAX between 2014 and 2017 in daily time frames. The fourth column implicates the period length for the DOW-JONES between 2014 and 2017 for hourly time frames and the last column includes the results for the hourly time frames of the DAX between 2014 and 2017. Even though the price sequence of the DOW-JONES and the DAX are quite different between 2014 and 2017, the period lengths of the *IMFs* for the daily time frames as well as the period length of the hourly time frames are quite similar. The quotient IMF_i/IMF_{i-1} between two consecutive *IMFs* is between 1.9 and 2.5. For daily time frames the quotients are a little bit larger on average than for the hourly time frames.

3.4   Number of *IMFs*

Since the quotient between two consecutive *IMFs* is on average around 2.3 and since the first period length starts with 3, the number of *IMFs* for each price sequence depends mainly on the size of the sequence, i.e. on the number of prices. The daily time frames from 2014 to 2017 contain about 1,000 prices, which makes for 6 *IMFs*, whereas the hourly time frames from 2014 to 2017 include about 17,000 prices and this causes 8 *IMFs*. If the interval size would have been expanded or the time frame reduced, both leading to more prices, more *IMFs* will emerge. On the other side, for a reduced interval or a larger time frame, meaning less prices, the number of *IMFs* will decline.

3.5   Amplitudes

The daily DOW-JONES price sequence for 2017 is depicted in Fig. 8. Figure 9 portrays the amplitudes of IMF_1 (red), IMF_2 (green) and IMF_3 (blue) for the daily DOW-JONES in 2017. The image is similar to Fig. 4 but for a larger time interval. Again, the amplitudes for each *IMF* are not constant but change from period to period. On average IMF_3 has a larger amplitude than IMF_2, which has a larger amplitude than IMF_1. Table 2 reveals the average amplitudes for the DOW-JONES and the DAX between 01.01.2014 and 31.12.2017 for daily and hourly time frames. Similar to the Dow Theory, were the slower waves are the main waves (main movement), which have larger amplitudes than the faster waves (medium and short swing) [12], each IMF_i has a larger amplitude than its predecessor IMF_{i-1} for both markets and for both time frames.

Again the similarity of the average amplitude sizes between DOW-JONES and DAX for the daily time frame as well as for the hourly time frame is striking. For the daily DOW-JONES two *IMFs* are eminent, since the amplitude for this *IMF* and the amplitude of its smaller predecessor have a greater quotient than on average: IMF_2 and IMF_4. For the daily DAX the major *IMFs* are IMF_2 and IMF_5. For the hourly DOW-JONES the major *IMF* changes to IMF_7 and for the hourly DAX the major *IMFs* are IMF_4 and IMF_6.

Table 1. Average period lengths of the *IMFs* for the DOW-JONES and DAX from 2014 until 2017 for daily and for hourly time frames

IMF	DOW JONES daily	DAX daily	DOW JONES hourly	DAX hourly
0	3	3	3	3
1	7	7	6	6
2	16	15	11	11
3	33	35	21	21
4	83	89	39	42
5	208	186	74	97
6	–	–	163	215
7	–	–	320	478

Table 2. Average amplitudes of the *IMFs* for the DOW-JONES and DAX from 2014 until 2017 for daily and for hourly time frames

IMF	DOW JONES daily	DAX daily	DOW JONES hourly	DAX hourly
0	119	114	24	24
1	129	138	28	28
2	238	230	39	37
3	278	339	52	51
4	634	437	72	83
5	755	764	103	124
6	–	–	148	203
7	–	–	225	263

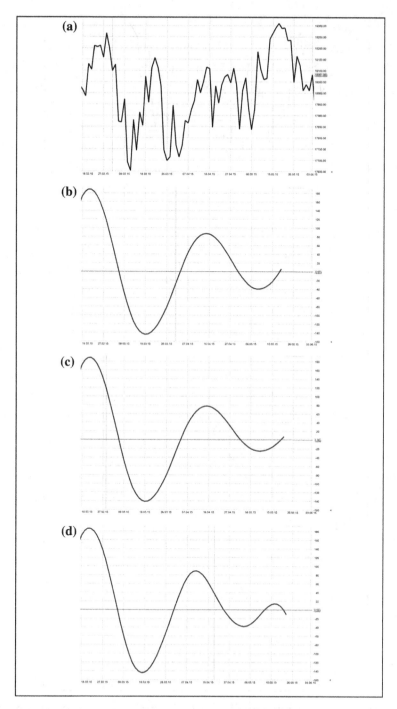

Fig. 6 (a) Price sequence DOW-JONES. (b) *IMF₃* between 18.02.2015 and 20.05.2015. (c) *IMF₃* between 18.02.2015 and 21.05.2015. (d) *IMF₃* between 18.02.2015 and 22.05.2015

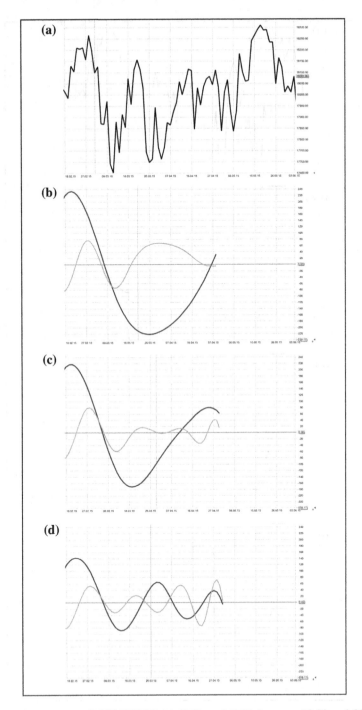

Fig. 7 (a) Price sequence DOW-JONES. (b) *IMF₂* and *IMF₃* between 18.02 and 28.04.2015. (c) *IMF₂* and *IMF₃* between 18.02 and 29.04.2015. (d) *IMF₂* and *IMF₃* between 18.02 and 30.04.2015

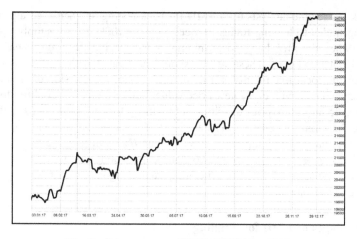

Fig. 8. Price sequence DOW-JONES for 2017

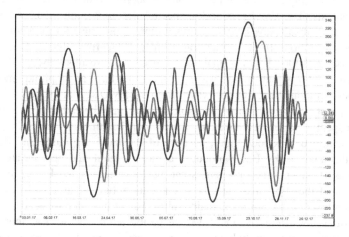

Fig. 9. IMF_1 (red), IMF_2 (green) and IMF_3 (blue) based on DOW-JONES in 2017 (Color figure online)

4 Using EMD for Trading

4.1 Disadvantages of EMD for Trading

As already mentioned above, the *IMF* signals can change considerably between two consecutive points of time. The value of IMF_i at time t_0 with $t_s < t_0 < t_e$ not only depends on $x(t)$ for all $t <= t_0$ but also on $x(t)$ with $t > t_0$. Therefore the EMD indicator is not a causal indicator. A non causal indicator causes problems when used for real time trading, as trading signals based on the indicator in the past tends to jump from one place to another place in the past calculated on two consecutive points of time. Therefore a non causal indicator can not be used for back tests as it disturbs the results of the back test. Some analysts used EMD for back-testing and achieved a percentage for winning trades to loosing trades between 90% to 100% [6] by simply opening a long trade when the *IMF* has a local minimum and closing the trade when the *IMF* reaches a local maximum. These results should be treated with caution as the final positions of the local maximums and minimum are not fixed inside the sequence of prices but can change with every new price value. Furthermore, it is doubtful to use the IMF_s for predicting future price development by using forward projections of the IMF_s as damped harmonic oscillations [7] as the IMF_s values on the end of the price sequence at t_e change and jump much stronger than *IMF* values in the middle or at the beginning of the sequence between two consecutive points of time. Therefore, the EMD should be used with care for generating trading signals, back tests or predicting future price development.

4.2   Advantages of EMD for Trading

Despite the fact that the EMD has many disadvantages for real time trading mainly because of the missing causality, it offers some properties which are very useful for the technical analysis. The EMD produces a spectral decomposition of the market price sequence into set of sub waves, which is much more appropriate for market prices than spectral decompositions from Fourier transform [4], Goertzel algorithm [3], MESA [13] or Autocorrelation [14]. The main difference of the results between these algorithms and the EMD is that the sub waves of the EMD have an amplitude modulation and a frequency modulation. The sub waves from the EMD start at the beginning of the price sequence at t_s and go through the whole interval until the end at t_e. The sub waves of the other spectral algorithms have only a very short length, many times the sub wave disappears within one period length, because of the fixed amplitude and frequency. Therefore the analysis by EMD produces a more natural and appropriate way for market prices. Two important properties can be harvested by the EMD: the average period length of the sub waves and the average amplitude of these sub waves. This information allows to determine the major sub waves of the price sequence. These sub waves are quite consistent and their average period lengths as well as their average amplitudes change only slightly between two consecutive points of time. For real time trading, band-pass filters with the period length of the major sub waves, calculated by the EMD, can be used in order to get consistent and causal trading signals.

5   Conclusion

The empirical mode decomposition (EMD) dismantles the stock market price into a set of intrinsic mode functions (*IMF*), each of which having an amplitude modulation and a frequency modulation. As a non causal indicator the EMD need to be used with caution if used for generating trading signals, back tests or predicting future prices. The main advantage of the EMD in the context of technical analysis is the calculation of the period length and the amplitudes of the major sub waves, which can not be achieved by the standard spectral algorithms using fixed frequencies and amplitudes. These properties promotes the EMD to a valuable and exceptional tool in the technical analysis.

References

1. Hurst, J.M.: The Profit Magic of Stock Transaction Timing. Prentice Hall Inc., Englewood Cliffs (1970)
2. Ehlers, J.F.: Rocket Science for Traders: Digital Signal Processing Applications. Wiley, New York (2001)
3. Engelberg, S.: Digital Signal Processing. Springer, London (2008)
4. Bracewell, R.: The Fourier Transform and Its Applications. McGraw-Hill, New York (1999)
5. Huang, N.E., et al.: The empirical mode decomposition and the hilbert spectrum for nonlinear and non-stationary time series analysis. Proc. R. Soc. Lond. Ser. A **454**, 903–995 (1998)
6. Dürschner, M.G.: Technische Analyse mit EMD: Die Anwendung der EMD auf Indizes, Rohstoffe, Währungen und Aktien. Wiley, Weinheim (2013)
7. Reiß, O.: Kursverlaufsprojektion auf Basis der Empirical Mode Decomposition, VTAD (2017). https://www.vtad.de/node/11527
8. Chan, R.H.F., et al.: Empirical mode decomposition and technical analysis. In: Technical Analysis and Financial Asset Forecasting Book, chap. 9. World Scientific Press (2014). https://doi.org/10.1142/9789814436250_0009
9. Nava, N., et al.: Financial time series forecasting using empirical mode decomposition and support vector regression. Risks **6**, 7 (2018). https://doi.org/10.3390/risks6010007
10. Murphy, J.J.: Technical Analysis of the Financial Markets. Prentice Hall Press, Upper Saddle River (1986)
11. Toraichi, K., Katagishi, K., Sekita, I., Mori, R.: Computational complexity of spline interpolation. Int. J. Syst. Sci. **18**(5), 945–954 (1987)
12. Rhea, R.: The Dow Theory. Stock Investing Barrons, New York (1932)
13. Burg, J.P.: Maximum Entropy Spectral Analysis, Stanford University (1975)
14. Ehlers, J.F.: Cycle Analytics for Traders. Wiley, New York (2013)

Enhancement of the Segmentation Framework for Rotated Iris Images

Fati Oiza Salami[1]([⊠]) and Mohd Shafry Mohd Rahim[2]

[1] Department of Computer Science, Kogi State College of Education,
Ankpa, Nigeria
fati.salami@kscoeankpa.edu.ng
[2] Universiti Teknologi Malaysia, 81310 Skudai, Johor, Malaysia

Abstract. Iris segmentation method is an important process to extract the features of iris for biometric identification system. It contributes to improve the accuracy of the systems. Several researches have been done to increase the accuracy, however there are still several remaining issues which require enhancement of segmentation method. In this research, the focus is to improve accuracy of segmentation method for rotated iris image. The current accuracy rate for the segmentation is around 94% and it must be improved. The proposed method in segmentation process utilized the integration of an optimized Hough integration of the optimized Hough circle transform with the integrodifferential operator enabled search for the iris location over a wider radii, detecting and localizing the iris region of the eye image by employing one center coordinates of the iris and pupil. This approach is found more effective in improving the accuracy of iris segmentation in rotated iris image. Evaluation was carried out at the end of the study using UBIRIS v2.0 Database and the approach achieved an overall recognition accuracy of 97.6%. The result of the experimental evaluation showed that the accuracy of the iris identification increased as compared to existing techniques. The researchers therefore, recommend that enhanced segmentation framework for rotated iris images should be adopted by government agencies and organizations in ensuring secured passage of persons across borders and effective forensic outcomes.

Keywords: Iris recognition · Hough Circle Transform · Segmentation

1 Introduction

The ease in the development of iris recognition systems as a very reliable means of personal identification and recognition has largely being due to the iris being a very unique feature of human beings. The iris has globular and planar shape which invariable makes it easier for segmentation and parameterization, it possesses a prevalent indiscriminating chaotic façade that does not change throughout the lifetime of an individual.

The iris capturing process involves the acquisition of the iris image via some data capturing media. In capturing the image of an iris, it can be done by employing the use of a camera that has the capacity of using both infrared and visible light. The iris

A. Alfaries et al. (Eds.): ICC 2019, CCIS 1098, pp. 16–29, 2019.
https://doi.org/10.1007/978-3-030-36368-0_2

capturing can either be acquired manually or using an automated system. This manual process of capturing the iris image which is often also referred to as controlled iris acquisition process is highly demanding and there is need to properly familiarize users beforehand. On the other hand, the automatic iris image capturing process also referred to as the uncontrolled acquisition process uses a collection of camera to locate the face and identify the iris automatically thereby simplifying the whole process and making it to be user friendly [1].

Several initiatives and recent research interest now lay more emphasis in the area of recognition and identification in an uncontrolled environment where the subject's iris image is acquired without the subject's awareness or without the subject's control, this approach of iris image acquisition in an uncontrolled environment is referred to as non-cooperative iris image acquisition. The non-cooperative iris acquisition approach enables the system of iris recognition to be applied to several domains in which the subject may not give his cooperation in the iris image acquisition.

However, several defects can arise from non-cooperative iris images. Through visual inspection, fourteen different factors were detected and categorized as either global or local based on the level or extent to which the degradation affects the iris image. The local degradation is referred to the degradation that occurs when part of the image is affected while global degradations are degradations that affect the overall iris image. The local classification comprises obstructed iris, reflections, off-angle images and partially captured images, while the global class is made up of rotated, poor focused, motion-blurred, improper lighting and out-of-iris images [2]. The defects that can arise from non-cooperative iris images are numerous. Through visual inspection, fourteen different factors were detected and categorized as either global or local based on the level or extent to which the degradation affects the iris image. The local degradation is referred to the degradation that occurs when part of the image is affected while global degradations are degradations that affect the overall iris image. The local classification comprises obstructed iris, reflections, off-angle images and partially captured images, while the global class is made up of rotated, poor focused, motion-blurred, improper lighting and out-of-iris images [2].

Having a stout iris recognition by using images degraded by any of the afore-mentioned defects may sprout quite a number of difficulties like false iris detection, incomplete iris detection providing insufficient information for segmentation hence, resulting in poor and unreliable segmentation and localization of the iris which will negatively affect the overall accuracy the of the iris recognition system. Several approaches have been developed to improve the accuracy of iris recognition system by optimizing the segmentation phase of the recognition system in resulting degraded images from the non-cooperative targets. [3] in their work, deployed a conventional gaze angle estimation which can be used for angle correction therefore important in correcting off angle iris images by using projective transformation to obtain the angle of rotation before carrying out the conventional pre-processing of the iris image. [4] laid emphasis on proper and efficient segmentation in a robust technique that combines the use of Gaussian filter, Hough transformation and canny edge detection in order to derive a substantial and useful amount of data from a degraded iris. [5] implemented a novel system of iris recognition based on multi iris images by using shape feature and integral imaging to detect the angle or rotation of the iris by implementing the two center positions of both pupils as detected by CEDs.

[6] proposed scale invariant feature transform (SIFT) technique in a non-cooperative human iris recognition implementing active contour model to identify the innermost boundaries of the iris and pupil. [7] proposed an iris recognition algorithm in which a set of iris images of a given eye are fused together to give a single template by extracting the most consistent feature data from each of the templates to be fused. A robust algorithm based on the Random Sample Consensus (RANSAC) for accurate localisation of non-circular iris boundaries which is one of the problems encountered in iris images acquired in non-ideal imaging conditions was projected by [8]. [9] involved the use of image registration techniques to normalize the extracted iris region and carry out the iris template registration by means of phase correlation base method. [10] implemented a three staged approach which included the use of AdaBoost eye detection in order to make up for the iris detection error, a color segmentation technique for detecting obstruction and lastly the extraction of corneal specular reflection to accurately extract iris regions from a non-ideal image quality.

Current study reveals that issues still exists in achieving high accuracy of iris segmentation when in an uncontrolled environment, hence, the need for improvement in the framework to carry out accurate iris segmentation in an uncontrolled environment is required. In this study, a framework for the improvement of the accuracy of segmentation in rotated iris images will be considered using the optimized Hough Circle Transform integrated with Daugman Integrodifferential Operator to accurately detect and segment the inner and outer boundaries of the rotated image acquired from a non-cooperative subject, (i.e. not placed under constrained environment) and extract reasonable amount of reliable and usable iris data which can be employed in iris recognition system to make flawless decision.

2   Proposed Approach

Figure 1 illustrates a frame work of the proposed scheme. It includes image preprocessing, segmentation, normalization, feature extraction and template matching which are detailed below.

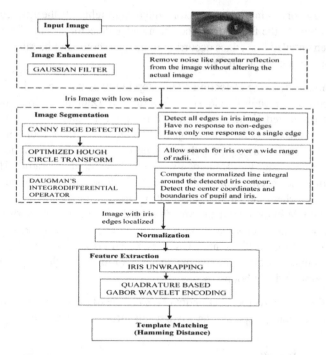

Fig. 1. Proposed enhancement of segmentation framework.

2.1   Image Enhancement

Image enhancement is the process of reducing unnecessary information in the image in order to increase the accuracy of the image data for further processing. Image enhancement is considered a necessary step in our procedure due to the non-ideal image environment in which our dataset images the UBIRIS v2.0 was acquired. All the images which were originally in RGB format were converted to grayscale images, this is a necessary step in order to be able to perform edge detection on the images.

The image enhancement was carried out using a 4×4 Gaussian kernel and a standard deviation (σ) of 3. The Gaussian low pass filter which is a non-uniform low pass filter was selected for the image enhancement due to its ability to remove small noises/details like specular reflections but does not alter the image itself.

2.2   Enhanced Iris Segmentation Process

Image segmentation describes the process of iris localization which constitutes the removal of unwanted information contained in the image and isolating the most useful portion of the iris from the eye image.

The segmentation process is explained in three stages below.

Edge Detection. The iris segmentation is the most important part of the overall pre-processing because a poorly segmented iris can lead to the generation of false or unreliable results. Therefore, the segmentation will begin with the binarization of the image by the use of Canny edge detector which highlights all the true edges in the image while subduing the false edges, the Canny edge detector was used due to its low error rate which entailed that edges occurring in images should not be missed and that it should have no responses to non-edges.

Outer and Inner Iris Edge Detection. This step involves the use of the combination of both an optimized Hough Circle Transform and the Daugman's Integrodifferential Operator. The optimized Hough circle transform is a technique which can be used to detect the boundaries of symmetrical objects like circles or lines found in an image. The research approach utilizes the hybrid of the optimized Hough Circle Transform function for circles and the Daugman's Integrodifferential operator. This hybrid approach enables the specification of the range of possible radii (i.e. the minimum and maximum radius) where the circular shape of the iris can be located regardless of the position of the circle in the eye image, in addition, the image output yields the original image overlapped with circles matching up with the edges of the outer and inner iris boundaries and the Integrodifferential Operator functions to calculate the normalized line integral around a circle, compute the center coordinates of the pupil and iris and calculate the pupil and iris boundary.

Iris Localization. The iris localization involves the use of the generated coordinates to efficiently and accurately separate the iris portion form the entire eye image.

2.3 Iris Normalization

Normalization refers to a standard used in defining the dimensions with which iris images are to be saved. In order to facilitate the matching process, the need arises to have a standard by which all the segmented irises are saved into the database and a standard that determines the size of iris templates to be made. It is necessary for all the templates to have the same matrix size in order to undertake template comparison. For this work, a standard iris model of 32 radial pixels versus 240 angular pixels was used as the standard size during the coding process for the normalization phase. This stage is necessary due to the fact that the images are captured under varying conditions like distance, angle etc. so the need arises to place the images on a uniform dimension.

2.4 Feature Extraction

Feature extraction is used to efficiently represent parts of interest in an image as well as acquire information from large sized images by reducing the feature representation to a compact dimension in order to carry out image matching, the feature extraction stage was split into two main processes viz;

Iris Unwrapping. In order for comparison to be possible, there arises the need to unwrap the localized circular iris unto a rectangular sheet of data as described by Daugman Rubber Sheet Model [11]. It is the translation of the circular shape of the normalized image to a rectangular image with fixed size radius that tallies with the length of the rectangular block.

Daugman's rubber sheet model uses polar unwrapping approach to map the iris after normalization. It assumes iris concentric circular boundaries with the column pixels corresponding to the radial pixel samples at each angle around the iris as shown in Fig. 2 below. The Daugman's rubber sheet model though an old technique, was adopted because it has the highest successful rate when compared with other techniques till date [1].

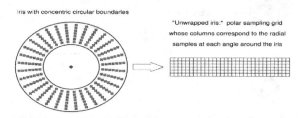

Fig. 2. The Classical Daugman rubber sheet model.

The Quadrature Based Gabor Wavelet Encoding. The Quadrature based Gabor Wavelet Encoding was implemented since we shall be testing our algorithm on the UBIRIS.V2 where the dataset members were acquired via visible wavelength. The Visible wavelength light is preferred due to the fact that most of the data will be acquired at long distance or off angle positions and as such can give a better quality image than the near infrared (NIR) light used in controlled environment.

The Quadrature based Gabor Wavelet Encoding functions by capturing the information contained in the iris texture and translate the information unto a fixed size template called the feature template. The feature template describes the bit positions corresponding to the position of every pixel value within the normalized iris image.

2.5   Template Matching

The template matching process entails showing the similarity in the features between two iris images. A prerequisite for iris template matching is iris template enrolment which refers to storing of the iris templates in a database where they can be accessed for matching with other templates. Distance metric or matching criteria is the main tool for retrieving similar images from databases. After the iris is normalized and its features or iris codes is extracted unto a fixed size template, the matching process is done using the Hamming Distance measure. The Hamming distance operation is performed on iris feature templates encoded in binary form. Equation 1 shows the formula for calculating the Hamming Distance.

$$HD = \frac{1}{N}\sum\nolimits_{J=1}^{N} X_j \oplus Y_j \tag{1}$$

The Hamming distance between two iris feature templates X_j and Y_j is defined as the number of bit positions at which the corresponding symbols are different between the two templates. In practical cases, the hamming distance value spans from the range of zero (0) to one (1). Figure 3 illustrates the steps involved in the process of template matching between two iris templates.

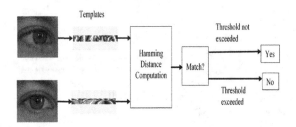

Fig. 3. Template matching process between two iris templates.

2.6 Evaluation

The process of evaluation to ascertain the level of performance will be carried out by the use of two parameters namely the false acceptance rate (FAR) and false rejection rate (FRR) attained by the recognition system.

False Acceptance Rate (FAR). The False Acceptance Rate will evaluate the recognition system by engaging it to compute the number of times an unenrolled iris template is recognised as an enrolled template thereby wrongfully granting access when the template should have been denied access. Equation 2 shows the equation for computing FAR.

$$FAR = \frac{No.\ of\ false\ acceptance}{Total\ no.\ of\ impostor\ testing} \tag{2}$$

False Rejection Ratio (FRR). The False Rejection Rate will evaluate the recognition system by computing the number of times an enrolled iris template is recognized as an unenrolled iris template thereby refusing the template from gaining access to the system when the template should have been granted access. FRR is calculated using Eq. 3.

$$FRR = \frac{No.\ of\ false\ rejection}{Total\ no.\ of\ genuine\ testing} \tag{3}$$

3 Data Preparation

Due to the fact that this work is focused on enhancing degraded images acquired from non-cooperative subjects, our data was acquired from UBIRIS.V2 dataset. This decision was made with respect to the fundamental characteristics that distinguished the UBIRIS.V2 from other datasets. UBIRIS V2 is a "noise induced iris image database" where the elements of the noise are encouraged and prompted, in order to create or replicate the non-cooperative image acquisition, some examples of noise found include obstructions of the iris, poor focusing, rotated and off-angle iris images etc. UBIRISV2 database is made up of 11,102 images which were gathered from 261 subjects with 522 irises. The exercise for the data capturing involved the subject of interest walking at a relatively slow pace (e.g. like taking a leisurely walk) and made to look at a number of adjacent marks causing the rotation of the head which inevitably leads to rotating the eyes, hence, allowing the possibility of acquiring 3 images per meter between the range of four to eight meters which resulted in the total of fifteen images per eye [12]. The total number of rotated iris images in the UBIRIS v2.0 is 157 images gathered from 25 subjects.

4 Experimental Results and Discussions

The experiment result show the efficiency and accuracy of the proposed approach on recognition of rotated iris image under non-ideal image conditions. Experimental results and analysis are presented for all the stages as depicted in the proposed framework.

This research made use of images obtained from the UBIRIS.v2 dataset. The UBIRIS.v2 dataset images were acquired using Canon EOS 5D camera with RGB color representation. The manually cropped resultant iris images was of size 300×400 in dimension and file format of .tiff extension. In order to enhance the ease of processing, the images were converted from RGB to grayscale and the dimension reduced to 240×320. Figure 4 shows the original eye image in RGB form and the grayscale of the original eye image after conversion.

4.1 Image Preparation

This research made use of images obtained from the UBIRIS.v2 dataset. The UBIRIS.v2 dataset images were acquired using Canon EOS 5D camera with RGB color representation. The manually cropped resultant iris images was of size 300×400 in dimension and file format of .tiff extension. In order to enhance the ease of processing, the images were converted from RGB to grayscale and the dimension reduced to 240×320. Figure 4 shows the original eye image in RGB form and the grayscale of the original eye image after conversion.

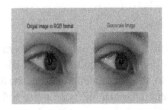

Fig. 4. Original (RGB) image and grayscale of the original image.

4.2 Image Enhancement

Enhancing an image involves improving on the overall quality of the image in order to ensure that the pre-processing of the image is effectively carried out. In this research work, the Gaussian filtering was implemented on the images. The effect of the Gaussian filter which is a low pass filter is to remove little details like specular noise without tampering with the image itself. Figure 5 shows the original eye image and its histogram after enhancement using the Gaussian filter.

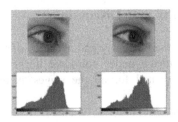

Fig. 5. Original image and Gaussian filtered image and their intensity histogram.

4.3 Segmentation Process

The segmentation of the eye image is the most important step in iris recognition system. Therefore, our segmentation consist of a two layered steps beginning with the binarization of the image by the use of Canny edge detector which highlights all the true edges in the image while subduing the false edges. The next step involves the use of the combination of both an optimized Hough Circle Transform and the Daugman's Integrodifferential Operator. Our approach utilize the hybrid of the optimized Hough Circle Transform function for circles and the Daugman's Integrodifferential operator. This hybrid approach enables the specification of the range of possible radii (i.e. the minimum and maximum radius) where the circular shape of the iris can be located regardless of the position of the circle in the eye image and the Integrodifferential Operator functions to calculate the normalized line integral around a circle, compute the center coordinates of the pupil and iris and detect the pupil and iris boundary. The generated coordinates is then used in efficiently localizing the iris portion form the entire eye image.

The segmentation process was divided into the following stages:

Edge Detection. The purpose of edge detection in eye image is to significantly reduce the amount of data in the eye image, while preserving the structural properties to be used for the segmentation process. The Canny edge detector operator is very effective in maximizing the probability of detecting real edge points while minimizing the probability of falsely detecting non-edge points, detect edges should be as close as possible to the real edges and ensuring that one real edge does not result in more than one detected edge.

Outer and Inner Iris Edge Detection. The iris and pupil are circular in shape and thus to be able to detect them, a circle detection function is to be used. This is carried out using the optimized Hough circle transform to detect the location of the inner boundary of the iris and outer boundary of the iris within the eye image based on the specified range of radii.

Iris Localization. Localisation of the iris involves separating the useful portion of the eye (i.e. iris) from the unwanted part of the eye image like the sclera. The Daugman Integrodifferential Operator functions to compute the center coordinates and boundaries of the detected pupil and iris and also isolate the computed pupil and iris boundary from the rest of the eye.

4.4   Iris Normalisation

Iris normalization involves the transformation of the iris region so that it has fixed dimensions to allow comparisons between same iris images. Iris normalization is a necessary step in the iris recognition process due to the inconsistencies between eye images caused by factors such as dilation of pupil from different illumination, eye rotation, camera rotation, head tilt and varying image distance. Iris normalization was done using the normalisation process as implemented by Libor Masek in his work [13]. The localised iris is translated into iris codes equivalent by translating the original cartesian coordinates for every pixel within the localised iris to the normalized polar coordinates equivalent.

4.5   Feature Extraction

The process of feature extraction which involves the retrieval of the iris codes from the eye image is implemented as two layered processes in the approach implemented by this study. The first stage involves unwrapping the iris into a rectangular sheet. The second stage implements the use of Quadrature based Gabor wavelet encoding to encode the extracted iris data into iris templates.

Iris Unwrapping. In order to make the iris images comparable, it is necessary to unwrap the circular normalized iris into a rectangular sheet of data as described by Daugman's rubber sheet model [11]. Daugman's rubber sheet model uses polar unwrapping approach to iris mapping. It assumes iris concentric circular boundaries with the column pixels corresponding to the radial pixel samples at each angle around the iris. The unwrapping function involves the unwrapping of the circular normalized iris structure into and equivalent fixed dimension rectangular structure.

Quadrature Based Gabor Wavelet Encoding. The 1-D Log Gabor wavelet was implemented to generate a flawless feature extraction tool for iris detection because of its quality that equates image analysis via Gabor wavelet to the human visual perception. The encoding function encodes the iris complex structure into two templates; the iris feature template which stores the actual encoded data and the noise template (mask) that describes how the noise contained in the image is distributed across the image.

4.6   Recognition Process

The recognition phase of the iris recognition process is comprised of two very important steps that must be conducted in order to successfully implement the recognition process. The first step is to determine the most suitable Hamming distance value which will serve as the threshold for acceptance or rejection of the iris. The second step is the matching process where the iris templates are actually compared and the outcome of the comparison will determine the decisions to be made based on the hamming distance value.

Hamming Distance Value. In order to execute the matching step, Hamming distance was chosen as a metric for recognition, in view of the fact that bit-wise comparisons will be carried out on the feature templates.

To select a suitable threshold value for the Hamming Distance, different values within the range of 0.2 to 0.5 were implemented to compute the Hamming distance for a sample of iris templates and the FAR and FRR at each threshold value was evaluated. The results obtained for the FAR and FRR at every iteration as depicted in Table 1 led to the decision to select 0.35 as the most suitable Hamming Distance threshold value.

Table 1. False acceptance and false rejection rates for different threshold.

Threshold value	FAR (%)	FRR (%)
0.20	0	26.5
0.25	0	12.21
0.30	0	6.84
0.35	**0**	**3.57**
0.40	0.135	1.78
0.45	17.45	0.14
0.50	89.5	0

Matching Process. In order to carry out the matching of iris templates successfully, it is necessary to first enroll the extracted iris templates in a storage location where it can be accessed for matching with other iris templates. Matching process entails showing the similarity in the features between two iris templates. Distance metric or matching criteria is the main tool for retrieving similar images from databases. The main purpose of the matching and recognition stage is to ascertain the authenticity of a person. This means to give access to the correct person and to prevent unauthorized persons from gaining access thereby ensuring security.

4.7   Implementation of the Recognition Process

The experiment performed was evaluated by implementing it on 145 iris templates obtained from 145 eye images from 25 subjects. The iris templates and their corresponding mask templates were divided into two categories. Category 1 (Enrolled category) was made up of 100 iris templates obtained from 20 unique subjects, each subject had 5 iris templates obtained at an interval of one metre between 4 to 8 m enrolled in the database. Category 2 (Testing category) was made up of 45 templates. 25 templates of the category 2 were obtained from 5 unique subjects whose iris templates were not enrolled into the database, 5 different template were obtained from each of the 5 subjects between 4 to 8 m at an interval of one metre. The remaining 20 templates for the category 2 was obtained from the 20 subjects already enrolled in the database, however, these 20 templates that will be used for testing are different from the 100 templates already enrolled in the database.

The category 2 (Testing category) iris templates were matched against the templates in the category 1 (Enrolled category), this is to observe if any of the iris templates in the category 2 can be accurately recognised when compared with all the templates in category 1. If a similar iris template match is found between the features of the template being tested and the features of any of the templates enrolled in the database, the matched template should be accurately identified and granted access and if no match is found for the template when compared with templates in the database (enrolled category) then the template should not be recognised or granted access.

The basis for the categorization is to critically observe the accuracy of our algorithm as regards the rate of false acceptance and false rejection. The Table 2 gives the summary of results obtained from the template matching for all the 145 tested templates.

4.8   Evaluation of Results

The results obtained by the implementation of the algorithm will be appraised by applying the false acceptance rate (FAR) and false rejection rate (FRR) as shown by a summary in Table 2.

Table 2. Summary of experimental results of the recognition accuracy based on the FAR and FRR.

Evaluation tool	Occurrence rate	Percentage accuracy	Percentage error
FAR	2 in 25	92.0%	8.0%
FRR	1 in 100	99.0%	1.0%
Successful decision	122 in 125	97.6%	2.4%

The probability that an enrolled individual is rejected by the system is 0.01, while the probability of an unenrolled person to be accepted by the system is also 0.08. The very low percentage obtained in the false acceptance and false rejection indicates the high accuracy rate of recognition achieved by the proposed approach based on the results obtained as shown in Table 2.

5   Conclusion and Recommendations

In this paper, we have proposed a new framework for the improvement of the accuracy of segmentation in rotated iris images and has been successfully implemented, using the optimized Hough Circle Transform integrated with Daugman Integrodifferential Operator to accurately detect and segment the inner and outer boundaries of the rotated image acquired from a non-cooperative subject. Therefore, the improved enhancement achieved in the iris segmentation by the implementation of this approach will be valuable in implementation on a wider range of degradations to further improve the accuracy of segmentation in degraded images. It will also be valuable in research work focused on optimizing the algorithm to enable a robust iris recognition system that can be implemented in the segmentation of iris acquired in an uncontrolled environment and it can enhance further research that will facilitate real time iris recognition in uncontrolled environments and non-cooperative subjects.

References

1. Shah, N., Shrinath, P.: Iris recognition system – a review. Int. J. Comput. Inf. Technol. 3(2), 99–106 (2014)
2. Proenca, H.: Non-cooperative iris recognition: issues and trends. University of Beira Interior, Department of Computer Science (2010)
3. Yang, T., Stahl, J., Schuckers, S., Hua, F., Boehnen, C.B., Karakaya, M.: Gaze angle estimate and correction in iris recognition. Int. J. Comput. Sci. Issues 8(4), 15–26 (2014)
4. Chawla, S., Oberoi, A.: A robust algorithm for iris segmentation and normalization using Hough transformation. Glob. J. Bus. Manage. Inf. Technol. 1(2), 69–76 (2011)
5. Kwang, S., Kim, Y., Yeong-Gon, K., Kang-Ryoung, P.: Enhanced iris recognition method based on multi-unit images. Opt. Eng. 52, 105–110 (2013)
6. Tan, T., He, Z., Sun, Z.: Efficient and robust segmentation of noisy iris images for non-cooperative iris recognition. Image Vis. Comput. 28, 223–230 (2014)

7. Desoky, A.I., Ali, H.A., Abdel-Hamid, N.B.: Enhancing iris recognition system performance using templates fusion. Ain Shams Eng. J. **3**(1), 133–140 (2012)
8. Li, P., Ma, H.: Iris recognition in non-ideal image conditions. Pattern Recogn. Lett. **33**, 1012–1018 (2011)
9. Nithyanandam, S., Gayathri, K.S., Priyadarshini, P.L.K.: A new iris normalization process for recognition system with cryptographic techniques. Int. J. Comput. Sci. **8**(4), 10–18 (2011)
10. Jeong, D.S., et al.: New iris segmentation method for non-ideal iris images. Image Vis. Comput. **28**, 254–260 (2010)
11. Daugman, J.: High confidence visual recognition of persons by a test of statistical independence. IEEE Trans. Pattern Anal. Mach. Intell. **15**(11), 1148–1161 (1993)
12. Proença, H.P., Filipe, S., Santos, R.J., Oliveira, J., Alexandre, L.A.: The UBIRIS.v2: a database of visible wavelength iris images captured on-the-move and at-a-distance. IEEE Trans. Pattern Anal. Mach. Intell. **32**(8), 1529–1535 (2010)
13. Masek, L.: Recognition of human iris patterns for biometric identification. Masters thesis, The University of Western Australia, 3 (2003)

Domain and Schema Independent Ontology Verbalizing

Kaneeka Vidanagea[✉], Noor Maizura Mohamad Noora[✉],
Rosmayati Mohemada, and Zuriana Abu Bakara

University Malaysia Terengganu, Kuala Terengganu, Malaysia
kaneeka.online@gmail.com,
{maizura,rosmayati,zuriana}@umt.edu.my

Abstract. The semantic web has gained vast popularity among current computer scientists and engineers, due to its remarkable attribute of machine readability and human readability. As evidence of witnessing that popularity, thousands of semantic web based knowledge models have been designed, to solve various problems emerging from different domains that are almost freely available in numerous repositories in the web. Semantic web based knowledge models also referred to as ontologies, are domain rich conceptualizations. Hence, they have been widely used to gain computational intelligence, related to areas such as medical sciences, law, management and many other disciplines. Nevertheless, the complexity associated with semantic web-based knowledge representations such as RDF and OWL act as a serious bottleneck in reusability and knowledge dissemination linked with the semantic web. Knowledge retrieval from an existing ontology solely depends on schematics understanding and writing of appropriate SPARQL or SQWRL queries. This would become a really challenging hurdle for non-computer specialists such as medical consultants, lawyers, criminologists who also wish to experience the benefits of semantic web-based technologies.

This research emphasizes on proposing a generalized verbalizer which could act as domain and schema independent ontology verbalizer for both RDF and OWL ontologies in human readable English. It is expected this generic verbalizer will widen the horizons of the semantic web-based technologies by opening new ventures for non-technical audiences.

Keywords: ACE · Ontology-verbalization · Object-properties · Semantics · Reasoning

1 Introduction

Introduction of the semantic web has made the internet, a web of knowledge. A most remarkable factor associated with semantic web is, it is machine-readable, as well as human-readable. Semantic web presented in form of a taxonomic structure makes it human understandable [1]. With the help of a tool like Protégé [2], the taxonomic structure can be graphically obtainable.

Resource Description Framework (RDF) and Ontology Web Language (OWL) are identified as the most popular formats of representing semantic web-based information

A. Alfaries et al. (Eds.): ICC 2019, CCIS 1098, pp. 30–39, 2019.
https://doi.org/10.1007/978-3-030-36368-0_3

[3]. As a result of richness associated in domain linked knowledge expressions, there is very high enthusiasm to use semantic web-based technologies to resolve numerous recurring issues experienced in day to day lives. Witnessing that popularity, currently, there are thousands of readily defined semantic web-based knowledge models available on the internet. Few repositories where these predefined ontologies are available will be Vocab.Org [4], Swoogle [5], LOV [6], Protégé Wiki [7], AberOWL [8] and BioPortal [9].

The semantic web can be used to present knowledge associated with any domain. When semantic web-based knowledge representation is used to depict knowledge associated with a specific domain, it will be referred to as an ontology. This makes ontologies to be domain rich conceptualizations. This is how Spasic et al. have defined ontologies in [10].

Creation of an ontology from scratch is not an easy task. Hence, once an ontology is created, the maximum of benefits should be derived through it, as still no 100% automated mechanisms for ontology construction are available. Human intervention is essential [12].

Though ontologies have many advantages, yet there are several complicated bottlenecks associated with retrieving knowledge from existing knowledge models (ontologies), which are freely available on the internet. This has adversely affected the reusability of the ontologies readily available in numerous repositories as claimed above. Authors of [11] have stated this is an utter cognitive wastage, as a valuable piece of knowledge presented in RDF/OWL formats will soon become stagnated in repositories, after serving only the purpose it had been created for.

One of the issues hindering the reusability of the existing ontologies is identified as the difficulty of understanding the schematic structure of a defined ontology. Because without knowing the schematic structure, knowledge retrieval from an existing ontology would not be feasible. Another problem is the requirement of high technical knowledge to understand a schema and necessity of writing SPARQL or SQWRL queries for knowledge retrieval [13–16].

Because we cannot always expect people seeking the benefits of ontologies are software experts or ontologists only. For instance, ontologies are widely used in the medical domain as a critical decision assistive tool for consultants. Lawyers use them for judicial judgement analysis. Police officers and detectives use them for criminal case assessments [17–19]. Therefore, how reasonable is it to expect from them to write a correct SPARQL or SQWRL query by understanding the schema of the ontology? Additionally, even for a computer scientist also, it is not an easy task to understand the schema of an ontology developed by someone else and to write the appropriate queries for knowledge retrieval. But what if there is a mechanism to extract out all required knowledge assertions from the RDF or OWL-based ontology file and to present them to the end user in natural language/readable English?

This will set up the pathway for the research question, which could be defined as, "how to propose a generic verbalizer, facilitating natural language based knowledge extraction from both RDF or OWL ontologies in a schema and domain independent basis"? In simple, verbalization, is the process of extracting knowledge from an RDF or OWL file and representing it in form of natural language.

The remaining section of the paper will discuss about related works, methodology, results and discussion and conclusion, respectively.

2 Related Work

Extracting knowledge from an RDF or OWL file and representing it in form of natural language is the process known as ontology verbalization. There are few prototypes developed on ontology verbalization by a few research groups. Even though, still no stable version is released as a product to be used, with documentation [20]. Among the verbalizers available so far, almost all are domain and schema dependent. This means, all the verbalizers defined are statically mapped to only one ontology, and they cannot be used to verbalize an ontology from any other domain. For example, verbalizers produced by [21] and [22] can only work with DBpedia and accommodation ontology only, as they both have a static mapping to their respective ontologies. As mentioned in [23], it was the only prototype which could verbalize knowledge in a domain-independent manner.

Nevertheless, the prototype has several limitations as it could work only with OWL ontologies and not be extended to work with both RDF and OWL ontologies. Furthermore, the natural language generation of that verbalizer results in an Attempt to – Control – English (ACE), which is not the proper English read and written. ACE is just some English statements, extracting out the triple arrangement in the knowledge file. MIKAT is another verbalizer which can work only in breast cancer domain, assisting the clinical decisions of the consultants examining a patient [24]. [25] elaborates another verbalizer which has been developed on the domain of colonoscopy, which is used to annotate video footages of colonoscopy.

Therefore, as conversed above in literature, there exists an apparent gap to be addressed on domain and schema independent ontology verbalization. Additionally, verbalizers which could work with both RDF and OWL formats to generate proper English could be understood even by non-technical specialists. As discussed so far, even the only located domain independent verbalizer in [23] also cannot produce colloquial English to disseminate the knowledge stored in the ontology files.

As already discussed in the introduction section, difficulty in understanding knowledge represented in semantic formats such as RDF and OWL, as well as the inability of writing complex SPARQL and SQWRL queries to retrieve knowledge from ontologies, act as main bottlenecks hindering the reusability of ontologies that already exist [13–16]. Because it's not practical to anticipate always that only IT experts or ontologists will seek for the potentials of the semantic web [17–19]. As explained in [26] it's not fair enough to expect from a non-tech expert as a medical, legal or etc. consultant to read and understand a complex schema written in RDF or OWL and to query it to get the required knowledge out of it.

Another important aspect, which authors of this paper are interested in pointing out is, the use of ontologies as a knowledge dissemination platform. Because an ontology is a domain rich conceptualization [10].

For instance, as one practical use case, assume the process of training criminology officers, detectives and investigators. They need to gain a comprehensive knowledge of crime types, evidence gathering procedures, crime analysis, etc. [27]. In fulfilling these purposes as already conversed, there are ample, carefully designed knowledge models available in popular semantic web formats on the internet, mostly free of charge [12]. If required formats of knowledge models are not available, these could be created through collaborative efforts of computer scientists and criminology domain specialist. In fact, this could be a one-time effort. Because the created knowledge models can be used again and again over batches of criminology students and specialists for effective knowledge dissemination assuring knowledge reusability aspects as well. This is only a one practical use case elaborating the benefits of a potential verbalizer. Ontology is a very rich domain constrained model, which can preserve domain constrained mappings assuring the proper context. Therefore, even existing compiles like LEX and YACC also incapable in handling this context preserved knowledge extraction and, it will become even more inefficient, as per the nature of this research problem, because it's domain and schema independent [36].

It's very apparent that there is a research gap to be addressed in proposing a domain and schema independent verbalizer which could work with both RDF and OWL, being the most popular and W3C accredited formats of semantic web representations [28]. Furthermore, a verbalizer is capable of producing colloquial English for the purpose of knowledge dissemination in ontology files.

3   Methodology

As the initial step of the methodology, the stipulated research question is justified via accessing latest research and journal publications (wherever possible) from established and credible research repositories such as Science Direct, ACM, IEEE Xplore and etc. Keywords such as 'ontology verbalizers', 'domain and schema independent verbalizers', 'natural language generation', 'ontology schema understanding' and etc. are used in querying the research repositories to gather a coherent collection of papers for the further assessment of the research question. Deductive research methodology is followed in conducting this research. Because the gap associated with this research domain is confirmed via assessment of multiples of literature [29].

4   Results and Discussion

After intense assessment of existing literature, ultimately, as denoted in Fig. 1 below, execution flow is derived for the proposed generalized ontology verbalizer, which is capable of domain and schema independent knowledge extraction and colloquial English based natural language generation.

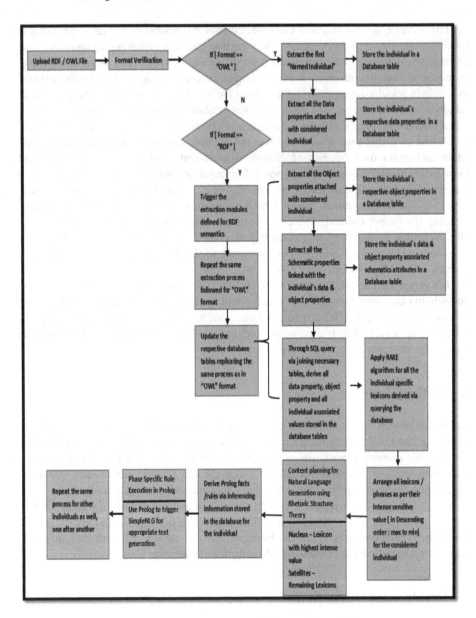

Fig. 1. Overall process flow of the generic verbalizer

Extracted information resulting out from the execution flow in Fig. 1, is stored in the database design depicted in Fig. 2 below.

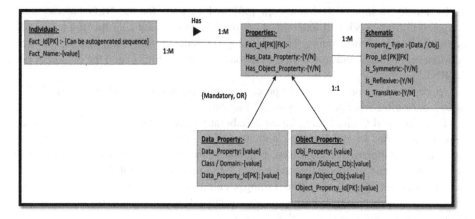

Fig. 2. Database schema

The proposed execution flow of the ontology verbalizer is capable of processing both RDF and OWL files, as it is one dimension expected to be addressed as a research gap in the problem statement. In achieving this goal, separate program design modules need to be introduced, hence the semantics associated with RDF and OWL are not identical. All extracted pieces of information will be stored in the above-proposed database design depicted in Fig. 2. This mechanism will facilitate the natural language generation (NLG) process, as whenever facts are required for the NLG process, those can be extracted out easily through simple SQL queries.

In achieving the requirement of deriving opinioned lexicons for the NLG process, RAKE algorithm is used. All data and object property associated values attached to one specific individual is mined via the RAKE algorithm. RAKE is a domain-independent and unsupervised keyword extraction algorithm which tries to determine important key phrases (not only words) by analyzing the frequency of the words appearing along with the co-occurrence with the other words in the given text [30]. The processed output of the RAKE algorithm will provide the considered individual's lexicons and phrases along with their intense values. Once the lexicons are arranged in descending order of the intense value, most important lexicon or phrase associated with the considered individual can be derived. This lexicon or phrase can be recognized as the nucleus, according to the Rhetorical structure theory (RST) proposed by Mann and Thompson in [31] and the remaining lexicons and phrases will become satellites. According to RST, the nucleus is the most important element and satellites will become the discourses elaborating the nucleus. Therefore, this RST theory will be very useful in content flow planning in NLG processes.

Subsequently, to intelligently govern the NLG process preserving coherence and relevance of the contents, Prolog inferencing will be used. First order logic based axioms and rule sets need to be created from the facts extracted and stored in the database. A dedicated program module needs to be designed and developed to address the feature of axioms and knowledge mapping to prolog based facts and rules. As this is going to be another complex research component, it will not be discussed under this publication.

Eventually, SimpleNLG framework [35] will be used for the NLG process and SimpleNLG framework will function as per the instructions and coordination provided by the Prolog [34] inferencing. Hence Prolog inferencing will solely depend on the information extracted and stored on the database design (in Fig. 2) and the outcomes of the RST.

As depicted in Fig. 1, the same process will be repeated for each and every individual, once after another in a sequential fashion.

This SimpleNLG and Prolog based collaborative operation can be carried out as a phased execution. In collaboration with the NLG process, multiple phases such as introduction, elaboration, comparison, conclusion, etc. These phases can be introduced to sequentially and methodically control the NLG process associated with a specified individual/axiom. SimpleNLG and Prolog's collaborative operation associated with phased NLG process will be separately discussed in another publication, as its digressing from the emphasis of this publication.

Eventually, the functionality of the proposed framework can be evaluated for the use case discussed above as per the process mentioned in Fig. 3 below.

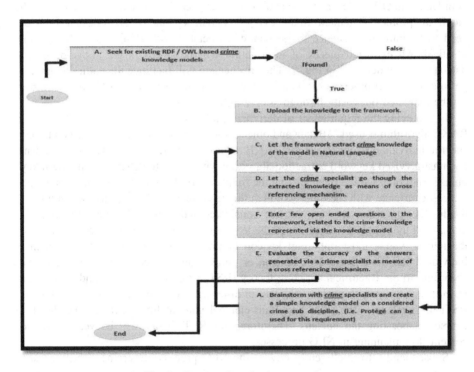

Fig. 3. Suggested evaluation procedure

5   Conclusion

This paper addresses a potential solution to overcome the research gap associated with domain and schema independent ontology verbalization, capable of producing colloquial English representations for both OWL and RDF semantic formats. As already conversed in the literature, this research gap has not been addressed as a single integrated solution.

It is not an easy task to extract knowledge from OWL and RDF based semantic web formats and to represent in conversational English. In relation to this aspect, in [32] group of researchers have discussed the "divide and conquer" concept. As pointed out by researches, attempting to fulfil all the tasks from one module will increase the complexity and coupling associated with the system. In [33] it further suggests that the definition of a complex problem space via multiple resolution layers will provide the opportunity of attention to detail in knowledge modelling and analysis aspects and it will further prevent the single module being flooded with information and resulting in complex schematic structures or conditions. Therefore, considering those suggestions, it is concluded that the proposed framework should also comprise of multiple resolution layers, addressing each of the specified part proposed in execution flow in Fig. 1.

Therefore, to attain all those aspects and to ensure the sequential and methodical execution of the entire process, as a future recommendation, it's determined to propose an instructional task-based upper ontology, which will act as the central controlling point via coordinating with multiple modules proposed to cover up the entire process.

Finally, it's anticipated that the introduction of this generalized verbalizer can address all specified research gaps discussed above to open new doors for non-technical audiences to enjoy the benefits of semantic web and it's also assumed this will escalate the reusability of the existing ontologies, facilitating efficient knowledge dissemination.

There are some more aspects to be discussed such as NLG process and Prolog based knowledge mapping features. Those aspects are too complex to be discussed within the same paper since it would cause to exceed the allowed page amount for the paper. Therefore, those aspects will be discussed in future as several separate publications.

References

1. Kashyap, V.: Ontologies and schemas. In: The Semantic Web, pp. 79–135. Springer, Heidelberg (2008). https://doi.org/10.1007/978-3-540764526_5
2. Protege: Protege (2019). https://protege.stanford.edu/. Accessed 16 Feb 2019
3. Caldarola, E.G., Rinaldi, A.M.: An approach to ontology integration for ontology reuse. In: 2016 IEEE 17th International Conference on Information Reuse and Integration (IRI) (2016). https://doi.org/10.1109/iri.2016.58
4. Davis, I.: vocab.org - A URI space for vocabularies (2014). http://vocab.org/. Accessed 16 Feb 2019
5. Yu, L.: Swoogle. In: Introduction to the Semantic Web and Semantic Web Services, pp. 145–157 (2007). https://doi.org/10.1201/9781584889342.pt3

6. Vandenbussche, P., Atemezing, G.A., Poveda-Villalón, M., Vatant, B.: Linked Open Vocabularies (LOV): a gateway to reusable semantic vocabularies on the Web. Semantic Web **8**(3), 437–452 (2016). https://doi.org/10.3233/sw-160213

7. Musen, M.A., The Protégé Team: Protégé Ontology Editor. Encyclopedia of Systems Biology, pp. 1763–1765 (2013). https://doi.org/10.1007/978-1-4419-9863-7_1104

8. Slater, L., Gkoutos, G.V., Schofield, P.N., Hoehndorf, R.: Using AberOWL for fast and scalable reasoning over BioPortal ontologies. J. Biomed. Semant. **7**(1) (2016). https://doi.org/10.1186/s13326-016-0090-0

9. National Center for Biomedical Ontology: NCBO BioPortal (2005). https://bioportal.bioontology.org/ontologies. Accessed 16 Feb 2019

10. Spasic, I., Ananiadou, S., McNaught, J., Kumar, A.: Text mining and ontologies in biomedicine: making sense of raw text. Brief. Bioinform. **6**(3), 239–251 (2005). https://doi.org/10.1093/bib/6.3.239

11. Zenuni, X., Raufi, B., Ismaili, F., Ajdari, J.: State of the art of semantic web for healthcare. Procedia Soc. Behav. Sci. **195**, 1990–1998 (2015). https://doi.org/10.1016/j.sbspro.2015.06.213

12. Trokanas, N., Cecelja, F.: Ontology evaluation for reuse in the domain of Process Systems Engineering. Comput. Chem. Eng. **85**, 177–187 (2016). https://doi.org/10.1016/j.compchemeng.2015.12.003

13. Chergui, W., Zidat, S., Marir, F.: An approach to the acquisition of tacit knowledge based on an ontological model. J. King Saud Univ. Comput. Inf. Sci. (2018). https://doi.org/10.1016/j.jksuci.2018.09.0129

14. Alavi, M., Leidner, D.E.: Knowledge management and knowledge management systems: conceptual foundations and research issues. Manag. Inf. Syst. Q. **25**, 107–136 (2001). https://doi.org/10.2307/3250961

15. Anderson, J.R.: The Architecture of Cognition. Harvard University Press, Cambridge (1983)

16. Gutierrez-Basulto, V., Ibanez-Garcia, Y., Kontchakov, R., Kostylev, E.V.: Queries with negation and inequalities over lightweight ontologies. SSRN Electron. J. (2015). https://doi.org/10.2139/ssrn.3199213

17. Ku, C., Leroy, G.: A decision support system: automated crime report analysis and classification for egovernment. Gov. Inf. Q. **31**(4), 534–544 (2014). https://doi.org/10.1016/j.giq.2014.08.003

18. Pinheiro, V., Furtado, V., Pequeno, T., Nogueira, D.: Natural Language Processing based on Semantic inferentialism for extracting crime information from text. In: 2010 IEEE International Conference on Intelligence and Security Informatics (2010)

19. Rusu, D., Dali, L., Fortuna, B., Grobelnik, M., Mladnnic, D.: Triple Extraction from sentences. Paper presented at Technical University of Cluj-Napoca, Romania

20. Williams, S., Third, A., Power, R.: Levels of organisation in ontology verbalization. ENLG (2011). https://www.semanticscholar.org/paper/Levels-of-organisation-in-ontology-verbalisation-WilliamsThird/08c6a058f5f78cf49701d2534bf9c6af3683f9e9

21. Habernal, I., Konopík, M.: SWSNL: semantic web search using natural language. Expert Syst. Appl. **40**(9), 3649–3664 (2013). https://doi.org/10.1016/j.eswa.2012.12.070

22. Poulovassilis, A., Selmer, P., Wood, P.T.: Approximation and relaxation of semantic web path queries. SSRN Electr. J. (2016). https://doi.org/10.2139/ssrn.3199265

23. Kaljurand, K., Fuchs, N.E.: Verbalizing owl in attempt to controlled English. In: Proceedings of Third International Workshop on OWL: Experiences and Directions, Innsbruck, Austria (6th–7th June 2007), vol. 258 (2007)

24. Bontcheva, K., Wilks, Y.: Automatic report generation from ontologies: the MIAKT approach. Nat. Lang. Process. Inf. Syst., 324–335 (2004). https://doi.org/10.1007/978-3-540-27779-8_28

25. Bao, J., Cao, Y., Tavanapong, W., Honavar, V.: Integration of domain-specific and domain-independent ontologies for colonoscopy video database annotation. Artificial Intelligence Research Laboratory-Iowa State University (2004)
26. Bojars, U., Liepins, R., Gruzitis, N., Cerans, K., Celms, E.: Extending OWL Ontology Visualizations with Interactive Contextual Verbalization. VOILA@ISWC (2016)
27. Smith, N., Flanagan, C.: The Effective Detective: Identifying the skills of an effective SIO. Police Research Series (2000). http://library.college.police.uk/docs/hopolicers/fprs122.pdf
28. Noy, N., McGuiness, D.: Ontology Development 101: A Guide to Creating Your First Ontology. Stanford University, Stanford (2001)
29. El Ghosh, M., Naja, H., Abdulrab, H., Khalil, M.: Towards a legal rule-based system grounded on the integration of criminal domain ontology and rules. Procedia Comput. Sci. **112**, 632–642 (2017). https://doi.org/10.1016/j.procs.2017.08.109
30. Rose, S., Engel, D., Cramer, N., Cowley, W.: Automatic keyword extraction from individual documents. Text Mining **1**, 1–20 (2010). https://doi.org/10.1002/9780470689646.ch1
31. Rhetorical structure theory: description and construction of text structures. Decision Support Syst. **3**(4), 360 (1987). https://doi.org/10.1016/0167-9236(87)90127-8
32. Yang, P., Tang, K., Yao, X.: Turning high-dimensional optimization into computationally expensive optimization. IEEE Trans. Evol. Comput. **22**, 143–15622 (2017)
33. Abeysiriwardana, P.C., Kodituwakku, S.R.: Ontology based information extraction for disease intelligence. Int. J. Res. Comput. Sci. **2**(6), 7–19 (2012). https://doi.org/10.7815/ijorcs.26.2012.051
34. SWI-Prolog (1987). http://www.swi-prolog.org/
35. SimpleNLG | DialPort (2019). http://dialport.ict.usc.edu/index.php/simplenlg/
36. Waite, W.: Beyond LEX and YACC: How to Generate the Whole Compiler (1996)

The Effect of User Experience on the Quality of User Interface Design in Healthcare

Hanaa Alzahrani and Reem Alnanih[✉]

Computer Science Department, Faculty of Computing and Information
Technology, King Abdulaziz University, Jeddah, Saudi Arabia
halzahrani0500@stu.kau.edu.sa, ralnanih@kau.edu.sa

Abstract. Electronic health records (EHRs) improve the quality of healthcare, prevent medical errors, and decrease paperwork. As EHR end users, the viewpoint of healthcare physicians, or user experience (UX), should be considered in the design of a user interface to help reduce their complex workloads.

The purpose of this study is to create two personas, one for pediatric cardiology and one for general physicians from different specialties in King Abdulaziz University Hospital (KAUH) in Jeddah, Saudi Arabia. The applicability of UX is explored as well as the ability of the personas to assist healthcare professionals and inform design decisions. The results of this study show no difference between the requirements of either persona, however there are differences in the priorities for each. In relation to design decisions, the researchers found that there are fundamental elements designers need to consider to ensure a highly efficient system that suits physicians and increases their effectiveness.

Keywords: Procedure booking software · User experience · Persona · User behavior · Design decisions

1 Introduction

Health information technology (HIT) is a broad concept that encompasses various technologies used to store, share, and analyze health information in an electronic environment. Electronic health records (EHRs) are an element of HIT that have many benefits. EHRs improve the general quality of healthcare, prevent medical errors, reduce healthcare costs, increase administrative efficiency, decrease paperwork, and expand access to affordable healthcare [1]. In relation to medical errors within order entry systems, medical record systems, and patient information systems, the reality is that errors are seldom the result of carelessness or negligence. More commonly, the errors are due to a variety of reasons, such as faulty system design (specifically faulty interface design) [2], using a manual system that decreases the level of quality, or by designing a user interface (UI) without considering user behavior [3]. Procedures booking software (PBS) is becoming increasingly popular in this era of technologically advanced healthcare. PBS affects healthcare delivery by improving healthcare efficiency, reducing costs, and improving health outcomes. With PBS, physicians can book patient appointments online. Patients receive a confirmation email with directions

A. Alfaries et al. (Eds.): ICC 2019, CCIS 1098, pp. 40–51, 2019.
https://doi.org/10.1007/978-3-030-36368-0_4

and other important instructions, and are reminded twenty-four hours and one hour before their scheduled appointment by text message. However, inappropriate software design for PBS means that physicians are forced to spend more time documenting the health related information of their patients. As a result, they prefer face-to-face interactions with their patients and ignore the technology [4]. Through the widespread use of this software, which has poor usability, the workload for the user (i.e., the healthcare physicians) increases, which leads to reduced efficiency [5]. The survey results by Hyppönen et al. [6] confirm the need for continuous monitoring of EHRs, including end user opinions of them. In addition, extensive development work needs to be undertaken to achieve the expected benefits of an EHR system. Such benefits include improving the efficiency of healthcare and communication, access to up-to-date information on patients, and increasing the quality of care. Thus, the physician's view, as EHR end user, should be considered and not underestimated. Consequently, designing a useful UI that considers UX and improves the quality of work done by healthcare professionals can reduce their complex workload.

1.1   Problem

In the department of pediatric cardiology at KAUH, the booking of cardiac catheterization procedures is recorded manually on a calendar booklet. The booklet is kept in the clinic and can only be checked or adjusted by visiting the clinic. There is no system of communication between the cardiologist, the calendar booklet and the hospital information software. As a result, any cancelations or adjustments can cause confusion for the cardiac catheterization team and in some cases lead to loss of hospital bed booking. Considering UX in healthcare can help users become more aware of their overall well-being. Designers however must understand human cognition and be acquainted with medical expressions. The engagement of patients and physicians in such research can provide substantial benefits to the creation of successful healthcare products.

1.2   Objectives

In this research study, the focus is on determining the applicability of UX and personas in informing designers and assisting in the creation of an interactive and easy-to-use UI for the PBS that serves the pediatric cardiology department at KAUH.

This research is based on user behavior and personas and explores the extent of user impact on the design of an interactive, easy-to-use UI for PBS. The objective of designing a PBS is to improve the quality of healthcare professionals by increasing their effectiveness, efficiency, and satisfaction, while also improving their time management and decreasing their stress levels. The objectives are to (1) carryout a literature review that focuses on the impact of personas (which are used to represent specific user groups and their special requirements, goals, and attitudes) and UX on design decisions, while also reviewing EHRs and their related benefits and challenges; (2) define the applicability of UX and personas in assisting and informing design decisions; and (3) create two persona templates, one for pediatric cardiology physicians and one for general physicians, and then compare them to investigate whether there are any significant differences between them.

The rest of the paper is organized as follows: Sect. 2, presents an overview of personas and user behavior, while Sect. 3 provides an overview of EHRs. In Sect. 4, the method of data collection and analysis used for the study is described. Section 5 discusses the research results. Finally, Sect. 6 concludes the paper.

2 Related Work

The literature review for this research focused on the impact of UX on UI design, including user behavior and personas. Some general topics were reviewed to determine how a successful UI is designed. Successful UI design requires a firm understanding and examination of user behavior that can be adapted to a specific persona. Solutions may then be developed to produce a design that suits the user for specific situations, thereby enhancing the user's execution of various tasks.

Recently, UX has received more attention from researchers in the field of human–computer interaction (HCI). According to Mirnig et al. [7], UX comprises an individual's opinions and reactions after using a product, software, or service. UX has emerged to reference the universality and multidimensionality of the user-software relationship as it has improved over time [8]. Measuring UX involves consideration of functionality (e.g., does it perform its tasks adequately?), sensory experiences (e.g., is it appealing to look at?), physical ease (e.g., is too much psychomotor interaction required?), cognitive requirements (e.g., is it understandable?), and psychological contentment (e.g., what are the feelings one gets from using it?). In HCI, the most widely accepted definition for UX is the one presented by the International Organization for Standardization (ISO). The ISO defines UX as the degree to which specific users effectively, efficiently, and satisfactorily use a product to accomplish a particular goal within a definitive framework. The design of UX refers to the development of software, resources, and processes to make them as user-friendly as possible. In addition, getting the UX right is vital to ensure user satisfaction; this means ensuring that the entire process is perfect [9].

In healthcare, UX has become an important issue due to the growing necessity of software, devices, and the interactions of patients and providers to diagnose, treat, and manage the disease. Product design affects the usability of healthcare systems. Improving UX for physicians is essential because it has beneficial effects for in-patient care and leads to the general contentment of physicians [10].

Many design models (like conceptual models) have been proposed and considered by researchers in this field. Increasing numbers of research studies have applied the user-centered design (UCD) method in product design. LeRouge et al. [11] investigated UCD as a practical means of designing and developing consumer health technologies (CHT) for elderly people. The adoption of user profiles and personas has not received much attention in health informatics research. As a result, LeRouge et al. [11] showed how user profiles and personas can be used to inform the requirements, design, and implementation decisions of a technology aimed at facilitating CHT adoption among elderly people.

Berry et al. [12] proposed a new design method based on a model of HIT systems. Their proposed model simplified the workflow of the outpatient. They also showed how a method generated for HIT UI design for a patient-centered case management system (P-CMS) was easy to use.

Finally, UX includes all the "user's emotions, beliefs, preferences, perceptions, physical and psychological responses, behaviors, and accomplishments that occur before, during and after use" [7]. The following subsections highlight the concept of personas and user behavior to better understand the design requirements. The subsections also highlight the importance of satisfying user requirements and healthcare objectives.

2.1 Personas

Personas is a technique being used by practicing software designers in interaction design [13]. It used in software design processes to characterize specific user groups and their special requirements, goals, and attitudes. Using personas facilitates communication about design choices [14]. In relation to certain issues, personas provide a similar language to discuss users and their needs. Moreover, they minimize conflict about user perceptions of certain goals in relation to the software, and they summarize data in an easily understandable template.

Recently, Pröbster et al. [14] conducted an empirical study of 59 participants. They used a persona introduced either as a "persona" or as a "real person." They tested whether the instructions that framed the use of the persona or the supposedly "real" user impacted on participant perception of the persona. Their results showed that participant perception did not depend on whether participants believed the user was a real person or a persona, thus demonstrating that a persona can be used to represent a certain category of users ensuring the success of the product.

Matthews et al. [15] presented the first study of how experienced UCD practitioners, who had previous experience in deploying personas, use and understand personas in industrial software design. They identified limits to the persona approach in the context studied. The practitioners used personas almost exclusively for communication but not for design. The participants specified four problems with personas, finding them abstract, impersonal, misleading, and distracting. They proposed a new approach to persona deployment and construction, which is to present user information to software designers in three easily separable layers: persona, user role, and user study data. Furthermore, Coorevits et al. [16] proposed a coupled, interactive, open-innovation method through iterative user involvement as a way of improving the effectiveness of personas. Their approach addressed user needs and created new opportunities (such as expanding potential, and providing extra content and collaboration options) by using a trial-and-error learning process. Also, Anvari et al. [17] empirically researched the concept of divergence in a conceptual design based on the personality of a persona. They conducted one study in Denmark and two in Australia. They gave four personas diverse personalities. The outcome of their studies indicated that participant views and prioritization of needs and system requirements were influenced by the personality traits of the persona. The results supported the proposal that personas with personality traits help software designers produce conceptual designs that cater to the needs of specific personalities.

The following subsection focuses on the concept of user behavior, the complement of personas.

2.2   Behavior

The influence and persuasion of human behavior through design are increasingly important topics in design research. However, there are few empirically grounded processes that support designers in realizing projects of behavioral change. Rodriguez and Boke's study [18], authors concerned with environmental design, highlighted that studying user behavior is the first step in offering solutions to decrease a product's environmental impact during the user phase. They demonstrated that studying user behavior is an important source of information for improving the environmental impact of products. Lockton et al. [19] presented the Design with Intent Method, an innovative tool for designers working in the banking industry. They applied this tool to an everyday situation of human-technology interaction: customers forgetting their bank cards inside automatic teller machines (ATMs). As a result of this study, they determined several possible design concepts comparable to existing developments in ATM design. This demonstrated that their approach could be developed and applied as part of a UCD process. Daae and Boke [20] focused on investigating issues that impact user behavior to aid designers in finding solutions to promote sustainability and prevent unsustainable behavior. Their results were compared with the results of two other user-focused studies. Their comparison highlighted the importance of differentiating between methods that are suitable for an examination of internal/external factors and conscious/unconscious factors. Cash et al. [21] proposed a behavioral design (BD) method by analyzing several projects in order to identify a general method for behavioral design. They found that several stages and activities were linked to the successful accomplishment of a project. This highlighted a new perspective, which allowed designers to combine certain core insights from the BD theory. However, most of the research in this area did not consider UX in terms of the persona or user behavior as a foundation for the creation of a health system that is adaptable to user needs.

Based on the comparison of the above studies in terms of modality, research purposes, techniques, results, and limitations, we note the following:

- UCD increases the robustness of UI software.
- There is a lack of UX studies combining personas and user behavior.
- There are many advantages to studying personas and user behavior prior to designing a system. Table 1 presents these advantages [11, 14–21].

Table 1. Advantages of studying personas and user behavior.

Ref.	Modality used	Advantages
[11]	Profiles and personas	Used to design, develop and implement a system leading to the adoption and use of said system
[14]	Persona	Used as a visible depiction of the needs and goals of a group of users
[15]	Persona	Allows designers to properly infer personas or other abstractions
[16]	Persona	Enhances the use and results of the use of personas in UX research and design
[17]	Persona	Improves target-user representation
[18]	User behavior	Provides solutions that reduce the environmental impact of the product during the use phase
[19]	User behavior	Guides designers to the use of a group of applicable methods from the outset
[20]	User behavior	Helps designers identify which techniques of user research are relevant, since an in-depth comprehension of the techniques is required to determine the relevance of the product
[21]	User behavior	Allows designers to identify arbitrary factors (e.g., social norms) and existing information that supports meta-analysis and ideation

3 Electronic Health Records

The meaning of EHRs is unstable since it has numerous functions that include many types of data. Häyrinen, Saranto, and Nykänen reviewed the literature relevant to EHR systems [22]. Their research determined several factors related to EHRs, including definition, structure, the context in which they are used, the people who gain access to them, and their data components. The authors conducted their research on PubMed, CINAHL, Eval and Cochrane. As a result, they defined an EHR as "a repository of patient data in digital form, stored and exchanged securely, and accessible by multiple authorized users." They determined that further studies are needed to overcome existing challenges, such as the use of international terminologies to achieve semantic interoperability. They proposed that future research be conducted to compare the documentation of different healthcare professionals with essential information about EHRs. They also proposed research that focuses on EHR content, specifically regarding nursing documentation and patient self-documentation.

An EHR system has the potential to improve the overall quality of health services, including the availability and reliability of health information. However, there are barriers to implementing an EHR system. One such barrier is user resistance [23]. The following studies examined the barriers to implementing EHR systems.

Kruse et al. [23] examined multiple databases, independently assessed the search results to determine the barriers of EHR, and chose several articles that were only relevant to their primary objective for review. Through many discussions, the researchers identified 39 barriers to adopting EHR. The most oft-repeated barriers were cost, technical concerns and support, and resistance to change. Ilie et al. [24] examined the accessibility of the development of electronic medical records (EMR) in terms of their physical and logical dimensions. There is no difference between EMR and EHR; the two terms are almost used interchangeably. EMR replaces the paper version of a patient's medical history and includes more health data, test results, and treatments. It also is designed to share data with other electronic health records so other healthcare providers can access a patient's healthcare data. In their study, physical access refers to the availability of physical objects, such as computers or mobiles, that can be used to access EMRs. Logical access refers to the ease or difficulty of logging into the system. The researchers concluded that accessibility is a necessary factor that can hinder the acceptance of complex technology.

Gagnon et al. [25] distributed online surveys to physicians in Quebec, Canada. Their research concluded that EHRs are more likely to be accepted by practitioners who find them straightforward, consistent with their social norms, and accepted by their colleagues. Akhu-Zaheya, Al-Maaitah and Hani's research [26] evaluated and compared the quality of paper-based records (PBRs) with EHRs. They found that EHRs were better in terms of process and structure, while PBRs were better in terms of quantity and quality of content. Their research confirmed the weaknesses of nursing documentation, the lack of knowledge and skills of nurses in dealing with both PBRs and EHRs in the nursing process. Ajami and Bagheri-Tadi [27] conducted an unsystematic review that identified the barriers doctors observe when adopting EHRs. They found that using EHRs requires the presence of certain user and system attributes. Many of the doctors had concerns about security, privacy, data entry, doctor-patient relationship interfaces, access to computers, computer literacy, data reliability, inadequate data exchange, system speed, interinstitutional integration, wireless connectivity and cost.

4 Data Collection and Results

In this section, we present the complete process of persona creation as follows [28].

4.1 Identification of Persona Data Sources and Establishment of User Categories

There are many ways to collect data. In this research, the data were collected by conducting interviews and distributing questionnaires to the participants. The target users were physicians working in KAUH. Two groups of physicians were selected. The first group was from the department of pediatric cardiology and consisted of 21 physicians; the second group was from a general department and consisted of 23 physicians.

4.2 Collection of User Data

Two methods were considered: interviews and questionnaires.

Interviews. Interviews were conducted with six doctors belonging to the department of pediatric cardiology, one consultant, three specialists, and two residents.

Questionnaires. We formulated a questionnaire consisting of two parts. The first part focused on general information, while the second focused on questions related to participant experience with an electronic health system. We received answers from all 21 physicians. Most of the responses were from males (85.7%), aged 30 to 39 years (47.9%), who worked full-time (95.2%) in KAUH. Their level of English in all responses was at a professional level (66.7%) and most were consultants (42.9%). From the other departments we received answers from all 23 physicians, most were from women (81.3%) aged 30 to 39 years (68.8%) who worked full-time (100%) in KAUH. Their level of English was also at a professional level (81.3%) and most were consultants (56.3%).

As indicated in Fig. 1(a), the results show that the pediatric cardiologists preferred to use PBS because it saved time, whereas the other general physicians preferred it because it facilitated information sharing.

Figure 1(b) shows that both pediatric cardiologists and general physicians viewed the many trials necessary to complete a task on PBS as the biggest impediment to its use. They viewed the lack of appropriate interface design as the second biggest impediment, while the third was the extensive time needed to complete a task. Finally, Fig. 1(c), shows that pediatric cardiologists believed the most important required improvement to PBS was a user-friendly design. The other general physicians viewed ease of access and use as the most important requirement. Finally, both the cardiologists and general physicians viewed the improved speed of PBS as the third most important requirement.

4.3 Prioritization of Responses

In this step, responses were given a priority level in terms of their importance to the PBS system. The personal information of users and their experiences with an electronic health system were our consideration.

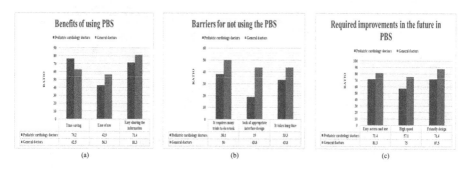

Fig. 1. (a) Benefits of using PBS (b) barriers to the use of PBS (c) required improvements for PBS in the future

4.4 Conversion of Responses to a Persona Template

In this step, the responses were converted to a persona document. During this process, imaginative elements, such as the person's name and image, were added to the responses. We created two personas: one for pediatric cardiologists (Fig. 2) and one for general doctors (Fig. 3).

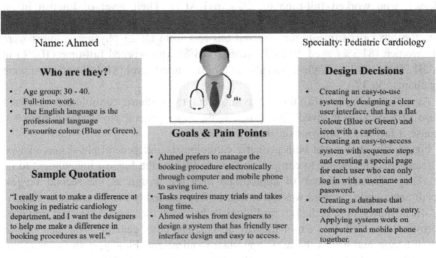

Fig. 2. The persona of a pediatric cardiology physician

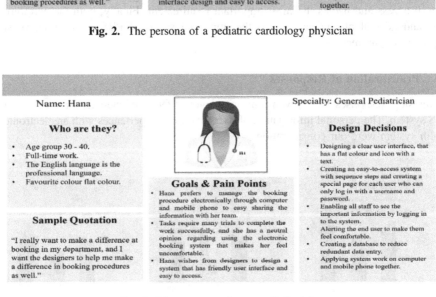

Fig. 3. The persona of a general physician

5 Results

From the previous results and following the creation of persona templates, we compared the persona of a pediatric cardiologist with the persona of a general physician. The results showed no fundamental differences in the system requirements, but there was a difference in the requirements in terms of the importance attributed to them. We found that when designing a system for health physicians, designers should consider the following fundamental elements:

- Physicians care about saving time, so designers should pay attention to accessibility and speed.
- Physicians care about ease of use, so the system design should contain icons with text or captions that ease usability. Colors must be comfortable and contrast with the background.
- Physicians care about accomplishing tasks quickly, so designers should not repeat data. Unimportant data should be removed.
- Physicians want the system to be easily available at all times, so the system must be usable on both computers and mobiles.

By adopting these fundamentals designers will ensure a highly efficient system that suits the personality of healthcare physicians. In turn, this will increase said physicians' effectiveness, efficiency and satisfaction, while improving their time management and reducing stress levels.

6 Conclusion

This paper proposed an interactive design for PBS based on personas and user behavior. Two templates were created, one for pediatric cardiologists and one for general doctors. The results confirmed that there was no fundamental difference in the requirements of the personas, but there was a difference in the priority of requirements, a consideration which designers should keep in mind when designing a health system to support UX. Finally, designing friendly UI facilitates information sharing, saves time, improves ease of use and access, improves time management and reduces stress.

In future work, we look forward to developing a PBS that considers all of the fundamental design implications discussed in this paper and applying them in real situations to prove the validity of the work.

Acknowledgements. I gratefully acknowledge the cardiovascular unit at KAUH for their cooperation in carrying out this research. I would also like to express my appreciation to my supervisor, Dr. Reem Alnanih for her support throughout this research project.

References

1. Smaradottir, B.F.: The steps of user-centered design in health information technology development. In: 2016 International Conference on Computational Science Computational Intelligence, pp. 116–121 2016
2. Ash, E., Berg, J.S., Coiera, M.: Some unintended consequences of information technology in health care: the nature of patient care information system-related errors. J. Am. Med. Inform. Assoc. **11**(2), 104–112 (2004)
3. Kaipio, J., et al.: Usability problems do not heal by themselves: national survey on physicians' experiences with ehrs in finland. Int. J. Med. Inform. **97**, 266–281 (2017)
4. Keefer, R.: Reducing stress in healthcare: evidence from using an integration design model. In: Proceedings of the Human Factors and Ergonomics Society Annual Meeting, vol. 61, no. 1, pp. 705–709. SAGE Publications, Los Angeles (2017)
5. Tu, Q., Wang, K., Shu, Q.: Computer-related technostress in China. Commun. ACM **48**(4), 77 (2005)
6. Hyppönen, H., Reponen, J., Lääveri, T., Kaipio, J.: User experiences with different regional health information exchange systems in Finland. Int. J. Med. Inform. **83**(1), 1–18 (2014)
7. Mirnig, A.G., Meschtscherjakov, A., Wurhofer, D., Meneweger, T., Tscheligi, M.: A formal analysis of the ISO 9241–210 definition of user experience. In: Proceedings of the 33rd Annual ACM Conference Extended Abstracts on Human Factors Computing Systems, CHI EA 2015, pp. 437–450 (2015)
8. Robert, J.M., Lesage, A.: 15 Designing and Evaluating User Experience. The Handbook of Human-Machine Interaction: A Human-Centered Design Approach (2012)
9. ISO: ISO 9241-11:2018: Ergonomics of human-system interaction—part 11: usability: definitions and concepts. International Organization for Standardization, Geneva, Switzerland (2018)
10. Viitanen, Johanna, Hyppönen, Hannele, Lääveri, Tinja, Vänskä, Jukka, Reponen, Jarmo, Winblad, Ilkka: National questionnaire study on clinical ICT systems proofs: physicians suffer from poor usability. Int. J. Med. Inform. **80**(10), 708–725 (2011)
11. LeRouge, C., Ma, J., Sneha, S., Tolle, K.: User profiles and personas in the design and development of consumer health technologies. Int. J. Med. Inform. **82**(11), e251–e268 (2013)
12. Berry, A.B., et al.: Using conceptual work products of health care to design health IT. J. Biomed. Inform. **59**, 15–30 (2016)
13. Chang, Y., Lim, Y., Stolterman, E.: Personas: from theory to practices. In: Proceedings of the 5th Nordic conference on Human-computer interaction: building bridges. ACM (2008)
14. Pröbster, M., Haque, M.E., Marsden, N., Functions, A.T.: Perceptions of personas: the role of instructions. IEEE International Conference on Engineering, Technology and Innovation (ICE/ITMC), pp. 1–8. IEEE, August 2018
15. Matthews, T., Judge, T., Whittaker, S.: How do designers and user experience professionals actually perceive and use personas?". In: Proceedings 2012 ACM Annual Conference on Human Factors in Computing Systems. CHI 2012, p. 1219 (2012)
16. Coorevits, L., Schuurman, D., Oelbrandt, K., Logghe, S.: Bringing personas to life: user experience design through interactive coupled open innovation. Pers. Stud. **2**(1), 97 (2016)
17. Anvari, F., Richards, D., Hitchens, M., Babar, M.A., Tran, H.M.T., Busch, P.: An empirical investigation of the influence of persona with personality traits on conceptual design. J. Syst. Softw. **134**, 324–339 (2017)
18. Rodriguez, E., Boks, C.: I A-2–2F: the environmental implications. Appliance, pp. 54–61 (2005)

19. Lockton, D., Harrison, D., Stanton, N.A.: The design with intent method: a design tool for influencing user behaviour. Appl. Ergon. **41**(3), 382–392 (2010)
20. Daae, J., Boks, C.: A classification of user research methods for design for sustainable behaviour. J. Clean. Prod. **106**, 680–689 (2014)
21. Cash, P.J., Hartlev, C.G., Durazo, C.B.: Behavioural design: a process for integrating behaviour change and design. Des. Stud. **48**, 96–128 (2017)
22. Saranto, K., Nyk, P.: Definition, structure, content, use and impacts of electronic health records: a review of the research literature, vol. 7, pp. 291–304 (2007)
23. Gesulga, J.M., Berjame, A., Moquiala, K.S., Galido, A.: Barriers to electronic health record system implementation and information systems resources: a structured review. Procedia Comput. Sci. **124**, 544–551 (2017)
24. Virginia, I., Van Slyke, C., Parikh, M.A., Courtney, J.F.: paper versus electronic medical records: the effects of access on physicians' decisions to use complex information technologies. Decis. Sci. **40**(2), 213–241 (2009)
25. Gagnon, M.P., et al.: Electronic health record acceptance by physicians: testing an integrated theoretical model. J. Biomed. Inform. **48**, 17–27 (2014)
26. Akhu-Zaheya, L., Al-Maaitah, R., Bany Hani, S.: Quality of nursing documentation: paper-based health records versus electronic-based health records. J. Clin. Nurs. **27**(3–4), e578–e589 (2018)
27. Ajami, S., Bagheri-tadi, T.: Barriers for adopting electronic health records (ehrs) by physicians. Acta Informatica Medica **21**(March), 129–134 (2013)
28. Pruitt, J., Adlin, T.: The Persona Lifecycle: Keeping People in Mind Throughout Product Design. Elsevier, Amsterdam (2010)

Saudi Arabia Market Basket Analysis

Monerah Alawadh[1(✉)], Israa Al-turaiki[2(✉)],
Mohammed Alawadh[3(✉)], and Shahad Tallab[1(✉)]

[1] Information Technology Department, College of Computer and Information
Sciences, King Saud University, Riyadh, Saudi Arabia
moalawadh@gmail.com, st.tallab@gmail.com
[2] IT Department, College of Computer and Information Sciences,
King Saud University, Riyadh, Saudi Arabia
ialturaiki@ksu.edu.sa
[3] Strategic Management & Marketing, College of Business Administration,
KSU, Riyadh, Saudi Arabia
malawadh@ksu.edu.sa

Abstract. Market Basket Analysis is one of the famous Data Mining applications, where is the later extract hidden and previously unknown patterns,
relationships and knowledge that are difficult to detect with traditional statistical
methods [1]. This type of analysis is rarely been applied in the Arab Markets
compared to the non-Arabic Markets. This paper will address the Saudi Arabia
Market Basket Analysis using real data from one of the biggest Supermarkets in
Saudi Arabia. At the end of this analysis study, we come up with a helpful
information and facts for Saudi Arabia Markets. Finally, we come up with new
knowledge about Saudi Arabia baskets which may help both marketers as well
consumers in the same time.

Keywords: Data mining · Saudi Arabia · FB-Grouth · Marketing · Consumers

1 Introduction

Data mining is the exploration of large datasets to extract hidden and previously
unknown patterns, relationships and knowledge that are difficult to detect with traditional statistical methods [1]. These analysis and findings of such trends, patterns,
correlations, and anomalies help business decision makers to make accurate and more
effective future decisions. Data mining is the most powerful tool that plays an important
role in the Market basket analysis. There are many non-Arabic Market Basket Analysis
studies published and made available on the web. In this project we gather its data from
the Saudi Market to be one of the few studies add to the Arabic market basket analysis
literature. The creative comparative analyze as well as the visualized results presented
in this project will be helpful information for Saudi Arabia Markets decision makers
and it will encourage researchers to do more studies and discover new knowledge about
Saudi Arabia baskets.

© Springer Nature Switzerland AG 2019
A. Alfaries et al. (Eds.): ICC 2019, CCIS 1098, pp. 52–59, 2019.
https://doi.org/10.1007/978-3-030-36368-0_5

1.1   The Problem

There are hundreds of studies related to market basket analysis that were published and made available on the web. However, few were done to the Arab Markets and less to the Saudi market. **Therefore**, this project will contribute to fill this gap and be good base for other studies to be done in this Saudi Market. The data collected in this project is a real data (Receipts) retrieved from one of the biggest Supermarket chains in Saudi Arabia.

1.2   The Importance of Analyzing Saudi Arabia Market Basket

The project aims to analyze the Saudi Arabia market basket to find out the hidden pattern regarding the trend of the Saudis shopping habits. Analysis, of the Saudi Arabia market data, will offer an insight of Saudi buyers' habits and consumer's behavior. Business decision makers, especially Marketing Managers are eager to know such behaviors in order to take the suitable marketing actions and decisions based on evidence and scientific studies and analysis of the market. Such results will help these marketers to know the best time to place an order for a specific product, when to announce sales promotions and merchandises, and what is the greatest way to organize products inside the super market to maximize profits of the business in one hand and made customers' convenience on the other hand.

2   Literature Review

Data mining has taken an important part of marketing literature for the last several decades [1]. Market basket analysis is one of the oldest areas in the field of data mining and is the best example for mining association rules. Market basket analysis defined as a technique for finding out relations or co-occurring items (correlations) in consumer shopping baskets [2].

According to [3] market basket analysis has been classified into two types: explanatory and exploratory. The main point in the exploratory type is that the discovering of purchase patterns will be from POS (point-of-sale) data. Exploratory approaches do not include information on consumer demographics or marketing mix variables [4]. On the other hand, explanatory models aim to pinpoint and measure cross-category selection effects of marketing variables. In this model dataset usually contains market basket data, product categories, customer attributes and marketing mix variables like, price, promotion and other marketing features. Most of the explanatory models rely greatly on regression analysis, profit and multivariate logistic model [5].

There are many exploratory techniques to uncover hidden frequent pattern of items in market datasets. The most famous and well known is the Apriori algorithm for mining frequent itemsets (items that happen together) [6]. This was proposed by Agarwal and Srikant in 1994 [7].

Apriori algorithm scans the dataset many time to find the frequent item sets [1]. This face memory and storage difficulties when dealing with larger datasets. FP-growth -frequent pattern growth- algorithm overcome this problem by scanning the database only twice, it represents the database in a compressed structure, organized, and easy to understand graph called FP-Tree [7]. Then, the FP-Tree is used to extract the association rules [8].

According to [7], to counter the drawbacks of Apriori performance, it was suggested to use an algorithm that will reduce the numbers of scans of the dataset by selecting fewer candidate items. In 2013, a thesis study applied market basket analysis and Apriori on beauty products as a mean to offer competitive edge to the companies [2]. Furthermore, the study focused on the probability of buying products at different times of the day and in different seasons. an analysis like this will offer markets and stores managers with knowledge on when is the best season for promotion of some product categories and at what time of the day customers are more likely to buy items from a specific product category.

Similarly, another study applied the market basket analysis to sport equipment's database in order to increase the sales using FP growth [9]. The study explains how to utilize the discovered information as to provide better recommendations and promotions for the customers. The study concluded with offering information about what spot items should be organized on the shelves together like towel, running shoes, socks etc.

Moving on to the second type of basket analysis, which is the explanatory analysis. A study [4] claimed that explanatory cross category market basket analysis is biased and inaccurate as it studies only a fraction of the market collection of data. Thus, the study proposes the use of Bayesian variable selection method to determine major cross category effect in multivariate model, and consequently allowing for deeper investigation of products and product categories than other previous researches.

Moreover, according to [10] there are number of Stores widely used the market basket analyses to manage the placement of goods in their store layout. Related products are placed together in such a manner that customers can logically find items he/she might buy which increases the customer satisfaction and hence the profit.

3   Software Used

For data presentation and simple modification and cleaning Microsoft Excel spreadsheet was used. For the knowledge extraction, we use free data mining tools available in the internet. The best tool is Rapid miner and we use it for the Knowledge extraction in this project.

4   Data Cleaning and Pre-processing

4.1   Cleaning and Translation Phase

In this phase we performed manual cleaning to unify items name using the find and replace function in excel. We also changed items name to English language and that was due to some difficulties we faced with encoding see Fig. 1.

Fig. 1. .

4.2   Extraction of Distinct Items Value Phase

As seen in the above figure, the data was normalized with each transaction repeated across multiple rows according to the number of items present in that transaction. We needed to extract a list of distinct items name to use as attribute headers. To do that we used the filter function in excel. Once we got the list of distinct items we created a new excel sheet and pasted the list. However, we want the list to be column headers not row values. So, we used "transpose" to switch axis. The dataset had the invoice id as the first column contains unique id for each transaction. The second is the city. Then each item name had a separate column with values either 0 or 1. 0 meant that the transaction did not contain that item, and 1 meant that the transaction contained that item. See the following Fig. 5 for the look of dataset at the end of this step.

5   Overview of Our Algorithm

FP-Growth:
FP-Growth allows frequent itemset discovery without candidate itemset generation. Two step approach:

Step 1:   Build a compact data structure called the FP-tree.

- Built using 2 passes over the data-set.

Step 2:   Extracts frequent itemsets directly from the FP-tree.

- Traversal through FP-Tree.

Evaluation Measures:
In order to evaluate, FP_grouth uses performance measures for the resulting models as follow:

Support

Support shows the frequency of the patterns in the rule; it is the percentage of transactions that contain both A and B, i.e.

Support = Probability (A and B).
Support = (# of transactions involving A and B)/(total number of transactions).

Confidence

Confidence is the strength of implication of a rule; it is the percentage of transactions that contain B if they contain A, i.e.

Confidence = Probability (B if A) = P(B/A).
Confidence = (# of transactions involving A and B)/(total number of transactions that have A).

Example:

Transaction ID	Item purchased	Item purchased
1604060010200200000	Yogurt	Beer
1604060010200300000	Salad	Soda
1604060010200400000	Yogurt	Soda
1604060010200500000	Salad	Tea

If A is "purchased Yogurt" and B is "purchased soda" then:

Support $= \mathrm{P(A\,and\,B)} = 1/4$, **Confidence** $= \mathrm{P(B/A)} = 1/2$

Confidence does not measure if the association between A and B is random or not.

6 Project Experiment

6.1 First Run All Cities

Extracting the association rules from all three cities (Riyadh, Jeddah, and Dammam). For this run we set the minsup to 0.08 and confidence to 0.5 to include more association's rules.

Association Rules for All Cities Run

Many rules are shows based on confidence of greater than 0.5, here we are showing the most important ones:

[Cheese] –> [Fresh milk, Industrial Bakery, Juice] **(confidence: 0.577)**
[Water] –> [yoghurt, Industrial Bakery, Juice] **(confidence: 0.597)**
[Washing Detergent] –> [Fresh milk, Juice, Chicken whole/parts] **(confidence: 0.623)**

Result Evaluation for This Run:

The association rules of this run clearly shows that people in the study are more into the industrial bakeries products such as, Lusinets beera, Kako pie, and seven days croissant. These products are known as low price products and suitable for breakfast/snack which could explain such behavior.

Another interesting observation is the people's value of cleanliness. That was clearly shown from the amount of washing detergents that found to be included in Saudi market basket. This can be explain by relating it to the teaching of the Mohammed prophet peace be upon him commanded Muslims to mind their personal hygiene especially during daily prayers.

Other prominent items in Saudi basket were fresh milk, and juice. And they seemed to accompany industrial bakeries most of the times. This can be related to the association of the drinks to some daily meals.

6.2   Second Run (Riyadh)

In the second Run we wanted to find the association rules related to Riyadh city only. To do that we used the filter highlighted in the above figure to select a range of rows based on city value equals to Riyadh. During this run we adjusted the minsup and confidence to be around .03 minsup and 0.5 for confidence as we were dealing with one third of our data.

Association Rules for Riyadh Only Run:

Many rules are shows based on confidence of greater than 0.5, here we are showing the most important ones:

[Fresh milk, Eggplant] –> [Cheese] **(confidence: 0.500)**
[Chocolate] –> [Juice] **(confidence: 0.510)**
[Chocolate] –> [Cheese] **(confidence: 0.510)**

Result Evaluation for Riyadh Only Run

From the sample of rules, we surmised that in Riyadh people like purchase fresh milk and eggplants are likely to buy cheese or onion with it. Also, those who like to buy chocolate with either cheese or juice.

To get this result, we started tweaking with value of minsup. We started at the same value for the first run (all cities) which was 0.08 and started to go down one digit at a time until 0.03 we reached a more diverse association rules from the first run.

6.3   Result Evaluation for Jeddah Only Run

In Jeddah, people like to buy bananas with fresh yogurt, milk, or juice. Moreover, those buy washing detergents are likely to buy chicken as well.

7 Comparative Analysis and Visualization

As stated above, one of our goals of the study was to perform some comparative analysis of our dataset. In order to explore another dimension of the data.

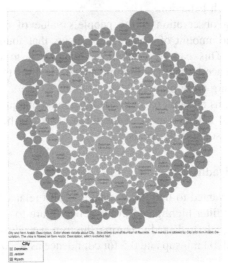

City and Item Arabic Description. Color shows details about City. Size shows sum of Number of Records. The marks are labeled by City and Item Arabic Description. The data is filtered on Item Arabic Description, which excludes Null.

City
▧ Dammam
▩ Jeddah
▦ Riyadh

Graph Observations

- People in Riyadh buy more biscuits and cheese than Jeddah or Dammam
- Both Riyadh and Dammam buy bread more that Jeddah.
- People in Dammam appear to purchase chocolate more followed by Riyadh the Jeddah.
- Riyadh buys chicken more than Dammam and Jeddah.
- Coffee is bought more in Dammam
- Industrial bakeries are purchased with similar frequencies across the cities under study.
- People of Dammam and Riyadh buy more juice than Jeddah
- Riyadh buys more pasta and potato.
- People in Dammam like to buy more spices and seasonings than Riyadh and Jeddah.

8 Conclusion and Future Work

The project went through main phases of data exploration, data collection, data cleaning, data mining, model evaluation, and knowledge discovery. The topic of our research was exploring frequent patterns of Saudi market basket, and to perform comparative analysis between shopping habits of three cities of Saudi Arabia. In our study we were able to find some interesting insights regarding Saudi shoppers' habits, and obtain some interesting association rules which will also help the marketers to do better business decisions. We think that this study will open the door to the future studies for the Saudi Markets.

As a future work, we can repeat the same experiment but with a substantial and huge amount of data, the association rules and comparative analysis would have been more accurate and truly indicative the hidden pattern in Saudi market basket.

Another dimension of the study that came to our mind, and would have liked to explored had there been enough time, was regarding finding statistical correlation between Saudi shopping habits and some health issues like the increasing high rates of obesity and diabetes in our county.

References

1. Gancheva, V.: Market basket analysis of beauty products. Master Thiese, pp. 16–20. Erasmus University Rotterdam (2016)
2. Gupta, S., Mamtora, R.: A survey on association rule mining in market basket analysis. Int. J. Inf. Comput. Technol. **4**(4), 409–414 (2014)
3. Master Thesis. Market basket analysis of beauty products, Docplayer.net (2016). http://docplayer.net/3183780-Master-thesis-market-basket-analysis-of-beauty-products.html. Accessed 4 Mar 2016
4. Dippold, K., Hruschka, H.: Variable selection for market basket analysis. Comput. Stat. **28**(2), 519–539 (2013)
5. Mild, A., Reutterer, T.: An improved collaborative filtering approach for predicting cross-category purchases based on binary market basket data. J. Retail. Consum. Serv. **10**, 123–133 (2003)
6. Agrawal, R., Srikant, R.: Fast algorithms for mining association rules. In: Proceedings of the 20th International Conference on Very Large Data Bases, VLDB, vol. 1215 (1994)
7. Pasquier, N., Bastide, Y., Taouil, R., Lakhal, L.: Efficient mining of association rules using closed itemset lattices. Inf. Syst. **24**(1), 25–46 (1999)
8. Strehl, A., Ghosh, J.: A scalable approach to balanced, high-dimensional clustering of market-baskets. In: Valero, M., Prasanna, V.K., Vajapeyam, S. (eds.) HiPC 2000. LNCS, vol. 1970, pp. 525–536. Springer, Heidelberg (2000). https://doi.org/10.1007/3-540-44467-X_48
9. Kaur, H., Singh, K.: Market basket analysis of sports store using association rules. Int. J. Recent Trends Electr. Electron. Eng. **3**(1), 81–85 (2013)
10. Charlet, L., Kumar, A.: Market basket analysis for a supermarket based on frequent itemset mining. IJCSI Int. J. Comput. Sci. **9**(5), 3 (2012)

Determining the Best Prediction Accuracy of Software Maintainability Models Using Auto-WEKA

Hadeel Alsolai[1,2]([⊠]) [ID] and Marc Roper[2] [ID]

[1] Computer Science and Information System,
Princess Nourah Bint Abdulrahman University, Riyadh, Saudi Arabia
hadeel.alsolai@strath.ac.uk
[2] Computer and Information Sciences, University of Strathclyde, Glasgow, UK
Marc.roper@strath.ac.uk

Abstract. Highly accurate prediction of software maintainability models is a significant requirement to achieve software quality assurance. Development an accurate prediction model may involve on trying several types of machine learning models with different configurations that include tuning parameters and selected features. However, this is a difficult and very time-consuming task to implement. In this paper, we report on the experience of using a new, rapid automated tool to identify the best prediction accuracy of a software maintainability model, namely Auto-WEKA, applied to sets of different models with various configurations. Auto-WEKA is applied to five datasets collected from real-world open-source software systems. The mean magnitude relative error (MMRE) value is used to evaluate the accuracy of predictive models, along with ZeroR model to compare selected model performance with the baseline. The results obtained from this study provide empirical evidence of the ability of Auto-WEKA to identify the best model to predict software maintainability. Auto-WEKA selected the following as the best prediction models: SMOreg in Eclipse JDT Core dataset, RandomSubSpace in Eclipse PDE UI dataset, KStar in Equinox Framework dataset, RandomForet in Lucene and Mylyn datasets. These selected models achieved a low MMRE value and improved performance of the accuracy prediction over the baseline. The proposed tool was found useful in identifying the best model in predicting software maintainability.

Keywords: Tuning parameters · Feature selection · Auto-WEKA · Software maintainability · Accuracy prediction · Machine learning

1 Introduction

Software maintainability is one of the significant attributes of software quality assurance [1] and is described as the ease to modify, improve or update a software system [2]. Software metrics are collected from source code software systems and can be used as predictors of the software maintainability [3–10]. Software maintainability prediction has been investigated in several studies using machine learning models [3–9]. However, the creation of a highly accurate prediction of software maintainability is a

© Springer Nature Switzerland AG 2019
A. Alfaries et al. (Eds.): ICC 2019, CCIS 1098, pp. 60–70, 2019.
https://doi.org/10.1007/978-3-030-36368-0_6

challenging task to implement, since the relationships between software quality attributes and their metrics are often complicated, nonlinear and lead to a reduction in the accuracy of prediction models [7].

Maintainability is commonly measured in several studies as the whole effort spent on changing a class [3–10]. These changes are indicated by a dependent variable, namely the CHANGE metric, that is calculated by counting the number of lines added or deleted in each class during a maintenance period [10]. A higher number of changes reflects low maintainability and high maintenance effort [9]. Object-oriented metrics, such as Chidamber and Kemerer (CK) metrics [11] and Li and Henry (LH) metrics [10] have been used by various studies as independent variables to predict software maintainability [3–9].

To build an accurate maintainability prediction model, prior studies have applied several types of machine learning models with configurations set manually (i.e. tuning parameters [12] or selected features [8]). However, this approach requires great time and effort. With the objective of determining the best prediction model of the software maintainability, this paper demonstrates the application of Auto-WEKA as a new, rapid and automated tool to help identify the best accurate prediction model among sets of models, with different parameters and features, using Bayesian optimisation [13, 14]. According to the best of our knowledge, there is no other work in the previous studies which have used the bug prediction datasets or the auto-WEKA tool to predict software maintainability. This work will contribute to enhancing the research in both the machine learning and software maintainability fields.

The rest of this paper is organised as follow: Sect. 2 presents related work. Section 3 reports the research methodology. Section 4 details the experimental setup. Section 5 discusses results and analysis, and we conclude in Sect. 6.

2 Related Work

Current related work is summarized as follows: (a) general approaches for machine learning models tuning and feature selection (b) studies which have created software maintainability prediction models, (c) studies which have applied tuning parameters in software maintainability prediction, and (d) studies which have performed feature selection for software maintainability prediction.

Recent studies have utilised various approaches for machine learning models tuning parameters. For example, Fernández-Delgado et al. created 179 classifiers and applied automatic parameter tuning using the R caret package [15]. Further, Olson et al. evaluated the ability of hyperparameter (i.e. algorithm parameter) tuning for 13 machine learning algorithms [16]. Both studies concluded the improvement of the prediction accuracy of the models with tuning parameters compared to the default setting of these models. Moreover, certain studies in the field the software defect prediction used different types of feature selection techniques such as greedy forward selection [17], automatic hybrid search algorithm [18] and correlation-based feature selection [19]. These techniques confirmed the effectiveness of the feature selection in this field.

Several studies have investigated software maintainability prediction using object-oriented metrics [3–10], such as (C&K) metrics [11] and (L&H) metrics [10]. Most of these studies applied different types of machine learning models on Quality Evaluation System (QUES) and User Interface System (UIMS) datasets [10]. Van Koten and Gray used a Bayesian network to develop a maintainability prediction model for an object-oriented software system [3]. Multivariate adaptive regression splines (MARS) were created by Zhou and Leung using the metric data collected from two different object-oriented systems [4]. MARS was compared with multivariate linear regression models, artificial neural network models, regression tree models, and support vector models, and the result indicates that MARS outperforms other models in both systems. Elish and Elish evaluated the ability of TreeNet model to increase accuracy prediction over widely used prediction models. The results provide confirmatory evidence that the TreeNet model is certainly a useful modelling technique for object-oriented software maintainability [5]. The Group Method of Data Handling model was explored by Malhotra and Chug to estimate software maintainability prediction [6]. The results suggests that the Group Method of Data Handling model achieved high accuracy against other compared models. Thwin and Quah compared the capability of two neural network models, namely, Ward neural network and General Regression neural network [7]. The result shows that General Regression neural network yield improved prediction accuracy over Ward neural network. Hybrid neural network and fuzzy logic models investigated by Kumar and Rath emphasise that the ability of the Neuro-Fuzzy model to predict software maintainability [8]. Alsolai compared sets of individual models (regression tree, multilayer perceptron, k-nearest neighbours and m5rules), with one an ensemble model (bagging). The findings obtained from the experiment provided empirical evidence of the ability of bagging model to increase accuracy prediction over almost all selected individual models [9]. However, since the implementation of a highly accurate prediction of software maintainability is a difficult task to achieve, there is a requirement to investigate other methods (e.g. tuning parameters or selected features) to improve accuracy prediction.

Even though tuning parameters is recommended by Fu et al. [20] to improve the performance of the prediction model, a limited number of studies have applied this approach for software maintainability prediction. For example, a study by Dahiya et al. [12] applied a genetic algorithm to optimise parameters of a fuzzy logic based maintainability metrics system. Moreover, research studies have investigated selected features as an alternative method to improve accuracy prediction. Kumar and Rath enhanced the performance of software maintainability prediction model using one method of feature selection, namely rough set analysis [8]. However, tuning parameters and selecting features requires many attempts and significant effort to obtain the optimal results. Therefore, Auto-WEKA has been recently proposed to resolve this problem and to provide mechanisms for both tuning parameters and selecting features [13, 14].

3   Research Methodology

This paper aims to use the Auto-WEKA tool to identify the best model to predict software maintainability. We apply Auto-WEKA on five datasets extracted from real-world software systems. With the goal of achieving the highest prediction accuracy, this tool tries several models with different tuning parameters and selected features.

The experiment is performed to respond to the following research questions:

RQ1) What is the best-selected model by Auto-WEKA to predict software maintainability in each dataset?

RQ2) How many configurations are tried to select the best model?

RQ3) What are the tuning parameter settings in the selected model?

RQ4) What are the selected features in the selected model?

RQ5) What is the MMRE value for the selected model?

RQ6) How much selected model increased the performance over the baseline (i.e. ZeroR)?

4   Experimental Setup

The following subsections identify the key elements in the study: the dataset collection, the dataset variables (dependent and independent), the Auto-WEKA tool and the evaluation measures.

4.1   Dataset Collection

We use five datasets collected from real-world software systems written in the Java language, namely the bug prediction datasets [21]. These datasets were collected at the class level and are composed of several metrics, bugs changes and version information about the system [21]. Moreover, these datasets have metrics that can be integrated to indicate CHANGE metric as the dependent variable. Besides, these datasets contain sets of object-oriented (OO) and CK metrics that can be used to predict software maintainability as independent variables. Previous studies used these datasets in software defect prediction [22, 23] but no studies have used them in software maintainability prediction. We apply pre-processing techniques to determine and remove outliers using the InterQuartileRange (IQR) and Removewithvalues filters in WEKA. Table 1 summarises the datasets used in this study.

Table 1. Summary of the datasets.

Dataset name	ID	Number of the original class	Number of class after removing outliers
Eclipse JDT Core	D1	997	695
Eclipse PDE UI	D2	1497	1209
Equinox Framework	D3	324	276
Lucene	D4	691	532

4.2   Dependent Variable: Maintainability

Maintainability is described in this study as the number of changes made in the class during the maintenance process. We determine the dependent variable (CHANGE) from the bug prediction datasets [21] by integrating two metrics: lines Added Until and lines Removed Until, which refer the lines inserted to or removed from the classes during maintenance period [21].

4.3   Independent Variables: Metrics

The independent variables include seventeen source code metrics that involve six CK metrics. Ambros et al. explain the details of extracting these metrics [21]. Table 2 lists a brief description of each independent variable used in this study.

Table 2. Summary of class level source code metrics [21].

CK metrics	
LCOM	Lack of Cohesion in Methods
NOC	Number of Children
DIT	Depth of Inheritance Tree
CBO	Coupling Between Objects
RFC	Response for Class
WMC	Weighted Method Count
OO metrics	
NOMI	Number of methods inherited
NOPM	Number of public methods
LOC	Number of lines of code
NOPRA	Number of private attributes
NOA	Number of attributes
FanIn	Number of other classes that reference the class
NOPRM	Number of private methods
NOM	Number of methods
NOAI	Number of attributes inherited
NOPA	Number of public attributes
FanOut	Number of other classes referenced by the class

4.4   Auto-WEKA

Auto-WEKA is an automatic tool that implements many types of machine learning models with integrated different selected features and tuning parameters in WEKA [13, 14]. This tool tries different hyperparameter settings and selected features for several models and provides the best model performance using the Bayesian optimisation method [13, 14]. Recently, Auto-WEKA is combined with WEKA as a package and is constructed to perform regression algorithms, performance metrics and parallel runs [13]. We used the default settings of this tool as suggested [14].

4.5   Evaluation Measurement

In this study we compare and evaluate prediction models by using one of the de facto standard prediction accuracy measures, namely Mean Magnitude of the Relative Error (MMRE) that is well-known and widely used when predicting software maintainability [3–5, 8, 24–26]. The MRE is computed by identifying the absolute difference between the actual values and predicted values divided by actual values [27]. Then, MMRE is computed by identifying the mean of MRE as indicated in the following equation:

$$\text{MMRE} = \frac{1}{n}\sum_{i=1}^{i=n}\text{MRE} \tag{1}$$

In addition, the baseline is considered as a benchmark to evaluate predicted models [28]. Previous studies utilised the baseline [15, 27, 29, 30], which depends on either the mean [29] or median [30] of the dependent variable. In this study, we use the ZeroR model to predict the mean value in the training data [31]. This model relies on the dependent variable only (i.e. CHANGE), and it is beneficial for identifying the baseline [32].

5   Results and Analysis

Table 3 provides the results of the best-selected model, along with numbers of attempted configurations, selected features and tuning parameters. This table answers **RQ1**, **RQ2**, **RQ3** and **RQ4**, and reveals in several findings. **First**, two individual models are selected as the best prediction accuracy models, namely SMOreg in D1, which is a support vector regression model, and KStar in D3, which is an instance-based model. **Second**, two meta models (i.e. ensembles) are chosen as the best prediction accuracy models, namely RandomSubSpace in D2, which creates a decision tree-based model and RandomForest in D4 and D5, which creates a forest of random trees. **Third**, the number of attempted configurations range from 134 to 428. **Fourth**, each selected model has specifically defined tuning parameters, while the selected features are applied only for D3 and D4 to determine the BestFirst filter for attribute search and the CfsSubsetEval filter for attribute evaluation.

Table 4 presents the results of the MMRE value to determine prediction accuracy achieved by the best-selected model, along with the baseline (i.e. ZeroR). It is apparent from this table that there was a difference between the MMRE values for selected models and MMRE values for ZeroR. Interestingly, the selected model in D3 achieved the best accuracy prediction, where the percentage of change was 89.78%.

Figure 1 shows a histogram of the MMRE value to compare the accuracy prediction between selected models and ZeroR models. The low value of this diagram indicates the better accuracy achieved by the prediction model. The results obtained from Fig. 1 established the evidence of the positive impact of using Auto-WEKA tool to select the best model in prediction software maintainability. It yields an improvement over the baseline (i.e. ZeroR) in the range 53.88% to 89.78%. The best-selected model in the D3 dataset achieved the lowest MMRE value, followed by the best-selected model in the D2 then D4 datasets.

Table 3. The best model selected in each dataset.

Dataset ID	Best-selected model/Numbers of tries configurations	Configurations	
		Selected features	Tuning parameters
D1	SMOreg/295	Null	[-C, 1.3565252749701955, -N, 0, -I, weka.classifiers.functions.supportVector. RegSMOImproved, -K, weka.classifiers.functions.supportVector. NormalizedPolyKernel -E 2.8518299249980115 -L]
D2	RandomSubSpace/134	Null	[-I, 53, -P, 0.37299422237345936, -S, 1, -W, weka.classifiers.functions. MultilayerPerceptron, −, -L, 0.6520314185757002, -M, 0.6694968982868784, -B, -H, i, -R, -D, - S, 1]
D3	KStar/428	Attribute search: BestFirst Attribute evaluation: CfsSubsetEval	[-B, 38, -M, n]
D4	RandomForet/321	Attribute search: BestFirst Attribute evaluation: CfsSubsetEval	[-I, 96, -K, 1, -depth, 12]
D5	RandomForet/162	Null	[-I, 136, -K, 7, -depth, 14]

Table 4. MMRE value for the selected model and ZeroR.

Datasets ID	MMRE for the best-selected model	MMRE for ZeroR	% of change
D1	6.36	13.79	53.88%
D2	0.79	6.12	87.09%
D3	0.57	5.58	89.78%
D4	5.21	15.18	65.68%
D5	1.54	5.92	73.99%

Figure 2 illustrates the residual box plots of the MRE values for selected and ZeroR models in each dataset. This diagram enables the visualization of the performance of all prediction models based on the MMRE value, which is indicated by an "X". The solid body of the boxes represents the spread of the middle 50% of the data (between the 1st and 3rd quartiles) and the solid line in this represents the median value. The vertical lines ("whiskers") show the spread of values that fall within 1.5 times the inter-quartile range, The prediction model which has lowest MMRE value and the narrowest box and smallest range is considered to be preferable.

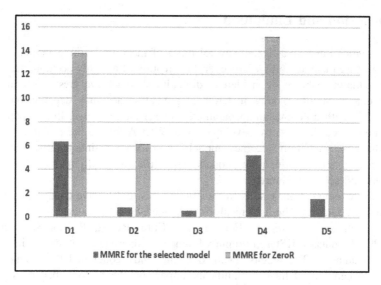

Fig. 1. MMRE value for selected and ZeroR models in each dataset.

In Fig. 2, there is a clear trend of a decrease in the MMRE value indicated by "X" in the diagram, after applying Auto-WEKA tool to all datasets. Moreover, each selected model had a reduction in the box spread.

The results obtained from this figure established the evidence of the positive impact of employing Auto-WEKA tool on all datasets. It yields an improvement of between (53.88%) and (89.78%), which is considered a high performance in the software maintainability prediction.

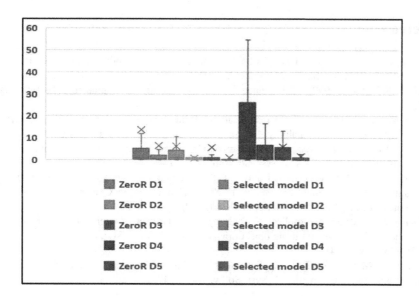

Fig. 2. Box plot of MRE for selected and ZeroR models in each dataset.

6 Conclusion and Limitation

Previous studies have investigated several types of machine learning models in predicting software maintainability. However, the creation of a highly accurate prediction of software maintainability is considered a difficult task to achieve. Best selection of the software maintainability models in terms of prediction accuracy depends on trying many models with different tuning parameters or selected features. In this paper, we have demonstrated the recently developed Auto-WEKA tool to the problem of identifying the best prediction accuracy model for software maintainability prediction among various machine learning models with different configurations for tuning parameters and selected features.

We have concluded our results from applying this tool on five datasets, called the bug prediction datasets. The final result has provided the best-selected models in each dataset, which are SMOreg in Eclipse JDT Core dataset, RandomSubSpace in Eclipse PDE UI dataset, KStar in Equinox Framework dataset, RandomForet in Lucene and Mylyn datasets. The results obtained in the study concluded that using Auto-WEKA tool can indeed have a significant impact on the performance of software maintainability prediction models. Therefore, we recommend that researchers should use Auto-WEKA tool to determine the best prediction accuracy model. As a part of future work, we will further investigate Auto-WEKA with different time settings and compare the performance of selected models against the default setting. Moreover, we will compare the results of Auto-WEKA with the ensemble models proposed in our research plan [33].

Acknowledgments. We gratefully acknowledge Princess Nourah bint Abdulrahman University for their support in pursuing this research. We thank the University of Strathclyde for providing several facilities in the production of this research paper.

References

1. Jung, H.-W., Kim, S.-G., Chung, C.-S.: Measuring software product quality: A survey of ISO/IEC 9126. IEEE Softw. **21**(5), 88–92 (2004)
2. IEEE Std 610.12-1990: IEEE Standard Glossary of Software Engineering Terminology. IEEE (1990)
3. van Koten, C., Gray, A.R.: An application of Bayesian network for predicting object-oriented software maintainability. Inf. Software Technol. **48**(1), 59–67 (2006)
4. Zhou, Y., Leung, H.: Predicting object-oriented software maintainability using multivariate adaptive regression splines. J. Syst. Software **80**(8), 1349–1361 (2007)
5. Elish, M.O., Elish, K.O.: Application of TreeNet in predicting object-oriented software maintainability: a comparative study. In: 2009 13th European Conference on Software Maintenance and Reengineering, pp. 69–78 (2009)
6. Malhotra, R., Chug, A.: Application of Group Method of Data Handling model for software maintainability prediction using object oriented systems. Int. J. Syst. Assur. Eng. Manag. **5**(2), 165–173 (2014)
7. Thwin, M.M.T., Quah, T.-S.: Application of neural networks for software quality prediction using object-oriented metrics. J. Syst. Softw. **76**(2), 147–156 (2005)

8. Kumar, L., Rath, S.K.: Software maintainability prediction using hybrid neural network and fuzzy logic approach with parallel computing concept. Int. J. Syst. Assur. Eng. Manag. J. Article **8**(2), 1487–1502 (2017)

9. Alsolai, H.: Predicting software maintainability in object-oriented systems using ensemble techniques. In: 2018 IEEE International Conference on Software Maintenance and Evolution (ICSME), pp. 716–721. IEEE (2018)

10. Li, W., Henry, S.: Object-oriented metrics that predict maintainability. J. Syst. Softw. **23**(2), 111–122 (1993)

11. Chidamber, S.R., Kemerer, C.F.: A metrics suite for object oriented design. IEEE Trans. Software Eng. **20**(6), 476–493 (1994)

12. Dahiya, S.S., Chhabra, J.K., Kumar, S.: Use of genetic algorithm for software maintainability metrics' conditioning. In: 15th International Conference on Advanced Computing and Communications (ADCOM 2007), pp. 87–92: IEEE (2007)

13. Kotthoff, L., Thornton, C., Hoos, H.H., Hutter, F., Leyton-Brown, K.: Auto-WEKA 2.0: automatic model selection and hyperparameter optimization in WEKA. J. Mach. Learn. Res. **18**(1), 826–830 (2017)

14. Kotthoff, L., Thornton, C., Hutter, F.: User guide for auto-WEKA version 2.3. Department of Computer Science, University of British Columbia, BETA lab, Vancouver, BC, Canada, Technical report, vol. 2 (2017)

15. Fernández-Delgado, M., Cernadas, E., Barro, S., Amorim, D.: Do we need hundreds of classifiers to solve real world classification problems? J. Mach. Learn. Res. **15**(1), 3133–3181 (2014)

16. Olson, R.S., La Cava, W., Mustahsan, Z., Varik, A., Moore, J.H.: Data-driven advice for applying machine learning to bioinformatics problems. arXiv preprint arXiv:1708.05070 (2017)

17. Laradji, I.H., Alshayeb, M., Ghouti, L.: Software defect prediction using ensemble learning on selected features. Inf. Softw. Technol. **58**, 388–402 (2015)

18. Gao, K., Khoshgoftaar, T.M., Wang, H., Seliya, N.: Choosing software metrics for defect prediction: an investigation on feature selection techniques. Softw. Pract. Experience **41**(5), 579–606 (2011)

19. Catal, C., Diri, B.: Investigating the effect of dataset size, metrics sets, and feature selection techniques on software fault prediction problem. Inf. Sci. **179**(8), 1040–1058 (2009)

20. Fu, W., Menzies, T., Shen, X.: Tuning for software analytics: is it really necessary? Inf. Softw. Technol. **76**, 135–146 (2016)

21. Ambros, M.D., Lanza, M., Robbes, R.: An extensive comparison of bug prediction approaches. In: 2010 7th IEEE Working Conference on Mining Software Repositories (MSR 2010), pp. 31–41 (2010)

22. Yang, J., Qian, H.: Defect prediction on unlabeled datasets by using unsupervised clustering. In: 2016 IEEE 18th International Conference on High Performance Computing and Communications; IEEE 14th International Conference on Smart City; IEEE 2nd International Conference on Data Science and Systems (HPCC/SmartCity/DSS), pp. 465–472 (2016)

23. Boucher, A., Badri, M.: Using software metrics thresholds to predict fault-prone classes in object-oriented software. In: 2016 4th International Conference on Applied Computing and Information Technology/3rd International Conference on Computational Science/Intelligence and Applied Informatics/1st International Conference on Big Data, Cloud Computing, Data Science & Engineering (ACIT-CSII-BCD), pp. 169–176 (2016)

24. Ahmed, M.A., Al-Jamimi, H.A.: Machine learning approaches for predicting software maintainability: a fuzzy-based transparent model. IET Softw. **7**(6), 317–326 (2013)

25. Kumar, L., Rath, S.: Predicting object-oriented software maintainability using hybrid neural network with parallel computing concept. In: Proceedings of the 8th India Software Engineering Conference, pp. 100–109. ACM (2015)

26. Kumar, L., Naik, D.K., Rath, S.K.: Validating the effectiveness of object-oriented metrics for predicting maintainability. Procedia Computer Science 57, 798–806 (2015)

27. Kitchenham, B.A., Pickard, L.M., MacDonell, S.G., Shepperd, M.J.: What accuracy statistics really measure [software estimation]. IEE Proc. Softw. 148(3), 81–85 (2001)

28. Shepperd, M., MacDonell, S.: Evaluating prediction systems in software project estimation. Inf. Softw. Technol. 54(8), 820–827 (2012)

29. Bi, J., Bennett, K.P.: Regression error characteristic curves. In: Proceedings of the 20th international conference on machine learning (ICML-03), pp. 43–50 (2003)

30. Mendes, E., Kitchenham, B.: Further comparison of cross-company and within-company effort estimation models for web applications. In: 10th International Symposium on Software Metrics, 2004. Proceedings, pp. 348–357. IEEE (2004)

31. Aher, S.B., Lobo, L.: Data mining in educational system using Weka. In: IJCA Proceedings on International Conference on Emerging Technology Trends (ICETT), vol. 3, pp. 20–25 (2011)

32. Venkatesh, A., Jacob, S.G.: Prediction of credit-card defaulters: a comparative study on performance of classifiers. Int. J. Comput. Appl. 145(7) (2016)

33. Alsolai, H., Roper, M.: Application of ensemble techniques in predicting object-oriented software maintainability. In: Proceedings of the Evaluation and Assessment on Software Engineering, Copenhagen, Denmark (2019)

Shark Smell Optimization (SSO) Algorithm for Cloud Jobs Scheduling

Yusra Mohamed Suliman[1], Adil Yousif[2(✉)],
and Mohammed Bakri Bashir[3]

[1] University of Science and Technology, Omdurman, Sudan
yosra_m_s@hotmail.com
[2] Najran University, Najran, Saudi Arabia
ayalfaki@nu.edu.sa, adiluofk@gmail
[3] Taif University, Taif, Saudi Arabia
mhmdbakri@gmail.com

Abstract. Cloud computing is an emerging technology based on moving the computing operations from the desktop computers to cloud providers through the internet. Typically, cloud providers on the internet process huge number of computing requests or jobs from enormous clients. Jobs scheduling in cloud computing is considered a crucial issue needs to be tackled. There are several methods available for jobs scheduling on cloud computing. However, there is a need for new mechanisms to reduce the job execution time and improve scheduling job process. This paper proposed a new job scheduling mechanism based on Shark Smell Optimization (SSO) algorithm. The proposed mechanism of job scheduling aims to find an efficient distribution of jobs based on SSO to mimic the behavior of sharks in the hunt wounded fish. Scheduling job in the proposed mechanism creates at first set of functions and resources to generate blood points by assigning jobs to resources randomly and assessing the blood points to find the place of a large amount blood points. The second phase repeats the regeneration of blood points based on the behavior of sharks to produce the best schedule for the jobs is that has the minimum execution time for jobs. Two experiments have been conducted to evaluate the proposed mechanism. The first stage of the evaluation process is a simple implementation scenarios using Java language. The second stage was a full simulation using CloudSim simulator toolkit. Several experiments scenarios using different numbers of jobs and resources are conducted. The simulation results revealed that the proposed SSO mechanism had outperformed Firefly Algorithm regarding the jobs execution time.

Keywords: Cloud · Job scheduling · Metaheuristic · Shark smell optimization

1 Introduction

Cloud computing is an emerging technology based on moving the computing operations from the desktop computers to cloud providers through the internet [1, 2].

The need for computing and storage are rapidly increasing. The cloud services are offered throughout the Internet networks. Cloud computing became one of the main

© Springer Nature Switzerland AG 2019
A. Alfaries et al. (Eds.): ICC 2019, CCIS 1098, pp. 71–80, 2019.
https://doi.org/10.1007/978-3-030-36368-0_7

models of computer science that utilize internet based model and provides three types of services software, platform and infrastructure.

Job scheduling process is one of the main issues need to be addressed in all the computing platforms [3, 4]. To effectively increase the advantages of cloud computing technologies, job scheduling is addressed in order to gain maximum benefits [5, 6].

The main aim of cloud job scheduling algorithms is to efficiently allocate the load on processors and optimize their utilization while minimizing the total job response time [7]. Applying optimization methods such as genetic algorithm, Firefly Algorithm and Glowworm optimization for cloud job scheduling process try to mimic the behavior of the natural environments [3, 4, 8].

In the job scheduling problem there are $R = \{r1, r2, r3 \ldots r$ are m cloud resources and $J = \{j1, j2, j3\ldots jm\}$ are clients jobs. The speed of each resource is stated in form of MIPS (Million Instructions Per Second), and the length of each job is stated in form of number of instructions. The job problem is how to distribute the client's jobs to the resources to reduce the jobs execution time.

The objective of this paper is to propose a new job scheduling method based on shark smell optimization (SSO) to minimize the execution time of the cloud jobs.

The rest of the paper is organized is follows. Section two illustrates the concepts and theories of cloud job scheduling. Section considers the related job scheduling methods. Section four explains in details the shark smell optimization algorithm and the proposed scheduling mechanism. Section five is the evaluation and experimentation part. We concluded in section six.

2   Cloud Job Scheduling

Cloud Job scheduling concerns with the allocation process of providers resources to user's jobs. Moreover, the required tasks can be finished in minimum time according to time defined in the user request. Several researches that considered job scheduling problem in grid computing can also be used in cloud computing setting [4, 9, 10]. The core task of job The main objectives of scheduling mechanisms is to locate the most suitable resources for the user's requests [11, 12].

The study by Pardeep Kumar and Amandeep Verma [5] proposed a new boost genetic algorithm for cloud job scheduling optimization. The new boost genetic algorithm produces the initial generation based on Min-Min and Max-Min instead of a random generation. This procedure for the initial population selection enhance the search process. Hence, the proposed boost genetic algorithm optimizes the scheduling process.

The study in [13] presented an Ant Colony Optimization as a policy for cloud computing job scheduling. The study handled the original ACO that was developed to handle the traveling salesman problem, by modifying some features of the ACO to fit the cloud computing job scheduling using simulator CloudSim. The modification was accomplished through extending the Datacenter Broker class for building the new cloud computing jobs scheduling policy based on ACO. The makespan (the total finish time of the tasks) is considered as evaluation criterion to assess the performance of the proposed job scheduling mechanism. The evaluation results revealed that the proposed

ACO scheduling policy reduces the makespan of the client's jobs submitted to the cloud providers.

The researchers in [14] proposed an ant colony algorithm for optimizing cloud computing job scheduling. The proposed method is called ACO-LB method, ant colony optimization for handling load balancing for cloud resources and virtual machines. The proposed ACO-LB decreased the makespan time and maintained the load balancing between resources.

A hybrid particle swarm optimization method is proposed by Shaobin Zhan and Hongying Huo to optimize cloud job scheduling [15]. Their mechanism merge particle swarm optimization and simulated annealing algorithm. The evaluation results of the merged mechanisms revealed that the average running time is decreased and the availability of resources is increased. The limitations of the merge mechanism is in balancing the load between the resources. Hence, the researchers recommended an enhancement to the algorithm through considering load balancing [15].

The research by Demyana et al. (2016), presented an enhanced firefly job scheduling optimization for cloud environment. The firefly algorithm for job scheduling is a population based optimization mechanism that uses firefly behavior to generate new solutions based on the fitness function [16].

The authors in [11, 12] proposed a new methods for job scheduling in cloud computing based on energy and fault tolerance aware techniques using clustering algorithms.

3 Shark Smell Optimization Algorithm

SSO is an optimization method based on the capability of shark, as a hunter in the sea water, for searching prey, which is based on the smell sense of shark and its movement to the smell source. A range of characteristics of shark within the search environment are modeled in the proposed shark smell optimization method. The efficiency of the proposed method is compared with several other optimization techniques using standard evaluation methodology. To test the applicability of the proposed shark smell optimization an illustration example using SSO is conducted for solving real-world problems. The proposed method is employed to solve load frequency control problem in electrical power systems. The results of the evaluation process revealed the validity of the proposed shark optimization method [17].

3.1 Formulation of the Proposed SSO Algorithm

To develop a mathematical model of the shark's search nature, some assumptions are deliberated as follows: The fish is injured and injects blood to the sea (search environment). So, the velocity of the fish movement is low and ignored against the shark's velocity [18–21]. Hence, the source (prey) is approximately assumed to be fixed. The blood is regularly injected to the sea and the effect of the water flows on distorting the odor particles is ignored. Therefore, nearer odor shark to the prey will be stronger. As a result, other by following the odor particles, the shark can approach the prey. One of the main assumptions of the SSO is only one injured fish in the search space [17].

The details of the proposed SSO method, based on the shark's search process, are described in the following subsections.

Step1: Get SSO algorithm parameters like α, β, M, NP, kmax η and NC.
Step2: Generate the initial population

$$X_i^1 = \left[x_{i,1}^1, x_{i,2}^1, \ldots, x_{i,ND}^1 \right], \quad i = 1, \ldots NP$$

$$[X_1^1, X_2^1, \ldots, X_{NP}^1], \quad NP = \text{Population Size}$$

Step3: initialize the stage counter: K = 1
Step4: Each component of the velocity vectors is calculated base on
Where
ηk: $\eta \in [0,1]$
αk: $\alpha \in [0,1]$
βk: is the velocity limiter ratio for stage k
Step5: new position of shark base o

$$Y_i^{k+1} = X_i^k + V_i^k \cdot \Delta t_k \quad i = 1, \ldots, NP \quad k = 1, \ldots, k_{max}$$

Where
tk indicates the time interval of the stage k.
Step6: if k equal kmax go to step 8
Step7: k = k+1 go to step 4
Step8: the best position of shark in the last stage (kmax) which has the highest OF value is selected as the final solution of the optimization problem
Step9: end

3.2   Pseudo Code for the Proposed Shark Smell Optimization

1. **Start**

2. *Get SSO algorithm parameters like α, β, M, NP, k_{max}, i, k, η and NC*

3. *Set NP=5, α=1, η=1, k_{max}=10, i=1, j=1 and k=1.*

4. *Generate R1, R2, and R3.*

5. *Generate the initial population of shark smell as allocation of job to resource*

   $$X_i^1 = [x_{i,1}^1, x_{i,2}^1, \ldots, x_{i,ND}^1], \quad i=1, \ldots NP$$

6. *Compute objective function OF(X_i^j)*

7. *Calculate the initial velocity vectors*

$$V_i^k = \eta_k.R1.\nabla(OF)|_{X_i^k}, \quad i=1,\dots,NP, \quad k=1,\dots,k_{max}$$

8. *While(k<=k_{max})*

   For i=1 to NP

$$|v_{i,j}^k| = \min\left[\left|\eta_k.R1.\frac{\partial(OF)}{\partial x_j}\Big|_{x_{i,j}^k} + \alpha_k.R2.v_{i,j}^{k-1}\right|, \left|\beta_k.v_{i,j}^{k-1}\right|\right]$$

$$Y_i^{k+1} = X_i^k + V_i^k.\Delta t_k \quad i=1,\dots,NP \quad k=1,\dots,k_{max}$$

   End for

K=k+1

End while

9. *the best position of shark in last stage (k_{max}) which has the highest OF value is selected as the final solution of the optimization problem*

$$|v_{i,j}^k| = \min\left[\left|\eta_k.R1.\frac{\partial(OF)}{\partial x_j}\Big|_{x_{i,j}^k} + \alpha_k.R2.v_{i,j}^{k-1}\right|, \left|\beta_k.v_{i,j}^{k-1}\right|\right]$$
$$j=1,\dots,ND, \quad i=1,\dots,NP, \quad k=1,\dots,k_{max}$$

4 Evaluation and Experimentation

To evaluate the proposed SSO method for cloud job scheduling this paper implemented the algorithm using CloudSim simulator. To handle a variety of characteristics of the proposed shark smell optimization different scenarios are configured. The execution time of each experiments is calculated as an evaluation criterion. The evaluation experimentations of the proposed shark smell optimization configured four simulation cases. 60 jobs, 15 resources and 10 bloods are considered in the first case. In the second case, the number of jobs was 150, the number of resources was 70 and the number of blood was 30. In the third case, comparison the execution times between Shark Smell Optimization (SSO) and firefly (FA) algorithm with the same number of jobs that is 80 described in [16], the number of resources 30. In the fourth case, compares the five execution times between SSO and FA algorithm with the different number of jobs and resources.

A suitable setting for the Firefly Algorithm parameter values are needed for the the simulation to work effectively. Before comparing the proposed mechanism with fireefly scheduling mechanisms, this research has conducted experiments to find out the most suitable parameter values for the firefly mechanism. In the following section, a discussion of some observations that have been collected during the process of setting parameter values for the proposed mechanism. To summarize the observations of the parameter settings, this research will use the finally selected parameter values as default values and change one value each time. The finally selected parameter values for firefly algorithm are:

- Population size: 10
- Iterations of firefly algorithmn: 10
- $\alpha = 0.9$
- $\gamma = 0.02$
- $\beta_0 = 1.0$

where β_0 is the firefly attractiveness value at $r = 0$, γ is the media light absorption coefficient and α is a randomization parameter.

4.1   The First Scenario

In this scenario, the study considered a number of 50 jobs and a number of 20 resources.

Table 1. Font sizes of headings. Table captions should always be positioned *above* the tables.

Iteration number	1	2	3	4	5	6	7	8	9	10
Execution time	296	296	296	294	294	291	287	285	285	283

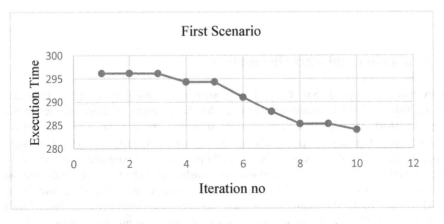

Fig. 1. CloudSim simulation result in first scenario

As described in Table 1 and Fig. 1 the results of the initial execution time is 296.17gradually decreased until it reached 283.98.

4.2   The Second Scenario

In this scenario, the study considered a number of 120 jobs and a number of 50 resources.

Table 2. The execution time of ten iterations in second scenario

Iteration number	1	2	3	4	5	6	7	8	9	10
Execution time	480	474	452	442	441	440	438	437	433	432

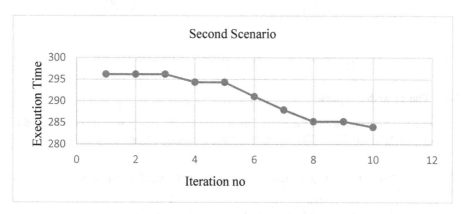

Fig. 2. CloudSim simulation result in second scenario

As described in Table 2 and Fig. 2 the result of the initial execution time is 480.07 gradually decreased until it reached 432.89.

4.3   The Third Scenario

In this scenario, a comparison of the execution time between SSO and FA algorithm is conducted with the same number of jobs and resources (100 jobs and35 resources).

Table 3. The comparison between SSO and FA algorithm

Algorithm	Execution time in seconds
FA	383.8034746697152
SSO	371.21539397038214

As shown in Table 3 and Fig. 3, this case is comparing SSO Algorithm and FA; SSO Algorithm performed better than FA Algorithm based on the execution time. The exaction time of the proposed SSO was 371.21 while the exaction time of FA was 383.80.

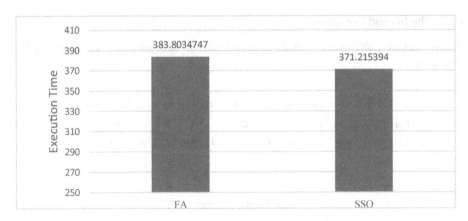

Fig. 3. Comparison of simulation result in the third scenario

4.4 The Fourth Scenario

To assess the performance of the shark smell method, the fourth scenario configured a number of jobs from 30 to 200 and a number of resources from 15 to 120.

Table 4. Average execution time between SSO and FA algorithm

Algorithm	FA	SSO
Time 1 (30 jobs and 15 resources)	72	55
Time 2 (50 jobs and 25 resources)	103	103
Time 3 (70 jobs and 35 resources)	170	157
Time 4 (100 jobs and 50 resources)	279	211
Time 5 (200 jobs and 120 resources)	656	576
Average time	256	221

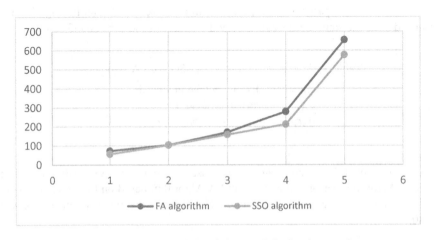

Fig. 4. Comparison of simulation result in fourth scenario

As described in Table 4 and Fig. 4 in this case comparison between the proposed SSO and FA algorithm is conducted. After calculating the average time for five executions, the SSO algorithm performed better than FA algorithm based on the execution time.

When there were 30 jobs and 15 resources the exaction time was 55.76 which is less than 72.77 obtained by FA. However, when there were 50 jobs and 25 resources the two mechanisms almost performed the same. In all remaining scenarios, the proposed SSO has shorter exaction time than FA. This indicates that proposed SSO is more effective when the load is heavy.

5 Conclusion

This paper proposed a new job scheduling mechanism to solve the scheduling problems by minimizing the execution time of jobs using Shark Smell Optimization (SSO).

The research work started with a mapping process to map the cloud job scheduling mechanism with the SSO. In this mapping, each job scheduling solution represents a position of shark. A random number of solutions have been selected to represent the initial position population. The execution time of each schedule is considered the objective function of the schedule (shark). For all iterations, the schedules (shark) move based on the current mode in which the position of shark the scheduling to generate a new population with enhanced objective function. To find the best solution in each iteration we choose the schedule that has the best objective function. Observably, as the number of jobs is increased the execution time grow to be longer than the execution times when the number of jobs is small. Nonetheless, the execution time of the shark smell optimization method is still less than Firefly optimization time. The evaluation of the proposed mechanism is implemented using Java language and CloudSim simulator and conducted several experiments. Empirical results proved that the proposed job scheduling mechanism outperforms FA. Furthermore, the proposed SSO minimized the execution time of jobs.

References

1. Rani, B.K., Rani, B.P., Babu, A.V.: Cloud computing and inter-clouds–types, topologies and research issues. Procedia Comput. Sci. **50**, 24–29 (2015)
2. Erl, T., Puttini, R., Mahmood, Z.: Cloud Computing: Concepts, Technology and Design. Prentice Hall PTR, Upper Saddle River (2013)
3. Esa, D.I., Yousif, A.: Scheduling jobs on cloud computing using firefly algorithm. Int. J. Grid Distrib. Comput. **9**, 149–158 (2016)
4. Esa, D.I., Yousif, A.: Glowworm Swarm Optimization (GSO) for cloud Jobs Scheduling. Int. J. Adv. Sci. Technol. **96**, 71–82 (2016)
5. Kumar, P., Verma, A.: Scheduling using improved genetic algorithm in cloud computing for independent tasks. In: Proceedings of the International Conference on Advances in Computing, Communications and Informatics, pp. 137–142 (2012)
6. Maqableh, M., Karajeh, H., Masa'deh, R.E.: Job scheduling for cloud computing using neural networks. Commun. Network **6**, 191 (2014)

7. Salot, P.: A survey of various scheduling algorithm in cloud computing environment. International Journal of research and engineering Technology (IJRET), ISSN, pp. 2319–1163 (2013)

8. Zhao, C., Zhang, S., Liu, Q., Xie, J., Hu, J.: Independent tasks scheduling based on genetic algorithm in cloud computing. In: 5th International Conference on Wireless Communications, Networking and Mobile Computing, 2009, WiCom 2009, pp. 1–4 (2009)

9. AbdElrouf, W., Yousif, A., Bashir, M.B.: High exploitation genetic algorithm for job scheduling on grid computing. Int. J. Grid Distrib. Comput. 9, 221–228 (2016)

10. Pan, G., Xu, Y., Ouyang, A., Zheng, G.: an improved artificial chemical reaction optimization algorithm for job scheduling problem in grid computing environments. J. Comput. Theor. Nanosci. 12, 1300–1310 (2015)

11. Latiff, M.S.A., Madni, S.H.H., Abdullahi, M.: Fault tolerance aware scheduling technique for cloud computing environment using dynamic clustering algorithm. Neural Comput. Appl. 29, 279–293 (2018)

12. Aghababaeipour, A., Ghanbari, S.: A new adaptive energy-aware job scheduling in cloud computing. In: International Conference on Soft Computing and Data Mining, pp. 308–317 (2018)

13. Wang, L., Ai, L.: Task scheduling policy based on ant colony optimization in cloud computing environment. In: Zhang, Z., Zhang, R., Zhang, J. (eds.) LISS 2012, pp. 953–957. Springer, Berlin (2013)

14. Xue, S., Li, M., Xu, X., Chen, J.: An ACO-LB algorithm for task scheduling in the cloud environment. J. Softw. 9, 466–473 (2014)

15. Zhan, S., Huo, H.: Improved PSO-based task scheduling algorithm in cloud computing. J. Inf. Comput. Sci. 9, 3821–3829 (2012)

16. Yousif, A., Esa, D.I.: Scheduling jobs on cloud computing using firefly algorithm. Int. J. Grid Distrib. Comput. 9(7), 149–158 (2016). 2016.9.7.16 2016

17. Abedinia, O., Amjady, N., Ghasemi, A.: A new metaheuristic algorithm based on shark smell optimization. Complexity 21(5), 97–116 (2014)

18. Rao, Y., Shao, Z., Ahangarnejad, A.H., Gholamalizadeh, E., Sobhani, B.: Shark Smell Optimizer applied to identify the optimal parameters of the proton exchange membrane fuel cell model. Energy Convers. Manag. 182, 1–8 (2019)

19. Hosseinzadeh, H.: Automated skin lesion division utilizing Gabor filters based on shark smell optimizing method. Evolving Systems, pp. 1–10 (2018)

20. Bagheri, M., Sultanbek, A., Abedinia, O., Naderi, M.S., Naderi, M.S., Ghadimi, N.: Multi-objective shark smell optimization for solving the reactive power dispatch problem. In: 2018 IEEE International Conference on Environment and Electrical Engineering and 2018 IEEE Industrial and Commercial Power Systems Europe (EEEIC/I&CPS Europe), pp. 1–6 (2018)

21. Abedinia, O., Amjady, N.: Short-term wind power prediction based on Hybrid Neural Network and chaotic shark smell optimization. Int. J. Precis. Eng. Manuf.-Green Technol. 2, 245–254 (2015)

A Visual Decision Making Support System for the Diabetes Prevention

Fatima Zohra Benhacine[✉], Baghdad Atmani[✉],
Mohamed Benamina[✉], and Sofia Benbelkacem[✉]

Laboratoire d'Informatique d'Oran (LIO), University of Oran,
1 Ahmed Benbella, BP 1524 EL Mnaouer, Oran, Algeria
benhacine.fatima@gmail.com, baghdad.atmani@gmail.com,
benamina.mohamed@gmail.com,
sofia.benbelkacem@gmail.com

Abstract. Our research is based on visualization of association rules for the diabetes prevention. In particular, we are interested in Gestational diabetes, which represents glucose intolerance that results in an increase in blood sugar levels in a pregnant woman. Treatment avoids complications for both mother and child. Data mining aims to extract as much relevant information as possible from a large amount of data. It is done automatically, or by exploring the data using interactive visualization tools. We propose a Visual Decision Making Support System to help experts in diabetes prevention. The main objective was to help experts study the impact of some criteria on the prevention of gestational diabetes in pregnant women. The article presents the application of our Visual4AR approach [1], which jointly uses 2D colored matrices and the Cellular Automaton CASI (Cellular Automaton for Symbolic Induction) for the diabetes prevention.

Keywords: Association rules · Data Mining · Visualization · Interactive visualization system · Cellular automaton · Colored 2D matrix · Boolean modeling · Gestational diabetes

1 Introduction

Diabetes, cardiovascular diseases, cancer and chronic respiratory diseases are the 4 non-communicable diseases identified by the World Health Organization (WHO). Diabetes is one of the world's leading killers today, 25 million people have diabetes worldwide according to the International Diabetes Federation and the WHO expects 622 million people with diabetes by 2040. Its progress is dazzling in developing countries, particularly in Africa. More than 2/3 of people with diabetes are undiagnosed. The complications of diabetes can take their toll. The reality of diabetes is unknown, underestimated and even ignored in a sadly and dangerously indifferent way in the word.

In the medical field, decision is the fundamental act of medicine. The medical decision-making process consists of choosing a mode of investigation, making a diagnosis and then proposing or postponing treatment. From there, medical decision support represents all the information management techniques that can help the doctor,

A. Alfaries et al. (Eds.): ICC 2019, CCIS 1098, pp. 81–92, 2019.
https://doi.org/10.1007/978-3-030-36368-0_8

partially or globally, in his decision-making process [2]. It is necessary to have the right decision support tools to ensure that the best decisions are made, visualization in clinical decision support system (CDSS) allows you to work in a visual way, so that relevant data is obvious. It highlights the elements relevant to the decision to be taken, and gives them meaning in such a way as to clearly and understandably reveal an often underlying structure within numerous and complex data [3].

Data Mining (DM) is a process of extracting knowledge from a very large amount of data. The principle is to search structures linking these data. This search can be done automatically, for example in medical field by using algorithms whose purpose is to find association rules such as Apriori [4]. An advantage of this algorithmic approach is its exhaustiveness, thanks to which all the association rules, which satisfy constraints on a set of metrics, will be found [5]. However, the number of rules built can sometimes be larger than the initial amount of data. In this case, we are faced with another problem of data mining, which consists in identifying the most relevant subsets of rules. To solve the problem of rule mass, visualization is presented as a potential solution in the post-processing of knowledge models. Indeed, the visualization of information helps human beings to acquire and increase their knowledge and to guide their reasoning through their perspective capacities.

Visual4AR [1] is an automatic data mining tool where knowledge extraction is done first with Boolean modeling using the CASI (Cellular Automata for Symbolic Induction) [6] and then visual exploration by rules selection.

The first part of this article deals with data mining visualization based on work related to visualization analysis and visual perception. Then, we detail our approach and show how to use the Visual4AR tool [1] to produce a Boolean visualization of association rules to explore and filter relevant rules for diabetes prevention. This paper is an application of the work done in [1].

2   Related Work

The clinical decision support system (CDSS), are playing increasingly important roles in medical practice by helping physicians or other medical professionals making clinical decisions. CDSS are having a greater influence about the care process. They are expected to improve the medical care quality; their impact should intensify due to increasing capacity for more efficient data processing [7].

Iram et al. [8] propose a CDSS for provide a recommendations and healthcare services for chronic disease patients by long term monitoring. To make their CDSS more intelligent, it induces the patients to interact with the system. By continuously learning and digesting patients' experience and knowledge, the knowledge base of their CDSS is self-evolutionary and dynamically enhanced.

Hussain et al. [9] design and develop the Smart Clinical Decision Support System (Smart CDSS) that takes input from diverse modalities, such as sensors, user profile information, social media, clinical knowledge bases, and medical experts to generate standards-based personalized recommendations. The authors test the system for 100 patients from Saint Mary's Hospital: 20 with type-1 diabetes, 40 with type-2 diabetes mellitus, and 40 with suspicions for diabetes but no diagnosis during clinical observations.

Alharbi et al. [10] present a diagnosis and treatment recommendation system for diabetes. The system considers patient information, symptoms and signs, risk factors and lab tests and suggests a treatment plan according to the diabetes type as recommended by the Clinical Practice Guidelines (CPG). The work consisted in the acquisition, modeling and implementation of diabetes domain expertise from experts, the CPG and other sources to develop a domain ontology and a decision support system to handle the diabetes in an early stage. The proposed system uses an ontology to allow a standard representation of domain concepts and relationships and enable clinical knowledge sharing, update and reuse.

El-sappagh et al. [11] propose a Clinical decision support system (CDSS) based on case-based reasoning (CBR) in early detection and diagnosis of diabetes. Building CBR's case-base knowledge is the most critical challenge. The authors propose a standard case-base relational data model for diabetes diagnosis. This model will collect all patient clinical data from distributed EHRs, and it will formulate it in the form of problem-solution. This case-base knowledge will be used as the knowledge base for a diabetes diagnosis CBR system.

Livvi Li et al. [12] develop a diabetes-specific clinical decision support system (Diabetes Dashboard) interface for displaying glycemic, lipid and renal function results, in an integrated form with decision support capabilities, based on local clinical practice guidelines. The clinical decision support system included a dashboard feature that graphically summarized all relevant laboratory results and displayed them in a color-coded system that allowed quick interpretation of the metabolic control of the patients. An alert module informs the user of tests that are due for repeat testing. An interactive graph module was also developed for better visual appreciation of the trends of the laboratory results of the patient.

Association rules are one of the most powerful models for data mining. Association rules allow large volumes of data to be processed and significant rules to be extracted. Nevertheless, this method produces a large and considerable number of rules, which makes it difficult for the human eye. This is why we are interested in the techniques of graphical representation of association rules. As we have pointed out in previous work [1], most visualization methods are not suitable for representing large sets of patterns. They become unusable when the number of patterns to be displayed is too large and few displays give an overview of the pattern sets. Finally, no method is suitable to really explain how to deduce certain rules or the presence of other rules [1].

In our work, we are interested on the Two Dimensional Matrix (2D) for the simplicity to represent the rules on two colors, blue for antecedent and red for consequent However, in the presence of a large number of association rules, this representation also becomes unreadable and the rules overlap. in order to overcome the problem of occultation and simplify the internal representation of manipulated knowledge we have opted for rule optimization using Boolean modeling offered by the Cellular Automaton (CASI) [6], and its inference engine to explain the reasoning of some deductions.

In our approach we based on some aspects of the CASI machine: its simplicity to express knowledge in rules and facts, its efficiency in optimizing storage space and execution time. The latter is a particular model of dynamic and discrete systems able to acquire, represent and process extracted knowledge in Boolean form [13].

The originality of Visual4ARis essentially in the combination between the 2D matrix and the CASI Cellular Automaton to prove its effectiveness in a new field which is visualization [1].

3   Proposed Approach

The proposed Visual Decision Making Support System (VDMSS) is based on the decisional visualization of association rules realized by Visaul4AR [1]. It is composed of 4 modules shown in Fig. 1: (1) Pre-processing module, (2) Data mining module, (3) Boolean modeling module, (4) Visualization module.

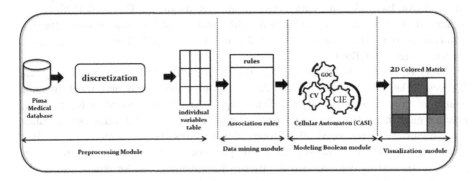

Fig. 1. VDMSS approach [1]

3.1   Gestational Diabetes

Globally, nearly half a billion people currently have diabetes. 327 million people with diabetes are between 20 and 64 years of age, while 123 million are over 65 years of age. In neighboring countries, about 1.65 million people have diabetes in Morocco while 762,000 people have diabetes in Tunisia. There are two types of diabetes. Type 1 diabetes, which is caused by the pancreas stopping the production of the hormone insulin, causing the body to become intolerant of glucose. More common, type 2 diabetes, also known as insulin resistance, is due to the misuse of insulin by the body's cells.

In pregnant women, there are two types of diabetes. The first (type 1 or 2) affects women before marriage, while the second occurs during pregnancy called gestational. The latter represents 15 to 20% of pregnant women in Algeria. Gestational diabetes develops during pregnancy (gestation). Like other types of diabetes, gestational diabetes affects how your cells use sugar (glucose) and causes high blood sugar that can affect your baby's health and your pregnancy.

In gestational diabetes, blood sugar usually returns to normal soon after delivery. But if you've had gestational diabetes, you're at risk for type 2 diabetes. You'll continue working with your health care team to monitor and manage your blood sugar. in this sense we must forward to the pregnant woman a prevention plan. In this work, we are interested in gestational diabetes.

We used Pima Indian Diabetes Dataset provided by the UCI repository (http://archive.ics.uci.edu/ml/), whose data set has a total of 768 Indian women (500 non-diabetic 268 Diabetic) described by 9 attributes (Table 1). The data used to test VDSS have been discretized [14].

Table 1. Attribute description [14].

Attribute	Abbreviation	Description
X1	Preg	Number of pregnancies
X2	Plas	plasma glucose concentration in 2 h
X3	Dias	diastolic blood pressure
X4	Tric	Triceps skin fold thickness, (mm)
X5	Ins	2-hour serum insulin, (mu U/ml).
X6	Mass	body mass index
X7	Pedi	Diabetes pedigree function
X8	Age	Age
Y	Plan	Treatment plan

Y represent a plan of treatment that takes its values from the set of diabetes care plans C = {Plan1, Plan2, Plan3, Plan4}, where Plan1 = Ace-inhibitor therapy; Plan2 = low fat diet; Plan3 = determine exercise regime and Plan4 = diabetes prevention program and Plan5 = prevention plan for non-diabetic individuals [14].

3.2   Datamining Process

Datamining is the center of the Knowledge Discovery in Databases process. Visual4AR [1] propose an application for data mining allowing the extraction of association rules from the volume of pre-processed data and implements the Apriori algorithm [4].

3.2.1   Apriori Algorithm

One of the important applications of data mining is to extract association rules from a large amount of data. In this study, we use the Apriori algorithm [4]. Proposed by Agrawal and Srikant [4] in 1994; APRIORI [4] represents the pioneering algorithm for searching frequent itemsets, it is a revolutionary approach in learning and exploring association rules. It takes its name from its heuristics, which use information known a priori on the frequency of items.

An association rule links different attributes describing the data. A rule $A \rightarrow B$ means: if the attributes contained in A are present in a given transaction, then the attributes contained in B are also present. Apriori [4] only takes into account nominal attributes.

Association rules are widely used in medical decision support. Data mining by association rules helps to build a disease prevention knowledge base that will help health care providers in tracking. The Apriori algorithm is the most used among the different association rule extraction algorithms.

The user intervenes at two distinct points in the process. First, it sets the support and confidence thresholds that will be used during the research. Once completed, it is the sole judge of the results that are presented, the direct consequence is that some items are not taken into account if they are not well represented in the database. To remedy this, the user can provide feedback by modifying the initial parameters and lowering the support, which shows the flexibility of our system [1].

Our VDMSS is applied to help experts in diabetes prevention. The main objective is to help experts in the field to study the impact of certain criteria on the prevention of gestational diabetes in pregnant women. We conducted a series of experiments on our pima database to choose the right model (Table 2).

Table 2. Experiences

Test	Support Min	Confidence Min	Rules number
Experience 1	10%	95%	1931
Experience 2	10%	90%	2495
Experience 3	10%	85%	2888
Experience 4	10%	80%	3443
Experience 5	9%	90%	3161
Experience 6	9%	80%	4355
Experience 7	9%	70%	6095
Experience 8	8%	90%	4036

3.2.2 Boolean Modeling

CASI [6] (Cellular Automata for Symbolic Induction) is a cellular automaton that simulates the basic operating principle of an inference engine using two finished layers of finite automata. A cellular automaton is a grid composed of cells that change state in discrete steps. After each step, the state of each cell is modified according to the states of its neighbors in the previous step. The cells are updated synchronously and transitions are performed, in theory, simultaneously.

The Cellular Automaton showed its evidence in several research studies in Data Mining: the urban transportation [15], the biology [16], ontologies fusion [13] …

The Boolean modeling used, which respects the principle of cellular automata, is described by four Boolean matrices and two transition functions that simulate the operation of an inference engine [1]. The initial state of the machine is given by the CelFact matrix expressing the fact base and the CelRule matrix expressing the rule. The initial configuration of the machine for the initial knowledge base is given by the initial state of CelFact and CelRule (Fig. 2) and RE and RS (Fig. 3).

The RE (Fig. 4) and RS (Fig. 5) incidence matrices represent the input/output relationship of the items and are used in forward chaining to move from premises to conclusions. In the transition functions $\delta fact$ and $\delta rule$, RE can also be used as an input relationship and RS as an output relationship to launch the backward chained inferences from the conclusions to the premises. In our case we will choose a rear chain for experiment N°1 and a front chain for experiment N°2.

For experiment N°1 we used the 7th series (Table 2) with 6095 interesting rules that we cannot all interpret, to retrieve the rules that can meet our objective which is the detection of the prevention plan and using the Boolean matrix and the 2D colored visualization to solve the occultation problem. In our case the fact (y = plan4) represents the Initial Fact to be established.

The CASI machine through its inference engine will allow us to refine all these rules by eliminating at each iteration the irrelevant rules according to the user's needs. By choosing the visualization by selection, the user validates his starting item; the rule to validate. The change of state of the machine, which behaves like a cellular automaton at this level, is done by transition functions whose role is to simulate the operation of a front linkage.

CELFACT	CELRULE	RE	RS			
FACT		EF	IF		SF	
x4='(24.5-inf)'		0	1		0	
x2='(-inf-103.5)'		0	1		0	
x4='(-inf-3.5)'		0	1		0	
y=plan4		1	1		0	
x4='(3.5-24.5)'		0	1		0	
x1='(6.5-inf)'		0	1		0	
x6='(-inf-26.35)'		0	1		0	
x5='(143-inf)'		0	1		0	
x6='(26.35-29.95)'		0	1		0	
x2='(154.5-inf)'		0	1		0	

Fig. 2. The G0 configuration, the CELFACT layer

CELFACT	CELRULE	RE	RS		
RULE	ER		IR		SR
R1	0		1		1
R2	0		1		1
R3	0		1		1
R4	0		1		1
R5	0		1		1
R6	0		1		1
R7	0		1		1

Fig. 3. The G0 configuration, the CELRULE layer

CELFACT	CELRULE	RE	RS							
RE	R1	R2	R3	R4	R5	R6	R7	R8	R9	f
x3='(-inf-91)'	1	0	0	1	1	0	1	0	0	
x7='All'	0	0	0	0	0	0	0	0	0	
x5='(-inf-143)'	0	1	0	0	1	0	0	0	1	
x1='(-inf-6.5)'	0	0	1	1	0	0	0	0	1	
y=plan5	0	0	0	0	0	1	1	0	0	
x6='(29.95-inf)'	0	0	0	0	0	0	0	1	0	
x2='(103.5-154.5)'	0	0	0	0	0	0	0	0	0	
x8='(28.5-inf)'	0	0	0	0	0	0	0	0	0	
x8='(-inf-28.5)'	0	0	0	0	0	0	0	0	0	

Fig. 4. The RE input matrix

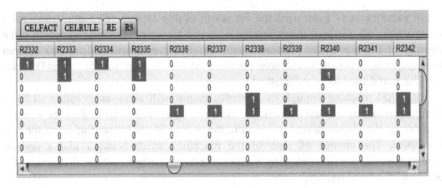

Fig. 5. The RS output matrix

In this case, we have defined two functions, δfact (1) and δrules (2) which operate on the CelFact and CelRule matrices respectively.

- The Transition Function δ_{fact} is given as follows:

$$(\text{EF, IF, SF, ER, IR, SR}) \xrightarrow{\delta_{fact}} \left(\text{EF, IF, EF, ER} + \left(R_E^t.\text{EF}\right), \text{IR, SR}\right) \tag{1}$$

- The Transition Function δ_{rules} is given as follows

$$(\text{EF, IF, SF, ER, IR, SR}) \xrightarrow{\delta_{rules}} (\text{EF} + (\text{RS.ER}), \text{IF, SF, ER, IR}, {}^{\wedge}\text{ER}) \tag{2}$$

Where the matrix RET refers to the transposition of RE and ^ER denotes the negation of the Boolean vector ER.

3.2.3   2D Visualization

VISUAL4AR [1] uses 2D visualization (rules-itemset), each line corresponds to an item and each column to a rule.

The premises are represented by the color blue and the conclusions are represented by a red color [17–19].

Matrices are certainly the most commonly used means of representing rules [17–19]. Boulicaut et al. [20] propose a Two-Dimensional Matrix (2D). A rule is represented by a cell, the antecedent is displayed on row and consequent is displayed in column. Ben Yahia and Nguifo [17] express the confidence of the rules by a gradual color of the cells. The greater the confidence, the darker the color of the cell, and an interface that allows interaction with the representation is provided.

4 Experimental Results

The rules triggered are R3489, R3491, R3492, R4377, R4378, R4379, R4380, R4383, R4384 (Fig. 6). These rules were presented to an expert who helped us interpret them.

The rule 3489 is interpreted as follows: y = plan4 → x3 = (inf-9.1), x6 = (29.95-inf) informs as who have completed a prevention program have a diastolic blood pressure lower than 9.1 and body mass index higher than a 29.95 and a plasma glucose concentration higher than 154.5.

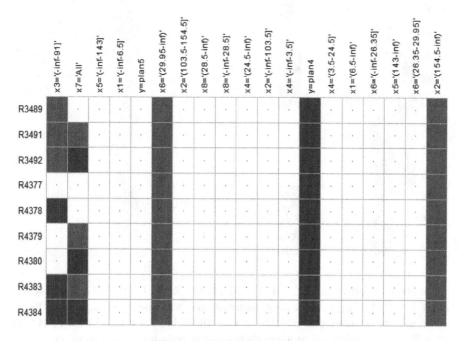

Fig. 6. Colored 2D visualization

For experiment N°2 we used the 1st series (Table 2) with 1931 rules, to retrieve the rules that can meet our objective which is the detection of the Plan4 which corresponds to a prevention plan, using the Boolean matrix and the 2D colored visualization.

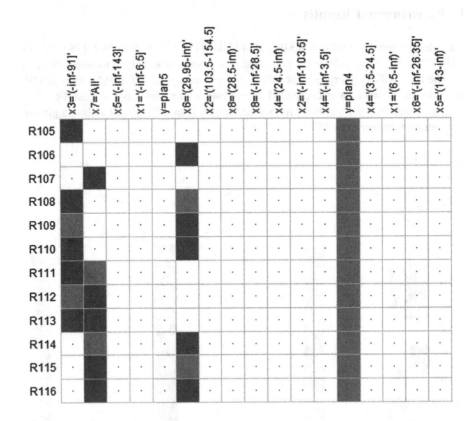

The rules triggered are R105, R106, R107, R108, R109, R110, R111, R112, R113, R114, R115, R116. These rules were presented to an expert who helped us interpret them:

The rule 105 is interpreted as follows: x3 = (inf-9.1) → y = plan4 informs as who have a diastolic blood pressure lower than 9.1 requires a prevention program.

The rule 106 is interpreted as follows: x6 = (29.95-inf) → y = plan4 informs as who body mass index higher than a 29.95 requires a prevention program.

The rest of the rules can be interpreted in the same way and it is clear that this result depends on the population and sample size of the study.

5   Conclusion

In this paper, we proposed a Visual Decision Making Support System to help experts in diabetes prevention. The main objective is to help experts study the impact of some criteria on the prevention of gestational diabetes in pregnant women. The Pima Indians Diabetes Data Set has been used for experimental purpose. The techniques of pre-processing applied were attributes identification, selection and discretization. We generate the rules by using the algorithm Apriori. We used an approach coupling a colored 2D matrix with a Boolean modeling to visualize association rules for diabetes prevention. The proposed visualization technique gives better results. The results confirm the results of a previous work realized by Benamina et al. [14].

The patients who have a diastolic blood pressure lower than 9.1 and body mass index higher than a 29.95 requires a prevention program. However, VDMSS has disadvantages related to the complexity of the domain of Diabetes Diagnosis. The results presented in this paper provide the basis for future research in several areas. Firstly, applicate the discretization with fuzzy logic [14] and secondly, evaluate association rules with the different measures and in different areas.

References

1. Benhacine, F.Z., Atmani, B., Abdelouhab, F.Z.: Contribution to the association rules visualization for decision support: a combined use between boolean modeling and the colored 2D matrix. Int. J. Interact. Multimedia Artif. Intell. **5**(5), 38–47 (2019)
2. Darmoni, S.: Titres et travaux, Informatique de santé, Sciences et Technologies de l'Information et de la Communication (2003)
3. Coninx, A., Bonneau, G., Droulez, J., Thibault, G.: Visualization of uncertain scalar data fields using color scales and perceptually adapted noise. In: Proceedings of the ACM SIGGRAPH Symposium on Applied Perception in Graphics and Visualization, pp. 59–66. ACM (2011)
4. Agrawal, R., Srikant, R.: Fast algorithms for mining association rules. In: Proceedings of the 20th International Conference Very Large Data Bases, pp. 487–499. VLDB (1994)
5. Bothorel, G., Serrurier, M., and Hurter, C.: From visualization to association rules: an automatic approach. In: Proceedings of the 29th Spring Conference on Computer Graphics, pp. 57–64. ACM (2013)
6. Atmani, B., Beldjilali, B.: Knowledge discovery in database: induction graph and cellular automaton. Comput. Inform. J. **26**(2), 171–197 (2007)
7. Leroy, G., Chen, H.: Introduction to the special issue on decision support in medicine. Dec. Support Syst. **43**(4), 1203–1206 (2007)
8. Iram, F., Muhammad, F., Donghai, G., Young-Koo, L., Sungyoung, L.: Socially interactive CDSS for u-life care. In: Proceedings of the 5th International Conference on Ubiquitous Information Management and Communication, p. 95. ACM (2011)
9. Hussain, M., et al.: Cloud-based smart CDSS for chronic diseases. Health Technol. **3**(2), 153–175 (2013)
10. Alharbi, R., Berri, J., El-Masri, S., Ontology based clinical decision support system for diabetes diagnostic. In: 2015 Science and Information Conference (SAI), pp. 597–602. IEEE (2015)
11. El-Sappagh, S., Elmogy, M., Riad, M.: A CBR system for diabetes mellitus diagnosis: case-base standard data model. Int. J. Med. Eng. Inform. **7**(3), 191–208 (2015)
12. Livvi Li, W., Kenneth, H.K.B., Tin, W.T., Sunil, K.S., Tze, P.L.: Development of a clinical decision support system for diabetes care: a pilot study. PLoS ONE **12**(2), e0173021 (2017)
13. Abdelouhab, F., Atmani, B.: Fusion cellular des ontologies. J. Dec. Syst. ISSN:1246-0125 (Print)2116-7052(Online). http://www.tandfonline.com/loi/tjds20
14. Benamina, M., Atmani, B., Benbelkacem, S.: Diabetes diagnosis by case-based reasoning and fuzzy logic. IJIMAI **5**(3), 72–80 (2018)

15. Amrani, F., Bouamrane, K., Atmani, B., Hamdadou, D.: Une nouvelle approche pour la régulation et la reconfiguration spatiale d'un réseau de transport urbain collectif. J. Dec. Syst. **20**(2), 207–239 (2011)
16. Mansoul, A., Atmani, B., Benbelkacem, S.: A hybrid decision support system: application on healthcare. CoRR abs/1311.4086 (2013)
17. Ben Yahia, S., Nguifo, E.: Emulating a cooperative behavior in a generic association rule visualization tool with Artificial Intelligence. In: ICTAI 2004. 16th IEEE International Conference (2004)
18. Zhao, K., Liu, B., Thomas, M., Tirpak, W.X.: Opportunity map: a visualization framework for fast identification of actionable knowledge. In: CIKM'05, Proceedings of the 14th ACM International Conference on Information and Knowledge Management. ACM Press, New York (2005)
19. Ounifi, M., Amdouni, S., Elhoussine, H., Slimane, R.: New 3D visualization and validation tool for displaying association rules and their associated classifiers. In: 20th International Conference on Information Visualization (IV), pp. 152–158. IEEE (2016)
20. Boulicaut, J., Marcel, P., Rigotti C.: Query driven knowledge discovery in multidimensional data. In: DOLAP 1999: Proceedings of the 2nd ACM International Workshop on Data Warehousing and OLAP, pp. 87–93. ACM Press, New York (1999)

Sensor-Based Business Process Model for Appliance Repair

Mayada Elsaid[✉], Ayah Alhamdan, and Sara Altuwaijri

Riyadh, Saudi Arabia
mayada.elsaidd@gmail.com

Abstract. The number of repair requests received by any manufacturing company is tremendous; therefore, automating part of the repair process will save both time and money for the company. In fact, the expansion of IoT capabilities reveals unseen opportunities to improve the repair process from the business perspective. Sensors placed within appliances will automatically do this by notifying the customer service about any abnormal behavior indicating an appliance malfunction. Using Business Process Management (BPM) Techniques, this research measures how effective will adding sensors be to the appliance repair process. Shedding the light on the consequences of such an action from the business process management viewpoint. With Bizagi, two business process models were built: one model showed the current situation where sensors are not involved and the other showed a proposed workflow with the help of sensors and software that add automation to the process. Comparison between simulation time and resource utilization for the two models indicated that the proposed model will save resources for the repair company, which is a positive effect on the business.

1 Introduction

Business project management (BPM) considers analyzing, monitoring, and improving current business processes in order to help companies and organizations achieve their goals and objectives. BPM includes creating many process scenarios, modelling them, then executing them to check for change effects and further improvements. The goal of BPM is to inspect the hidden reasons for delays and repetitive work in any business process that may affect the quality of the final service or product in a way that reduces the customer's satisfaction and the organization's sales rate. With regards to the context of manufacturing and repairing appliances, there are many obstacles that cause delays in the process and may negatively affect the quality of the final results of such processes. The process of appliance repair starts when the customer finds out that the machine is not working properly, then the customer would probably research the problem and try to find a simple solution for it. If it's not easy enough, the customer will refer to the customer service of the company to get some help. The customer service employee will arrange a proper time for both the customer and the technician for a site visit. At the site visit day, the technician will diagnose the appliance, check the customer's warranty status, and decide on a solution for the appliance to be either fixed on site or to be taken to the factory for major defects handling. Since the process

© Springer Nature Switzerland AG 2019
A. Alfaries et al. (Eds.): ICC 2019, CCIS 1098, pp. 93–102, 2019.
https://doi.org/10.1007/978-3-030-36368-0_9

involves several manual actions, there are drawbacks in terms of time and cost that show up when considering repairing an appliance. However, a solution for the observed problems in the appliance repair process will be proposed by applying the Internet of Things technology. Internet of Things is an environment of system of interconnected machines, sensors, computing devices, or objects with unique identifiers. All interrelated objects with their identifiers are connected via network to interact and communicate with each other. These devices communicate with each other by sending data through the network, then perform actions responding to some conditions on a programmed system. Sensors in these smart devices collect data, analyze it, and send an alarm if an emergency situation is observed. This paper is structured as follows: first, related work is discussed. Then, the research problem is described in detail. Third, a solution for the research problem is proposed. Last, the results and conclusion are discussed.

2 Related Work

Gjoni [3] discussed the issues of the companies that don't focus on the business logic in the development process of information systems. Organizations focus more on the technical perspective most of the time, which negatively affects the quality of the final software product. Oskeol Gjoni explained the concept of Model Driven Architecture (MDA) approach that mainly focuses on the business logic rather than the technical implementation. Oskeol Gjoni claims there should be a new approach for developing information systems that separates the technical implementation from the business logic. The author used the typical user access management (UAM) flow business process to automate a process. It was modeled in two different forms, UML, and BPMN. This business process is followed by all employees to gain access to perform some actions. The author explained the steps for automating the UAM process with the help the modeling software kit (MOSkitt), UML diagrams, and Bizagi business process management suite. The author also explained in details the steps followed in Bizagi studio for process automation. The steps include process modelling, data modelling, defining forms, defining business rules, defining the performers, integration, and executing. The author concluded that a high-quality software such as a web application could be automatically built with read, create, update, delete, and export functionalities.

Additionally, Dumas and Maggi [6] proposed a study on Business Process Management (BPM) based on evidence to instill a data-driven approach to the traditional business process improvement lifecycle. Traditional business process management practices have relied largely on rough estimates and manual data collection techniques which can be effective in capturing and conceptualizing a process' "happy paths", but they are short of providing a thoroughly detailed picture of it, including exceptions. On the other side, process mining is concerned with analyzing the collections of event records produced during a business process execution. A process mining technique's main input is a business process event log, which is a collection of relevant event records for a given business process. Of the proposed descriptive process mining approaches are automated process model discovery and process performance analytics. If evidence-based BPM becomes part of the management culture of the organization,

BPM will reach the level of modern marketing approaches, often driven by data. Every business process redesign decision will be made with data in an ideal evidence-based organization, backed up by data, and continually questioned based on data.

Another research paper by Kumar et al. [7] focuses on the business process management (BPM) from the customer's perspective, specifically concentrating on the customer's satisfaction. In order to compete with competitors in the business and reach high standards, business owners must put their customers as a priority. The service profit chain theory explains how the satisfaction of staff leads to customer satisfaction which results in high quality service, this positive linear relationship will definitely lead to profitability. In this study, it is suggested that businesses should make the process management as their main concern instead of only focusing on functional perspective. Service providers should get their customers feedback and act upon them in order to ensure high quality deliverables. The authors also stress out on the importance of applying different analytical methods such as structural equation modeling (SEM) tool to investigate the business processes' main issues and perform some statistics to reinforce proper solutions.

Moreover, Patel, Vyas, and Dwivedi [2] described how the process of repairing minor appliances defects can be simplified. The authors proposed a solution of repairing a damaged appliance by installing sensors into them to help the customer to fix the problem. The detection and fixing process is achieved by the help of sensors combined with expert system. Sensors have the ability to calculate many surrounding measurements like, humidity, temperature, and pressure. These abilities can be used to enhance the appliances capability to make them smarter. An expert system uses the technology of artificial intelligence to help making the decisions of fixing the problem. After collecting the sensed data from the surrounding environment, the expert system analyzes the problem and sends the solution on how to fix it to the customer. The solution provided by the expert system is supposed to contain easy and clear instructions with images for any kind of user to be able to fix it in home without external help. If a problem is not known or identified by the expert system, it will be sent to a human expert from the vendor company to send a proper solution via SMS or email. This method will save time and money for users to fix minor problems instead of contacting the manufacturing company or the vendor, which will be more complicated. The communication between the sensors in the appliances and the expert system is done by wireless connection. To apply such a solution, first is the deployment of sensors in heterogeneous home areas. Each sensor is installed inside an appliance and connected to the expert system. Next is data sensing phase where every sensor is sensing the surrounding activities and environment and collecting data about them. Then, in the data transmission phase, sensors send alarms, data about noticed defects and unexpected behavior by the appliance to the expert system to notify it that a problem is happening. After that comes the noise removal phase to generate the original data without the noise that may be generated by the sensors. Last, there is the expert system phase where intelligent decisions are made by using decision trees and pre-defined instructions and rules for any specific device. The authors discussed how improving the appliances' intelligence will make them more user-friendly and valuable.

Another study was conducted by Davis et al. [4] to investigate sending appliance diagnoses information via sensors that are located inside home equipment scheduled for repair. The sensors gather pieces of information regarding the equipment' status and if there are any occurrences of malfunction. This information includes data about temperature, amount of electric current flowing, as well as the speed of the compressor. These collections of data can be analyzed to detect any occurrences of failure. As soon as a failure is spotted, the smart home controller notifies the service provider. The information sent to the manufacturing company involves diagnostic information, the cause of failure, equipment identification number, and operating characteristics of the home device in addition to the location of the equipment. A request for repair is also automatically sent to the service provider to schedule an available time to fix the malfunction. The smart home controller is also capable of discovering faults or errors that can lead to potential failure before the owner notices any defect. This is done by having a communication network where all devices' information is transmitted through sensors.

3 Research Problem

3.1 Appliance Repair

Home appliances such as ovens, refrigerators, microwaves, washing machines, etc. sometimes fail to operate normally. In fact, many people have experienced having a malfunctioning appliance at least once. Appliance Repair includes diagnosing the malfunction and fixing it, either during a technician's visit to a person's home or after being taken to the manufacturer factory. According to the United States News and World Report [1], an average homeowner spends 1% to 4% of their annual home value on maintenance and repairs. The amount of money spent is an indicator of the frequency of repair requests. Therefore, to be able to handle such a tremendous number of repairs. A repairing company must optimize the repair process in order to save time, cost and effort.

3.2 Appliance Repair Process

Nowadays, the appliance repair process requires a lot of manual tasks, that are mostly slow in nature. After discovery of a malfunction, a customer calls the customer service to describe the problem he/she noticed in the appliance. The manufacturer company receives the claim where an employee from the customer service will ask the client some questions to understand more about the malfunction. Most people cannot discover the cause of the problem easily, this could be a challenging process for individuals who are not experts in the field. After collecting required information from the client, the customer service employee will then check for technicians' availability, assign one to the mission and schedule for site visit after receiving the customer's location details. During site visit day, the technician will diagnose the appliance problem. This process usually takes time especially when a general technician is assigned to the task. In many situations, a lot of time get wasted just for the technician to understand the root of the problem, this is due to the fact that he is not a specialist. Furthermore, usually technicians come to the site visit with a minimal tool kit where he then needs to leave the site and go back to his workstation to get equipment needed. After understanding the main problem of the device, the technician will know if the appliance is in a condition where the problem can be solved or not. If not, the client will be informed of the situation and that he needs to completely replace the device. On the other hand, if the malfunction was solvable, the technician will first check the client's warranty for expiration date. If the customer did not have a valid warranty, the technician will inform him/her with estimated cost of the service and any additional fees. After the client approves of the admission, the process will be taken to the repair phase where the specialized technician further examines the appliance and check if the condition status is a minor or major malfunction. If the appliance contained a slight problem, the technician will get the equipment needed to fix the device on site and issue bill. However, if the appliance problem was major, the customer will be informed that it has to be taken to the factory, schedule another visit to pick up appliance as well as checking time for transport. When the pickup day arrives, the appliance is taken pack to the manufacturer company to start the repair process. After the malfunction is fixed, the machine will be dropped off back to the customer, then the bill is issued. The client will be informed of payment status. If this service is not covered by warranty, the required payment will be deducted first, then a repair warranty is issued. Finally, the records will be studied and analyzed to keep track of the company's performance (Figs. 1 and 2).

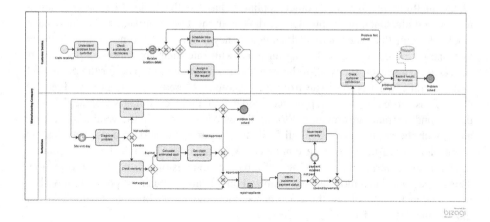

Fig. 1. As-Is main process

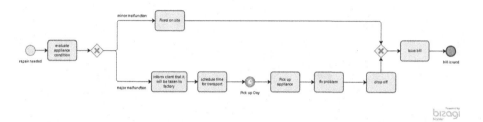

Fig. 2. As-Is sub process

4 Methodology

This study is approached using a mixed methodology. Quantitative and qualitative methods were combined to analyze outcomes: Qualitative analysis was performed through a research study where related works were reviewed to (1) show the value of business process management, and (2) prove that the proposed solution is technically feasible. Moreover, a quantitative analysis was done where statistical information was gathered using the modelling tool, Bizagi. Business Process Modeling Notation (BPMN) was used to build the current and proposed models of the appliance repair process. Then, the time and resource utilization for both models were compared to shed light on the effectiveness of the proposed model. All analysis done for this research are from the business point of view, where the end target is to improve the repair company business process in terms of time, cost, and quality.

4.1 Description of the Proposed Process

According to the time issues that were observed after simulating the As-Is process, a more effective and efficient process model is proposed. The idea of the proposed model is based on the concept of Internet of Things. The proposed process model suggests that appliances may have IoT sensors inside them to detect any special case that may be a sign of having an issue in the appliance. After that, the company is aware of the type of the malfunction that a customer appliance has, so that a lot of time is reduced regarding understanding the problem or diagnosing it. For example, an oven may have smoke detector that when activated, an emergency alarm is sent to notify the company that one of the customers is having an issue with one their appliances. Since data is collected by a sensor, the type of the problem is known and no need for the process of understanding what is the issue from the customer. Moreover, sensors have IDs and each ID is stored with the appliance model and type, customer's contact/location details, and warranty information. Storing the customer's data in the vendor's database along with the appliance details will facilitate the communication process between the client and the customer service employee. Appliance details could be the appliance model, manufacturing date, warranty information, and customer's contact information. This process has been modeled and analyzed only from the business point of view. The resources in the model are the customer service and the technician. Figure 3 below display the details of the main process.

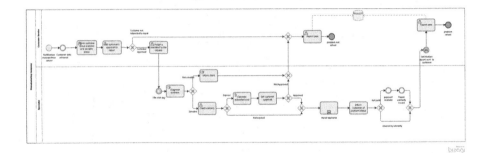

Fig. 3. Proposed main model

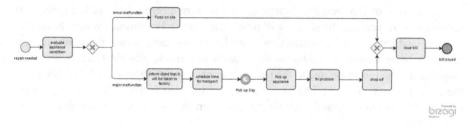

Fig. 4. Proposed sub process

The proposed model starts when a notification is received from the customer's appliance sensor, which indicates some issue was detected from the appliance. After that, the customer's information is retrieved from the vendor's database to contact the customer and discuss the issue. The customer service employee informs the customer about the problem that was detected and the warranty status. After getting the approval from the customer, instead of assigning a general technician to the site visit as in the As-Is model, a specialist to that specific issue is assigned to fix it. On the site visit day and after the diagnosing, it's either ends up being solvable or not. For solvable problems, the customer's warranty is checked first to calculate the estimated cost and get the customer's approval if it's expired. Next, the repair appliance subprocess starts. Activities and process flow is shown in the Fig. 4 above.

The malfunction should be classified either as major or minor problem. Minor issues can be easily fixed on site by the specialist. Otherwise the customer will be notified that the appliance should be taken to the factory for further repair, and the time for transport is scheduled. It's picked up on the scheduled day and fixed in the factory. After dropping off, bill is issued. For the payment process, it's checked first if the bill is covered by the warranty or not, and customer will be informed. If it's not covered, payment will be received from the customer and a warranty for the repair done will be issued.

4.2 Redesign Details

The paper introduces several modifications to the current present model to eliminate its limitations. First, since the proposed process starts with a notification from a sensor within an appliance, there will be no need for the customer to call the manufacturer company to complain about a malfunction or to provide the location or warranty details. In fact, the customer service will have to call the customer to ensure his willingness to repair and to inquire about the preferred time for a visit.

Another critical improvement is automation to several tasks with an automation software. After receiving the notifications from the sensors, a repair request is initiated, and the customer is assigned a specialist technician automatically based the sensor-identified problem and the customer's preferred time matched with technicians' available times. During interaction with the customer, the assigned technician will then record the actions taken on the appliance on a company's software so that repair cost calculation and repair warranty preparation will be automatic, and final repair case report will be ready at the end of the repair process. Moreover, instead of the manual task of calling a customer to receive feedback, automatically sent questionnaires are sent to the customer once a repair case is closed.

The effects of the mentioned changes to the current repair process is expected to prevent rework because the sensor will provide the needed confirmation that the device is fixed, and the customer satisfaction is no longer the determinant if the repair case needs to be reopened. In addition, time taken to execute several tasks is reduced, resulting in cost reduction due to the reduced number of employees needed to complete the same amount of work. The process quality will also increase with the increased customer satisfaction about the speedy process; therefore, an increase in repair revenues is expected.

5   Results

After improving the model of the process using Bizagi tool, scenarios were set, executed, and analyzed. Bizagi modeler handles the simulation of each case or customer to be an instance, and the simulation of 500 instances was done. The results of executing the instances showed improvements in terms of resource utilization and the full process completion time average. In the As-Is process, the resource utilization for the 5 customer service employees was 11.50% and 41.40% for the 15 technicians. However, in the proposed process model, it was 59.31% for 10 technicians and 11.50% for 1 customer service, as shown in Fig. 5. Furthermore, the maximum completion time for the proposed process model got improved from two days and nine hours, to be one day and five hours. The minimum time was 43 min and it changed to be seven minutes. In general, the average completion time for the process got reduced from 13 h to 5 h. Figure 6 shows summary of full process completion time statistics.

All changes and improvements that were implemented on the business process had many effects on the time, cost, flexibility, and quality. Some changes affected the process positively, negatively, or did not have any effect (Fig. 7). In general, the reduced time of the proposed model caused increased quality resulting from increased customer satisfaction and reduced cost resulting from reduced number of employees.

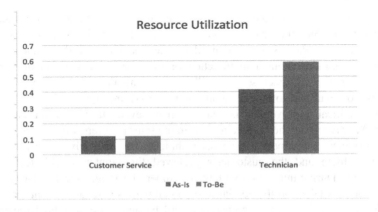

Fig. 5. Resource utilization

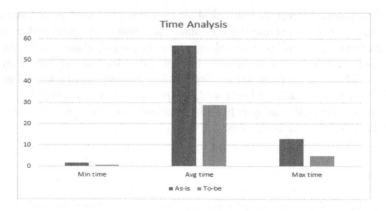

Fig. 6. Time analysis

Change	Time	Cost	Flexibility	Quality
Removing understand problem task that was done by the customer service. **(Task Elimination)**				
Remove the task of receiving location details that was done by the customer service. **(Task Elimination)**				
The loop back after checking customer satisfaction is removed, eliminating rework. **(Task Elimination)**				
Automate the task of checking availability of technicians that was done previously by the customer service. **(Automation)**				
Repair cost calculation is done by the system once the specialist records the fixes that is be done to the machine. **(Automation)**				
Issue repair warranty becomes an event that is automatically done by the system. **(Automation)**				
The task of making a report of the repair case has been automated. **(Automation)**				
Customer feedback can be collected by automatically shared questionnaires. **(Automation/ communication optimization)**				
Checking warranty repair warranty at customer site will not take time. **(Communication Optimization)**				
The task of assigning a general technician will change to assigning a specialist. **(Specialization)**				
For the same number of started process instances, the number of customer service is reduced to (1) and the number of technicians is reduced to (10). **(Resource Optimization)**				

Fig. 7. Effect on devil's quadrangle

6   Conclusion

The appliance repair business process can be optimized by applying some changes to its activities and using the techniques of Business Process Management. The purpose of applying BPM on the activities of any process is to increase the customer's satisfaction and reduce the cost and time for both the customer and the vendor company. The main improvement done on the process is automation with the use of Internet of Things sensors that collect data in the surrounding environments to detect potential threat. Other secondary heuristics that have been used on the appliances' repair business process, are Task Elimination, Communication Optimization, Specialization, and Resource Optimization. Using Bizagi modeling tool, the process was modeled before and after the improvements, and statistical analysis was conducted to understand the changes' effects on time and resource utilization. According to the generated reports by Bizagi, there was many indicators that demonstrate the positive change in the proposed process, like, variances in average time. In conclusion, literature reviews prove the technical feasibility of the proposed solution and Bizagi analysis proves its advantages over the current solution. That being said, the proposed solution which is based on qualitative and quantitative analysis from the business's point of view will be helpful if implemented in the repair companies.

References

1. Gordon, K.: Topic: home appliance industry (n.d.). http://www.statista.com/topics/1068/home-appliances/
2. Patel, Y.S., Vyas, S., Dwivedi, A.K.: A expert system based novel framework to detect and solve the problems in home appliances by using wireless sensors (2015). https://ieeexplore-ieee-org.ezproxy.psu.edu.sa/stamp/stamp.jsp?tp=&arnumber=7155039
3. Gjoni, O.: Comparison of two model driven architecture approaches for automating business processes, Moskitt Framework and Bizagi Process Management Suite (2015). http://www.mcser.org/journal/index.php/mjss/article/view/5853/5638
4. Davis, J., et al.: Systems and methods for sending diagnostic information during scheduling of home equipment repair (2019). https://patents.google.com/patent/US10229394B1/en
5. Turin, J.L., et al.: System and method for collecting and disseminating household information and for coordinating repair and maintenance services (2005). https://patents.google.com/patent/US6853958B1/en
6. Dumas, M., Maggi, F.M.: Evidence-based business process management (2015). https://www-sciencedirect-com.ezproxy.psu.edu.sa/science/article/pii/B9780127999593000173
7. Kumar, V., Smart, P.A., Maddern, H., Maull, R.S.: Alternative perspectives on service quality and customer satisfaction: the role of BPM (2008). https://www.emeraldinsight.com/doi/abs/10.1108/09564230810869720

A Multi-labels Text Categorization Framework for Cerebral Lesion's Identification

Hichem Benfriha[1,2]([✉]), Baghdad Atmani[1], Belarbi Khemliche[3],
Nabil Tabet Aoul[4], and Ali Douah[4]

[1] Laboratoire d'informatique d'Oran (LIO),
Université d'Oran 1 Ahmed Benbella,
BP 1524 El M'naouer, 31000 Oran, Algeria
hichem.benfriha@gmail.com, baghdad.atmani@gmail.com
[2] Département des Sciences Techniques,
Université Mustapha Stambouli de Mascara, BP 305, Mascara, Algeria
[3] Réanimation Médicale, Etablissement Hospitalo-Universitaire, Faculté de
Médecine, Université d'Oran 1 Ahmed Benbella, Oran, Algeria
khemliche_belarbi@yahoo.fr
[4] Réanimation Polyvalente Pédiatrique EHS Canastel, Faculté de Médecine,
Université d'Oran 1 Ahmed Benbella, Oran, Algeria
tabetrea@yahoo.fr, douah-ali@hotmail.fr

Abstract. Road traffic accidents in Algeria are a major public health problem for children, since they are among the leading causes of death starting from the age of 1 year. Among these victims, traumatic brain injuries (TBIs) causing several sequelaes, which are the frequent causes of consultation in children. For a better support of these cases, we propose a Multi-Label Text Categorization (MLTC) framework to help health professionals for the best cerebral lesions' identification found in TBIs that appear simultaneously. The aim through this article development is to evaluate a set of multi-label (ML) transformation approaches to detect cerebral lesions' from medical reports collecting from the pediatric intensive care unit of Oran hospital -Algeria.

Keywords: Head injury · Road accidents · Multi-labels learning · Text categorization · Data mining · Machine learning

1 Introduction

In Algeria, traffic accidents are a social problem, and an economic hemorrhage hindering the country's development. In his report, the National Centre for Road Safety and Prevention[1] estimates that 3,639 people died and 36,287 were injured in 25,038 road accidents recorded during the year 2017, 2548 died and 17883 were injured during the year 2018, and among those injured 26.79% in 2017, and 15.98% in 2018 are children under 15 years of age of whom 80% are traumatized children. The main trauma risks for car occupants depend on the interaction between the vehicles and the

---

[1] http://www.cnpsr.org.dz/.

A. Alfaries et al. (Eds.): ICC 2019, CCIS 1098, pp. 103–114, 2019.
https://doi.org/10.1007/978-3-030-36368-0_10

roadside during a frontal or lateral collision. In these serious accidents, the intensive care unit in Oran is mainly responsible for brain, thoracic and abdominal trauma care. Among the traumatic brain injuries are those which occupies an important place and they are responsible for serious brain injuries representing an important cause of morbidity and mortality. Cerebral lesions are numerous in these patients and cause serious squeals such as consciousness disorders, epilepsy, amnesia, loss of consciousness and headaches [1]. The identification of lesions automatically and simultaneously from clinical reports is an essential and a necessary step for health professionals in the intensive care unit. To deal with this problem and throw this paper a set of ML transformation approaches is used to identify the TBIs of road accidents during childhood.

In recent years, the demand for the use of ML techniques has been increasing in various fields [2] particularly in the medicine. Many methods have been developed to solve ML categorization problems, where an patient can suffer from several diseases or present various diagnostics. In medical Text categorization (TC), clinical report are classified into one or more of predefined categories based on their contents and can be seen as the prediction of the target label sequence given a source text [3]. Over past years, many works have been adopted for dealing with unstructured clinical reports associated with more labels. Somme of them are presented bellow. The rest of the paper is organized as the following: in Sect. 2 we present some related works. We give some notions on ML classification problems in Sect. 3. In Sect. 4 we give a description of the proposed MLTC framework. In Sect. 5 we introduce the dataset of head trauma, then we give a presentation of experimentation, interpretation and comparisons of results. Finally, we present conclusion and future works in Sect. 6.

2 Related Works

Many works have been proposed in the medical MLTC field, and many evaluations exist in the literature. Baumel et al. [4] attempted to identify ICD code assignment based on ML classification of patient notes. In this study authors apply recurrent networks with hierarchical sentence and word attention to classify ICD9 diagnosis codes.

In the same context, Mullenbach et al. [5] proposed a convolutional neural network for ML classification on patient text discharge summaries from intensive care unit. Pereira et al. [6] proposed an automated ICD-9-CM medical coding of diabetic patient of clinical reports using ML learning. Results in this study shown that the convolutional neural network with three parallel convolutional layers achieves the best performances. As well, Zhang et al. [7] used the convolutional neural network for ML classification from clinical report to predict diagnoses. The purpose of this study is to encode the plain text into a fixed-length sentence embedding vector. Experimental results demonstrate the superiority of the proposed model. Pestian et al. [8] proposed the use of ML techniques to assign to clinical radiology report codes from a set of ICD-9 codes.

Baumel et al. [9] used ML classification methods to assign codes of patient notes. The best results have been obtained when a hierarchical approach to tag a document by identifying the relevant sentences for each label has been exploited. One more work for the use of ML classification from medical report is presented in [10], Glinka et al. focused on feature selection techniques investigating different approaches of transformation methods in order to improve the ML classification task.

To classify free text clinical report, Zhao et al. [11] proposed two techniques of ML classification: Sampled Classifier Chains (CC) and Ensemble of Sampled Classifier Chains (ECC) to obtain a relationship between disease and classification. Berndorfer et al. [12] explored various text representations and ML classification techniques for assigning ICD-9 codes to discharge summaries from the Medical Information Mart for Intensive Care III. Best results was obtained by combining models built using different representations. With the Medical Information Mart for Intensive Care II dataset Bromuri et al. [13] experimented ML classification techniques by means of combinations of bag-of-words models, and adopt time series and dimensionality reduction approaches.

3 Multi-labels Classification

According to [14–17], ML classification concerns supervised learning problems in which each observation may be associated to multiple labels simultaneously. his objective is to detect the most appropriate class labels for each observation as possible at the same time.

Formally, let $O(x_1, x_2, x_3, .., x_n, L_i)$ is the set of observations, whereas $(x_1, x_2, x_3, ..., x_n)$ represent the attributes and L_i represents the target class label, for a given instance O_i in O. In single label binary classification task $L_i = 2$ takes only two modalities, O_i will belong to only one value of L_i. In single label multi-class classification, $L_i > 2$ takes more than two values, O_i belongs to one of the values of L_i. In ML classification, there is more than one target class $L_i, L_j, ..., L_n$. In this case, each target label is binary and takes only values 0 or 1; each data instance will belong to more than one target class. Table 1 shows the multi-label data set.

Table 1. Sample of multi-label dataset

Obs	Attributes					Labels			
	x_1	x_2	x_3	.	x_n	L_1	L_2	.	L_n
o_1	0	1	0	..	1	1	0	0	1
o_2	1	1	0	..	0	1	0	1	1
o_3	1	0	0	..	1	0	1	0	1
..									
o_n	0	1	1	..	1	1	1	1	1

ML classification is classified into two major groups : problem transformation methods which transform the multi-label problem into a series of single-label problems which are then solved using existing single-label learning methods while the second one is method adaptation in which existing single label classifier models are enhanced to deal with ML data directly [18].

3.1   Problem Transformation Methods

The first approach to realize ML classification was based on data transformation techniques [19], these are leved to produce binary datasets from the multi-label original ones. It's a relatively straightforward way to do ML classification through traditional classifiers. The main data transformation approaches are:

- **Binary Relevance (BR):** This technique is extended in the ML applied to take into account that several labels can be relevant at once. Therefore, a binary classifier is trained for each label [19]. This approach has a drawback of not considering the association between labels, indeed it treats each label individually [17].
- **Classifier Chains (CC):** transforms the ML classification task into a chain of binary classification problems to model the correlations between labels [20].
- **Label Powerset (LP):** This technique creates one binary classifier for every label combination attested in the training set [2, 17].

3.2   Algorithm Adaptation Methods

The second solution is an alternative to the data transformation techniques. This approach is named adaptation methods [17]. This solution solves the ML problems directly by adapting existing methods for single-label learning. Its aim is to prepare existing classification algorithms to make them able to manage instances with several outputs, so it's comprises the algorithms designed to directly handle the ML data set. Herrera et al. [2] proposed many algorithms for this task.

3.3   Evaluation Methods

To evaluate and compare the performance of the combination of the considered classifieur and ML approach, we applied six evaluation metrics: accuracy, average precision, F-Measure, Hamming Loss, Ranking Loss and One-Error (I.e. have a look on [17]).

4   Text Categorization Framework

The proposed framework called Multi-Label for Text Categorization (ML4TC) consists of two complementary modules as shown in Fig. 1. The first, is the preprocessing module that produces an index of words and the second is the learning process.

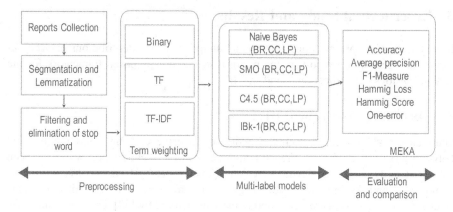

Fig. 1. ML4TC architecture.

4.1 Preprocessing

In text categorization, the step of preprocessing builds a representation of the selected documents [3]. The classifiers cannot operate on the reports as they are introduced; the reports must be given internal representations so that the classifier can make sense of, once the classifier build them. It is thus customary to transform all our medical reports into internal representations.

This preprocessing will be performed in three steps:

1. **Segmentation and lemmatization**: this step is done by the Tree Tagger[2], which is a tool for annotating text with part-of-speech and lemma information.
2. **Filtering and elimination of stop word**: cleaning is performed to remove the non-representative to retain only text content.
3. **Term weighting**: is a step that takes place during our preprocessing in order to assess the value of each term to the report. it's the assignment of numerical values to terms that represent their importance in a report in order to improve text categorization. For each term weighting schemes are used such as binary, term frequency (TF) and frequency-inverse document frequency (TF-IDF) weightings.

4.2 Approach ML and Classifier

This works initiates the discussion of ML learning in the domain of TBIs. Specifically, we perform the ML classification technique known as problem transformation which is discussed in Sect. 3-A. After several experimentations using different data mining methods on MEKA platform [21], only SMO (Sequential minimal optimization), C4.5 (decision tree), NB (naive Bayes) and kNN (k-nearest neighbours with k = 1) gave the highest performances. Cross-validation is used for evaluation with ten folds.

---

[2] http://www.ims.uni-Stuttgart.de/projekte/corplex/TreeTagger.

5   Experimental Study and Results

In this section we present our experimental study. First, we describe our dataset collection and second we report on the performance of our proposed framework for the cerebral lesions' identification found in TBIs.

5.1   Dataset of Head Trauma (HT)

Our dataset was collected from the pediatric intensive care unit of Oran hospital between 2017 and 2018. This French corpora contains 120 child report who have been subjected to HT associated with 4 lesions (labels): cerebral edema, fracture, brain hemorrhage and foreign substance. There are two measures for evaluating the characteristics of a dataset: cardinality and density as defined by [22] The cardinality of a dataset S is the mean of instances' labels numbers that belong to S, defined by (1), and the density of S is the mean of instances' labels numbers that belong to S divided by L, defined by (2). Table 2 provides the HT label cardinality and density.

$$Cardinalite(s) = \frac{1}{n} \sum_{i=1}^{n} |Y_i| \qquad (1)$$

$$Density(s) = \frac{1}{n} \sum_{i=1}^{n} \frac{|Y_i|}{L} \qquad (2)$$

Table 2. ML Dataset of HT

Instance	Terms	Labels	Cardinality	Density
120	1307	04	1.585	0.156

5.2   Results and Discussion

In this section, comparisons in terms of *six* evaluating metrics for the ML transformation approach, *four* other algorithms and three weighting schemes are presented for the best cerebral lesions' identification from the HT dataset. Tables 3, 4, 5, 6, 7 and 8 show the performance of the ML approach and Figs. 2, 3, 4, 5, 6 and 7 shows the comparative analysis.

From the observation of the previous results, the accuracy based on BR approach with NB classifier and TF weighting outperforms other ones with 64,8%. On the other hand the use of TF-IDF weighting, C4.5 classifier and BR approach gave best performance in terms of average precision with 81,6% and in term of F-Measure, TF weighting, NB classifier, BR and CC approach gave best performance with 70,2%.

Table 3. Accuracy (↑)

Classifiers	ML approach	Term weighting		
		Binary	TF	TF-IDF
NB	**BR**	0,625	**0,648**	0,616
	CC	0,625	0,647	0,616
	LP	0,462	0,578	0,589
SMO	BR	0,588	0,555	0,566
	CC	0,588	0,555	0,565
	LP	0,558	0,592	0,587
C4.5	BR	0,491	0,610	0,563
	CC	0,491	0,606	0,563
	LP	0,506	0,549	0,509
IB1	BR	0,566	0,552	0,550
	CC	0,563	0,552	0,550
	LP	0,563	0,552	0,550

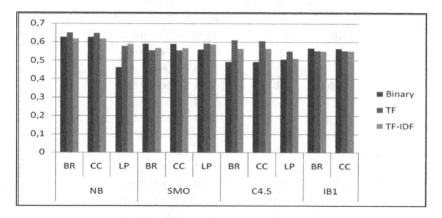

Fig. 2. Accuracy.

Table 4. Average Precision (↑)

Classifiers	ML approach	Term weighting		
		Binary	TF	TF-IDF
NB	**BR**	0.764	0.640	0.621
	CC	0.764	0.640	0.621
	LP	0.774	0.681	0.676
SMO	BR	0.757	0.728	0.740
	CC	0.748	0.727	0.764
	LP	0.568	0.558	0.560
C4.5	BR	0.796	0.794	**0.816**
	CC	0.796	0.788	0.674
	LP	0.701	0.674	0.662
IB1	BR	0.666	0.729	0.706
	CC	0.667	0.729	0.706
	LP	0.729	0.729	0.706

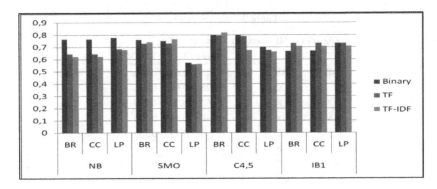

Fig. 3. Average Precision.

Table 5. F-Measure (↑)

Classifiers	ML approach	Term weighting		
		Binary	TF	TF-IDF
NB	**BR**	0.670	**0.702**	0.666
	CC	0.670	**0.702**	0.666
	LP	0.475	0.604	0.608
SMO	BR	0.624	0.602	0.613
	CC	0.624	0.602	0.613
	LP	0.577	0.631	0.624
C4.5	BR	0.544	0.647	0.608
	CC	0.544	0.644	0.608
	LP	0.543	0.605	0.552
IB1	BR	0.586	0.602	0.600
	CC	0.586	0.602	0.600
	LP	0.586	0.602	0.600

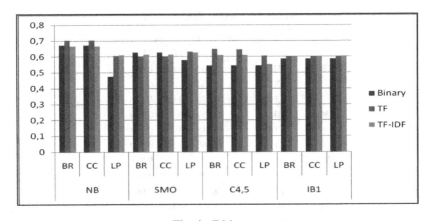

Fig. 4. F-Measure

Table 6. Hamming Loss (↓)

Classifiers	ML approach	Term weighting		
		Binary	TF	TF-IDF
NB	**BR**	**0.165**	0.193	0.201
	CC	**0.165**	0.193	0.201
	LP	0.207	0.192	0.198
SMO	BR	0.179	0.186	0.186
	CC	0.183	0.187	0.178
	LP	0.195	0.184	0.184
C4.5	BR	0.213	0.188	0.205
	CC	0.224	0.197	0.203
	LP	0.233	0.233	0.238
IB1	BR	0.200	0.229	0.228
	CC	0.203	0.229	0.228
	LP	0.203	0.229	0.228

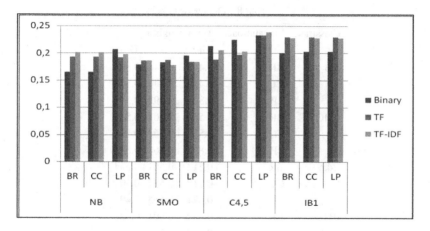

Fig. 5. Hamming Loss

Table 7. Ranking Loss (↓)

Classifiers	ML approach	Term weighting		
		Binary	TF	TF-IDF
NB	BR	0.136	0.194	0.219
	CC	0.136	0.194	0.219
	LP	0.357	0.244	0.244
SMO	BR	0.220	0.232	0.222
	CC	0.229	0.231	0.218
	LP	0.369	0.378	0.374
C4.5	**BR**	**0.134**	0.149	0.149
	CC	**0.134**	0.156	0.147
	LP	0.251	0.276	0.311
IB1	BR	0.287	0.232	0.256
	CC	0.289	0.232	0.256
	LP	0.291	0.232	0.256

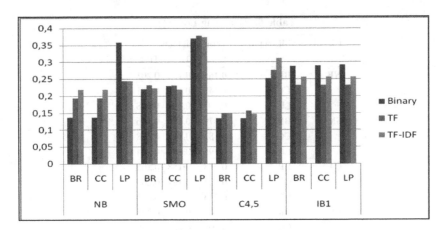

Fig. 6. Ranking Loss

Table 8. One-error (↓)

Classifiers	ML approach	Term weighting		
		Binary	TF	TF-IDF
NB	**BR**	**0.472**	0.544	0.568
	CC	**0.472**	0.544	0.568
	LP	0.803	0.592	0.571
SMO	BR	0.530	0.561	0.544
	CC	0.530	0.561	0.538
	LP	0.818	0.800	0.800
C4.5	BR	0.512	0.561	0.544
	CC	0.512	0.532	0.503
	LP	0.621	0.663	0.496
IB1	BR	0.632	0.601	0.626
	CC	0.632	0.601	0.626
	LP	0.635	0.601	0.626

The hamming loss should be less or equal to zero for the best classifier. According to results, it is noticed that BR, CC approach with NB classifier and Binary weighting show better performance with 16,5%. Similar to hamming loss, Rankin loss and One-Error measure must be small for efficient classifier. In term of Rankin loss, results demonstrate that BR, CC approach with C4.5 classifier and Binary weighting show better performance with 13,4%. Finally, best result in term of One-Error is done with BR, CC approach, NB classifier and Binary weighting with 47,2%. LP performed poor for all metrics, the reason can be that the fours classifiers may not be able to use the label relationship to the required extent when used with LP approach. Also, dataset size and number of models used with LP may be small enough to not consider label correlation properly, that's why BR and CC approach have given the best results.

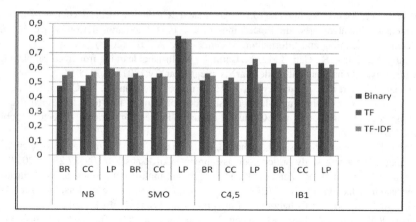

Fig. 7. One-error

6 Conclusion and Future Works

In this paper, A Multi-label Text Categorization framework has been proposed. An attempt has been made to identify the cerebral lesions from HT clinical French report collected from the pediatric intensive care unit of Oran hospital using ML classification algorithms. The task has been carried out with different problem transformation based methods such as BR, CC and LP with a variety of base classifiers and different weightings schemes.

The performance of the classifiers is analyzed using performance metrics like accuracy, average precision, F-measure, hamming loss, ranking loss and one-error. It is noticed from the results that the BR and CC classifier with NB and C4.5 base classifier provide a significantly better performance compared to other classifiers. In future research works, the focus will be made on the extension of MLTC which can be extended by using other ML transformations (ECC, CLR, Rakel, Homer, …) [23] and adaptations approaches [2] to improve the performance.

References

1. Campbell, J.E., Alson, R.L.: International Trauma Life Support for Emergency Care Providers, 8th edn. Pearson Education (2016). ISBN 978-0-13-413079-8
2. Herrera, F., Charte, F., Rivera, Antonio J., del Jesus, María J.: Multilabel Classification. Springer, Cham (2016). https://doi.org/10.1007/978-3-319-41111-8
3. Sebastiani, F.: Machine learning in automated text categorization. ACM Comput. Surv. **34** (1), 1–47 (2002)
4. Baumel, T., Nassour-Kassis, J., Elhadad, M., Elhadad, N.: Multi-label classification of patient notes a case study on ICD code assignment. In: AAAI Workshop on Health Intelligence (2018)
5. Mullenbach, J., Wiegreffe, S., Duke, J., Sun, J., Eisenstein, J.: Explainable Prediction of Medical Codes from Clinical Text. arXiv [Cs.CL] (2018). http://arxiv.org/abs/1802.05695

6. Pereira, V., Matos, S., Oliveira, J.L.: Automated ICD-9-CM medical coding of diabetic patient's clinical reports. In: Proceedings of the First International Conference on Data Science, E-Learning and Information Systems - DATA 2018 (2018)
7. Zhang, X., Henao, R., Gan, Z., Li, Y., Carin, L.: Multi-label learning from medical plain text with convolutional residual models. arXiv preprint arXiv:1801.05062.2018
8. Pestian, J.P., Brew, C., Matykiewicz, P., Hovermale, D.J., Johnson, N., Cohen, K.B., et al.: A shared task involving multi-label classification of clinical free text. In: BioNLP 2007: Biological. Translational and Clinical Language Processing, Prague, Czech Republic, pp. 97–104 (2007)
9. Baumel, T., Nassour-Kassis, J., Elhadad, M., Elhadad, N.: Multi-label classification of patient notes a case study on icd code assignment. CoRR abs/1709.09587.2017 (2017)
10. Glinka, K., Woźniak, R., Zakrzewska, D.: Improving multi-label medical text classification by feature selection. In: 2017 IEEE 26th International Conference on Enabling Technologies: Infrastructure for Collaborative Enterprises, pp. 176–181. IEEE (2017)
11. Zhao, R.W., Li, G.Z., Liu, J.M., Wang, X.: Clinical multi-label free text classification by exploiting disease label relation. In: 2013 IEEE International Conference on Bioinformatics and Biomedicine (BIBM), pp. 311–315. IEEE (2013)
12. Berndorfer, S., Henriksson, A.: Automated diagnosis coding with combined text representations. Stud. Health Technol. Inform. **235**, 201–205 (2017). ISSN: 0926-9630. eprint: 28423783
13. Bromuri, S., Zufferey, D., Hennebert, J., Schumacher, M.: Multi-label classification of chronicallyill patients with bag of words and supervised dimensionality reduction algorithms. J. Biomed. Inform. **51**, 165–175 (2014)
14. Gibaja, E., Ventura, S.: A tutorial on multi-label learning. ACM Comput. Surv. **47**(3) (2015)
15. Reyes, O., Morell, C.: Sebasti: an Ventura, Effective active learning strategy for multi-label learning, Neurocomputing. https://doi.org/10.1016/j.neucom.2017.08.001.2017
16. Tsoumakas, G., Katakis, I., Vlahavas, I.: Mining multi-label data. In: Maimon, O., Rokach, L. (eds.) Data Mining and Knowledge Discovery Handbook, pp. 667–685. Springer, Boston (2010). https://doi.org/10.1007/978-0-387-09823-4_34
17. Zhang, M., Zhou, Z.: A review on multi-label learning algorithms. IEEE Trans. Knowl. Data Eng. **26**(8), 1819–1837 (2014)
18. Madjarov, G., Kocev, D., Gjorgjevikj, D., Dzeroski, S.: An extensive experimental comparison of methods for multi-label learning. Pattern Recogn. **45**(9), 3084–3104 (2012)
19. Barot, P., Panchal, M.: Review on various problem transformation methods for classifying multi-label data. Int. J. Data Mining Emerg. Technol. **4**(2), 45–52 (2014)
20. Read, J., Pfahringer, B., Holmes, G., Frank, E.: Classifier chains for multi-label classification. Mach. Learn. **85**, 333–359 (2011)
21. Read, J., Reutemann, P.: MEKA multi-label dataset repository. http://sourceforge.net/projects/meka/files/Datasets/
22. Tsoumakas, G., Katakis, I.: Multi-label classification: an overview. Int. J. Data Warehouse. Min. **3**(3), 1–13 (2007)
23. Tidake, V.S., Sane, S.S.: Evaluation of multi-label classifiers in various domains using decision tree. In: Bhalla, S., Bhateja, V., Chandavale, Anjali A., Hiwale, Anil S., Satapathy, S.C. (eds.) Intelligent Computing and Information and Communication. AISC, vol. 673, pp. 117–127. Springer, Singapore (2018). https://doi.org/10.1007/978-981-10-7245-1_13

Fuzzy Adaptation of Surveillance Plans of Patients with Diabetes

Mohamed Benamina[1(✉)], Baghdad Atmani[1], Sofia Benbelkacem[1], and Abdelhak Mansoul[1,2]

[1] Laboratoire d'Informatique d'Oran (LIO),
University of Oran 1 Ahmed Benbella, Oran, Algeria
benamina.mohamed@gmail.com, baghdad.atmani@gmail.com,
sofia.benbelkacem@gmail.com, mansoul21@gmail.com
[2] Department of Computer Sciences, University of Skikda, Skikda, Algeria

Abstract. Reuse past experiences in solving new problems is common in the everyday lives, since it is well obvious and legitimate that similar problems have similar solutions and we are often confronted with a problem already met. The case-based reasoning (CBR) as a powerful design methodology of intelligent systems can be strengthened in the different stages of process by techniques for optimization. In a previous work [10], an approach guided by case-based reasoning based on retrieval by fuzzy decision tree has been proposed. In this paper, we propose a medical decision support system to assist physicians by adapting monitoring plans. The case-based reasoning process involves through several steps, we are interested in the adaptation phase which is to reuse totally or partially a solution of the selected case to solve the new problem. FUZZY DTA offers a medical decision making support system using a fuzzy reasoning for diabetes surveillance plans.

Keywords: Case-based reasoning · Diabetes · Adaptation · Fuzzy reasoning · Planning · Fuzzy decision tree

1 Introduction

Case-based reasoning is a powerful and natural reflex that aims the reuse of experiences in solving emerging problems. The general idea is that the ability of a human to act in the presence of an unprecedented situation is linked to its ability to explain it and this process of explanation involves his knowledge and his memory. Research on case-based reasoning saw the emergence of several under discipline which are distinguished by the characteristics of the developed systems.

Medical data suffers, in general, at least from a type of imperfection such as for example the vagueness and uncertainty. For these reasons, the uncertainty aspect must be taken into account in the development of CBR systems designed to provide diagnostic aid to physicians. We propose a new adaptation technique in case-based reasoning based on fuzzy logic in the medical field: diagnosis of diabetes by classification of diabetics. This adaptation requires a set of knowledge, and for software to be able to

© Springer Nature Switzerland AG 2019
A. Alfaries et al. (Eds.): ICC 2019, CCIS 1098, pp. 115–125, 2019.
https://doi.org/10.1007/978-3-030-36368-0_11

manipulate knowledge, it should be known to represent it symbolically. This is one of the most important areas of research in AI.

We have introduced the foundations of fuzzy logic [12–14] for knowledge representation and fuzzy decision tree for the knowledge management. The purpose of the previous work [10] was to improve the response time and the accuracy of the retrieval step, while the aim of the proposed FUZZY DTA is assisting physicians by proposing surveillance plan after CBR adaptation.

This document is organized as follows. Section 2 presents a state of the art of adaptation techniques. Section 3 explains the FUZZY DTA approach. In Sect. 4, we present and discuss the results of the experiments. Finally, in Sect. 5, we give a conclusion and some perspectives.

2   State of the Art

Adaptation is one of the most important steps of case-based reasoning. This step has been the subject of various works. Smyth and Keane [1] proposed a technique of retrieval guided by adaptation. This technique suggests using the knowledge of adaptation during the retrieval. The chosen case is the one that reduces the effort of adaptation and helps to better solve a new problem. This technique is applied to the design of industrial control software.

Maher and de Silva Garza [2] offered a technique that uses genetic algorithms to perform the adaptation of the case. Selected cases during the retrieval phase form the initial population for genetic algorithms. Two types of adaptation are used to change the contents of retrieved cases until a solution satisfies the constraints of the scope: (1) structural: by combination or crossing, (2) parametric: by mutation.

Corchado et al. [8] proposed a technique that uses an artificial neural network of type RBF (Radial Basis Function) to carry out the task of adaptation: learning of the network is directed by a set of source cases similar to the new problem, selected during the retrieval phase by the k-nearest neighbours method. The target problem is represented at the entrance to the network and its solution is recovered at its output. This technique performs well the acquisition of adaptation knowledge. The adaptation function is well controlled by neural network through source cases selected in the retrieval phase which are used in the learning network. The major problem with this technique is that after each resolution, no adaptation knowledge will be retained by the system. In other words, a neural network is used only to solve a given problem and it will be rejected. The field of application of this technique is the prediction of ocean temperature to a fixed depth for the next kilometers travelled by a ship.

Qi et al. [9] proposed a new method of case adaptation that uses support vector machine (SVM) incorporating knowledge related to adaptability provided by case snippets, called Adaptability-SVM (ASVM). This work consists of two parts. The first is to explore the adaptable property of old cases by using the decision tree method. Differences between the tests and extracts are used to assemble data from ground to accommodate the model of ASVM training. The second is to study the construction of ASVM adaptation in terms of extracted case model. Results show that ASVM is feasible and valid for the adaptation of cases.

The compositional adaptation is another way used to solve adaptation problems. In compositional adaptation, solutions from multiple cases are combined to produce a new composite solution. Arshadi and Badie presented a new approach for compositional adaptation since many cases at the same time can be similar to the user request, and through this way, the possibility will exist to combine the corresponding solutions (books' chapters in their study) in an efficient way yielding the final solution. This solution was used in Tutoring Library [15].

Schmidt and Vorobieva, developed ISOR, a system for endocrine therapy support, especially for hypothyroidism based on Compositional adaptation [16]. Jurisica et al. used a system (TA3-IVF) to modify in vitro fertilization treatment plans, relevant similar cases are retrieved and compositional adaptation is used to compute weighted average values for the solution attributes [17]. Schmidt and Gierl used also another system (TeCoMed) an early warning system concerning threatening influenza waves. The compositional adaptation is applied on the most similar former courses to decide whether a warning against an influenza wave is appropriate [18].

3   Proposed Approach FUZZY DTA

The proposed adaptation approach "FUZZY DTA" is illustrated in Fig. 1. The case-based reasoning process involves through several steps, we are interested in the adaptation phase which is to reuse totally or partially a solution of the selected case to solve the new problem. We use for the adaptation of the case the principle of inference by fuzzy decision rule for adaptation from a fuzzy decision tree [10]. The decision tree for adaptation FDTA is constructed from only similar cases.

We exploited the Pima Indians Diabetes Dataset of the UCI database library [24] to construct our initial case base that will be used under Jcolibri and Fispro processes. The problem part of cases is described by eight descriptors given in Table 1 and the solution part is given in the form of a treatment plan Y which takes its values in the set of diabetes care plans C = {Plan1, Plan2, Plan3, Plan4}. Where Plan1 = "Ace-inhibitor therapy"; Plan2 = "low fat diet"; Plan3 = "determine exercise regime" and Plan4 = "diabetes prevention program".

FisPro is an open source tool for creating fuzzy inference systems (FIS) to be used for reasoning purposes, especially for simulating a physical or biological system [19]. It includes many algorithms (most of them implemented as C programs) for generating fuzzy partitions and rules directly from experimental data. In addition, it offers data and FIS visualization methods with a java-based user-friendly interface. We make use of the Fuzzy Decision Trees (FDT) algorithm provided by FisPro [20].

Table 1. Attributes of PIDD [6, 7].

Abbreviation	Full name	UoM
Pregnant	Number of times pregnant	–
Glucose	Plasma glucose concentration in 2-hours OGTT	mg/dl
DBP	Diastolic blood pressure	mmHg
TSFT	Triceps skin fold thickness	mm
INS	2-hour serum insulin	mu U/ml
BMI	Body mass index	Kg/m^2
DPF	Diabetes pedigree function	–
Age	Age	–
DM	Diabetes Mellitus where 1 is interpreted as tested positive for diabetes	

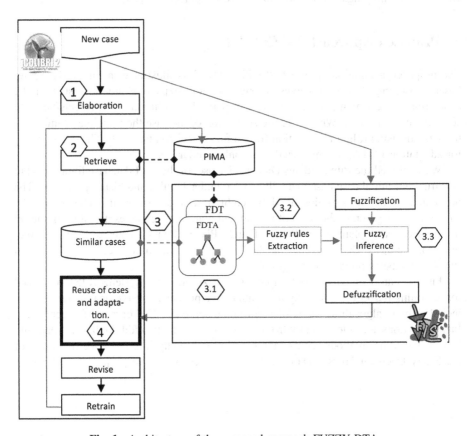

Fig. 1. Architecture of the proposed approach FUZZY DTA

3.1   The Reasoning Process

The process of case-based reasoning goes through several steps. We are interested in the adaptation step, which consists in reusing the solution of the selected case totally or partially in order to solve the new problem. We use in our paper, the adaptation of the cases by the principle of the inference by fuzzy decision rules deduced from a fuzzy decision tree for adaptation. The different steps of the proposed approach are described by the following pseudo algorithm:

Pseudo Algorithm: FUZZY DTA Reasoning Process
Input: PIDD, New Case
Output: Solution
1. *FDT=Create_FDT (PIDD)*
   Begin
2. *New_Case=**Elaboration**()*
3. ***Memorizing***
   Similar_Cases=Jcolibri2.k-nn(PIDD, New_case, k)
   Fispro.FDTA=Create_FDTA(Similar_Cases)
   Fispro.Fuzzy_Rules=Extraction(FDTA)
   Fispro.Fuzzification(New_Case)
   Fispro.Fuzzy_Inference(New_Case)
4. ***Reuse of cases and adaptation***
   Adapted_Case.Solution =Fispro.Defuzzification(New_Case)
   k-nn.Solutions=Extract_Solutions(Similar_Cases)
   Classified_Case=Classification(FDT, New_Case)[10]
   Compare(Adapted_Case.Solution; Classified_Case.Solution; k-nn.Solutions)
5. ***Revision**(Adapted_Case.Solution)*
6. ***Learning**(PIDD, Adapted_Case, Solution)*
   End

3.2   Fuzzy Set

Fuzzy logic is based on fuzzy set theory which is a mathematical theory that provides approximate reasoning modes rather than accurate. It is mainly the mode of reasoning used in most cases in humans. Thus, it avoids the inadequacies of the traditional theory regarding the treatment of this kind of knowledge [10].

A fuzzy set is defined by its membership function corresponding to the notion of characteristic function in classical logic; it measures the degree of membership of an element to the fuzzy set. A membership function of a fuzzy set is generally denoted by where x refers to the characterized variable. The most commonly used membership functions in the fuzzy sets are trapezoidal and triangular [10].

Various operations can be applied on fuzzy sets [11]. Let A and B be two fuzzy sets with and respectively their membership functions. Union, intersection and complement of fuzzy sets are deducted using their membership functions. In our study the parameters are fixed with Minimum value, Mean, Standard Deviation, Maximum value for each variable and then the membership function $\mu(x)$ of the triangular fuzzy number used by Benamina [10].

3.3 Fuzzy Decision Tree

Fuzzy decision trees originate from the classical theory of binary trees [4]. They require a predetermined fuzzy partitioning to be implemented. In fuzzy trees, each node is associated with a variable, and each branch will be assigned to a fuzzy subset (SEF) of this variable, which means that every path to a leaf corresponds to a fuzzy rule. A SEF is a modality of a variable; e.g., the variable *Plasma* has 3 SEF: *low*, *medium* and *high* [10].

There are several implementations for fuzzy decision trees. The one we have chosen can be considered as an extension of ID3. Each node is associated with a variable whose domain variation is cut by a strong fuzzy partition. Tests conducted to a node give the degrees of belonging to different fuzzy sets and its branches are activated by these membership degrees.

From the case base it built a fuzzy decision tree by the definition of fuzzy membership input and output functions. Each node is associated with a variable whose domain variation is cut by a strong fuzzy partition. Tests conducted at a node give the degrees of belonging to different fuzzy sets and branches from the node are activated by these degrees of membership. The membership functions may have different shapes [10].

We opted for triangular functions [6] because they allow easy implementation and fuzzification step then requires little computation time when evaluated in real time. Starting from the resulting fuzzy decision tree we launch an extraction of fuzzy rules. The important point in the extraction of rules and especially for the case of fuzzy rules induction is the choice of the fuzzy terms, since it represents the language aspect in the fuzzy reasoning. A fuzzy modality or fuzzy subsets with the attributes forms a rule of the form: If K is SEF i and K' is SEF i' Then $class_c$. We conclude that a rigorous selection of the fuzzy terms should be strongly required in order to talk about success rules induction. In our approach this knowledge results in a set of rules $\{R_1, R_2,...\}$ as shown in the following example:

R_1: If Plasma = "low" Then *Class_1*
R_2: If Plasma = "medium" and BMI = "medium" Then *Class_4*
R_3: If Plasma = "medium" and BMI = "high" and Age = "young" Then *Class_1*

The inference rules include intermediate steps that allow passing from real to fuzzy variables and vice versa; these are the steps of fuzzification and defuzzification. After fuzzification of the attributes of the new case in linguistic values, we launch the inference of fuzzy classification rules. Defuzzification of the conclusions obtained by fuzzy inference is the fuzzy adaptation. It is a transformation of the fuzzy information from the inference into deterministic information directly applicable to the process.

3.4 Integration of Diabetes Surveillance Plan

Type 2 diabetes is defined as a higher glucose 1.26 g/l (7 mmol/l) after fasting for 8 h at two different examinations or greater than 2 g/l (or 11, 1 mmol/l) two hours after controlled sugar ingestion. In this disease, there are two types of anomalies: insulin secretion by the pancreas is modified and the effects of insulin on tissues are modified (insulin resistance).

Diabetes usually begins between 40 and 50 years but the average age of diagnosis is between 60 and 65. As type 2 diabetes is symptom-free at the beginning of the disease, it is considered that more than a third of people are unaware of their disease. Self blood glucose monitoring allows glucose at any time using devices measuring blood sugar. For this we integrate a monitoring plan in our approach to this type of diabetes: a fasting blood glucose test should be done every three years; an induced hyperglycemia test can be undertaken to analyze more thoroughly in order to establish the diagnosis; weight control, healthy diet and physical exercise.

However, the induction in humans is often approximate rather than exact. Indeed, the human brain is able to handle imprecise, vague, uncertain and incomplete information. Also, the human brain is able to learn and to operate in a context where uncertainty management is indispensable. To optimize our diagnostic aid, our approach aims to determine the adequate monitoring of diabetes plan for each patient.

4 Experiments and Discussion

We applied our approach on the database Pima Indian Diabetes (PID) available on the official website of UCI machine learning repository [24]. This database is a collection of medical diagnostic reports of 768 women including 268 with diabetes and 500 without diabetes. Each case w_i is described by eight attributes: X_1: plasma glucose concentration, X_2: insulin dose, X_3: Body mass index, X_4: Diabetes pedigree function (heredity), X_5: Age, X_6: number of pregnancies, X_7: diastolic blood pressure, X_8: skin fold thickness of the triceps. Each case is assigned a diagnostic with a binary value (0 for non diabetic patient, 1 for diabetic patient) that indicates whether the patient shows signs of diabetes according to the criteria of the World Health Organization.

In our case, we used the relevant descriptors provided by Kalpana and Kumar [6]. After discussions with experts, we associated with each diagnosis a diabetes type and the best monitoring plan, based on various factors that are involved including glucose, insulin, body weight and age. In order to establish the correct diagnosis, the result of our approach is a value between 0 and 1 that represents the percentage of persons with diabetes. To test the effectiveness of our approach, we carried out experiments with two techniques.

1st Technique. Finding a Solution to the Target Case
We launched the same experiments with our FUZZY DTA approach, k-nn [3] method and classification by fuzzy decision tree. The goal of these methods is to find a solution to the target case. FUZZY DTA uses the classification model by fuzzy decision tree [10] constructed from only similar cases in order to propose a solution to the target case (find the type of diabetes: Type 2, Gestational), the degree of having this disease (linguistic variable with a percentage) and a monitoring plan. k-nn method uses similarity measures to search the similar cases to the target case and offers a binary solution: 0 for non-diabetic and 1 for diabetic. Table 2 shows a comparison between the three methods: FUZZY DTA, k-nn and classification by fuzzy decision tree general (FDT [10]) on a set of given target cases w_i.

Table 2. Results of the 1st experiments.

	k-nn	FDT [10]	FUZZY DTA
w_1	1	0,452	0,27
w_2	0	0,468	0,58
w_3	1	0,175	0,83
w_4	1	0,504	0,56
w_5	1	0,545	0,91

The three methods did not offer the same solutions; k-nn gives traditional solution (0 or 1) without any precision. However, the fuzzy decision tree method provides a solution between 0 and 1, but with a loss of certainty since it is generated from all the cases of the base, i.e. its construction has no relation with the descriptors of the target case. This is the problem that we have tried to solve with our approach FUZZY DTA which gave a complete and accurate solution.

2nd Technique. Comparing Solutions to the Physician Solution
In order to validate the result, we tested it in relation to the solution of the physician. Indeed, the classification by general fuzzy decision tree constructed from all the cases of the database gives a solution to the source case according to 5 classes given as output variables 'Verylow', 'Low', 'Medium', 'High', 'Veryhigh' based on the relevant descriptors proposed in the article 'Fuzzy Expert System for Diagnosis of Diabetes Using Fuzzy Determination Mechanism' [6]. Table 3, provides a comparison of the three experiments: FUZZY DTA is the classification model by fuzzy decision tree, 'Fuzzy Expert System by the Determination Mechanism 2011' [6], and 'Fuzzy Expert System by Fuzzy Assessment Methodology 2012' [7].

Table 3. Results of the 2nd experiments.

	Plas	Insu	Mass	Pedi	Age	Result
FUZZY DTA	172	579	42,4	0,702	28	High (0, 91)
Fuzzy expert system 2011	172	579	42,4	0,702	28	Medium (0, 46)
Fuzzy expert system 2012	172	579	42,4	0,702	28	Medium (0, 53)
Physician decision	172	579	42,4	0,702	28	Person is diabetic (1)

To validate our approach, we applied it on the same database Pima Indian Diabetes used by recent work: [6] and [7]. Figure 2 shows the comparison between FUZZY DTA and other works. We note that the result of our approach has given a result very close to the physician's decision. FUZZY DTA provided the solution: high diabetes with 91%, while other approaches have proposed that the patient is diabetic with less accuracy (medium with 46% and 53%). The decision of the doctor from his expertise provided the solution diabetic. This shows that the approach FUZZY DTA gives acceptable solutions compared to other approaches viewpoints precision and certainty.

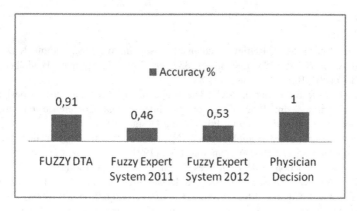

Fig. 2. Graphical representation of accuracy for the 2nd experiments

5 Conclusion

We have proposed a new technique of adaptation based on the fuzzy reasoning by decision tree and fuzzy inference that we named FUZZY DTA. The goal of our approach of fuzzy adaptation FUZZY DTA is to provide assistance to practitioners by providing a monitoring plan after diagnosis of diabetes in order to improve the quality of medical care. During their practice, practitioners use not only theoretical knowledge, but also their experience.

To this end, it is appropriate to exploit the fuzzy reasoning based on cases for medical surveillance assistance. We therefore based our approach on the fuzzy case-based reasoning which is a paradigm of solving problems based on past experience. We used the technique of fuzzy decision tree to extract knowledge. The main advantage of fuzzy decision tree is the interpretability of the results and also the ability to extract knowledge from a base of cases similar to the new case, which is a major interest in a diagnostic aid system [5]. We compared our approach with recent work.

We deduce from this comparison that the adaptation by inference rules is similar to the expert decision which optimizes the computation time. This is an advantage for our approach especially in the medical field it is important to get a result quite quickly with great precision and certainty.

Later, it would be interesting to use monitoring plans [23] in the solution part of the source cases to apply our fuzzy adaptation on these plans, to inform the patient not only of the type of diabetes that he has and to propose a general plan to follow, but also propose him a plan adapted to his own case (according to the degree of his diabetes), that is to say an application of fuzzy adaptation on surveillance plans. And to optimize response time and complexity we propose a Boolean modeling of induction and rule inference [21–23].

References

1. Smyth, B., Keane, M.T.: Retrieving adaptable cases. In: Wess, S., Althoff, K.D., Richter, M.M. (eds.) EWCBR 1993. LNCS, vol. 837, pp. 209–220. Springer, Heidelberg (1994). https://doi.org/10.1007/3-540-58330-0_88
2. Maher, M.L., de Silva Garza, A.G.: The adaptation of structural system designs using genetic algorithms. In: Proceedings of the International Conference on Information Technology in Civil and Structural Engineering Design (1996)
3. Dasarathy, B.V.: Nearest Neighbour (NN) Norms: NN Pattern Classification Techniques. IEE Computer Society Press, Washington, D.C. (1991)
4. Quinlan, J.R.: Induction of decision trees. Mach. Learn. 1, 81–106 (1986)
5. Pach, F.P., Abonyi, J.: Association rule and decision tree based methods for fuzzy rule base generation. Int. J. Comput. Electr. Autom. Control Inf. Eng. 2, 45–50 (2008)
6. Kalpana, M., Kumar, A.V.S.: Fuzzy expert system for diagnostics of diabetes using fuzzy determination mechanism. Int. J. Comput. Sci. Emerg. Technol. 2, 39–45 (2011)
7. Kalpana, M., Kumar, A.V.S.: Design and implementation of fuzzy expert system using fuzzy assessment methodology. Int. J. Sci. Appl. Inf. Technol. 1, 39–45 (2012)
8. Corchado, J.M., Aiken, J., Rees, N.: Artificial Intelligence Models for Oceanographic Forecasting. Plymouth Marine Laboratory, Plymouth (2001)
9. Qi, J., Hu, J., Peng, Y.: Incorporating adaptability-related knowledge into support vector machine for case-based design adaptation. Eng. Appl. Artif. Intell. 37, 170–180 (2015)
10. Benamina, M., Atmani, B., Benbelkacem, S.: Diabetes diagnosis by case-based reasoning and fuzzy logic. Int. J. Interact. Multimed. Artif. Intell. 5(3), 72–80 (2018)
11. Jain, V., Raheja, S.: Improving the prediction rate of diabetes using fuzzy expert system. Int. J. Inf. Technol. Comput. Sci. 10, 84–91 (2015)
12. Benbelkacem, S., Atmani, B., Benamina, M.: Planning based on classification by induction graph. In: International Conference on Data mining and Knowledge Management Process, Dubai (2013). ISBN 978-1-921987-15-1
13. Atmani, B., Benbelkacem, S., Benamina, M.: Planning by case-based reasoning based on fuzzy logic. In: International Conference on Computational Science and Engineering, Dubai, pp. 53–64 (2013)
14. Mokeddem, S., Atmani, B.: Assessment of clinical decision support systems for predicting coronary heart disease. In: Fuzzy Systems: Concepts, Methodologies, Tools, and Applications, vol. 184 (2017)
15. Arshadi, N., Badie, K.A.: Compositional approach to solution adaptation in case-based reasoning and its application to tutoring library. In: Proceedings of 8th German Workshop on Case-Based Reasoning, Lammerbuckel (2000)
16. Schmidt, R., Vorobieva, O.: Adaptation and medical case-based reasoning focusing on endocrine therapy support. In: Miksch, S., Hunter, J., Keravnou, E.T. (eds.) AIME 2005. LNCS (LNAI), vol. 3581, pp. 300–309. Springer, Heidelberg (2005). https://doi.org/10.1007/11527770_42
17. Jurisica, I., Mylopoulos, J., Glasgow, J., Shapiro, H., Casper, R.F.: Case-based reasoning in IVF: prediction and knowledge mining. Artif. Intell. Med. 12(1), 1–24 (1998)
18. Schmidt, R., Gierl, L.: Prognostic model for early warning of threatening influenza waves. In: Minor, M., Staab, S. (eds.) Proceedings of German Workshop on Experience Management, pp. 39–46. Köllen, Bonn (2002)

19. Guillaume, S., Charnomordic, B.: Learning interpretable fuzzy inference systems with FisPro. Inf. Sci. **181**(20), 4409–4427 (2011)
20. Alonso, J.M., Magdalena, L.: Generating understandable and accurate fuzzy rule-based systems in a java environment. In: Fanelli, A.M., Pedrycz, W., Petrosino, A. (eds.) WILF 2011. LNCS (LNAI), vol. 6857, pp. 212–219. Springer, Heidelberg (2011). https://doi.org/10.1007/978-3-642-23713-3_27
21. Atmani, B., Beldjilali, B.: Knowledge discovery in database: induction graph and cellular automaton. Comput. Inform. **26**(2), 171–197 (2012)
22. Barigou, F., Atmani, B., Beldjilali, B.: Using a cellular automaton to extract medical information from clinical reports. J. Inf. Process. Syst. **8**(1), 67–84 (2012)
23. Benamina, M., Atmani, B.: Définition d'un modèle booléen de raisonnement flou adapté à la planification. In: EGC, pp. 553–554 (2012)
24. http://www.diabetes.co.uk/
25. https://archive.ics.uci.edu/ml/datasets/pima+indians+diabetes

Arabic Real-Time License Plate Recognition System

Shaimaa Ahmed Elsaid[1,2(✉)], Haifa Alharthi[1], Reem Alrubaia[1],
Sarah Abutile[1], Rawan Aljres[1], Amal Alanazi[1],
and Alanoud Albrikan[1]

[1] Department of Information Technology,
College of Computer and Information Sciences, Princess Nourah Bint
Abdulrahman University, Riyadh, Kingdom of Saudi Arabia
saelsaid@pnu.edu.sa
[2] Electronics and Communications Department, Faculty of Engineering,
Zagazig University, Zagazig, Egypt

Abstract. Protection of homeland territory requires the capability to secure national borders in both the land and maritime domains. Assuring borderline security, denying illegal entry of people can be achieved by applying Automatic License Plate (ALP) recognition systems. In this paper, a Real-Time License Plates Recognition (RTLPR) system is proposed and applied to Saudi Arabian LPs. This system recognizes both Arabic and Indian numerals as well as limited Arabic and Latin alphabets. The developed system locates Saudi license plates in a captured image regardless of the time of day or license plate scale. It consists of five basic stages; preprocessing, license plate localization, character segmentation, features extraction, and characters recognition using Optical Character Recognition (OCR). To show the efficiency of the proposed system, it was tested on 470 LP images captured in outdoor environment including various types of vehicles with different shadow, skewness and noise effects. The experimental results yield 96% segmentation accuracy and 94.7% recognition accuracy. The recognition process takes 2 s to recognize plate information. Most of the elapsed time used is for the license plate extraction and rotation adjustment. The results show the feasibility of the methodology followed in this paper under different lighting conditions and shows the high robustness of the proposed algorithm.

Keywords: Secure national borders · Saudi license plates · Automatic License Plate (ALP) · Automatic vehicle identification · License plate detection · Optical Character Recognition · Character segmentation · Plate localization

1 Introduction

Assuring borderline security, denying illegal entry of people and goods as well as countering terrorist activities and movements are the main objectives of Border Police or Border Guard Authorities. Auto detector is a robust and highly reliable system that uses advanced technologies to perform embedded OCR processing. It can read vehicle license plates at access gates or during patrolling. License Plate (LP) is an unparalleled

© Springer Nature Switzerland AG 2019
A. Alfaries et al. (Eds.): ICC 2019, CCIS 1098, pp. 126–143, 2019.
https://doi.org/10.1007/978-3-030-36368-0_12

identification document for vehicles. It should be legitimate to be used in the public traffic; has the right shape and size, contains both alphabets and numbers, and should be fixed onto the car body (at both front and back sides). In recent years, the number of vehicles has largely increased in Saudi Arabia because of the growth of the urban population and the power of purchasing becomes stronger. In fact, the manual methods for identifying this large number of vehicles are so inefficient. So, this leads to difficulties in the management of vehicles and leads to many shortcomings such as the poor working environment, intensive labor, tedious work, and low efficiency. Due to the previously mentioned problems and to improve the efficiency of vehicle management and traffic control there is a need for automatic LPR system for the automatic identification of vehicles. LPR system (see Fig. 1) [1] is an image-processing technology used to identify vehicles by their license plates, or in other words, is a method used by a computer to convert digital images of vehicle license plates into text. It has a wide range of applications; traffic control, parking, access control, border control, and stolen cars tracking. It is considered as one of the most important topics of using computer vision and pattern recognition.

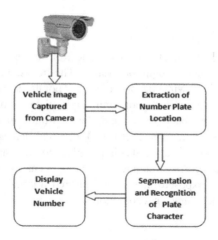

Fig. 1. General LPR system.

LPR systems have a wide impact in people's life as their scope is to improve transportation safety and mobility and to enhance productivity using advanced technologies. They have advances in navigation systems, Electronic toll collection systems, Assistance for safe driving, Optimization of traffic management, and Support for emergency vehicle operation. It should operate fast and accurate enough to satisfy the needs to it. Automatic License Plate Recognition (ALPR) is a widespread research area in many countries because of its importance. Due to the presence of various types of license plates, ALPR system may be different from one country to another. Figure 2 shows different license plates from different countries.

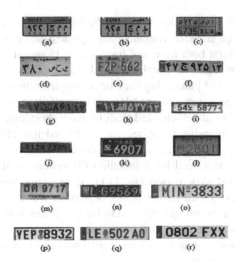

Fig. 2. Samples of license plates of different countries

1.1   Problem Statement

Detecting the accurate location of a license plate from a vehicle image is the most crucial step of a license plate recognition system. The license plate localization stage may be affected by the following factors; the view point changes (angle), when the vehicle body and LP have similar color, multi-style plate formats of license plates, distance changes, complex background and the non-uniform outdoor illumination conditions during image acquisition. Dirt (dust), physical damage, and unpredictable shadows screws and bolts (used to attach the plate to the car), may decrease the segmentation performance. Also, damaged or bent license plates, degrade images (including under or over exposed images, and blurred images). Problems of peel-off paint are exclusive to the character recognition.

2   Related Work

LP recognition requires high accuracy when considering busy roads or parking in Arabian countries. The recognition process in these places may not be possible manually as the human being become fatigues because of the job monotonous nature. Also, it is impossible to keep track of a vehicle when there are multiple vehicles passing in a very short time. To overcome these difficulties, many attempts have been made by the researchers across the globe for last decades. In [2], Integrated Municipal Provincial Auto Crime Team as a part of a more general response to auto theft, began to examine the utility and feasibility of ALPR. The authors discuss the results of the initial phase of the testing of this technology and its effectiveness in assisting police to respond to auto theft and other auto-related offences. In [3], the LPR system is stated to be appropriate for usage in Egypt and Saudi Arabia and a number of other Arabic countries. This system uses a new approach that begins directly after the license plate extraction phase.

The time taken to recognize a license plate 1.6 ms. The accuracy of recognition in the system is 90%. In [4], The authors approach the problem of real-time LPR by utilizing the NI LabVIEW software. Their method has proven to be surprisingly fast compared to other systems, with an average processing speed of 38 ms/image, and an average success rate of 84% under different conditions. The simplicity of the system and its low computational load makes it very attractive for real-time applications. In [5], the authors focus to recognize the vehicles by identifying the LP. The accuracy of the system is 96.53% average recognition rate using double hidden layer and 94% using single hidden layer. This system is basically used for traffic and security purposes. The project of [6] discusses the license plate detection and localization system (LPDL) which is used in Jordan. LPDL works perfectly on all kinds of license plates with 93.43% efficiency rate. However, the main disadvantage of the system is that the results can be affected by the clearance of the photo taken of the vehicle. In [7], it is stated that the license plate recognition system used in Iraq is License Plate Character Recognition (LPCR) based on Support Vector Machines (SVMs). The system performs well on various types of Iraqi plates, even on scratched, scaled plate numbers. However, SVMs are slower than other neural networks for a similar generalization. The accuracy of the system show that their system method produced 20% better accuracy for both numbers Indian and Arabic. In [8], a Shadow Aware License Plate Recognition (SALPR) system is proposed to recognize Egyptian LP. This system achieves high recognition rate through applying shadow detection and removal, rotation adjustment and using Multilayer perceptron as a powerful tool to perform the recognition process. The experimental results yield 95.5% recognition accuracy. The recognition process takes 1.6 s to recognize plate information. Performance comparison between SALPR and other LP recognition techniques shows that for most of the cases, SALPR performs better than other techniques under different lighting conditions and it shows the high robustness of the proposed algorithm.

3   Subjects and Methods

This section provides information about the overall architecture of the RTLPR system, Database design, and methods used in the proposed system.

3.1   Databases

The recognition phase goes through two main stages of database matching. The first one is a Character Template matching database which contains 27 saved characters represented as zeroes and ones each of size 42×24. The second one is the Identity database which is a structure to save the owner's information of different tested LP for the retrieval process. The LP will be recognized only and only if the system correctly matched the characters and found its corresponding owner from the Identity database. Otherwise, the system will show an error message.

3.2   Cross-Correlation Function (CCF)

Cross-correlation function (CCF) is a measurement of the similitude or similar properties between two parts. In signal processing, CCF is a measure of similarity of two signals as a function of a time-lag to one of them. Also, it is known as a sliding dot product or inner-product. CCF is used for checking a long-duration waveform for a shorter known feature. It also has many applications in various fields; pattern recognition, single particle analysis, electron tomographic averaging...etc.

3.3   Optical Character Recognition (OCR)

OCR is needed when the information should be readable to humans and machine while alternate inputs cannot be described in advance. Comparing it with other ALPR techniques, OCR is unique in that it does not demand control of the information production process.

The main idea in automatic patterns recognition, is to train the machine which classes of patterns that may occur and what they look like. In OCR, the patterns may be numbers, letters, or some special symbols like question marks, commas, ... etc., while each class corresponds to similar characters. The training of the machine is done by teaching the machine samples of characters of the different classes. Depending on these samples the machine constructs a prototype or a description for each class. Then, during recognition, the unknown characters are compared to the previously obtained descriptions, and assigned the class that gives the best match. In most commercial systems for character recognition, the training process has been performed in advance. Some systems do however, include facilities for training in the case of inclusion of new classes of characters.

A correlation approach is most commonly used, wherein the designated character to be recognized is overlaid on each of a set of candidate characters of similar size. The CCF of the two characters is computed, and the character with the highest CCF number is then chosen as the specified character.

4   The Proposed System

In this paper, a Real-Time License Plates Recognition (RTLPR) system is proposed. The proposed recognition system is applied to Saudi Arabian LPs which have two different formats. So, the proposed RTLPR system recognizes both Arabic and Indian numerals as well as Arabic and Latin alphabets. The developed system locates Saudi license plates in a captured image regardless of the time of day or license plate scale. It consists of five basic stages; preprocessing, license plate localization, character segmentation, features extraction, and characters recognition using Optical Character Recognition (OCR). The RTLPR system's flowchart shown in Fig. 3 illustrates the system architecture besides all the processes involve in the proposed system implemented in Matlab software. It explains how the flow of data in the system will be handled in order. Starting from getting the image, going through all the procedures and techniques of license plate handling which involves detection, extraction, segmentation to finally recognizing the plate and getting the output which specifies the owner's information.

The proposed RTLPR system flowchart illustrates all processes involved in the identification of the car owner. The first process is start or the system initialization. Once ready, the RTLPR system is started with Matlab software and launch a simple interface by using GUI function that asks for admin login user name and password. Once the ALPR system start up, the GUI interface will pop up with multiple boxes [9]. The first box will display the captured image Fig. 4 from the camera which is connected wirelessly to the computer.

4.1 Image Preprocessing Stage

After the image is loaded, the preprocessing steps are started to enhance the image quality to be able to extract the plate region from the original image accurately. It consists of eight minor processes which are Grayscale, Binarization, Median Filtering, Edge Detection, Dilation, Convolution, Flood Fill, and Image Cropping.

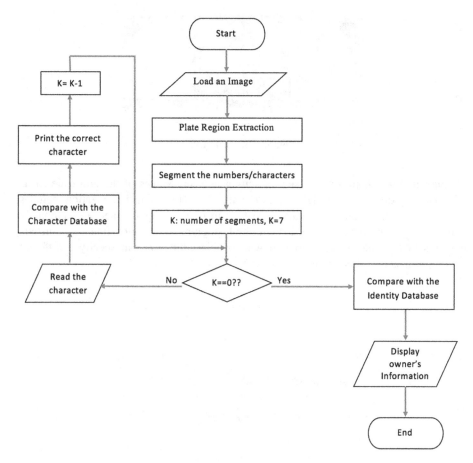

Fig. 3. System architecture.

Fig. 4. The captured image

Grayscale Process: Grayscale process is a method to process and turn the image into gray based color. The grayscale image is important to generate a clean and sharp binary image in the next process. Once the LP is segmented and cropped, it is processed into grayscale as shown in Fig. 5.

Fig. 5. Grayscale LP.

Histogram Equalization: The step of setting intensity values of the grayscale LP is automatically done by using Histogram Equalization. Histogram Equalization includes transforming these values so that the histogram of the output image approximately coincides a given histogram. By default, the histogram equalization function, "histeq" attempts to coincide a flat histogram with 64 bins, but you can specify a different histogram instead. This process is shown as in Figs. 6, 7, and 8.

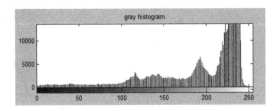

Fig. 6. Histogram of gray image.

Fig. 7. Histogram equalization image.

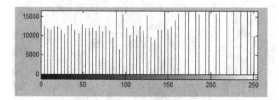

Fig. 8. Histogram equalization.

Binarization Process: The third process in Preprocessing stage is Binarization. This process will convert or turn the gray image into a binarized image consisting of only white and black pixels for the LP image. The system will process and generate the binarized image as shown in Fig. 9.

Fig. 9. Binarized LP.

Median Filtering Process: After the LP image become as binarized image which consists only of white and black pixel, the image need to go through median filtering process to make the image smoothens from contour of an object, breaks narrow isthmuses, and eliminates thin protrusions as shown in Fig. 10.

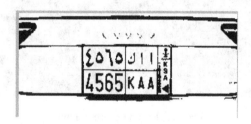

Fig. 10. LP image after Median Filtering.

Edge Detection: Edge is a curve that follows a path of rapid change in image intensity. Edges are related to the boundaries of objects in a scene. Edge detection is utilized to identify the edges in an image. The most powerful edge-detection technique is Canny. Canny technique varies from the other edge-detection techniques in that it uses two distinct thresholds (to detect strong and weak edges), and contains the weak edges only in the output if they are connected to strong edges. This method is therefore less likely than the others to be fooled by noise, and more likely to detect true weak edges as shown in Fig. 11.

Fig. 11. Edge detection step's output.

Dilation Process: Dilation process is the next process that executed to the image after median filtering and edge detection process. This is one of special technique in morphological algorithm in image processing with the aim to dilate the character image with the structural element. This ensures that the image is becoming more dilated and thicker from its original size for a better result.

Convolution Process: Convolution always applied to any image after dilation process, because convolution is brightening up the edges of any image. In this experiment, the image will be executed with the convolution process in each digit or character in the plate region to make all the edges of the characters look brighter.

Erosion Process: After the image has gone through the convolution process, another minor technique in morphological algorithm is applied which is Erosion technique. It is quite like Dilation technique, but Erosion technique is technically used to remove irrelevant details thus eliminating unnecessary pixels from the binary image. The output of the applied algorithm is shown in Fig. 12.

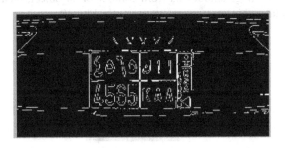

Fig. 12. Erosion process output.

Flood Fill Process: After the Erosion process, the displayed image will look better, but somehow it is normally containing several holes or unfilled areas in any of the characters especially in the white pixels' area. To overcome this problem and produce a better result, Flood Fill technique is identified to be used in this stage. Generally, Flood Fill process is a simple technique in image processing to fill all the holes as shown in Fig. 13.

Fig. 13. Flood fill output.

4.2 Plate Region Localization and Cropping Stage

The second stage of the proposed RTLPR system is the plate region cropping process. This process determines and identify the middle area of the image to carry and extract out the plate region area that has been gone through all the processes as mentioned above. Image Cropping is a special technique algorithm to focus on only a Region of Interest (ROI) in an image, it is used to crop the plate region by using some of the Dilation function to the pixels. The Image Cropping process output is shown in Fig. 14.

Fig. 14. Plate region cropping output.

4.3 Character Segmentation Stage

The objective of this stage is to segment every single character into the boundary box to compare it with the Database later. To execute this phase, all characters that are in the cropped LP image will be segmented with a specific segmentation technique. The approach used in this work for character segmentation is based on thresholding and Connected Component Analysis (CCA); discussed previously in Sect. 3. In binary image processing, CCA is a significant technique that scans and tags the pixels of a binary image into components based on pixel connectivity. Each pixel is tagged with a value according to the component to which it was assigned. The connected components are then analyzed to clear out long and wide components. The CCA function separates the characters one by one, and put each one in a boundary box as seen in Fig. 15.

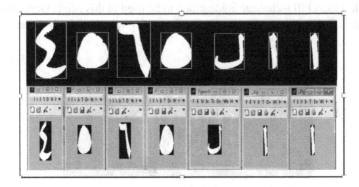

Fig. 15. Segmented characters

4.4 Characters' Features Extraction Stage

The features of each segmented character are extracted using Regionprops Matlab function in which it returns measurements for the set of properties specified for each 8-connected component (object) in the binary image. According to our approach each alphanumeric character has a unique set of properties associated with it, which differentiates it from the rest of the characters. Features are extracted from each character and saved in a database as pixel values in range between 0 and 255 changing from one character to another. This process matches pixel by pixel value of input image with template image. compare and find the closest match of the features vector from the database.

4.5 Car Owner Identification Stage

This is the final stage of the proposed RTLPR system. Characters recognition by comparing the features of each character to those features stored in the characters' database (discussed later in details) using Template Matching and Cross Correlation function [10]. After recognizing the LP's characters, it is compared to the LP's characters that are stored in the car owners' database to identify the car owner with more information about the car specifications.

4.6 The RTLPR System's GUI

Figure 16 shows the main GUI interface for our proposed ALPR System. The first process is to capture the image automatically. Once the image has been loaded, the captured image will appear in (Original Plate) box. The second step will execute the plate Region and the image will appear in (ROI) box. The next process is Segmentation where characters get segmented, features are extracted then compared and matched automatically with the Character Template then it will appear in (Segmentation) box. The final process, which is Plate Recognition phase, is also executed automatically by comparing the results of the previous step with another database to retrieve the owner's information of recognized plates only. The result will be shown in (Plate Information) space. Also, the proposed system checks if he is allowed to cross the border and gives alarm if he is unauthorized person. All these processes can be executed for so many times by loading/capturing different images.

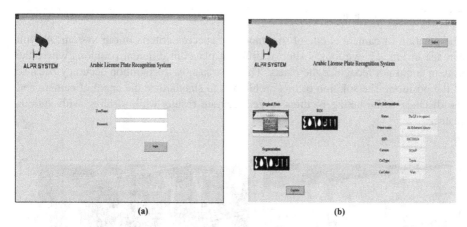

Fig. 16. The RTLPR system's GUI; (a) Log in screen, and (b) The detection and recognition screen

5   Experimental Results

To show the efficiency of the proposed system, experiments have been done on numerous captured images including various types of vehicles with different lighting and noise effects. Eight sets of vehicle images are used in our experiments as discussed later in Subsect. 5.2. These experiments have been executed by following two major phases which are characters segmentation and characters recognition.

5.1   Test Plan

In our project, we have created a database that includes a set of LP taken pictures considered as a Train set to the system, then we gathered another collection of LP images to test the performance of the ALPR system. In addition, some of the LP images that is in the test collection are already used in the database, and some of them are not. To get the accurate percentage for every phase of process, the following Eqs. (1) and (2):

1. Accuracy of the Segmentation Phase

$$= (\text{Number of Correct Segmentation Output}/\text{Total Input Data}) * 100\% \quad (1)$$

2. Accuracy of the Recognition Phase

$$= (\text{Number of Correct Recognition Output}/\text{Total Input Data}) * 100\% \quad (2)$$

5.2   Test Cases Case 1

The position of camera is one of the important success criteria in our system. As you can see in Fig. 17, we took a shot of different plates in different positions where the system could not recognize the plates. This case has 0% recognition accuracy because of the position. The solution of this problem is to standardize the angel of camera and the distance while taking pictures to get accurate results while dealing with various plates.

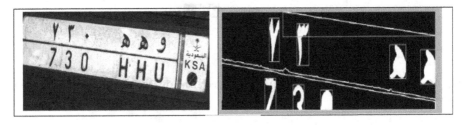

Fig. 17. Case 1

Case 2: The brightness (due to the sun or flash) and shadow sometimes affect the plates during recognition phase as you see in Fig. 18. In this case, the shadow masked some parts of the LP characters which led to inaccurate results. This case has 0% Segmentation accuracy because the shadow hides the letters so the system cannot extract them from the plate.

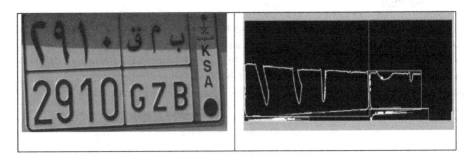

Fig. 18. Case 2

Case 3: License plates could also be physically damaged. As in our next case in Fig. 19, two spikes on the corners are affecting the alphanumeric plate. It creates additional spots that might be detected incorrectly as part of the characters in the recognition process. This case has 66% recognition accuracy because the damage so the system cannot extract the letters correctly from the plate.

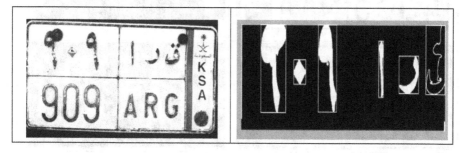

Fig. 19. Case 3

Case 4: Rain, Dust, and Mud affect the plates and cause noise that might erase some characters during processing. This case has 0% Segmentation accuracy because of the noise so the system cannot extract it from the plate. Figure 20.

Fig. 20. Case 4

Case 5: The following figures are some of standard plates that are recognized successfully. The right angle of camera was the key of success. Also, the noise filters that have been added to make the plate clearer. This case has 100% recognition accuracy (See Fig. 21).

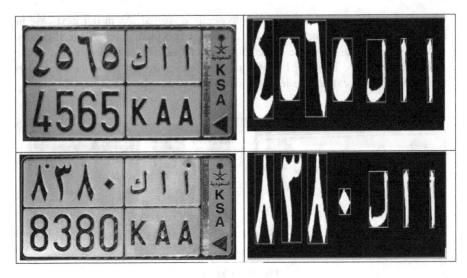

Fig. 21. Case 5

Fig. 22. Case 6

Fig. 23. Case 7

Case 6: regardless of the position and the number of alphanumeric which may be less than the standard plate that equal to 7 characters, our technique recognizes the plate correctly as in Fig. 22. In this case, the result of recognition is 100%.

Case 7: The physical bolts (used to attach the plate to the car) may decrease the segmentation performance. In our system, we have improved the process of localization and segmentation where those bolts get removed and the plates extracted correctly. In this case the recognition accuracy is 100% (See Fig. 23).

Case 8: Even though there is a slight slope in the position of the LP in Fig. 24, our system localized it and recognized it accurately with 100% without any errors.

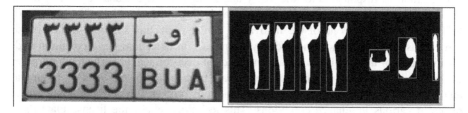

Fig. 24. Case 8

5.3 Test Results

This subsection analyzes the overall performance of RTLPR program by measuring its accuracy and effectiveness. This is to ensure that this project has achieved the main objectives and purposes. The results to evaluate the algorithm performance is measured by three main LPR program phases which are Plate Region Extraction and Character Segmentation, and Character Recognition phase. These major phases results are analyzed and calculated based on the accuracy of the output with the original data in preprocessing stage. Figure 25 shows the recognition accuracy results for the eight test cases mentioned above.

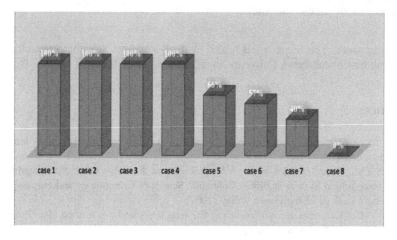

Fig. 25. Recognition accuracy for the 8 test cases.

Using 470 random images from the previous eight test categories both the segmentation stage and the recognition stage of the proposed system are tested. The test results are 96% segmentation accuracy and 94.7% recognition accuracy.

6 Conclusions and Future Works

Saudi Arabia is responsible for the safety and security of its citizens. It protects them against organized crime, drug trafficking and illegal immigration. The proposed RTLPR system offers one of the innovative border protection solution to the armed forces, customs, the police and security agencies. On detection, the recognition and identification of targets allows instant and efficient decision making. The main purpose of this paper is to detect an Arabic license plate from an image provided by a camera automatically in real time. An effective technique is proposed to detect Arabic license plates in various luminance conditions. This technique elicits the license plate data from an image and provides it as an input to the LP Recognition step. The image of a vehicle is given as an input from the camera. Extracted plate information and the car's owner can be seen on screen for verification purposes. To show the efficiency of the proposed system, experiments have been done on numerous captured images. The system is tested on 470 LP images captured in outdoor environment including various types of vehicles with different lighting, shadow, skewness and noise effects. The experimental results yield 96% segmentation accuracy and 94.7% recognition accuracy. The recognition process takes 2 s to recognize plate information. Most of the elapsed time used is for the license plate extraction and adjustment.

To enhance the recognition, our future research is directed towards:

- Minimize the errors due to stains, smudges, blurred regions & different font style and sizes.
- The proposed approach has been applied for Saudi licenses only. It can be extended to cover more Arabic countries.

Acknowledgments. This research was funded by the Deanship of Scientific Research at Princess Nourah bint Abdulrahman University through the Fast-track Research Funding Program.

References

1. Bhat, R., Mehandia, B.: Recognition of vehicle number plate using matlab. Int. J. Innovative Res. Electr. 1 (2014)
2. Cohen, I.M., Plecas, D., MoCormic, A.V.: A Report on the Utility of the Automated License Plate Recognition System in British Columbia. School of Criminology and criminal Justice University College of the Fraser Valley (2007)
3. Khalil, M.I.: Car plate recognition using the template matching method. Int. J. Comput. Theory Eng. 2(5), 683–687 (2010)
4. Al-Juraifani, A., Al-Audah, Y., Al-Zuhair, A.: A Real-Time Recognition System for Saudi License Plates using LabVIEW. King Fahd University for Petroleum and Minerals (2012)

5. Meenakshi,R.B.D.: Vehicle license plate recognition system. Int. J. Adv. Comput. Res. (2012)
6. Moustafa, A., Jaradat, M.: A new approach for license plate detection and localization: between reality and applicability. Int. Bus. Res. 8(11), 13 (2015)
7. Abed, M.A.: New Hybrid SVMS-BCOA architecture for Iraqi vehicles license plate recognition. Eur. J. Comput. Sci. Inf. Syst. 3(1), 73–86 (2015)
8. Elsaid, S.A.: Shadow aware license plate recognition system. Soft. Comput. 19(1), 225–235 (2015)
9. Gonzalez, R.C., Woods, R.E., Eddins, S.L.: Digital Image Processing Using MATLAB. United States of America (2009)
10. Dey, S., Choudhury, A., Mukherjee, J.: An efficient technique to recognize license plate using morphological edge detection and character matching algorithm. Int. J. Comput. Appl. (0975 – 8887) 101(15) (2014)

Exploring Barriers Mobile Payments Adoption: A Case Study of Majmaah University in Saudi Arabia

Rana Alabdan[⊠]

Department of Information Systems, Faculty of Sciences and Information Technology College, Majmaah University, Al Majma'ah 11952, Saudi Arabia
r.alabdan@mu.edu.sa

Abstract. Mobile payment is the new paradigm shift to use as an efficient electronic method to pay in daily life as an alternative of cash, debit or credit. This study explores the barriers of mobile payment adoption among Saudi individuals in Majmaah University either students, staff, or faculty. The researcher conducted a survey among participants in Majmaah University, only 198 completed the survey. The researcher studied the mobile payment among this population specifically because there is no prior study investigated of this topic. It is also a developing city which is the future of Sudair. It is improving very quick in all areas especially education, industrial, and digitally. The survey conducted in October 2018 until December 2018. The author acquired the following results, it identified security was a barrier to adopt mobile payment in Majmaah University.

Keywords: Mobile payment · Security risk · Quantitative study

1   Introduction

Mobile payment is a paradigm shift method of payment which increases due to the smartphone and technology emerging every year. Individuals might adopt or not adopt mobile payment due to set of influential factors that influence those individuals. Saudi individuals are willing to use new innovation such as mobile payment and they prefer to used smartphone to make payment [1,2]. Statista [2] quantified, the usage of smartphones in the Kingdom of Saudi Arabia increased from 19 million in 2015 to 21 in 2018, it is also estimated to be 24 million by 2022. This study emphasizes on the non-adopters or early adopters who are reluctant to use mobile payment regularly. The researcher investigates the barriers that prevent individuals in Majmaah University from adopting mobile payment. These barriers constructed from previous conducted study Pinchot et al. [3].

Mobile payment is different than online banking, it is defined as the method of payment where individuals use electronic device such as smartphones, tablet,

A. Alfaries et al. (Eds.): ICC 2019, CCIS 1098, pp. 144–160, 2019.
https://doi.org/10.1007/978-3-030-36368-0_13

or PDA to pay for a product, or item. You can also send money electronically for your relatives or friends via mobile payment. Saudi users enticed to use new technology and preserve new smartphones. In addition, Saudi individuals believe in the positive impact of new technology and the importance to shift to electronic services "four-fifth of respondents believe that digital services will be used by more people and spread to more areas of life" (Alarabiya [1], para. 4). There is high percentage among Saudi individuals to use their smartphone for mobile banking either online banking via internet browser or on the smartphone app, which is %51 and %44 respectively [1]. However, the researcher conducted a short poll via Twitter on April 5 that showed %62 of Saudi do not use mobile payment, the total vote were 21 users. This result is different than the findings in the previous studies.

To understand the community of this study, will explain about Majmaah City and the university. Majmaah is the capital city of Sudair, which is northern region of Riyadh. The modern improvement this city had in the couple years ago is interesting. It has also Majmaah University which is established in 2009, followed by multiple colleges and departments. Even though Majmaah is a small city, it is well developed in education, industrial and soon digitally. It is the future city of industry and business sector. Thus, it is vital to understand the attitude of the population regard the adoption of mobile payment especially in Majmaah city which is still developing city.

The purpose of this study is to explore the barriers which influence Saudi faculty, staff, and students to adopt mobile payment services in Majmaah University. This study is replication of Pinchot study which is study the barriers of mobile payment among United Stated students. However, this study expands the sample to include the faculty and staff. The research questions for the study are as the following:

- **RQ1**: What are the barriers that influence adoption of mobile payment from individuals in Majmaah University?
- **RQ2**: What can be done to encourage individuals in Majmaah University to adopt mobile payments?

This paper organized as the following, it starts with the introduction section followed by literature review, factors that influence mobile payment, and trust in m-payment. The following section will be methodology including data collection and analysis. Then, the findings will be discussed in the result section. The last section will be discussion section which includes implications and limitation of the study.

2   Literature Review

2.1   Examining Mobile Payment Using TAM

Mobile payment adoption increases especially with the new shifting to electronic service around the world. In this paper, the researcher examined the literature from different perspective by classifying this section into multiple section that provide a review of the mobile payment in general and specifically in the Middle East and the Kingdom of Saudi Arabia.

Technology acceptance Model (TAM) was widely used among the researchers in the literature to investigate mobile payment. The researcher will investigate the studies that use TAM as a theoretical framework then converse the other type of the model. Dastan [4] conducted a study using a technology acceptance model to investigate the factors influence mobile payment adoption in Turkey. Dastan found that trust, mobility and attitude have positive influence of mobile payment while usefulness and ease of use does not affect m-payment. In addition, Barkhordari, Nourollah, Mashayekhi, Mashayekhi, and Ahangar [5] conducted a similar study in Iran to investigate the critical factors influence trust in mobile payment. An online survey distributed among 246 of Iranian customers. Barkhordari et al. argued consumers perceived security can be improved by access to the security guidelines, technical and transaction procedures. The second factor is access to and security including security guidelines, which is the most significant factor influence trust. Security has positive influence on the adoption of mobile payment.

In addition, Lwoga and Lwoga [6], investigates users' behavioral intention regard the usage of mobile payment services in Tanzania. The authors argued the influence of four factors which includes security, user-centric, system characteristics and gender effect. Kim, Mirusmonov, and Lee [7] conducted a survey over the 12 weeks as well as e-mail surveys and interviews in Korea, the sample was 269. They differentiate between early and late adopters of this service. Early adopters influenced by ease of use, whereas late adopters influenced by usefulness, reachability, and convenience of mobile payment. Bailey, Pentina, Mishra, and Ben Mimoun [3], investigated the relationship amongst mobile payment, anxiety, technology, privacy, and self-efficacy by using TAM model to study the mobile payment adoption. The study discovered adoption of mobile payment "tap-and-go payment" , amongst the US users. Thus, mobile payment affected by self-efficacy, ease of use, usefulness, intention to use it, and privacy concerns.

2.2 The Influencing Factors of Mobile Payment

Chachage, Kamuzora, and Malim [8], evaluated factors that influence mobile payment acceptance services among students of higher education especially Ruaha University College of Saint Augustine University of Tanzania. They distributed an online survey amongst 441 randomly students from Tanzania, Ruaha University College (RUCO). The results showed that majority of individuals were male aged between 20–29 years. The study identified multiple factors influence behavior to adopt mobile payment, which are as following: performance expectancy, social influence, and effort expectance. However, Pinchot et al. [3] explored the barriers that influence mobile payment adoption among students in the U.S. Pinchot et al. [3], identified security, awareness, and availability as barriers which affect mobile payment adoption.

A study by Dastan [4], investigated the factors which influence the adoption of mobile payment. Dastan survey 225 participant in Turkey. Dastan found that trust mobility and attitude influence mobile payment. Luna, Montoro-Ríos, Liébana-Cabanillas, and Lun [9] investigated the acceptance of Near-field communication (NFC) technology for mobile payment from a Brazilian perspective, which emphasis on exploring the factors which influence acceptance of NFC directly or indirectly. Thy used questionnaire with 423 users in Brazil. The results illustrated that the willingness of users to use IT, innovation influenced individuals to use NFC technology, and usefulness, which represents 74%, 56%, and 43%.

2.3 Trust and Security Issues of Mobile Payment

Trust is a vital factor that influence users to use mobile payment or not, which is a barrier that prevent mobile payment from being widely used for Gao and Waecht [10] identified the lack of user trust as the main significant barrier for mobile payment success. The researcher distributed a survey among 1155 of Australian individuals. The researcher argued the quality of the system and information is related to trust as a positive influential factor. Trust has a positive effect on the usage of mobile payment which perceived convenience. Barkhordari et al. [5] accented how trust is a critical factor to adopt mobile payment and it was influenced by security Barkhordari et al. [5] either accessing to the guidelines or transaction. Security and trust are crucial factors that influence individuals to adopt mobile payment or not.

The attitude of users regarding mobile payment is different among new adopters or existing users. Existing users has more trust than new adopters who has some doubt in mobile payment. Hillma and Neustaedter [11] studied mobile payment within two groups of individuals, the first group who use mobile payment to buy from online stores via app, i.e., Amazon. The second group who use mobile payment to buy from physical store via app i.e., Starbucks app [11]. The group who use payment through online stores has no trust issues with the mobile payment especially they have trust in the brands/products or recommendation from others [11]. The second group has some concerns regarding information access which influence their trust to adopt this technology [11]. However, authors believe that mobile payment will be prominent in North America.

The researchers agreed upon the importance of trust as a factor that influence the users to adopt/not adopt mobile payment. The companies who use mobile payment or the banking system need to enhance the level of trust in this service. When the trust is increased, the usage might be increased as well.

3 Methodology

3.1 Data Collection

A survey distributed to the faculty, staff, and students (males and females) in Majmaah University, Saudi Arabia. In this study a convenience sample was selected due to the relevance of the sample specifically to study mobile payment barriers among this environment, which is in a rural area. Convenience sample is appropriate because it is suite the study because it is focusing on a group of individuals within the university. Thus, it the sample was chosen according to convenience and availability of the individuals [12]. The researcher collected the sample from Majmaah University specifically, because educated individuals are more persuasive to approve new technology such as mobile payment. The sample is over 18 years, which represents different generations. This variation of ages and job status provides the uniqueness for the study. It will demonstrate the different barriers among these individuals, where it can be compared and contrast.

This survey is adapted from Pinchot [3] study and translated to Arabic to be more convenient to the sample who speaks Arabic as a native language. The researcher distributed the survey within the Majmaah University to examine the barriers that influence mobile payment adoption. The researcher sought the approval from Ethics committee in Majmaah university to distribute the survey that is approved in September 2018.

The researcher structured the questioner using five-point Likert scale: strongly agree, agree, neutral, disagree, and strongly disagree. This kind of scale is appropriate to the study to increase response rate, quality, and to be more contented to the participants [13,14]. The survey developed to measure three main factors: awareness, availability, and security.

In 2019, the total population in Majmaah University, specifically colleges located in Majmaah is 7940 among faculty, staff, and students. The population is divided as the following: faculty is 304 males and 122 females; staff is 336 male, 336 females, while undergrad students are 3324 male, 3309 females; 191 grad male and 18 grad females. The researcher selects Majmaah university as the target of the population because it is small city and we need to explore the mobile payment adoption amongst its individuals, which will add to the body of knowledge in this specific field (*see* Tables 1 and 2).

Table 1. The demographic table.

	Female	Male
Faculty	122	304
Staff	336	336
Students	Grad	
	18	191
	Undergrad	
	3324	3309

Table 2. Questionnaire (Pinchot et al. [3]).

Construct	Item
Awareness	I am not aware of mobile payment services that are available for use on my smartphone
	I do not really understand all the different mobile payment options
	I do not know how to use mobile payment services on my smartphone
Availability	I do not think mobile payments are accepted by enough retailers to make their use worthwhile
	The places I shop don't accept mobile payments
	I do not have the necessary feature on my phone to use mobile payment services
Security	I do not think that my personal payment information is kept safe when I use a mobile payment service to pay for a purchase
	I am concerned about the security of mobile payments
	I am concerned about someone intercepting my payment information or other data if I use mobile payment services

4 Results

A total of 257 responded to the survey two of them do not use smartphones, so 255 participants have smartphones. Out of 255 who use smartphones only 198 completed the full survey which excluded 57 responses that is incomplete. Out of 257 only 198 completed the full survey but 145 who use mobile payment services among these 198. Table 3 below showed that female participants more than male where it is 60.61%, 39.39% respectively. The sample was from the younger generation, as shown in Table 4. The age group from 25–34 has the highest percentage among the participants by 38.38% followed by 18–24 with 33.33%. The highest participation has a bachelor degree which is 35.86% where is diploma is the lowest percentage by 4.55%. Below are the complete summary results of the data taken and analyzed by SurveyMonkey.

Table 3. Participants by gender

Gender	Number of participants	Percentage (N = 198)
Male	78	39.39
Female	120	60.61

The individuals are using smartphone more than seven years by 141 out of 198 participants which represents 71.21% of the sample. Moreover, the individuals use smartphone the most in social media where 139 out of 198 answered which is 70.20%. However, the least usage was in mobile payment and online shopping

Table 4. Number and percentage of participants by age groups

Age	Number of participants	Percentage (N = 198)
18–24	66	33.33
25–34	76	38.38
35–44	47	32.74
45–54	8	4.04
55 or older	1	0.51

Table 5. Number and percentage of participants by job status

Job status	Number of participants	Percentage (N = 198)
Students	95	47.98
Administrative staff	47	23.74
Faculty	56	28.28

which represents 3.03% for each. The first group which represents 145 out of 198 are aware of the apps they can use on their mobile devices to make purchases rather than using a credit or debit card. The other group who is not aware of this service represents 53 totals of 198. That means Saudi individuals in Majmaah City are aware of mobile payment services and its usage. The survey also revealed that iPhone were the most used smartphone device among participants which is 110 whereas Android only 35. It is interesting that individuals in Majmaah do not use other type of smartphone beside iPhone and Android (Tables 5 and 6).

Apple Pay was the most mobile payment used among the individuals by 90 out of 145 (62.07%), where is the least was Samsung Pay by 4 (2.76%). Google Wallet and Android Pay has the same percentage which is 6.21% of the sample. Accordingly, Apple products are more popular usage among the individuals as it is shown in the survey results. The individuals divided into two groups, one who did not use mobile payment services via smartphones which represents 57.24%. The other group who used the services is 42.76%. For the first group the possibility to use mobile payment services in the future is very

Table 6. Number and percentage of participants by education levels

Education level	Number of participants	Percentage (N = 198)
High School or equivalent	59	29.80
Diploma	9	4.55
Bachelor	71	35.86
Master	32	16.16
PhD	27	13.64

likely 54.22%, 45 out of 83. The second group who uses mobile payment is aware of the service agreed by 41.38% and strongly agreed by 35.86% (Figs. 1, 2, 3, 4, 5, 6, 7, 8, 9, 10, 11, 12, 13, 14, 15, 16, 17, 18, 19 and 20).

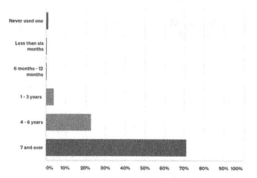

Fig. 1. Q7: A smartphone is a moble phone with features that may enable it to access the web, send emails, download apps, and interact with computers. How long have you been using a smartphone?

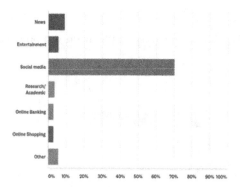

Fig. 2. Q8: Which of the following types of apps do you use regularly on your smartphone?

5   Discussion

The previous analysis of the survey approved that individuals in Majmaah have awareness of mobile payment services and its availability. Majority of the participants are iPhone users may be due the easiness of the iOS in comparison to the Android system. Even though, Saudi in Majmaah inclined to use the mobile payment service and aware of it, 59.31% of the individuals in Majmaah University use mobile payment once a month.

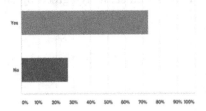

Fig. 3. Q9: Are you aware that there are apps you can use on your smartphone to make purchases rather than using a credit or debit card?

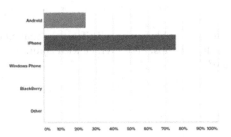

Fig. 4. Q10: Which type of smartphone do you primarily use?

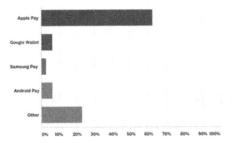

Fig. 5. Q11: Mobile payment services offer the ability to pay for purchases using your smartphone as an alternative to a credit or debit card. Typically, you download an app to your smartphone and the app is loaded with your banking, credit card, or debit card information. You then use the app to pay for a purchase at a retailer by opening the app on your smartphone and tapping it to the payment device at a cash register instead of swiping your card. Are you familiar with any of the following mobile payment services?

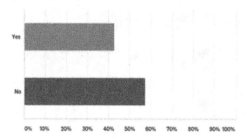

Fig. 6. Q12: Have you ever used a mobile payment service to make a purchase?

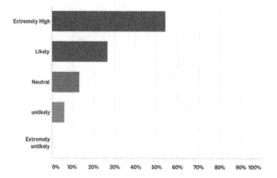

Fig. 7. Q13: How likely are you to use mobile payment services in the future?

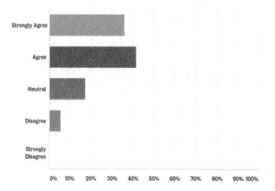

Fig. 8. Q14: I am aware of mobile payment services that are available for use on my smartphone.

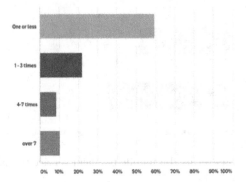

Fig. 9. Q15: Number of times you use smartphone for mobile payment per month.

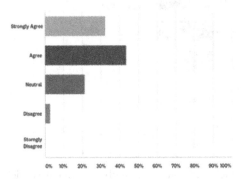

Fig. 10. Q16: I think mobile payment services are simple to understand and use on my smartphone.

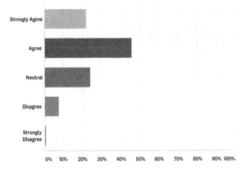

Fig. 11. Q17: I think mobile payments are accepted by enough retailers to make their use worthwhile.

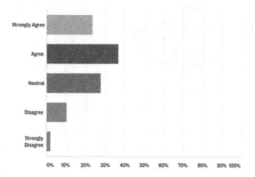

Fig. 12. Q18: I think that my personal payment information is kept safe when I use a mobile payment service to pay for a purchase.

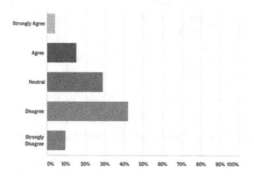

Fig. 13. Q19: It is difficult to set up and use mobile payment services.

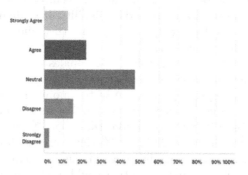

Fig. 14. Q20: The places I shop do not accept mobile payments.

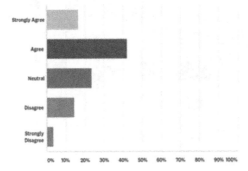

Fig. 15. Q21: It is easier for me to pay with cash or a credit/debit card than to use mobile payment services.

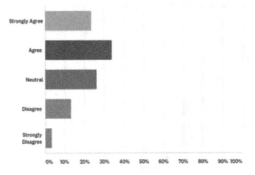

Fig. 16. Q22: I am concerned about the security of mobile payments.

The researcher found that the only barrier is security, where three items are concerning the individuals in Majmaah University (see Table 7). This finding is consistent with the literature [5,6]. Security influences Saudi (faculty, staff, and students) to adopt mobile payment in their daily life. Thus, this study findings are consistent with Pinchot et al. [3], findings in security as a barrier while it is not on the other barriers: awareness and availability. It is almost the half of the participants in Majmaah University who are concerned about their information and the security of the mobile payment.

In security factor, it is been noticed that females are inclined to trust the mobile payment than males, see to the statistics of the Table 8 below.

There is a gender impact on adoption of the mobile payment in Majmaah university. The percentage of using online banking among males and females are 3.85%, 2.50% respectively. In addition, the usage of news is higher among males than females which was 19.23%, 2.50%. However, females use other service more than males such as social media entertainment and online shopping. Males are aware more of mobile payment app that could use for mobile payment than females, 83.33%, 66.67%. In addition, the process of purchase using mobile payment was higher among males than females, 49.32%, 37.50%. The total number

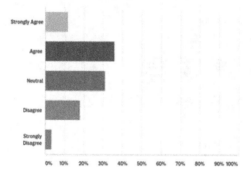

Fig. 17. Q23: I do not really understand all the different mobile payment options.

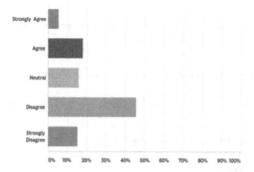

Fig. 18. Q24: I do not have the necessary feature on my phone to use mobile payment services.

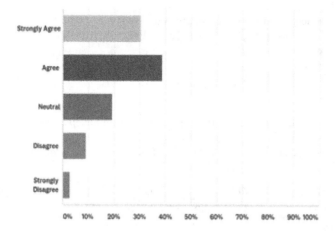

Fig. 19. Q25: I am cocerned about someone intercepting my payment information or other data if I use mobile payment services.

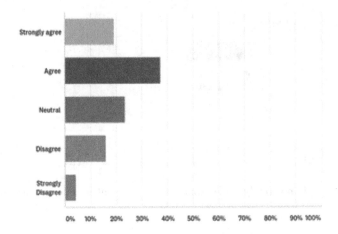

Fig. 20. Q26: I know how to use mobile payment services on my smartphone.

Table 7. Security factor as a barrier among Majmaah individuals

Survey item	Number (198)	Percentage (%)
I think that my personal payment information is kept safe when I use mobile payment	Strongly Agree (34) Agree (53) = 87	23.45%–
I am concerned about the security of mobile payment	Strongly Agree (34) Agree (49) = 83	23.45% 33.79%
I am concerned about someone intercepting my payment information	Strongly Agree (44) Agree (56) = 100	30.34% 38.62%

Table 8. I don't think my information is kept safe

Gender	Strongly agree	Agree	Neutral	Disagree	Strongly disagree	Total
Male	24.62%	36.92%	25.15%	12.31%	0%	44.83%
	16	24	17	8	0	65
Female	22.5%	36.25%	28.75%	8.75%	3.75%	55.17%
	18	25	23	7	3	80
Total	34	53	40	15	3	145

of usages among males per month was higher than females, for example, males use the mobile payment services more than seven time a month by 15.38% while females only 6.25%.

According to the participants, they will be encouraged if the security is increased, provide the services in more stores, compensation if there is some hacked or stolen situations. The sample was limited only to Majmaah university and the complete answers was only 198 in total of 257 participation. Also, the number of females' participants are more than males which may affect the result.

Further study should be conducted on Saudi individuals around the Kingdom to compare the difference between these studies. The researchers also need to analyze the gender influence on adoption of mobile payment among Saudi.

Acknowledgement. The author would like to thank Deanship of Scientific Research at Majmaah University for supporting this work under Project Number No. 1439-45.

References

1. Alarabiya. Most Saudi consumers prefer payment with mobile phones (2016). https://english.alarabiya.net/en/business/technology/2016/10/03/Most-Saudi-consumers-prefer-payment-with-mobile-phones.html. Accessed 4 Apr 2019
2. Statisctica. Number of smartphone users in Saudi Arabia from 2017 to 2023 (in millions)* (2019). https://www.statista.com/statistics/494616/smartphone-users-in-saudi-arabia/. Accessed 5 Feb 2019
3. Pinchot, J.L., et al.: Exploring barriers to adoption of mobile payments for university students: lack of awareness, lack of availability, and perceived security risks. Issues Inf. Syst. **173**, 20–30 (2016)
4. Daştan, İ., Gürler, C.: Factors affecting the adoption of mobile payment systems: an empirical analysis. EMAJ: Emerg. Mark. J. **61**, 17–24 (2016)
5. Barkhordari, M., et al.: Factors influencing adoption of e-payment systems: an empirical study on Iranian customers. Inf. Syst. e-Bus. Manag. **151**, 89–116 (2017)
6. Lwoga, E.T., Lwoga, N.B.: User acceptance of mobile payment: the effects of user-centric security, system characteristics and gender. Electron. J. Inf. Syst. Dev. Ctries. **81**(1), 1–24 (2017)
7. Kim, C., Mirusmonov, M., Lee, I.: An empirical examination of factors influencing the intention to use mobile payment. Comput. Hum. Behav. **26**(3), 310–322 (2010)
8. Chachage, B., Kamuzora, F., Malima, G.: Factors influencing acceptance of mobile money services amongst students of higher learning institutions in Tanzania with special reference to Ruaha University College. ANVESHAK Int. J. Manag. **2**(2), 9–18 (2013)
9. Luna, I.R.D., et al.: NFC technology acceptance for mobile payments: a Brazilian perspective. Rev. Bras. Gest. Neg. **1963**, 82–103 (2017)
10. Gao, L., Waechter, K.A.: Examining the role of initial trust in user adoption of mobile payment services: an empirical investigation. Inf. Syst. Front. **19**(3), 525–548 (2017)
11. Hillman, S., Neustaedter, C.: Trust and mobile commerce in North America. Comput. Hum. Behav. **70**, 10–21 (2017)
12. Babbie, E.R.: Survey Research Methods. Wadsworth, Belmont (1990)

13. Babakus, E., Mangold, W.G.: Adapting the SERVQUAL scale to hospital services: an empirical investigation. Health Serv. Res. **266**, 767 (1992)
14. Bouranta, N., Chitiris, L., Paravantis, J.: The relationship between internal and external service quality. Int. J. Contemp. Hosp. Manag. **21**(3), 275–293 (2009)

A Method for 3D-Metric Reconstruction Using Zoom Cameras

Boubakeur Boufama[1(✉)], Tarik Elamsy[2], and Mohamed Batouche[3]

[1] School of Computer Science, University of Windsor, Windsor, Canada
boufama@uwindsor.ca
[2] Department of Software Engineering, Al Ain University, Al Ain, UAE
Tarik.elamsy@aau.ac.ae
[3] College of Computer and Information Sciences, Princess Nourah University,
Riyadh, Kingdom of Saudi Arabia
mabatouche@pnu.edu.sa

Abstract. We propose in this work a practical method to compute the Euclidean (metric) 3D reconstruction of a scene, observed by a stereo pair of static, off-the-shelf, zooming cameras. The proposed method does not assume any form of explicit, pattern-based, calibration. The stereo system acquires a set of pairs of images, at different zooming levels, making it possible to obtain an affine calibration. The latter is obtained by taking advantage of the translation motion of the principal plane of each zooming camera. In particular, each pair of zoom images provides a pair of parallel planes that intersect at infinity. This makes it possible to estimate the principal point of each camera. Finally, a 3D metric reconstruction is calculated. Extensive experiments on both indoor and outdoor images have demonstrated the viability and accuracy of the proposed method.

Keywords: Artificial 3D vision · 3D visual processing and artificial intelligence

1 Introduction

While humans can easily recognize and understand a complex scene from a single visual glance, this same ability remains an ultimate long-term goal for machine vision. Despite the remarkable progress made so far, artificial vision successes remain limited, when target scenes consist of unknown objects in a cluttered real-world environment. The recovery of the three-dimensional structure from two-dimensional images is an ultimate goal in computer vision. Once the intrinsic and the extrinsic parameters of a stereo system are known, image-features can be easily matched and depth information can be estimated [4]. Although classical, pattern-based, calibration allows for accurate estimation of the intrinsic and extrinsic parameters of a stereo system, such calibration will be lost once cameras move or change their settings. In particular, such calibrated stereo system can neither move nor adjust its lenses configuration.

© Springer Nature Switzerland AG 2019
A. Alfaries et al. (Eds.): ICC 2019, CCIS 1098, pp. 161–173, 2019.
https://doi.org/10.1007/978-3-030-36368-0_14

While there is a wide range of commercial stereopsis systems nowadays [9], they are limited to certain domains of applications and cannot be used outdoor in general. Ideally, we want to be able to use off-the-shelf cameras and to obtain automated self-calibration capabilities allowing us to adjust at will cameras' settings, location and orientation. Hence, self-calibration is the only ultimate optimal solution for a flexible and usefull stereo-vision system. Although the camera self-calibration problem is by nature nonlinear [2,3,10], taking advantage of zoom capabilities in zooming cameras, together with a simple and realistic assumption, can transform this problem into a linear one citeElamsy2014.

In this paper, we tackle the possibility of developing a simple stereo system, consisting of two off-the-shelf cameras with motorized (computer controlled) zooming capabilities. Our aim is to obtain metric 3D reconstruction of observed scenes (feature points of the scene), once the system is calibrated, for various simple vision tasks. The proposed system is capable to self-calibrate on site, once turned-on, allowing the user to adjust the stereo system orientation, position, and settings, as needed, prior to actual operation. The consequences of this are highly demanded for practical vision systems. In particular, it allows placing your cameras anywhere and start using them on the fly, as the computer will take care of calibrating itself and performing 3D interpretation. When the system need to self-calibrate, each camera acquires two images at different unknown zoom settings (zoom in/zoom out). The main advantage of this system is its simplicity as it does not require any special motion of the rig [1,6]. This makes it ideal for several online applications such as 3D gesture interpretation used in interaction within virtual realities, e.g. virtual white-board applications and video games, where extreme accuracy is not mandatory.

2   Background

2.1   Notations and Basic Principles

In this paper we consider a static scene observed by a stereo rig of uncalibrated cameras with motorized zooming capabilities. The pair of cameras are placed at distinct positions with different orientation. We assume that the stereo rig remains stationary during the self-calibration process. Each camera i $(i = 1, 2)$ captures two images of the static scene at different settings in the subset $\mathcal{S}_i = \{1, 2, ...\}$ of the unknown possible zooming configurations of its lenses. It is important to note that although the cameras and the scene neither rotate nor translate when self-calibrating, the geometry of each camera changes under zooming effect. Thus for simplicity, we assume that images captured by the same camera with distinct zoom settings as if they had been captured by distinct cameras each of which following the well-known pinhole model [4]. At any given zoom setting $s \in \mathcal{S}_i$, a camera i maps a world point Q onto the image point $q_{i,s}$. Expressing world and image points by their homogeneous coordinates, this mapping is described - up to a scale factor - through a 3×4 camera matrix $\mathsf{P}_{i,s}$ as follows

$$q_{i,s} \sim \mathsf{P}_{i,s}Q \tag{1}$$

where ($\sim$) represents the equality up to a non-zero scale factor. The notation $P_{i,s}$ is used to denote the perspective projection matrix of camera i under the sth zoom setting. We assume throughout this paper that all camera matrices $P_{i,s}$ have been calculated from point correspondences with respect to a common projective reference frame. While such set of camera matrices can be obtained using virtually any off-the-shelf method [4], we have used in the present work the method of Rothwell et al. [8]. The resulting matrices allow only for the recovery of the scene and cameras up to a common but unknown projective ambiguity.

In a metric case, each camera $P_{i,s}$ can be factorized as follow:

$$P_{i,s(metric)} = K_{i,s}[\ R_{i,s}\ |\ t_{i,s}\ ], \tag{2}$$

where $R_{i,s}$ denotes a 3×3 rotation matrix and $t_{i,s}$ a 3 translation vector representing the orientation and position of the camera. The upper triangular calibration matrix $K_{i,s}$ encodes the intrinsic parameters of the camera:

$$K_{i,s} = \begin{bmatrix} \tau f_{i,s} & \gamma & u_{i,s} \\ & f_{i,s} & v_{i,s} \\ & & 1 \end{bmatrix}, \tag{3}$$

where $f_{i,s}$ denotes the focal length, $(u_{i,s}, v_{i,s})$ the principal point, τ the aspect ratio, and γ the skew factor.

3 Affine Self-calibration

Affine calibration is equivalent to estimating the plane at infinity. The process of estimating the plane at infinity can be done via a linear method when using a pair of zooming camera. In the following, we briefly review the aforementioned linear method and highlight our novelty.

3.1 Zooming Cameras Model

Consider a camera that is physically fixed in space while capturing two images at different zoom settings. At any given setting $s \in \mathcal{S}_i$ of its zoom lens, a camera i , $(i = 1, 2)$ is described by its image plane $\mathcal{I}_{i,s}$ and by its optical center $C_{i,s}$ (see Fig. 1). The optical center $C_{i,s}$, in which all light rays emanating from the scene intersect, is located at a focal distance $f_{i,s}$ from the image plane, along the optical axis of the camera. The optical axis of the camera perpendicularly intersects $\mathcal{I}_{i,s}$ in the principal point $c_{i,s}$.

Under the effect of zooming, the optical center $C_{i,s}$ translates to a new location $C_{i,s'}$ at a focal distance $f_{i,s'}$ from the image plane. This repositioning of the lens affect the focal length of the pinhole camera. Based on this description, the zooming process incorporates displacing the camera center to a new location whilst preserving camera orientation (i.e. no rotation). This displacement of the camera center in general alters three out of the main five intrinsic parameters: the skew and aspect ratio remain very stable while the principal point and focal

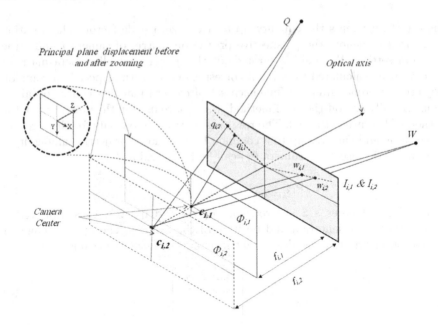

Fig. 1. Zooming camera model

length vary. For simplicity, we employ a weaker assumption here. We rely only on the fact that the optical center is displaced along the $Z-$ axis but assume that the camera center doesn't shift along the $X-$ and $Y-$ axes. Thus the principal point before and after zooming remains fixed. Under these assumptions, both of the principal planes passing through the camera center before and after zooming are parallel to the image plane, and thus parallel to each other.

3.2   Estimation of the Infinity Plane

Let the $\Phi_{i,s}$ and $\Phi_{i,s'}$ denotes the homogeneous coordinate 4-vectors of the principal planes at two distinct zoom settings of a camera i. The two planes represented by these coordinates are parallel if considered in any metric or affine frame and hence intersect the plane at infinity in a line. Although parallelism is not preserved under projective transformations, the linear relationship

$$\alpha_{i,s,s'}\Phi_{i,s} + \alpha_{i,s',s}\Phi_{i,s'} = \Pi_\infty. \tag{4}$$

still holds, for some non-zero scalars $\alpha_{i,s,s'}$ and $\alpha_{i,s',s}$, regardless of the frame in which the coordinate vectors $\Phi_{i,s}$, $\Phi_{i,s'}$ and Π_∞ may be expressed.

Note that the coordinate vectors of the principal planes may be obtained from the last rows of the associated projective camera matrices $P_{i,s}$ and $P_{i,s'}$ whose calculation only requires feature correspondences across images. When considering a single camera i at two distinct zoom settings, the linear relationship (4) provides four independent equations in six unknowns: $\alpha_{i,s,s'}$, $\alpha_{i,s',s}$ and the 4 coordinates of the plane at infinity Π_∞. These equations define a one-parameter family of points describing the line on the plane at infinity at which $\Phi_{i,s}$ and $\Phi_{i,s'}$ intersect. All principal planes originating from the same camera meet in this line. Two such cameras, in general position, provide 8 independent linear equations in 8 unknowns, allowing us to solve a linear system of equations and hence, recover the plane at infinity Π_∞.

3.3 Affine Upgrade

Once the coordinates of Π_∞ are estimated, the projective ambiguity that affects the scene structure and the cameras can be reduced to an affine one, by means of an adequate transformation T represented by a 4×4 matrix in the form of

$$T \sim \begin{bmatrix} P \\ \Pi_\infty^\intercal \end{bmatrix}. \tag{5}$$

The transformation matrix T is obtained by stacking a 3×4 matrix, arbitrarily chosen in the set of camera matrices $P_{i,s}$, and the row homogeneous coordinate vector $\Pi_\infty^\intercal$ of the plane at infinity. While every scene point Q is mapped by T to its new location TQ, the camera matrices in the affine frame are given by $P_{i,s}T^{-1}$. In particular, the 3×3 matrix $H_{i,s}$ where

$$H_{i,s} = P_{i,s}T^{-1}[\, I \mid 0\,]^\intercal \tag{6}$$

represents the inter-image homographies induced by the plane at infinity, also known as *infinity homographies*, which relates the reference image and the image captured by the ith camera at the setting s of its zoom. Note that I and 0 respectively denote the 3×3 identity matrix and the null 3-vector.

4 Metric Self-calibration

4.1 Estimation of the Principal Points

According to the pinhole model, the principal point is the pixel coordinate point at which the principal axis intersect the image plane. Under the considered zooming camera model, discussed in Subsect. 3.1, a direct estimation of the principal point of a camera from two images taken at different zoom/focus setting is possible. This has been illustrated in several works, see for example [7] and [5]. The idea is simple under the assumed pinhole model of a stationary camera. The effect of zooming/focusing, while camera not moving, can be interpreted as a displacement of the camera center along the principal axis. This indicates that the principal point position remains fixed regardless of the current zoom setting. If one considered laying two or more such images on top of each other and linking each corresponding image point across the overlaid images with a line, see Fig. 2, the principal point can be determined as the common point of intersection between all these lines. In ideal cases, two such lines are enough to determine the principal point. In practice, due to noise and mechanical errors, one should use all available lines in a least square fitting approach to obtain reasonable estimation of the point of intersection (i.e. the principal point). This process has to be done for both cameras of the stereo rigs.

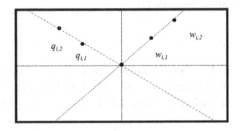

Fig. 2. Principal point estimation by zooming

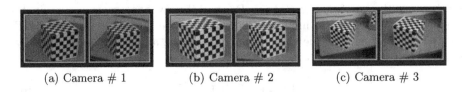

(a) Camera # 1   (b) Camera # 2   (c) Camera # 3

Fig. 3. The 3 pairs of zoom images: each pair was captured from a different camera mounted on a tripod.

4.2   Estimation of the Focal Length

The computed infinity homographies, $H_{i,s}$, can be used to self-calibrate the stereo rig and hence to upgrade the scene's structure and cameras to metric. These matrices satisfy the relationship

$$H_{i,s}^{-T} \omega H_{i,s}^{-1} \sim \omega_{i,s} \tag{7}$$

between the Image of the Absolute Conic (IAC) ω in the reference image and its corresponding conic $\omega_{i,s}$ in the image captured by camera i under the sth zoom setting. The IAC in each image, including the reference image, is solely dependent upon the intrinsic parameters of the imaging camera. It is represented by a 3×3 symmetric positive-definite matrix that can be factored into $\omega_{i,s} \sim K_{i,s}^{-T} K_{i,s}^{-1}$ and whose inverse allows to recover the 3×3 upper-triangular intrinsic parameters matrix, $K_{i,s}$, through Cholesky factorization.

All self-calibration techniques are achieved by placing some constraints on the intrinsic camera parameters. It is quite safe with today's CCD camera to consider square pixel sensors i.e unit aspect ratio $\tau = 1$ and zero skew $\gamma = 0$. Further simplification can be carried on by shifting the image origin $(0, 0)$ to the principal point position. This can be done either by assuming that the principal point is at the middle of the image (i.e. $u = width/2, v = height/2$) or as previously described in Subsect. 4.1. Doing so will significantly simplify the intrinsic matrix parameterizations in (3) to

$$K_{i,s} = \begin{bmatrix} f_{i,s} & 0 & 0 \\ & f_{i,s} & 0 \\ & & 1 \end{bmatrix}, \tag{8}$$

In order to upgrade the scene and cameras to a metric frame, it only suffices to recover the intrinsic parameters matrix K of the reference camera or, equivalently, ω's entries. Under the zero skew, unit aspect ratio, and known principal point assumptions, each image provides the following four linear equations:

$$e_1^T H_{i,s}^{-T} \omega H_{i,s}^{-1} e_1 - e_2^T H_{i,s}^{-T} \omega H_{i,s}^{-1} e_2 = 0 \tag{9}$$

$$e_1^T H_{i,s}^{-T} \omega H_{i,s}^{-1} e_2 = 0, \tag{10}$$

$$e_1^T H_{i,s}^{-T} \omega H_{i,s}^{-1} e_3 = 0, \tag{11}$$

$$e_2^T H_{i,s}^{-T} \omega H_{i,s}^{-1} e_3 = 0, \tag{12}$$

in the unknown entries of ω. The element at the last row and last column of $\omega_{i,s}^2$ is fixed and set to 1. The vectors e_1, e_2, and e_3 are the canonical basis vectors $e_1 = (1,0,0)^T$, $e_2 = (0,1,0)^T$, and $e_3 = (0,0,1)^T$ respectively. Combining the constraints from all images provide an over determined system of 16 linear equation which can be solved for the element of ω. The initial estimate of the plane at infinity and intrinsic parameters can be refined through a nonlinear optimization for optimal results. The optimal results reported in the present paper have been obtained using the Levenberg-Marquardt algorithm. The interested reader may refer to [4] for more details regarding the affine and metric upgrades of projective reconstructions.

5   Experiments and Results

We have conducted several experiments using real images carried out in a laboratory setup and with a real outdoor scene. From matched image points across the different images, projective camera matrices were calculated using the method described in [8]. As customary, data normalization has been used throughout. Proper transformation is carried out to shift the image origin to the estimated principal point, as described in Subsect. 4.1 or to the middle of the image dimensions (we tried both ways). We start with a linear estimation of the plane at infinity by solving (4). Then, an initial estimation of the intrinsic parameters is obtained by solving (9–12) for the IAC. Finally, the obtained results are nonlinearly refined using the Levenberg-Marquardt algorithm.

Indoor Experiments. We carried out an experiment using real images in a laboratory setup to validate our proposed self-calibration method. Three low-end consumer digital cameras with motorized zoom lenses have been used: a *Kodak EasyShare*, a *Sony Cyber-shot DSC-S930* and a *Canon PowerShot SX150 IS*. Each camera was placed on a tripod in front of a 21 × 21 × 21 cm cube-shaped calibration object exhibiting 30 × 30 mm black and white squares on each face. The distance between any two given cameras was roughly between 30 and 60 cm and oriented toward the calibration cube. Two images at different zoom settings were captured by each camera, as shown on Fig. 3. The ground truth knowledge of the Euclidean structure of the calibration cube was determined in the lab to measure the resulting 3D reconstruction errors. The calibration cube was treated as an unknown scene when applying our self-calibration method. A total of 108 points, located on 3 mutually orthogonal faces of the cube, were matched across the images obtained by all cameras at both zoom settings. We applied our self-calibration method for the three possible pairs of stereo camera systems, i.e., pair of cameras 1 & 2, 1 & 3, and 2 & 3). In each test, an estimate of the intrinsic parameters have been calculated linearly in two different ways:

– *"p.p. at the middle"* refers to principal point assumed at image centre.
– *"estimated p.p."* refers to principal point estimated as described in Subsect. 4.1.

Table 1. Relative 3D RMS errors % using the calibration cube.

Used stereo		p.p. at the middle		estimated p.p.	
Left view	Right view	Linear	Refined	Linear	Refined
1	2	4.85%	4.41%	4.92%	1.98%
1	3	9.59%	1.15%	9.59%	0.92%
2	3	13.26%	3.29%	13.29%	0.93%

The initial linear estimates were optimized by non-linear refinement. Table 1 provides the 3D RMS error (in %) - relative to the cube's diagonal - of the 3D reconstruction calculated linearly and after the nonlinear refinement considering the three different stereo pairs and the two principal point estimation methods. The ground truth data are the measurements we obtained from the cube using an office ruler. For convenience, we provide in Fig. 4 the 3D structures obtained from stereo pair # 2 & 3 for linear and optimized results. The results show that for both used principal point estimation methods, the linearly calculated 3D metric reconstruction quality is relatively the same. The obtained error for the initial linear calculation are within 4.8% and 13.3% acceptable bounds. It is also clear that in all cases, the non-linear refinement led to better quality. However, using the "estimated p.p." method, the non-linear refinement produced lower error % for all of the three evaluated stereo pairs.

Table 2. Calculated intrinsic parameters corresponding to the first image of each pair.

Stereo pair		Viewpoint #1 PowerShot 1600 × 1200 pixel					Camera #2 Cyber-shot 3648 × 2736 pixel					Viewpoint #3 EasyShare 2592 × 1944 pixel				
		τf	f	γ	u	v	τf	f	γ	u	v	τf	f	γ	u	v
	Pattern	5407	5378	5	923	482	5883	5862	-15	1637	1301	9933	9885	-3	1423	854
1 & 2	Linear	2535	2535	0	801	612	3670	5107	0	5880	1568	-	-	-	-	-
	Refined	4235	4216	-85	803	598	5456	5458	75	1813	1252	-	-	-	-	-
1 & 3	Linear	5189	5189	0	801	612	-	-	-	-	-	30336	30663	0	10563	5824
	Refined	6093	6093	0.2	801	588	-	-	-	-	-	12045	12031	-2	1433	980
2 & 3	Linear	-	-	-	-	-	22819	5998	0	3509	12105	3571	3571	0	1301	977
	Refined	-	-	-	-	-	6007	6018	58	1810	1251	9490	9455	-86	1296	979

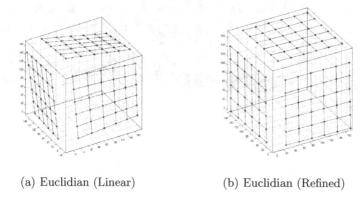

(a) Euclidian (Linear)   (b) Euclidian (Refined)

Fig. 4. 3D reconstruction from stereo pair (cameras 2&3).

In addition, the intrinsic parameters of the cameras, corresponding to the first image of each pair (left-most image in each sub-figure of Fig. 3) captured at each tested pair of cameras, are reported in Table 2. We also report in this table the intrinsic parameters obtained when calibrating the camera using the cube object as a calibration pattern with 108 known 3D points to estimate the Euclidean camera matrix from which the parameters are extracted ("Pattern"). For the three different stereo pairs of cameras, we report the linearly estimation intrinsics ("linear") and after the non-linear optimization ("Refined"). It can be seen that the intrinsic parameters obtained after refinement are always close to those obtained though the pattern-based calibration. However, the obtained "Linear" parameters are less acceptable. The errors on the "Linear" parameters estimation are correlated to camera #3. Some of the estimated focal lengths and principal points obtained linearly for stereo pairs involving camera 3 (i.e. stereo pair #1 & camera #3 and #1 & camera #2), were found far from the assumed ground truth value. For the other two cameras (camera #2 & camera #2), the estimated intrinsics were relatively close. This explains why the linearly estimated RMS error for the stereo pair (#1 & #2) was relatively acceptable (RMS < 5%) in comparison with the RMS error estimated with stereo pairs which involve camera #3 (RMS error between 9.59% and 13.3%). However, these errors remain acceptable in the sense that the parameters linearly retrieved still allow the refinement step to converge as desired. Although the true principal point does not necessarily coincide with the image center, the results reported here show that, for all the cameras we have used, this point consistently falls within a reasonable distance from it.

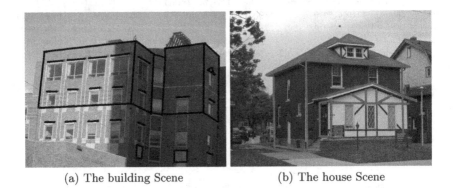

(a) The building Scene   (b) The house Scene

Fig. 5. The two outdoor scene models used in the experiments.

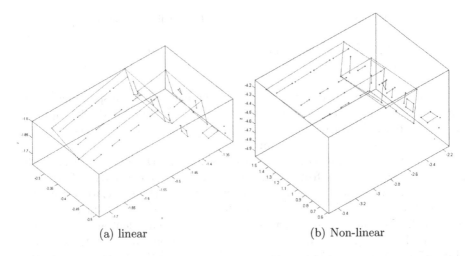

(a) linear   (b) Non-linear

Fig. 6. Sample wireframe model of metric 3D reconstruction of the building scene.

Outdoor Scene Experiments. Several additional experiments were conducted on different outdoor real scenes but we report hear only two of them. In each experiment, a pair of cameras on a tripod were used. At each viewpoint position, the considered camera captured 2 images at different settings of its zoom lens. As ground truth data is not available for those models, we only report

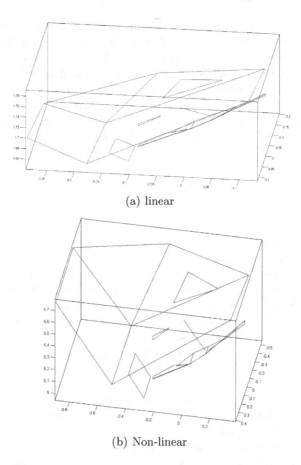

(a) linear

(b) Non-linear

Fig. 7. Sample wireframe models of metric 3D reconstruction of the house scene.

the 3D metric reconstruction of the scene in a wireframe model representation. In each experiment, a number of feature points were extracted and manually matched across all 4 images using mouse clicks. Certain line segments have been chosen to provide "visually" meaningful wireframe model of the recovered scene.

Building Scene Experiment: Two different cameras, the Sony Cyber-shot and the Kodak EasyShare, were used to capture images of a large building shown in Fig. 5(a). The two camera's were a few meters apart from each other and roughly 50 m away from the building Each considered camera captured 2 images at different settings of its zoom lens. A total of 71 feature points were extracted and matched. We apply our proposed method and compute the metric 3D reconstruction for the selected feature points. Figure 6 shows a wireframe model of the metric 3D reconstruction computed linearly and after non-linear refinement. Visual assessment of the linearly produced 3D metric shows acceptable quality while the non-linear refinement remarkably enhanced it.

House Scene Experiment: In this experiment, the Sony Cyber-shot was used to capture 2 images at different zoom setting of a house, shown in Fig. 5(b), from two distinct positions few meters apart from each other and roughly 25 m away from the scene. A total of 42 points were extracted and matched across the 4 images. Figure 7 shows the wireframe metric 3D reconstruction of the house. As shown, the linear 3D estimation of the house are acceptable but suffered from significant skewness for some of the right angles. However, the non-linear refinement produced excellent quality and adjusted the structure to match what it appears to be in reality.

6   Conclusion and Future Work

This paper proposed a new linear technique to obtain the 3D metric structure of a scene, observed using a set of two noncalibrated zoom cameras. In particular, the proposed method does not require prior knowledge on the cameras or on the scene. More importantly, the cameras are free to adjust their zoom settings and are not restricted to be fixed. The self-calibration technique follows a stratified approach in which a linear estimation of the plane at infinity is obtained utilizing the parallelism of the principal planes of the zoom images. Having the plane at infinity allows the obtention of 3D structure in the affine space. An approximate estimation of the unknown principal point can be computed linearly under the simple and realistic assumption of nonchanging principal point for zoom images. The affine projection matrices can then be transformed into metric space, using linear constraints for square pixels interior. In addition to the simplicity of our self-calibration method, the obtained results, using low-end zooming cameras, are very good for most applications.

Future work could target the pixel correspondence problem between multi-zoom images, a problem not addressed in the literature. Although there are several existing methods for performing pixel matching, all of them only consider the case of images with very similar zoom setting (scale).

References

1. Agapito, L., Hayman, E., Hartley, R.I.: Linear self-calibration of a rotating and zooming camera. In: Proceedings of the IEEE Conference on Computer Vision and Pattern Recognition, vol. 1, p. 1015 (1999)
2. Brückner, F.B., Denzler, J.: Intrinsic and extrinsic active self-calibration of multi-camera systems. Mach. Vis. Appl. **25**(2), 389–403 (2014)
3. Führ, G., Jung, C.R.: Camera self-calibration based on nonlinear optimization and applications in surveillance systems. IEEE Trans. Circuits Syst. Video Technol. **27**(5), 1132–1142 (2017)
4. Hartley, R.I., Zisserman, A.: Multiple View Geometry in Computer Vision, 2nd edn. Cambridge University Press, Cambridge (2004)
5. Li, M.: Camera calibration of a head-eye system for active vision. In: Eklundh, J.-O. (ed.) ECCV 1994. LNCS, vol. 800, pp. 541–554. Springer, Heidelberg (1994). https://doi.org/10.1007/3-540-57956-7_62

6. Luong, Q.T., Faugeras, O.D.: Self-calibration of a stereo rig from unknown camera motions and point correspondences. In: Gruen, A., Huang, T.S. (eds.) Calibration and Orientation of Cameras in Computer Vision. Springer Series in Information Sciences, vol. 34, pp. 195–229. Springer, Heidelberg (2001). https://doi.org/10.1007/978-3-662-04567-1_8

7. Pollefeys, M., Van Gool, L., Moons, T.: Euclidean 3D reconstruction from stereo sequences with variable focal lengths. In: Li, S.Z., Mital, D.P., Teoh, E.K., Wang, H. (eds.) ACCV 1995. LNCS, vol. 1035, pp. 405–413. Springer, Heidelberg (1996). https://doi.org/10.1007/3-540-60793-5_94

8. Rothwell, C.A., Faugeras, O.D., Csurka, G.: Different paths towards projective reconstruction. In: Proceedings of the Europe-China Workshop Geometric Modelling and Invariance Computer Vision (1995)

9. Schoning, J., Heidemann, G.: Taxonomy of 3D sensorsa survey of state-of-the-art consumer 3D-reconstruction sensors and their field. Mach. Graph. Vision **24**(3), 57–117 (2016)

10. Urban, S., Wursthorn, S., Leitloff, J., Hinz, S.: Multicol bundle adjustment: a generic method for pose estimation, simultaneous self-calibration and reconstruction for arbitrary multi-camera systems. Int. J. Comput. Vision **121**(2), 234–252 (2017)

Bellman-Ford Algorithm Under Trapezoidal Interval Valued Neutrosophic Environment

Said Broumi[1(✉)], Deivanayagampillai Nagarajan[2],
Malayalan Lathamaheswari[2], Mohamed Talea[1], Assia Bakali[3],
and Florentin Smarandache[4]

[1] Laboratory of Information Processing, Faculty of Science Ben M'Sik,
University Hassan II, B.P 7955 Sidi Othman, Casablanca, Morocco
broumisaid78@gmail.com, taleamohamed@yahoo.fr
[2] Department of Mathematics, Hindustan Institute of Technology and Science,
Chennai 603 103, India
dnrmsu2002@yahoo.com, lathamax@gmail.com
[3] Ecole Royale Navale, Boulevard Sour Jdid, B.P 16303 Casablanca, Morocco
assiabakali@yahoo.fr
[4] Department of Mathematics, University of New Mexico,
705 Gurley Avenue, Gallup, NM 87301, USA
fsmarandache@gmail.com, smarand@unm.edu

Abstract. The shortest path problem has been one of the most fundamental practical problems in network analysis. One of the good algorithms is Bellman-Ford, which has been applied in network, since the last some years. By virtue of complexity in the decision making process, the decision makers face complication to express their view and judgment with an exact number for single valued membership degrees under neutrosophic environment. Though the interval number is a special situation of the neutrosophic, it is not solved the shortest path problems in an absolute manner. Hence, in this work, we have proposed the trapezoidal interval valued neutrosophic version of Bellman's algorithm to solve the shortest path problem absolutely.

Keywords: Bellman's algorithm · Trapezoidal interval valued neutrosophic number · Ranking method · Shortest path problem · Network

1 Introduction

A set which is defined in terms of 'affiliation function' is called fuzzy set (FS) in 1965 [1] and mainly deals with which handles with numerous real world situations, where the data possesses some sort of uncertainty. The notion of FS is concern about only the membership value of each and every element not about the non-membership. This issue was sorted out by intuitionistic fuzzy set (IFS) introduced by Atannasov in 1975 [2] which allows the membership function and non-membership function as well. Since the real world situations may contain indeterminacy in the data, FS and IFS could not deal with indeterminacy. This problem was rectified by neutrosophic set (NS), generalization of FS and IFS, introduced by Smarandache [3]. NS is a set in which, all the elements

© Springer Nature Switzerland AG 2019
A. Alfaries et al. (Eds.): ICC 2019, CCIS 1098, pp. 174–184, 2019.
https://doi.org/10.1007/978-3-030-36368-0_15

have degree of membership, indeterminate membership and non-membership and the sum these membership functions (MFs) should be less than or equal to 3. All the three MFs are independent to each other. Uncertainty can be captured for the elements using fuzzy numbers and intuitionistic fuzzy numbers. In the same way, neutrosophic numbers are useful in capturing uncertainty and indeterminacy of the elements. And hence it is a special case of the NS which enhances the domain of real numbers to neutrosophic numbers.

Shortest path problem has been solved by many researchers under fuzzy and intuitionistic fuzzy environments [5–8]. The concept of Bellman's algorithm has been applied in a fuzzy network [9] for solving shortest path problem and it is not applied in neutrosophic network so far. Distance measure can be obtained using single and interval valued trapezoidal neutrosophic numbers in a multi attribute decision making problem. Dijkstra algorithm is very useful and optimized one to solve the shortest path problem but cannot able to handle negative weights where as Bellman can able to deal negative weights. SPP also can be solved by using single valued neutrosophic graph [11–16].

Hence for the first time, the interval valued trapezoidal neutrosophic portrayal of Bellman's algorithm is applied here to solve neutrosophic shortest path problem [17, 18]. An extension of fuzzy sets called type-2 fuzzy sets and its special cases called interval type-2 fuzzy sets have growing applications in control systems, image processing and other medical fields. Shortest path problems can be solved using triangular and trapezoidal interval neutrosophic environments as an extension of neutrosophic sets. From the overview of solving shortest path problem under various sets environments one can understand the difference and capacity of handling uncertainty with various level [19–26].

In this paper, we are motivated to present a new version of Bellman's algorithm for solving the shortest path problem on a network where the edge weight is characterized by interval valued trapezoidal neutrosophic number. The rest of this paper is organized as follows. In Sect. 2, some concepts and theories are reviewed. Section 3 presents the neutrosophic version of Bellman algorithm. In Sect. 4, a numerical example is provided as an application of our proposed algorithm. Section 5, shows the advantages of the proposed algorithm. The last but not least the section, in which the conclusion is drawn and some hints for further research is given.

2 Overview on Trapezoidal Interval Valued Neutrosophic Number

In this section, we review some basic concepts regarding neutrosophic sets, single valued neutrosophic sets, trapezoidal neutrosophic sets and some existing ranking functions for trapezoidal neutrosophic numbers which are the background of this study and will help us to further research.

Definition 2.1 [3]. Let ξ be a of points (objects) set and its generic elements denoted by x; we define the neutrosophic set A (NS A) as the form $\overset{...}{A} = \left\{ <x : T_{\underset{A}{..}}(x), \right.$ $I_{\underset{A}{..}}(x), F_{\underset{A}{..}}(x) > , x \in \xi \}$, where the functions T, I, F: $\xi \to]^-0,1^+[$ are called the truth-membership function, an indeterminacy-membership function, and a falsity-membership function respectively and they satisfy the following condition:

$$^{-}0 \le T_{\overset{..}{A}}(x) + I_{\overset{..}{A}}(x) + F_{\overset{..}{A}}(x) \le 3^{+}. \tag{1}$$

The values of these three membership functions $T_{\overset{..}{A}}(x), I_{\overset{..}{A}}(x)$ and $F_{\overset{..}{A}}(x)$ are real standard or nonstandard subsets of $]^{-}0,1^{+}[$. As we have difficulty in applying NSs to practical problems. Wang et al. [4] proposes the concept of a SVNS that represents the simplification of a NS and can be applied to real scientific and technical applications.

Definition 2.2 [4]. A single valued neutrosophic set $\overset{...}{A}$ (SVNS $\overset{...}{A}$) in the universe set ξ is defined by the set

$$\overset{...}{A} = \left\{ <x : T_{\overset{..}{A}}(x), I_{\overset{..}{A}}(x), F_{\overset{..}{A}}(x) > , x \in \xi \right\} \tag{2}$$

Where $T_{\overset{..}{A}}(x), I_{\overset{..}{A}}(x), F_{\overset{..}{A}}(x) \in [0, 1]$ satisfying the condition:

$$0 \le T_{\overset{..}{A}}(x) + I_{\overset{..}{A}}(x) + F_{\overset{..}{A}}(x) \le 3 \tag{3}$$

Definition 2.3 [10]. Let x be trapezoidal interval valued neutrosophic number (TrIVNN). Then its truth membership function are given by

$$T_x(z) = \begin{cases} \frac{(z-a)t_x}{(b-a)}, & a \le z < b, \\ t_x, & b \le z \le c \\ \frac{(d-z)t_x}{(d-c)}, & c \le z \le d \\ 0, & otherwise \end{cases} \tag{4}$$

Its indeterminacy membership function is

$$I_x(z) = \begin{cases} \frac{(b-z)+(z-a)i_x}{(b-a)}, & a \le z < b \\ i_x, & b \le z \le c \\ \frac{z-c+(d-z)i_x}{d-c}, & c < z \le d \\ 0, & otherwise \end{cases} \tag{5}$$

And its falsity membership function is

$$F_x(z) = \begin{cases} \frac{b-z+(z-a)f_x}{b-a}, & a \le z < b \\ f_x, & b \le z \le c \\ \frac{z-c+(d-z)f_x}{d-c}, & c < z \le d \\ 0, & otherwise \end{cases} \tag{6}$$

Where $0 \leq T_x(z) \leq 1, 0 \leq I_x(z) \leq 1$ and $0 \leq F_x(z) \leq 1$ and also t_x, i_x, f_x are subset of $[0, 1]$ and $0 \leq a \leq b \leq c \leq d \leq 1$. $0 \leq \sup(t_x) + \sup(i_x) + \sup(f_x) \leq 3$; Then x is called an interval trapezoidal neutrosophic number $x = ([a, b, c, d]; t_x, i_x, f_x)$ we take $t_x = [\underline{t}, \overline{t}]$, $i_x = [\underline{i}, \overline{i}]$ and $f_x = [\underline{f}, \overline{f}]$.

Definition 2.4 [10]. Let $\tilde{a}$ and $\tilde{r}$ be two TrIVNNs, the ranking of $\tilde{a}$ and $\tilde{r}$ by score function and accuracy function is described as follows:

1. *if* $s(\hat{r}^N) \prec s(\hat{s}^N)$ *then* $\hat{r}^N \prec \hat{s}^N$
2. *if* $s(\hat{r}^N) \approx s(\hat{s}^N)$ *and if*
   a. $a(\hat{r}^N) \prec a(\hat{s}^N)$ *then* $\hat{r}^N \prec \hat{s}^N$
   b. $a(\hat{r}^N) \succ a(\hat{s}^N)$ *then* $\hat{r}^N \succ \hat{s}^N$
   c. $a(\hat{r}^N) \approx a(\hat{s}^N)$ *then* $\hat{r}^N \approx \hat{s}^N$

Definition 2.5 [17]. There are some advantages of using interval valued trapezoidal neutrosophic number as follow.

- Interval trapezoidal neutrosophic number is a generalized form of single valued trapezoidal neutrosophic number.
- In this number, the trapezoidal number is characterized with three independent membership degrees which are in interval form.
- The number can flexibly express neutrosophic information than the single valued neutrosophic trapezoidal number.
- Therefore the number can be employed to solve neutrosophic multiple attribute decision making problem, where the preference values cannot be expressed in terms of single valued trapezoidal neutrosophic number.

3 Proposed Concepts

Definition 3.1. Score Function of IVTrNN. Let $x = ([a, b, c, d]; [[\underline{t}, \overline{t}], [[\underline{i}, \overline{i}], [\underline{f}, \overline{f}])$ be a IVTrNN then its score function defined by,

$$S(x) = \frac{1}{16}(a + b + c + d)(2 + \underline{t} + \overline{t} - \underline{i} - \overline{i} - \underline{f} - \overline{f}), S(x) \in [0, 1]$$

Here we take $0 \leq a \leq b \leq c \leq d \leq 1$, t_x, i_x, f_x are subset of $[0,1]$ where $t_x = [\underline{t}, \overline{t}], i_x = [\underline{i}, \overline{i}]$ and $f_x = [\underline{f}, \overline{f}]$.

Property 3.2. Score function is bounded on [0, 1].

Proof:

$$0 \leq a \leq b \leq c \leq d \leq 1$$
$$\Rightarrow 0 \leq a + b + c + d \leq 4 \tag{7}$$

Now,

$$-4 \leq \underline{t}+\bar{i}-\underline{i}-\bar{i}-\underline{f}-\bar{f} \leq 2$$
$$\Rightarrow 2-4 \leq 2+\underline{t}+\bar{i}-\underline{i}-\bar{i}-\underline{f}-\bar{f} \leq 4 \tag{8}$$
$$\Rightarrow -2 \leq 2+\underline{t}+\bar{i}-\underline{i}-\bar{i}-\underline{f}-\bar{f} \leq 4$$

Multiplying (7) and (8) we get,

$$0 \leq (a+b+c+d)(2+\underline{t}+\bar{i}-\underline{i}-\bar{i}-\underline{f}-\bar{f}) \leq 16$$
$$\Rightarrow 0 \leq \frac{1}{16}(a+b+c+d)(2+\underline{t}+\bar{i}-\underline{i}-\bar{i}-\underline{f}-\bar{f}) \leq 1$$

Therefore, score function is bounded.

Example: Let a = ([0.1, 0.2, 0.3, 0.4]; [0.1, 0.2], [0.2, 0.3], [0.4, 0.5])

$$Sc(a) = \frac{1}{16}(0.1+0.2+0.3+0.4)(2+.1+.2-.2-.3-.4-.5) = 0.07875$$

Definition 3.3. Accuracy function. Let $x = ([a,b,c,d]; [\underline{t},\bar{t}], [\underline{i},\bar{i}], [\underline{f},\bar{f}])$ be a IVTrNN then its accuracy function defined by,

$$Ac(x) = \frac{1}{8}(c+d-a-b)(2+\underline{t}+\bar{i}-\underline{f}-\bar{f}), Ac(x) \in [0, 1]$$

Here we take $0 \leq a \leq b \leq c \leq d \leq 1$, t_x, i_x, f_x are subset of [0, 1] where $t_x = [\underline{t},\bar{t}]$, $i_x = [\underline{i},\bar{i}]$ and $f_x = [\underline{f},\bar{f}]$.

Property: Accuracy function is bounded on [0, 1].

Proof:

$$0 \leq a \leq b \leq c \leq d \leq 1$$
$$= > -2 \leq c+d-a-b \leq 2 \tag{9}$$

$$-2 \leq \underline{t}+\bar{i}-\underline{f}-\bar{f} \leq 2$$
$$\Rightarrow 0 \leq 2+\underline{t}+\bar{i}-\underline{f}-\bar{f} \leq 4 \tag{10}$$

Multiplying (9) and (10)

$$0 \le (c+d-a-b)(2+\underline{t}+\overline{t}-\underline{f}-\overline{f}) \le 8$$
$$\Rightarrow 0 \le \frac{1}{8}(a+b+c+d)(2+\underline{t}+\overline{t}-\underline{f}-\overline{f}) \le 1$$

Therefore, accuracy function is bounded.

Example: Let x = ([0.1, 0.2, 0.3, 0.4]; [0.1, 0.2], [0.2, 0.3], [0.4, 0.5])

$$Ac(x) = \frac{1}{8}(0.1+0.2+0.3+0.4)(2+.1+.2-.4-.5) = 0.175$$

4 Computation of Shortest Path Based on Interval Valued Trapezoidal Neutrosophic Number

This section introduces an algorithmic approach to solve NSPP. Consider a network with 'n' nodes where the node '1' is the source node and the node 'n' is the destination node. The neutrosophic distance between the nodes is denoted by d_{ij} (node 'i' to node 'j'). Here $M_{N(i)}$ denotes the set of all nodes having a relation with the node 'i'.
We begin with the following definition.

Bellman Dynamic Programming
Given an acyclic directed connected graph G = (V, E) with 'n' vertices where node '1' is the source node and 'n' is the destination node. The nodes of the given network are organized with the topological ordering (E_{ij}: i < j). Now for the given network the shortest path can be obtained based on the formulation of Bellman dynamic programming by forward pass computation method.
The formulation of Bellman dynamic programming is described as follows:

$$f(1) = 0$$
$$f(i) = \min_{i<j}\{f(i) + d_{ij}\}$$

where d_{ij} = weight of the directed edge E_{ij}
$f(i)$ = length of the shortest path of ith node from the source node 1.

Applying the concept of Bellman's algorithm in neutrosophic environment, we have

Neutrosophic Bellman-Ford Algorithm:
1. $nrank[s] \leftarrow 0$
2. $ndist[s] \leftarrow$ *Empty* neutrosophic number.
3.   Add s into Q
4.   **For** each node i (except the s) in the neutrosophic graph G
5. $rank[i] \leftarrow \infty$
6.   *Add* i into Q
7.   **End For**
8. $u \leftarrow s$
9.   **While**(Q is not empty)
10.   remove the vertex u from Q
11. **For** each adjacent vertex v of vertex u
12.   relaxed$\leftarrow$*False*
13. $temp\_ndist[v] \leftarrow ndist[u] \oplus edge\_weight(u,v)$ //$\oplus$ represents the addition *of* neutrosophic//
14. $temp\_nrank[v] \leftarrow$ rank_of_neutrosophic(*temp_ndist[v]*)
15.   If $temp\_nrank[v]$<$nrank[v]$ **then**
16. $ndist[v] \leftarrow temp\_ndist[v]$
17. $nrank[v] \leftarrow temp\_nrank[v]$
18. $prev[v] \leftarrow u$
19.   **End If**
20. **End For**
21.   **If** relaxed equals False **then**
22. exit the loop
23.   **End If**
24. $u \leftarrow$ Node in Q with minimum rank value
25. **End While**
26.   **For** each arc*(**u**,**v**)* in neutrosophic graph G do
27.   **If** $nrank[v]$> rank_of_neutrosophic(ndist[u] $\oplus$ edge_weight(u,v))
28. return false
29. **End If**
30. **End For**
31. The neutrosophic number *ndist[u]* is a neutrosophic number and its represents the shortest path between source node s and node u.

In the following, we will provide a simple example for a better understanding as follows.

5 Illustrative Example

For this purpose, a numerical problem from [11] is taken to prove the inherent application of the proposed algorithm.

Example 1: Consider a network (Fig. 1) with six nodes eight edges and the edge weights are characterized by IVTpNNs, where the first node is the source node and the sixth node is the destination node. Trapezoidal interval valued neutrosophic distance is given in Table 1.

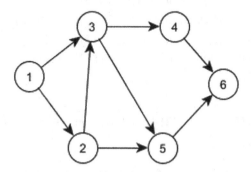

Fig. 1. A network with six vertices and eight edges (Broumi et al. [11])

In this situation, we need to evaluate the shortest distance from source node i.e. node 1 to destination node i.e. node 6 (Table 2)

Table 1. The details of edges information in terms of TrIVNNs

Edges	Trapezoidal interval valued neutrosophic distance
1–2 (e_1)	$\langle(0.1,0.2,0.3,0.4);[0.1,0.2],[0.2,0.3],[0.4,0.5]\rangle$
1–3 (e_2)	$\langle(0.2,0.5,0.7,0.8);[0.2,0.4],[0.3,0.5],[0.1,0.2]\rangle$
2–3 (e_3)	$\langle(0.3,0.7,0.8,0.9);[0.3,0.4],[0.1,0.2],[0.3,0.5]\rangle$
2–5 (e_4)	$\langle(0.1,0.5,0.7,0.9);[0.1,0.3],[0.3,0.4],[0.2,0.3]\rangle$
3–4 (e_5)	$\langle(0.2,0.4,0.8,0.9);[0.2,0.3],[0.2,0.5],[0.4,0.5]\rangle$
3–5 (e_6)	$\langle(0.3,0.4,0.5,1);[0.3,0.6],[0.1,0.2],[0.1,0.4]\rangle$
4–6 (e_7)	$\langle(0.7,0.8,0.9,1);[0.4,0.6],[0.2,0.4],[0.1,0.3]\rangle$
5–6 (e_8)	$\langle(0.2,0.4,0.5,0.7);[0.2,0.3],[0.3,0.4],[0.1,0.5]\rangle$

Table 2. The details of deneutrosophication value of edge (i, j)

Edges	Score function	Edges	Score function
e_{12}	0.05625	e_{34}	0.416875
e_{13}	0.48125	e_{35}	0.56375
e_{23}	0.6075	e_{46}	0.85
e_{25}	0.44	e_{56}	0.36

According to the algorithm method proposed in Sect. 4, the shortest path from node one to node six can be computed as follows:

$$f(1) = 0$$
$$f(2) = \min_{i<2}\{f(1)+c_{12}\} = c_{12}^* = 0.05625$$
$$f(3) = \min_{i<3}\{f(i)+c_{i3}\} = \min\{f(1)+c_{13}; f(2)+c_{23}\}$$
$$= \{0+0.48125, 0.05625+0.6075\} = \{0.48125; 0.66375\} = 0.48125$$
$$f(4) = \min_{i<4}\{f(i)+c_{i4}\} = \min\{f(3)+c_{34}\} = \{0.48125+0.416875\} = 0.89$$
$$f(5) = \min_{i<5}\{f(i)+c_{i5}\} = \min\{f(2)+c_{25}; f(3)+c_{35}\}$$
$$= \{0.05625+0.44; 0.48125+0.56375\} = \{0.49, 1.045\} = 0.49$$
$$f(6) = \min_{i<6}\{f(i)+c_{i6}\} = \min\{f(4)+c_{46}; f(5)+c_{56}\}$$
$$= \{0.89+0.85; 0.49+0.36\} = \{1.74, 0.85\} = 0.85$$

thus,

$$f(6) = f(5)+c_{56} = f(2)+c_{25}+c_{56} = f(1)+c_{12}+c_{25}+c_{56}$$
$$= c_{12}+c_{25}+c_{56}.$$

Therefore, the path P: $1 \rightarrow 2 \rightarrow 5 \rightarrow 6$ is identified as the neutrosophic shortest path, and the crisp shortest path is 0.85.

6 Advantages of the Proposed Algorithm

The proposed Bellman algorithm under trapezoidal interval valued neutrosophic environment has the following advantages.

(i) indeterminacy of the information can be dealt effectively
(ii) cost of the neutrosophic shortest path can be minimized
(iii) the performance of the network can be maximized though the data have Indeterminacy
(iv) Indeterminacy can be captured and shortest path can be obtained by splitting the various paths and hence performance of the system can be increased.

7 Conclusion

Here in this work, proposed the definitions of score function and accuracy functions and their properties. Also proposed the neutrosophic version of Bellman's algorithm based on the trapezoidal interval valued neutrosophic number (TrIVNN) which expresses the flexibility of the neutrosophic information absolutely under trapezoidal interval valued neutrosophic environment. Also, one numeric example is presented. In future, bipolar neutrosophic version of Bellman algorithm can be introduced.

References

1. Zadeh, L.A.: Fuzzy sets. Inf. Control **8**(3), 338–353 (1965)
2. Atanassov, K.T.: Intuitionistic fuzzy sets. Fuzzy Sets Syst. **20**(1), 87–96 (1986)
3. Smarandache, F.: Neutrosophy: neutrosophic probability, set, and logic. In: ProQuest Information and Learning, Ann Arbor, Michigan, USA, p. 105 (1998)
4. Wang, H., Smarandache, F., Zhang, Y., Sunderraman, R.: Single valued neutrosophic sets. Multispace Multistruct. **4**, 410–413 (2010)
5. De, P.K., Bhincher, A.: Dynamic programming and multi objective linear programming approaches. Appl. Math. Inf. Sci. **5**, 253–263 (2011)
6. Kumar, G., Bajaj, R.K., Gandotra, N.: Algorithm for shortest path problem in a network with interval-valued intuitionistic trapezoidal fuzzy number. Procedia Comput. Sci. **70**, 123–129 (2015)
7. Meenakshi, A.R., Kaliraja, M.: Determination of the shortest path in interval valued fuzzy networks. Int. J. Math. Arch. **3**(6), 2377–2384 (2012)
8. Elizabeth, S., Sujatha, L.: Fuzzy shortest path problem based on interval valued fuzzy number matrices. Int. J. Math. Sci. Eng. Appl. **8**(I), 325–335 (2014)
9. Das, D., De, P.K.: Shortest path problem under intuitionistic fuzzy setting. Int. J. Comput. Appl. **105**(1), 1–4 (2014)
10. Biswas, P., Pramanik, S., Giri, B.C.: Distance measure based MADM strategy with interval trapezoidal neutrosophic numbers. Neutrosophic Sets Syst. **19**, 40–46 (2018)
11. Broumi, S., Bakali, A., Talea, M., Smarandache, F., Vladareanu, L.: Computation of shortest path problem in a network with SV-trapezoidal neutrosophic numbers. In: Proceedings of the 2016 International Conference on Advanced Mechatronic Systems, Melbourne, Australia, pp. 417–422 (2016)
12. Broumi, S., Bakali, A., Talea, M., Smarandache, F., Vladareanu, L.: Applying Dijkstra algorithm for solving neutrosophic shortest path problem. In: Proceedings of the 2016 International Conference on Advanced Mechatronic Systems, Melbourne, Australia, 30 November–3 December, pp. 412–416 (2016)
13. Bellman, E.: On a routing problem. Q. Appl. Math. **16**(1), 87–90 (1958)
14. Wikipedia article. https://en.wikipedia.org/wiki/Bellman%E2%80%93Ford_algorithm
15. Broumi, S., Bakali, A., Talea, M., Smarandache, F., Kumar, P.K.: Shortest path problem on single valued neutrosophic graphs. In: 2017 International Symposium on Networks, Computers and Communications (ISNCC) (2017)
16. Broumi, S., Singh, P.K., Talea, M., Bakali, A., Smarandache, F., Venkateswara Rao, V.: Single-valued neutrosophic techniques for analysis of WIFI connection. In: Ezziyyani, M. (ed.) AI2SD 2018. AISC, vol. 915, pp. 405–412. Springer, Cham (2019). https://doi.org/10. 1007/978-3-030-11928-7_36
17. Broumi, S., et al.: Shortest path problem in fuzzy, intuitionistic fuzzy and neutrosophic environment: an overview. Complex Intell. Syst. **5**, 371–378 (2019)
18. Broumi, S., Nagarajan, D., Bakali, A., Talea, M., Smarandache, F., Lathamaheswari, M.: The shortest path problem in interval valued trapezoidal and triangular neutrosophic environment. Complex Intell. Syst. **5**, 1–12 (2019). https://doi.org/10.1007/s40747-019-0092-5
19. Deli, I.: Some operators with IVGSVTrN-numbers and their applications to multiple criteria group decision making. Neutrosophic Sets Syst. **25**, 33 (2019)
20. Giri, B.C., Molla, M.U., Biswas, P.: TOPSIS method for MADM based on interval trapezoidal neutrosophic number. Neutrosophic Sets Syst. **22**, 151–167 (2018)

21. Deli, I., Subas, Y., Cagraman, N.: Single valued interval valued trapezoidal neutrosophic numbers and SVIVTN multi attribute decision-making method. In: International Conference on Mathematics and Mathematics Education (ICMME-2016), 19–20 May 2016 (2016)

22. Nagarajan, D., Lathamaheswari, M., Sujatha, R., Kavikumar, J.: Edge detection on DICOM image using triangular norms in type-2 fuzzy. Int. J. Adv. Comput. Sci. Appl. **9**(11), 462–475 (2018)

23. Lathamaheswari, M., Nagarajan, D., Udayakumar, A., Kavikumar, J.: Review on type-2 fuzzy in biomedicine. Indian J. Public Health Res. Dev. **9**(12), 322–326 (2018)

24. Nagarajan, D., Lathamaheswari, M., Kavikumar, J., Hamzha: A type-2 fuzzy in image extraction for DICOM image. Int. J. Adv. Comput. Sci. Appl. **9**(12), 352–362 (2018)

25. Lathamaheswari, M., Nagarajan, D., Kavikumar, J., Phang, C.: A review on type-2 fuzzy controller on control system. J. Adv. Res. Dyn. Control Syst. **10**(11), 430–435 (2018)

26. Sellappan, N., Nagarajan, D., Palanikumar, K.: Evaluation of risk priority number (RPN) in design failure modes and effects analysis (DFMEA) using factor analysis. Int. J. Appl. Eng. Res. **10**(14), 34194–34198 (2015)

Design and Implementation of Secured E-Business Structure with LTL Patterns for User Behavior Prediction

Ayman Mohamed Mostafa[1,2(✉)]

[1] College of Computer and Information Sciences, Jouf University, Sakakah,
Kingdom of Saudi Arabia
amhassane@ju.edu.sa
[2] College of Computers and Informatics, Zagazig University, Zagazig, Egypt
am_mostafa@zu.edu.eg

Abstract. E-business applications are implemented for performing services of user transactions. Analysis performance of customer preferences can be enhanced based on E-business structure and predefined formula patterns. Linear temporal logic (LTL) provides multiple formula patterns for obtaining better query of user requirements. Protecting and verifying users' preferences and transactions are major concerns for enhancing E-business applications. This paper presents a design of a secured B2C and G2C E-business framework based on 3D secure mechanism. Advanced formula patterns are applied to the secured E-business structure for enhancing analysis performance and predicting users' behavior. Enhanced web server logs are generated and optimized with an authentication algorithm to record and secure infinite traces of event actions. The secured E-business framework is implemented for optimizing key metrics of user behavior and enhancing business analysis and user insights. Experimental results are conducted for displaying the efficiency for the enhanced web server logs and flag parameter algorithms.

Keywords: E-business · Linear temporal logic · 3D secure · Web server log · Authentication algorithm · User behavior

1 Introduction

E-business consists of a set of frameworks, methodologies, applications, and processes for helping organizations performing their financial transactions [1]. Different types of E-business applications have been developed and implemented based on the roles of E-business partners such as: consumer, business, and government. The construction of E-business web services has emerged technologies and models for enhancing the analysis performance of E-business transactions and services. As presented in [2], the quality of E-business web services is considered a primary concern in maintaining secrecy and integrity of large amount of data and information. The lack of control and monitoring of E-business transactions and services may lead to violation of confidentiality and information leakage [3]. In addition, current E-business frameworks are implemented for private environment and special purpose processes. As a result, limited number of customers is utilized for the analysis process. The security of E-business transactions is

© Springer Nature Switzerland AG 2019
A. Alfaries et al. (Eds.): ICC 2019, CCIS 1098, pp. 185–200, 2019.
https://doi.org/10.1007/978-3-030-36368-0_16

considered one of the challenging processes in current E-business researches. As presented in [4], an E-business application has been implemented with a digital signature model for preserving the confidentiality of E-business transactions. As shown in [5], an E-business framework is applied that obtains web service design and security parameters. The authors of [6] provide an E-business application for measuring the interaction of students to E-business services. The contributions of this paper are as follows:

- A security framework for protecting user transmissions for both B2C and G2C subsystems is proposed.
- We proposed applying multi-layer authentication mechanism for securing customer information in G2C subsystem.
- We proposed implementing a 3D secure system for the B2C and G2C subsystems for protecting acquirer, issuer, and interoperability sides.
- A structured web server log for recording the viewing and transaction operations in user sessions is developed.
- We proposed analyzing users' behavior by enhanced set of mathematical formula patterns based on linear temporal logic (LTL) and Declare patterns.
- An authentication algorithm is designed and implemented for authenticating user during payment process.
- Experimental results are conducted for displaying the efficiency of proposed algorithm and enhanced web server structures.

2   Related Works

With the significant increase of E-commerce and its applications in real life, the importance of E-business application has been emerged due to its great importance in saving time and effort in the operations of buying and selling and the implementation of government transactions. As presented in [7], the design of E-commerce and E-business web services is improved using web usage mining. A pre-processing of data, mining of data and data analysis are applied to an E-commerce web site called "OrOliveSur". In this web site, a K-means clustering technique and an Apriori algorithm of association rule mining technique are applied to the collected data set to measure the significance, unusualness, sensitivity, and fuzzy confidence. Another method to discover different clusters of E-commerce interest patterns was presented in [8]. This method is based on measuring the frequency of page visits and the time spent in each product category. Based on this approach, the user's behavior of the web service structure can be analyzed and measured. As presented in [9], different mining operations are explained for building user sessions from web server log. The mining operations are classified to three main categories: web content mining, web structure mining, and web usage mining. The web content mining is based on using the web application content for mining processes. Web structure mining identifies the structure of the hyperlinks for mining processes while web usage mining is based on mining the records of the web server log for predicting user behavior.

Another framework for selecting sample size of E-business application data was presented in [10]. In this framework, a two-fold sample size is selected for measuring the degree of trust to all E-business applications. One of the recent researches for analyzing users' behavior in E-business and E-commerce web sites was presented in [11]. The authors of this research developed a web server log for storing user tracing records. A data preprocessing is applied to a ready-made E-commerce web site for identifying users' behavior patterns and considering different actions performed in user sessions. The increasing availability of data recorded into the event logs of E-business applications makes the analysis, mining, and prediction of user behavior a complex task [12]. Each event recorded into the event log is called an activity and is related to a specific action or process in the E-business application. Additional information is stored into the event log such as timestamp of the process, the user who initiating the process, and browsing history. This information is easy to be recorded but hard to be processed and analyzed. For tracking and analyzing different user transactions in E-business web services, different patterns are implemented based on mathematical formulas. Declare patterns contain a set of constraints called templates. Each template has a specific semantic through LTL formulas that should obtain a front-end graphical user interface and must be understandable by users. Each LTL mathematical formula can specify certain constraint based on the ordering of activities [13]. Declare patterns provide an obvious front-end translation to the formal back-end LTL formula patterns. The effectiveness and the interoperability should also be maintained in recent E-business applications. One of the recent researches for reviewing E-business interoperability frameworks are presented in [14]. The authors of that research define the interoperability as the ability of information and business processes to be exchanged. Different interoperability levels are explained in that research in regard to different E-business frameworks such as application and software framework, ATHENA framework, enterprise framework, and grid wise context setting framework. The paper concludes that an E-business interoperability framework should be simple, understandable, should be enhanced easily, and must ensure consistency and avoid redundancy.

3   E-Business Authentication Mechanism

In our proposed E-business framework, two main processes are provided. The first process is the G2C and B2C user transactions. The second process is the authentication mechanism for securing both inner user operations and electronic payment transmissions. As shown in Fig. 1, the entire E-business framework is based on government-to-consumer (G2C) and business-to-consumer (B2C). The G2C subsystem presents a set of governmental services embedded into the overall system. The presented governmental services are the payment of electricity, water, Internet, car violations, school fees, and flight reservation. In G2C, each customer is considered as an administrator of the subsystem. The B2C subsystem presents an online shopping application for managing sales and ordering of a set of products. In B2C subsystem, all user processes are recorded into the web server log that will be analyzed and managed using Modern Checking Analysis (MCA) technique for analyzing users' behavior.

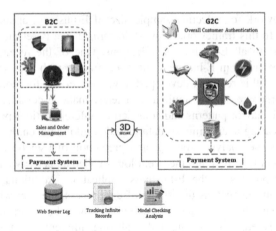

Fig. 1. E-Business security framework

The authentication mechanism in the E-business framework is based on two layers. In the first layer of G2C subsystem, the customer registers with an authentic username, password, and email. Each time the customer logs in into the G2C subsystem; a secret key is randomly generated and is sent to the customer email. This can prevent brute force attacks of customer credentials. In the second layer of G2C subsystem, the customer creates a unique username and password for each G2C service. The customer has the authorization to proceed into any single service inside the G2C application using a two-factor authentication (2FA) mechanism. As presented in Fig. 2, the customer needs a username, password, and a second factor key called token to perform a transaction for any service. The second factor key is automatically generated based on the unique password of the customer and a predefined formula.

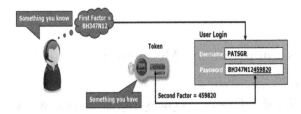

Fig. 2. Two-factor authentication mechanism

4   Administration and Secure Transmission

The security parameters of E-business application are developed based on three basic procedures. These parameters are system administration, customer authorization, and transmission security.

4.1 E-Business Administration

In E-business administration, the database administrator is responsible for several operations such as:

- Adding, removing, or modifying posts for overall B2C E-business application.
- Adding or removing new services in the G2C application.
- Storing all user accounts with their verification code in the database server.
- Tracing and monitoring all manipulation and shopping records for both G2C and B2C subsystems that are recorded into a web server log.

Table 1. Encrypted user accounts

Id	Email	EmailConfirmed	PasswordHash	AccessFailedCount	IsActive	CreationDate	VerifioCode
1	1fae2582-ed18-4Ga4-9065-f97369672dcc	sysadmin@gmail.com	1	AJc6QJMuDNqYiLxjpOMTFX76of+Ap+OxNv65BHvDQK1wa0UW9...	0	1	2017-08-03 11:37:50.273	YCNVLj0u82wHeV1317fmTNAc
2	29f0a9eb-9781-44c8-b72c-f1ab445e7d43	aymanm62@gmail.com	1	AHEgDVBAtCUaBxd1R9k4HGm9f5H23/HV4Na4n9H8LEReMZSw/...	0	1	2018-09-30 22:22:33.123	Za/ncvoBgp7qXeddEOO0LmG
3	6383cc97-034c-41a4-bf68-01179a6e6819	alatigmy@gmail.com	0	Alz3eGL/KVjeCLwegR6MyseDXTjmUrTxCDfqQFrpl0YZ0cXCa+pwM...	0	0	2018-08-17 15:50:42.090	NULL
4	a5dc78f2-2537-4142-92fc-274e8caf7241	ahmedrefaiyandroid@g...	1	AB9MP3g9f1l2/ooUi/QU4+rhmL+mmPFs4cW1OZaVk-/RLqi5/Mbswk...	0	1	2018-07-16 20:08:44.237	vGqWj7dR93JayonY8nBopS9oV
5	b52c188e4310-4030-9d6d-5a9a11db8866	aymanm62@gmail.com	0	ALc0jpGE6CVNWbEb1tK2bxXZMDFD2m7LWtJeo5eU6l0kyzvRzG8...	0	0	2018-09-30 22:22:33.123	NULL

As presented in Table 1, the authentication process stores and encrypts all parameters of user accounts in the database server based on three stages:

- In stage 1, once a user account is created, the email, creation date, user name and password are stored. The user password is encrypted using MD5 hash function and is stored in the password hash field. The "access failed count" field is used to count the possible number of failed attempts on the system.
- In stage 2, after passing the first layer, a unique verification code or token is sent to the user email to register the second authentication layer. This token is generated using OAuth 2.0 authorization protocol. Once the verification code or token is sent to the user email, the "email_confirmed" field is converted in the user account table from "0" to "1". As explained in Table 1, if a verification code is not sent to the user email, the value will be NULL and the "email_confirmed" field will be "0".
- In stage 3, the user creates a unique username and password for each G2C service. An additional authentication factor (secret key) is generated by concatenating the last 3 digits of both username and password. As presented in Algorithm 1, the username and password are encrypted using MD5 hash function and are compared with the hashed username and password entered during the payment process. If both hashes matched, the "Isactive" field in Table 1 is updated to "1"; otherwise the value is set to "0".

Algorithm 1: Authentication Factor
1. **Start** G2C Service
2. Input Username $\leftarrow U_1$
3. Input Password $\leftarrow P_1$
4. Generate $\rightarrow$ Hash (U_1)
5. Generate $\rightarrow$ Hash (P_1)
6. Generate Security Key (SK_1)
7. Set $SK_1 = U_1 \| P_1$
8. Generate $\rightarrow$ Hash (SK_1)
9. **Start** Payment Proceed
10. Input Username $\leftarrow U_2$
11. Input Password $\leftarrow P_2$
12. Generate $\rightarrow$ Hash (U_2)
13. Generate $\rightarrow$ Hash (P_2)
14. **If** Hash (U_1) = Hash (U_2) & Hash (P_1) = Hash (P_2) **Then**
15.   Set Payment = True
16.   Set SK_1 = True
17.   Update User Account Table
18.   Set Isactive = True
19. **Else**
20.   Set Payment = False
21.   Set SK_1 = False
22.   Update User Account Table
23.   Set Isactive = False
24. **End If**
25. **End** Payment Proceed
26. **End** G2C Service

4.2 User Authentication Mechanism

In the E-business application, each customer is considered as an administrator for his/her own G2C or B2C subsystem. The time schedule for each G2C service can be updated or disabled based on the customer's preferences. The customer has the authority to perform the following operations:

- Generating new or modifying existing authentication parameters for the main G2C subsystem.
- Recording all successful and failed attempts on the G2C service.
- Changing authentication parameters for each distinct G2C service.
- Creating a time schedule for each G2C service for automatic payment.
- Activating an alarm procedure for notifying the customer before executing the automatic payment.

As presented in Fig. 3, the G2C service determines each successful and failed login attempt by identifying the IP address, browser type, device type, and timestamp for each user.

Fig. 3. Successful and failed login attempts

As presented in Fig. 4, a time schedule for performing an automatic payment is developed and implemented. In this figure, the user must determine the payment date, apply the automatic payment procedure, and determine the payment system date whether it is daily, monthly, or annually.

APPLY BILL DATE & MAKE PAYMENT ⊕

CHANGE PAYMENT SECRET INFORMATION (USERNAME & PASSWORD ⊠

10/08/2018	Payment Date
ayman	User Name
••••••	Password
Yes	Apply Automatic Payment
Monthly	Based on Payment Date, the Automatic Payment will be

PAYMENT

Fig. 4. Automatic payment process

4.3   Transmission Security

As presented in Fig. 1, the payment system for both G2C and B2C transactions are executed using 3D secure system. The 3D secure is a protocol based authentication system for online credit card transactions. The protocol transmits XML authentication messages through an SSL connection with client authentication for ensuring the server and the client. Three participants of the payment process are shared for securing the transmission. These participants are:

- Acquirer side that is considered the destination domain for receiving transactions.
- Issuer side that is considered the source domain for sending the transaction.
- Interoperability side is the access control server for supporting 3D secure.

We assume that the connection between the three participants is protected against any kind of attacks by using an SSL connection which is a realistic assumption in security mechanisms.

4.4   Behavioral Pattern Analysis

Based on our paper presented in [15], the linear temporal logic (LTL) is a model checking analysis (MCA) technique that uses formula patterns for enhancing the queries of customer preferences [16]. The predefined formula patterns are used for recording and analyzing user processes and transactions over an extended period of time for unlimited event streams [17]. Customer preferences are recorded into the web server log for predicting user's behavior and enhancing the E-business application structure. An enhancement of declarative approaches is presented by applying a set of formula patterns for predicting users' behavior and enhancing E-business structure. As shown in Fig. 5, the web service structure consists of different secondary sections related to the main section. The main sections of the B2C structure starts with the homepage with level 0. Level 1 consists of a set of categories from C1 to Cn such as Mobiles, Electronics, etc. Each category contains a set of related products from P1 to Pn as shown in level 2. In level 3, the products are composed of a set of interrelated items from I1 to In. In level 4, the items are composed of a set of interrelated sub-items from S1 to Sn. The shaded circle refers to the leaf items that have no sub-items. The items that have no sub-items are stored in the web server log with a NULL value. To identify a specific product or item, the B2C structure depends on the formula $L_{i,j}$ where i refers to the structure level and j refers to the product or item number in the web server log. For each category, the process of tracking users' behavior consists of five sequential event actions. These event actions are viewing (V), revision (R), payment (P), execution (E), and item return (IR). A counting process is executed for determining the customer preferences for tracing users' behavior.

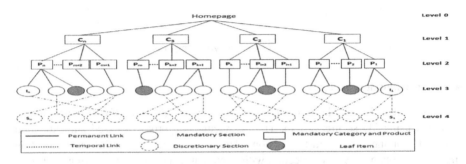

Fig. 5. Proposed B2C structure

4.5 Flag Parameter Log

As shown in the flag parameter algorithm presented in our paper [15], each transaction being executed is recorded based on a specific flag parameter. Two main levels can be sequentially executed: viewing level and action level. The view level VL_i is divided into category, product, item, and sub-item such that $VL_i \in S$ where S is the main or secondary web level. The event action $\mathbb{V}_A$ is divided into two flags: viewing flag (VF) and action flag (AF) where each visited service page updates the flag value to 1 based on the proposition formula $S_i(\mathbb{V}_{At})$.

4.6 Web Server Customer Log

The behavior patterns presented in [11] is based on showing the percentage of total number of events and the percentage of appearances in sessions without tracking the customer viewing and action patterns. The web log record architecture presented in [9] is based on registering requests and responses through the web server by storing the host address, request type, and browser type but it eliminates the viewing of multi-level web structure and action procedures from reviewing to payment process. In open systems such as E-commerce and E-business websites, the discovery of process-oriented model for tracing users' behavior becomes difficult [18]. As shown in Table 2, all customers' usernames are grouped to categorize their viewing transitions and action operations. The web server customer log can simplify and enhance the performance of E-business structure based on a categorization process. The categorization process is based on grouping the username and MAC address of each customer with their viewing and action operations in each category and product. The return item rate (RT %) records 4% for the customer "Jones" with MAC address "74-C4-3B-52-33-51" while the return item (RT %) records 2.7% for the customer "Adam" with MAC address "34-81-2B-13-A2-62". The high percentage of return item can be considered evidence to the low quality of the item or the high requirements of the customer. Future offers can be presented to all customers with high return item rate.

Table 2. Web server customer log

User name	MAC address	Category	Product	Item	Sub-item	Count	Viewing %			Action %			
							PL %	IL %	SL %	R %	PT %	E %	RT %
Adam	34-81-2B-13-A2-62	Mobile	Sony	Xperia	XZ3	32	90.6%	59.6%	51.3%	13.5%	8%	8%	2.7%
Jones	74-C4-3B-52-33-51	Electronics	DELL	Inspiron	XPS 13	25	88%	68%	48%	8%	4%	4%	4%

4.7 Web Server Item Log

The most used methods for processing the web server log is by cleaning unwanted and duplicated entries [19]. For obtaining high analysis performance, the web server log is formalized based on the item log. In this case, as long as the item/sub-item level is accessed, the category level will be already accessed because the category level is considered as the root of the item. As presented in Table 3, the web server item log summarizes all viewing and action transitions for each item/sub-item. The viewing and action logs are executed as follows:

- The viewing log percent is measured for product logs (PL), item logs (IL), and sub-item logs (SL). Each one indicates the viewing percentage from the overall category counter.
- The action log percent calculates all action operations for each item/sub-item based on the requirement revision percent (R) and payment process percent (P).

The execution percent is divided into accumulated executes and net execute. Accumulative executes (AE) refers to the overall number of executes from the total category counter while the net execute (NE) refers to the actual execution from payment process. Accumulative executes are calculated in Eq. (1) as follows:

$$Accumulative\ Execute\ (AE) = \frac{Execution\ Counter}{Category\ Counter} \tag{1}$$

The net execute is calculated in Eq. (2) as follows:

$$Net\ Execute\ (NE)\% = \frac{Execution\ Counter}{Payment} \tag{2}$$

The return item percent is divided into accumulative return and net return. Accumulative return (AR) refers to the overall number of returning item from the total category counter while the net return (NR) refers to the actual return from the net execution process. The accumulative return is calculated in Eq. (3) as follows:

$$Accumulative\ Return\ (AR) = \frac{Return\ Counter}{Category\ Counter} \tag{3}$$

The net return is calculated in Eq. (4) as follows:

$$Net\ Return\ (NE)\% = \frac{Return\ Counter}{Net\ Execute} \tag{4}$$

Based on both net execute (NE) and net return (NR), an offer priority rate is established to verify whether the return rate is high or low. As a result, if the return rate is high, then the offer priority will be high and vice versa. The offer priority rate can be dynamically changed based on the number of transactions executed. As presented in Table 3, the accumulative return is considered low for all items and sub-items but it varies in net return because the net return (NR) refers to the real return value divided by the actual net execute. As a result, the offer priority is identified based on the net return value. The net return achieves high rates with 8.03%, 12.57%, 1.38% and 9.88%. This means that additional offers should be presented to customers to enhance E-business structure. The net return achieves low rates with 1.38%. This means that no additional offers will be presented.

Table 3. Web server item log

Item/Sub-item	Category Counter	Viewing Log Percent			Action Log Percent						Offer Priority
	CL	PL	IL	SL	R	PT	Accu. E	Net Execute	Accu.RT	Net Return	
Huawei	1127	94.9%	84.1%	78%	16.6%	12.95%	12.16%	91.9%	0.98%	8.03%	Ⓗ
Samsung	1653	95.5%	88.5%	80.9%	24.9%	11.86%	10.1%	85.16%	1.27%	12.57%	Ⓗ
IPhone	2561	97.2%	94.2%	92.5%	25.3%	18.6%	16.95%	93.13%	0.23%	1.38%	Ⓛ
Sony	1537	96.9%	83.7%	73.9%	13.9%	11.52%	10.54%	89.79%	1.04%	9.88%	Ⓗ

5 Experimental Results

To visualize the performance analysis of user behavior, the E-business structure and the multiple web server logs have been implemented using Microsoft Visual Studio.net 2013 with Microsoft SQL Server 2012 database. The experimental results were conducted on Intel ® Core i5 CPU 1.8 GHz machine and 8 GB RAM. Datasets of 9680 transactions have been selected based on viewing and action processes. The datasets are divided into two categories; the first category was *Mobile* with a total of 6878 transactions and the second category was *Electronics* with a total of 2802 transactions. Different data mining techniques such as classification, clustering, association rule mining, and sequential pattern mining are used to analyze users' behaviors [20]. As presented in Fig. 6, the viewing and action flags for customer preferences are computed based on product log (PL), item log (IL), sub-item log (SL), revision (R), payment (P), accumulative execute, and accumulative return for *Mobile* category. The viewing and action flags are decreased linearly and recorded 96.13%, 87.63%, 81.33%, 20.18%, and 13.73%, 12.44%, and 0.88% respectively. The accumulative execute and accumulative return; are computed based on the presented Eqs. (1) and (3) for identifying the overall number of executed transactions and the overall number of return items from the total customers' transactions of this category.

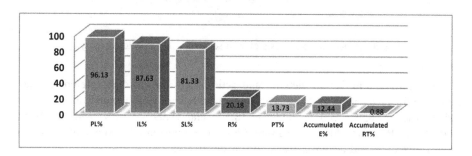

Fig. 6. Viewing and action flags for mobile category

For verifying the net execute and net return transactions, Eqs. (2) and (4) are computed. The net execute is computed by dividing the number of executed transactions by the number of payment transactions. The net return is computed by dividing the number of accumulative return by the net execute value. As shown in Fig. 7, using the payment percentage of 13.73% as a main parameter with 944 transactions, the net executed transactions records 90% with 850 transactions. Rollback executed transactions records 2.03% with 19 transactions while the net return records 7.97% with 75 transactions.

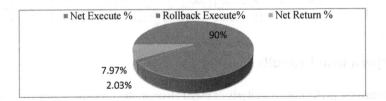

Fig. 7. Net execute and return for mobile category

The analysis performance of the structured web server log explains the processing percentage of transactions for each individual stage. As presented in Fig. 8, by merging Eqs. (1), (2), (3) and (4), the processing percentage of transactions recorded 23.43%, 21.36%, 19.8%, 4.9%, 3.34%, 3.02%, 22%, 0.21%, and 1.94% for product log (PL), item log (IL), sub-item log (SL), revision (R), payment (P), accumulative execute, net execute, accumulative return, and net return respectively.

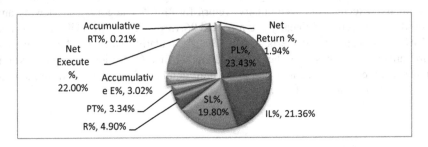

Fig. 8. Performance analysis of web server log for mobile category

As shown in Fig. 9, the viewing and action flags for customer preferences are computed for *Electronics* category. The viewing and action flags are decreased linearly and recorded 87.85%, 75.02%, 34.05%, 18.3%, and 12.09%, 9.78%, and 0.64% for product log (PL), item log (IL), sub-item log (SL), revision (R), payment (P), accumulative execute, and accumulative return respectively.

The accumulative execute and accumulative return; are computed based on Eqs. (1) and (3) for identifying the overall number of executed transactions and the overall number of return items from the total customers' transactions of this category. The net execute and net return transactions are computed based on Eqs. (2) and (4). As shown in Fig. 10, using the payment percentage of 12.09% as a main parameter with 339 transactions, the net executed transactions records 78.75% with 267 transactions.

Rollback transactions records 13.43% with 46 transactions and the net return records 7.82% with 26 transactions.

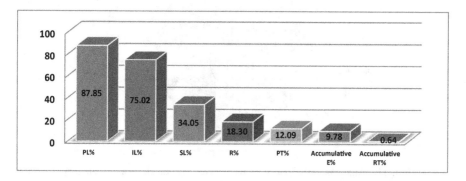

Fig. 9. Viewing and action flags for electronics category

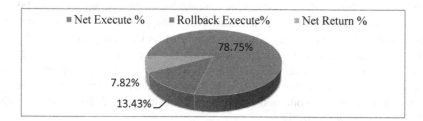

Fig. 10. Net execute and return for electronics category

The performance analysis of the web server log explains the processing percentage of transactions for each individual stage. As shown in Fig. 11, by merging Eqs. (1), (2), (3) and (4), the processing percentage of transactions recorded 27.1%, 23.13%, 10.49%, 5.64%, 3.72%, 3.02%, 24.3%, 0.2%, and 2.4% for product log (PL), item log (IL), sub-item log (SL), revision (R), payment (P), accumulative execute, net execute, accumulative return, and net return respectively.

Figure 12 concludes the viewing and action flags for both *Mobiles* and *Electronics* using a linear scatter diagram. As shown, all viewing and action processes are decreased linearly with respect to browsing sessions. The general statistics of online viewing and payment (action) are presented in Fig. 13. On a parameter of >=90% on a product level (PL), mobile shopping exceeded the rate with 96.13% while electronics shopping are below the rate with 87.85%.

As presented in Fig. 12, the scatter diagram showed a decreasing linear order. So, the parameters of Fig. 13 will be decreased linearly through the browsing and action processes. On a parameter of >=80% on item level (IL), mobile shopping exceeds the rate with 87.63% while electronics shopping are below the rate with 75.02%. On a parameter of >=70% on sub-item level (SL), mobile shopping exceeds the rate with 81.33% while electronics shopping are still below the rate with 34.05%.

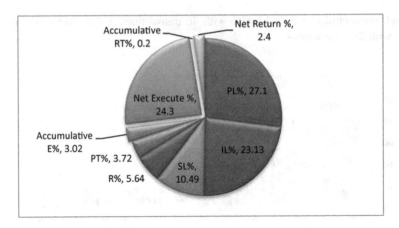

Fig. 11. Analysis performance of web server log for electronics category

As presented in [21], many users may face some concerns in regard to online payment with at least 30% of products are returned back. On a parameter of >=25% on revision level (RL), both mobile and electronics shopping are below the rate with 20.18% and 18.3% respectively. On a parameter of >=10% on payment level (PL), both mobile and electronics shopping exceeded the rate with 13.73% and 12.09% respectively while on a parameter of >=5% on execute level (E), both mobile and electronics shopping exceeded the rate with 12.44% and 9.78% respectively. Finally, for return item level (RI) both mobile and electronics shopping are below the rate with 0.88% and 0.64% respectively.

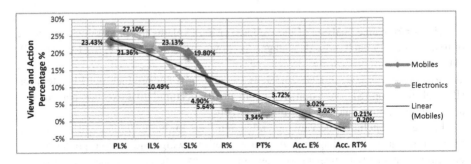

Fig. 12. Scatter diagram for viewing and action percentage

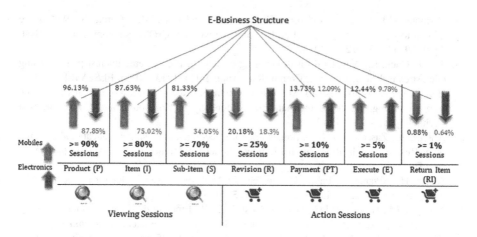

Fig. 13. Summary of customer choices

6 Conclusions

This paper presented a structured framework for B2C and G2C subsystems for tracking, analyzing and securing customer services by applying authentication mechanisms based on 3D secure system. Analyzing infinite customer browsing and transactions is considered a very complex task. In this paper, an E-business framework with security features is designed and implemented for analyzing and predicting user behavior based on user transactions that have been recorded using mathematical formula patterns. Experimental results are conducted to prove the adaptability, efficiency, and performance of the secured E-business structure. Future directions of this research focus on building recommender systems based on the recorded customer preferences and user's behavior.

References

1. Ciarniene, R., Stankeviciute, G.: Theoretical framework of E-Business competitiveness. In: International Scientific Conference of Economics and Management, Procedia - Social and Behavioral Sciences, Elsevier, vol. 123, pp. 734–739 (2015)
2. Chao, K.: E-services in E-business engineering. J. Electron. Comm. Res. Appl. **16**(2), 77–81 (2016). ELSEVIER
3. Basu, A., Muylle, S.: Assessing and enhancing E-Business processes. J. Electron. Comm. Res. Appl. **10**(4), 437–499 (2011)
4. Saha, G., Desai, M., Ghosh, A., Saha, N.: Digital signature modeling in E-business. In: IEEE International Conference on E-business Engineering, pp. 350–354 (2014)
5. Ping, G.: Analysis the application of E-business for the tourism enterprises' performance evaluation in China. J. Energy Procedia **5**, 849–854 (2011). ELSEVIER
6. Ahrens, A., Zascerinska, J.: A comparative study of engineering and business students' attitude to E-business application. In: IEEE International Conference on E-Business, pp. 31–38 (2014)

7. Carmona, C.J., Ramirez, S., Torres, F., Bernel, E., Del Jesus, M.J., Garcia, S.: Web usage mining to improve the design of an E-commerce website: OrOliveSur.com. J. Expert Syst. Appl. **39**, 11243–11249 (2012)

8. Su, Q., Chen, L.: A method for discovering clusters of E-commerce interest patterns using click-stream data. J. Electron. Comm. Res. Appl. **14**(1), 1–13 (2015). ELSEVIER

9. Hemapriya, A., Bhuvaneswari, M., Muneeswaran, K.: Reconstruction of user sessions from web server log. In: IEEE International Conference on Computing and Communication Technologies, pp. 37–42 (2015)

10. Ahrens, A., Zascerinska, J.: A framework for selecting sample size in educational research on E-Business application. In: IEEE International Conference on E-Business, pp. 39–46 (2014)

11. Sergio, H., Alvarez, P., Fabra, J., Ezpeleta, J.: Analysis of users' behavior in structured E-commerce websites. IEEE Trans. Access J. **5**, 1–17 (2017)

12. Maggi, F.M., Bose, R.P.J.C., van der Aalst, W.M.P.: Efficient discovery of understandable declarative process models from event logs. In: Ralyté, J., Franch, X., Brinkkemper, S., Wrycza, S. (eds.) CAiSE 2012. LNCS, vol. 7328, pp. 270–285. Springer, Heidelberg (2012). https://doi.org/10.1007/978-3-642-31095-9_18

13. Zugal, S., Pinggera, J., Weber, B.: The impact of testcases on the maintainability of declarative process models. In: Halpin, T., Nurcan, S., Krogstie, J., Soffer, P., Proper, E., Schmidt, R., Bider, I. (eds.) BPMDS/EMMSAD -2011. LNBIP, vol. 81, pp. 163–177. Springer, Heidelberg (2011). https://doi.org/10.1007/978-3-642-21759-3_12

14. Rezaei, R., Chiew, T., Lee, S.: A review on E-business interoperability frameworks. J. Syst. Softw. **93**, 199–216 (2014). ELSEVIER

15. Mostafa, A.M., Alroudhan, J., Hassan, M.M.: LTL formula patterns for enhancing the performance analysis for e-business structure. J. Theor. Appl. Inf. Technol. **97**(8), 2429–2439 (2019)

16. Alvarez, P., Fabra, J., Hernandez, S., Ezpeleta, J.: Alignment of teacher's plan and students' use of LMS resources: analysis of moodle logs. In: IEEE International Conference on Information Technology Based Higher Education and Training, pp. 1–8 (2016)

17. Burattin, A., Cimitile, M.: Online discovery of declarative process models from event streams. IEEE Trans. Serv. Comput. **8**(6), 1–14 (2015)

18. Poggi, N., Muthusamy, V., Carrera, D., Khalaf, R.: Business process mining from E-Commerce web logs. In: Daniel, F., Wang, J., Weber, B. (eds.) BPM 2013. LNCS, vol. 8094, pp. 65–80. Springer, Heidelberg (2013). https://doi.org/10.1007/978-3-642-40176-3_7

19. Colaco, J., Mittal, J.: An efficient approach to user navigation pattern prediction. In: IEEE International Conference on Advances in Electrical, Electronics, Information, Communication, and Bioinformatics, pp. 420–424 (2016)

20. Zhang, Q., Segall, R.: Web mining: a survey of current research, techniques, and software. Int. J. Inf. Technol. Decis. Making **7**(4), 683–720 (2008)

21. El Haddad, G., Aïmeur, E., Hage, H.: Understanding trust, privacy and financial fears in online payment. In: IEEE International Conference on Trust, Security and Privacy in Computing and Communications, pp. 28–36 (2018)

Association Rules for Detecting Lost of View in the Expanded Program on Immunization

Fawzia Zohra Abdelouhab[✉], Baghdad Atmani,
and Fatima Zohra Benhacine

Laboratoired' Informatiqued' Oran, University of Oran1 Ahmed Ben Bella,
BP 1524 EL Mnaouer, Oran, Algeria
fzabdelouhab@gmail.com, baghdad.atmani@gmail.com,
benhacine.fatima@gmail.com

Abstract. According to the Expanded Program on Immunization (EPI), all children are entitled to a series of vaccination from the first week of birth to 11 months. A policy that aims to reduce the impact of major deadly diseases for children. The EPI faces to major childhood diseases most responsible for mortality in children. Unfortunately, a problem arises: all children who present for the first vaccination one week after birth no longer receive all vaccines, and this, for many reasons; These are the lost of view. A real problem for health authorities. In this study, we present a cellular Matching method for detecting lost of view using association rules.

Keywords: Process ontology · Boolean modeling · Ontology alignment · Association rule · CASI machine · Lost of view · Expanded Program on Immunization · Immunization coverage

1 Introduction

In knowledge based engineering framework and more exactly in the heterogeneous data integration with ontologies, our approach implements a new extensional ontology matching technique based on Boolean modeling CASI (Cellular Automata for Symbolic Induction) [4]. Our approach merges two important areas such as data mining and mathematical modeling. From the first one, we exploit association rules paradigm to extract correspondences between the ontologies from the vocabulary used to describe their instances. And from the second, we take advantage of the dynamic and discreet formalism of the cellular automatons to implement our approach. The latter allows us to optimize the complexity in time and in space by the use of the simple local transitions synchronous function.

To integrate data from different and distinct ontologies it would be necessary, at first, to find semantic links between their entities and match them. Then, we talk about ontology alignment or Matching [12].

Ontologies are currently at the heart of all the work on the knowledge to uncover semantic and syntactic ambiguities. Their scope is constantly expanding and covers decision-support systems, problem-solving systems or knowledge management systems [9, 10, 12]. A Closed connectivity is created, in particular between ontologies

A. Alfaries et al. (Eds.): ICC 2019, CCIS 1098, pp. 201–213, 2019.
https://doi.org/10.1007/978-3-030-36368-0_17

and datamining so that much ontology has proven their competences in mining extracting association rules [7, 15, 16].

Reciprocally, others works use association rules to improve the use of ontologies. For example, use association rules for assessing the overall quality of data [14] or for the construction of models for the detection of anomalies and data contradictions [8]. And finally, the association rules for matching ontology by AROMA method [11]. This method allows detection of involvement relations between entities from two hierarchies of text or of ontology based on textual data in the extension (instances) and annotations (name, comment, etc.). We are largely inspired by this method, considered by OAEI among the best alignment systems, to develop our own approach of extensional alignment of ontologies.

In this article we will describe the deployment of our approach that we realized in a real case of preventive medicine during our participation in the National Research Project (PNR) entitled "Service-Oriented Architecture for the Expanded Program of Vaccination" developed within the AIR team of which we are part, "Automatic Learning, Artificial Intelligence and Reasoning" of the Oran LIO Computer Laboratory. In this project, it was mainly a matter of automating the vaccination process of the Epidemiology and Preventive Medicine Services (SEMEP) to highlight cases lost to follow-up during vaccination coverage.

This paper is structured as follows: At first, we present the vaccination in Algeria then we briefly introduce the SEMEP services and their mission in the survival of the child. We continue with the characteristic properties of a vaccination system and describe the ontological model that we propose. The fourth section presents our cell alignment approach that we developed. Finally, a discussion and some critics will conclude this study.

2 Vaccination in Algeria

In the last twenty years or so, the computer access to medical knowledge is a major challenge for health professionals as well as to the general public. Face to the proliferation of potentially accessible information sources and face to the dizzying increase of textual production, limitations of information processing tools have appeared. They do not come from their performance to store and quickly process large volumes, but their inability to take into account the specificities of user business vocabulary [6].

We addressed this issue by participating in the National Research Project (NRP) entitled "Architecture Oriented Services for the Expanded Program on Immunization" developed within the AIR team to which one belongs, "Machine Learning, Artificial Intelligence and Reasoning" from Computer lab Oran LIO. In this project, it was mainly question to automate the vaccination process to highlight the case of lost sight in immunization coverage.

Vaccination in Algeria is a fairly complex process involving cooperation several types of stakeholders and several systems, difficult to synchronize starting from services of the wilaya up to the public health services. For this, the services of Epidemiology and Preventive Medicine (SEMEP) will need to coordinate the different underlying information systems to all services involved in this vaccination. This process involves the vaccination history, consults the vaccine supply, and uses geolocation influences epidemiology etc. As many systems and services to move towards a quality vaccination. Like a chain reaction, it is clear that the success of vaccination, which depends on that of the EPI is closely linked to the quality of coordination and the rates of involvement of each subsystem participating.

Our contribution in this project is to provide semantic interoperability among different subsystems intervening to EPI process. This allows us to have constantly all immunization data available for better exploitation by SEMEP. In practice, this translates into the implementation a platform for monitoring, scalable, capable of integrating knowledge from the various vaccination centers called PMIs (Protection Maternal and Child). This knowledge and the resources used, are necessarily heterogeneous, make their understanding and analysis very difficult. Preserve the meaning of the information exchanged is then an important problem. This is what is called semantic interoperability [13]. Consideration of this semantic allows different PMI and the SEMEP to combine the received information with local information and treat all in a coherent way.

The statistics of last years show that it is difficult to achieve reasonable immunization rates due to several factors including the lost of view. The lost of view is the situation of a child who has had at least one contact with immunization services but that has not finished his series of five contacts (Table 1). Those adversely affect the coverage of different antigens. This results in a decrease in coverage of total immunization minimizing the efforts in favor of child survival. Therefore, we are interested in this study to identify cases of dropouts and help in the adaptation strategies that can reduce them in children 0 to 11 months using engineering knowledge technical and datamining.

In knowledge based engineering framework and more exactly in the heterogeneous data integration with ontologies, our approach implements a new extensional ontology matching technique based on Boolean modeling CASI (Cellular Automata for Symbolic Induction). Our approach merges two important areas such as data mining and mathematical modeling. From the first one, we exploit association rules paradigm to extract correspondences between the ontologies from the vocabulary used to describe their instances. And from the second, we take advantage of the dynamic and discreet formalism of the cellular automatons to implement our approach. The latter allows us to optimize the complexity in time and in space by the use of the simple local transitions synchronous function.

3 SEMEP and His Mission

The SEMEP is defined as a medical center that coordinates, amongst other the action and the operation of PMIs on a circumference encompassing several wilayas.

PMI are welcome points of individuals for vaccinations, medical monitoring etc. In this sense, they represent for SEMEP its main sources of information it needs for its making eventual decisions. The quality of the decision that it is collaborative and/or cooperative depends on the quality of interactions between PMI and SEMEP.

Considerable efforts are continuously made by SEMEP, to fight against some devastating diseases and this, by the implementation of the EPI.

However, Algeria today is far from that of the sixties. Population increased because the demography has exploded and is spread over a larger area. This new situation poses problems at the SEMEP for socio-demographic and socio-economic causes such as:

The geostrategic partitioning of the territory gives rise to very remote and rural areas difficult to access.

The social-professional development in large cities causes permanent and significant exodus of the population making it difficult to follow the medical record of a person.

The presence of bygone computing resources no longer meets the continued growth of the population and the specific needs of users.

Among the most important tasks of the SEMEP is EPI whose objectives are directed to:

- An increase in immunization coverage: This point is undoubtedly the most important in the overall EPI process. It mainly concerns the function of PMI by the act of vaccination whether in group (companions of school hygiene) or individual, in the center or at home. Individual vaccination, called routine (Table 1) is based on a specific vaccination calendar and the vaccination of door to door enables for isolated populations of low accessibility to health facilities, to enjoy the benefits of vaccination.
- Weight reduction of certain diseases: This point is automatically deducted from the first one. Good coverage presupposes already a polio eradication, elimination of measles, a control on neonatal tetanus etc.
- The safety of vaccinations, sustainability of program.

Table 1. Calendar of routine immunization

Contact	Age	Recommended antigens
1	Birth	BCG, Polio0
2	8 weeks	DTCoq1, Polio1
3	12 weeks	DTCoq2, Polio2
4	16 weeks	DTCoq3, Polio3
5	9 month	Measles

4 Description of the Proposed Approach

Our project aims to improve the exchange between the PMI on one side and SEMEP on the other side and also to assist the EPI in its immunization campaign. This goal took place in two stages: First, ensure the structural and semantic interoperability of data which circulates within SEMEP and PMI services to ensure perfect synchronization between them. For this, we had to restructure existing local databases into PMI in ontologies of vaccination to support the semantics of data and homogenize the vocabulary used. Given the decentralized nature of the PMI, we are find with several modular ontologies produced independently but the SEMEP had inevitably need to assemble, exchange and share.

A reconciliation of ontologies was necessary for develop a shared universal ontology and adopted by all users SEMEP that we have realized through our cell fusion system of ontologies [1]. Secondly we focused on the issue of lost of view. It is clear that the failure of any immunization system is caused by the cases that begin the vaccination program but who do not complete for various reasons. For SEMEP this is a real challenge to combat these causes in order to reduce these cases of abandons and at the same time succeed its immunization coverage. This is our second goal.

Our, eventual solution resides in a new technology of alignment extensional ontology based on a Boolean modeling CASI. Our approach combines two important areas such as datamining and mathematical modeling. First, we use the paradigm of association rules for extracting correspondences between ontologies from the vocabulary used in descriptions of their instances. And second, we enjoy the dynamic formalism and discrete cellular automata to implement our approach. These we optimize the complexity in time and space by the use of simple functions synchronous of local transitions.

The idea inherent in our approach is to exploit and analyze instances of different immunization ontologies we developed upstream. These instances are, in reality, different children in the vaccination program. Our intuition is that if we apply some datamining in this group of children we can through association rules detect a certain implicit and tacit knowledge that SEMEP can exploit it to mark the abandons.

4.1   The Ontology of Vaccination

As we have explained before we generated our ontology from different relational databases located at the IMPs. We used for it a set of rules to transform the builders of the relational database to SQL file format to builders semantically equivalent in the ontology. These rules are based on an analysis of relations, keys and inclusion dependencies. That is to say transform relationship, attributes and key to concepts, properties and axioms.

4.2   Vaccination Process

Immunization coverage (CV) is a mathematical model subdivides the population into three groups of individuals:

- Totally Vaccinated (TV) set of all children (individuals) who received all vaccines. They have 5 contacts.
- Partially vaccinated (PV) set of all children who received vaccination number belonging to [1, 2]. They have not yet completed their vaccinations.
- Not Vaccinated (NV) all children who received no vaccination.

An individual moves from NV state to PV state by a first vaccination and PV state to TV state after 5 vaccinations as is shown below.

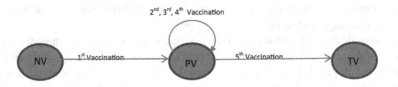

The risk factors considered events, maintain a causal relationship with the vaccination process.

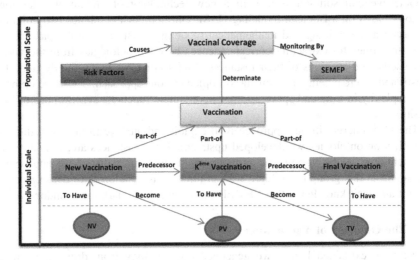

Fig. 1. Process of vaccine coverage

To make more efficient our ontology, we've added a "Causes" concept that defines the different causes of vaccination abandons. These causes can be divided into three categories:

- Related To Parents: For example,
  - Temporary or permanent absence of the mother with her child.
  - Lack of time to bring the child to the vaccination.
- Related To the services: For example:
  - Coordination between curative and preventive health services is often inadequate; health workers are unable to properly follow the immunization calendar, especially if several vaccines must be given at different times.
  - The disorder, queues, lack of friendliness of staff are responsible for missed appointments.
  - Insufficient training of health workers in vaccine management (waste).
  - Absence of vaccinator agent.
  - Lack of vaccine in the vaccination centers.
  - Related to Beliefs: For example Child repressed for various reasons (illness, carelessness etc.).

We also added an important property to the class Vaccination is "NumContact" that lets to know the status of the child vaccinated (NV, PV or TV).

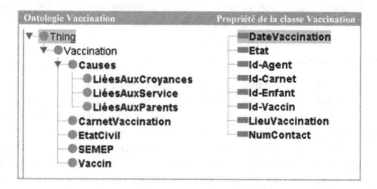

Fig. 2. Ontology of vaccination given by Protégé 3.1

The process of vaccination is a complex process that has two complementary aspects: the static aspect described by the ontology domain (Fig. 2) and the dynamic aspect describes by a process ontology generated by querying the domain ontology. A SPARQL query is run that defines the different states of children vaccinated according to the value of the property "NumContact". The entire population will be divided into three categories, each of which will instantiate the concepts of a process ontology (Fig. 3).

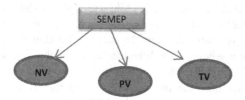

Fig. 3. A process ontology associated to the domain ontology of vaccination

The process of vaccination coverage that we have developed is a cellular process that is repeated at each SEMEP and follows a real process of extracting knowledge in four major phases:

- Phase 1: Preparation of data in which patterns of inputs ontologies are converted into Boolean matrix.
- Phase 2: Extraction association rules into binary principle.

- Phase 3: Cellular Inference. A stage dedicated to cellular inference motor, who using transition functions, determines the points of correspondence between instances of ontologies with an optimal set of association rules.
- Phase 4: Interpretation and analysis: semantic of correspondences links established in the treatment phase and their taking into account.

4.3 Data Preparation

Our approach adopts a Matching said holistic that consider in input over than two ontologies each belonging to a SEMEP. The set of instances of all input ontologies are grouped in a single database called for this occasion, learning database. The principle is to induce the eventual relationship between the entities based on their extensions respective. However, a constraint makes this simple principle not applicable as it is. Indeed, it is rare for two or more ontologies share the same extensions. To solve this problem, the extensional approaches perform preprocessing on ontologies to make them comparable [7]. There are three possible approaches:

- Reduce their extension (and their indexing relation) to $O1 \cap O2$.
- Increase their extension (and their indexing relation) to $O1 \cup O2$.
- Extract another representation of extensions and thus another indexing relationship.

The first approach, (one adopted in our work) is the simplest to set up. The second approach relies on supervised classification and the last one completely changes the indexing relationship by the extraction and selection of descriptors issued from the content analysis of instances.

The common set of instances will contain children who have circulated from one SEMEP to another (for some reasons) and thus have multiple states according to their position in each SEMEP. For example: a child with code E0158 is a new vaccinated in the town of Oran where the mother was staying there temporarily. His state in SEMEP Oran is NV. Before reaching the next booster vaccination her mother has already moved to Mostaganem where she will reside for 8 months. Following immunization contacts will be at the SEMEP Mostaganem and the state of the child E0158 passes from NV to PV. After that, the mother will goes definitely to Algiers because his husband was promoted to the ministry; his child will complete his immunization in SEMEP Algiers. During immunization coverage, this child will be lost from sight at the SEMEP Oran and Mostaganem. This example shows the complexity of the real system that is difficult to detect it when it is concerned a big data exceeding thousands of instances.

To explain the principle of our approach we have taken a sample of 12 individuals from the learning database built from SEMEP1 of Oran, SEMEP2 of Mostaganem and SEMEP3 of Algiers (Fig. 4).

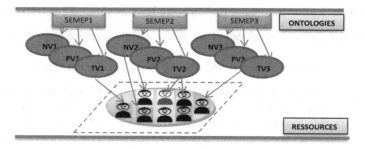

Fig. 4. Extract of the process ontology of vaccination

From here we give the transaction table (Table 2) which is extracted from a sample of 12 tuples.

Table 2. Table of transactions

N°	Transactions
1	E0101
2	E0202
3	E0406
4	E1258
5	E485
6	E3259
7	E845
8	E0125
9	E365
10	E0895
11	E01144
12	E6548

4.4 Generating Association Rules

Notion of Association rule is defined to a context of a search of a set of individuals described by a set of variables called a table (or a set of joined tables) issue from a relational database. As part of the alignment of ontologies, our search context or learning is consisting of the terms of the components of the ontology, i.e., each ontology represents a predictive attribute whose modalities shall be its different concepts.

Formally, an association rule is a couple of variable noted a → b, where a and b are disjoint itemsets, called respectively premise and conclusion. There are two key issues that must be considered when using association rules. First extraction of motifs (more or less frequent) can be numerically expensive if all instances (databases) is large. Second, some association rules are potentially false or irrelevant.

To provide a solution to these problems we have established certain assumptions:

1. The desired rules are binary rules i.e. they have only one variable in premise and in conclusion.
2. Premises and conclusion are issued respectively from disjoint sets of variables.

Datamining that we apply proceeds as follows: First we fixe an attribute whose modalities will form the different premise of association rules. This is reflected in our case by processing a search on a given SEMEP. Then we'll see what attributes that correspond him by an alignment. For this we use the following algorithm that extracts association rules.

```
Function : RuleExtract
INPUT : (1) List of concepts of the first ontology
        (2) List of itemsets
OUTPUT: List of association rules
Begin
K=1; // number of rules
While (true)
{Read (Itemseti);
SupportItemset ← GetSupport(Itemseti);
l=1;
For j=1 to n do Item ← GetConcept(Itemseti(j));
If Item ∈ ListConceptPremise Then Premise ← Item;
                      SupportItem ←GetSupport(Item);
                      Else Conclusion(l)← Item;
EndIf;
l++;
EndFor;
For j=1 to l do Rule(k)←Premise+'→'+Conclusion(l);
Support(Rule(k))=SupportItemset/N;
Confiance(Rule(k))=SupportItemset/SupportItem;
k++; }
```

The sequence of the algorithm on our transaction table gives us the following association rules:

Table 3. Association rules

Rule	Meaning
If NV1 Then PV3	A new vaccinated in SEMEP1 continues his contacts in SEMEP3
If PV1 Then TV2	A vaccinated in SEMEP1 ends its immunization in SEMEP2

The set of rules generated forms the new knowledge base. The latter contains an important set of rules, many of them are redundant and others without important meaning.

4.5   Cellular Machine CASI and Boolean Matching

CASI machine developed by Atmani [4] is a cellular automaton described by four Boolean matrices and two transition functions that simulate the operation of an inference engine.

CASI machine has proven itself in several applications of datamining in particular for controlling and reconfiguring collective urban transport networks [3], for text categorization [5], and in the Boolean representation of the association rules for the biological datamining. [10]. We use the CASI machine to extract association rules while ensuring optimization in the storage space, the runtime and programming complexity. In general, the operation of the machine CASI is using two main functions:

1. The Match() function that compares the rules and eliminates redundant.
2. The Merge() function that merges the valid rules with same premise. She allows to build a new rule from the rules with same premise by the combination of their respective conclusions.

4.6   Results Interpretation

The rules generated by CASI machine represent the state of immunization coverage. Once submitted to an expertise some reports can be established. This expertise could infer the following explicit knowledge:

- Identify the current case (PV): Show the children already registered who have not yet received all of their doses.
- Compute the coverage rates. Immunization status of children of a given group can be calculated automatically.
- Identify latecomers. Children, who missed a dose of vaccine, can be easily identified.
- To have more accurate coverage rates.
- More importantly, the expertise may deduct the following implicit knowledge.
- The analysis of immunization records reveals in greater detail the reasons why some children are not vaccinated, to which community they belong to, and how important is the role played by reasons such as parental refusal (the reasons for refusal of vaccination are instances of the concept reasons in the ontology of vaccination).
- Ensuring that all children are vaccinated.
- Vaccine stock management and its use.
- Predict the number of children vaccinated each month, the quantities of vaccine to be distributed, the reserve stock and the minimum stock.

5   Conclusion

We presented in this paper our approach that allows us to mark cases of abandons of vaccination for a SEMEP given, through the analysis and search instances of ontology. We presented our problematic as an eventual solution to the problem of alignment of data and their semantics. Our study is part of an original perspective centered around cellular automata to model multiple ontologies in association rules base and implement algorithms of extensional matching with low complexity.

We hope our approach solves the problem of lost sight of, and facilitates the response to the fateful question that could pose any responsible of SEMEP. "What are the reasons that make many children 0 to 11 months who received the first dose of vaccine are not reviewed in the other immunization sessions?".

However, our approach as a method of aligning ontologies is subject to possible improvements. Serious reflections can be made to infer links other than subsumption or implication links between concepts such as so-called semantic rhetorical relations (e.g., "is-synonym-of," "part-of," etc.). In our approach we considered the alignment of ontologies sharing the same instance store, it would be interesting to do this for ontologies that do not share the same set of instances. In this case, a reindexing of the data is necessary.

Our approach, unlike other alignment approaches, adopts a holistic Matching that considers more than two ontologies. This point is certainly interesting, but remains no less problematic. The set of instances of all ontologies in entries is grouped in a single database called for the occasion, learning base. This learning base becomes, then, very quickly voluminous. A volumetry that slows the extraction times of the association rules considerably due to many reading of the database.

References

1. Abdelouhab, F., Atmani, B.: Fusion cellulaire des ontologies. Journal of Decision Systems (2016). ISSN: 1246-0125 (Print) 2116-7052. http://www.tandfonline.com/loi/tjds20
2. Abdelouhab, F. Atmani, B.: Intégration automatique des données semi-structurées dans un entrepôt cellulaire. ASD'2008, ISBN 978-9981-1-3000-1, dépôt légal: 2168/2008, pp. 109–120 (2008). http://eric.univ-lyon2.fr/ ~ asd/asd2008
3. Amrani, F., Bouamrane, K., Atmani, B., Hamdadou, D.: Une nouvelle approche pour la régulation et la reconfiguration spatiale d'un réseau de transport urbain collectif. JDS 20(2), 207–239 (2011)
4. Atmani, B., Beldjilali, B.: Knowledge discovery in database: induction graph and cellular automaton. Comput. Inform. J. 26(2), 171–197 (2007)
5. Barigou, F., Atmani, B., Bouziane, Y., Barigou, N.: Accélération de la méthode des K plus proches voisins pour la catégorisation de textes. EGC 2013, 241–246 (2013)
6. Baneyx, A.: construire une ontologie de la pneumologie aspects théoriques, modèles et expérimentations. PhD. thesis. Université Paris, 6 (2007)
7. Bellandi, A., Furletti, B., Grossi, V., Romei, A.: Ontological support for association rule mining. In: Proceedings of the 26th IASTED pp. 110–115 (2008)
8. Berti-Equille, L.: Data quality awareness: a case study for cost optimal association rule mining. Knowl. Inf. Syst. 11(2), 191–215 (2007)
9. Brahami, M., Atmani, B., Matta, N.: Dynamic knowledge mapping guided by data mining: application on healthcare. JIPS 9(1), 1–30 (2013)
10. Brisson, L., Collard, M.: An ontology driven data mining process. In: Proceedings of the 10th International Conference on Enterprise Information Systems, Barcelona, Spain, pp. 54–61
11. David, J., Guillet, F., Briand, H.: Association rule ontology matching approach. Int. J. Semant. Web Inf. Syst. 3(2), 27–49 (2007)

12. Euler, T., Scholz, M.: Using ontologies in a KDD workbench. Workshop on Knowledge Discovery and Ontologies at ECML/PKDD, pp. 103–108. Pisa, Italy (2004)
13. Hajjam, A.: Ontologies and Cooperation of Distributed Heterogeneous Information Systems for Tracking Chronic Diseases, 01/2013. https://doi.org/10.1007/978-3-319-00375-7_5. ISBN: 978-3-319-00374-0 (2013)
14. Hipp, J., Güntzer, U., Grimmer, U.: Data Quality Mining Making a Virtue of Necessity (2001)
15. Hou, X., Gu, J., Shen, X., Yan, W.: Application of data mining in fault diagnosis based on ontology. In: Proceedings of the Third International Conference on Information Technology and Applications, Washington, USA, pp. 260–263 (2005)
16. Zeman, M., Ralbovský, M., Svatek, V., Rauch, J.: Ontology-driven data preparation for association mining. In: Proceedings of the 8th Znalosti Conference, Brno, pp. 1–12 (2009)

Hybrid Model Architectures for Enhancing Data Classification Performance in E-commerce Applications

Ayman Mohamed Mostafa[1,2(✉)], Mohamed Maher[1], and M. M. Hassan[1(✉)]

[1] Faculty of Computers and Informatics, Zagazig University, Zagazig, Egypt
am_mostafa@zu.edu.eg
[2] College of Computers and Information Sciences, Jouf University, Sakakah, Kingdom of Saudi Arabia
amhassane@ju.edu.sa

Abstract. Data mining algorithms are used for analyzing and extracting large volume of data from different sources. Applying data mining in e-commerce applications can help making better decisions for new integrated technologies. Data mining create a way for decision-makers to make their decision more effective for improving businesses. In this paper, a framework is proposed to enhance the performance of classification techniques that are applied to an online shopping agency dataset by applying the best hybrid algorithm called EMLMT algorithm. Another proposed model framework is built to enhance the performance and decrease the execution time of the classification techniques that have been applied on a real dataset for easy cash company by applying the best hybrid algorithm which called DBKNN algorithm on this dataset. The conducted experimental results of the two proposed model architectures achieved high rates in accuracy, precision, recall, F-measure, and ROC when compared to classification only algorithms.

Keywords: E-commerce · Data mining · Classification · EMLMT algorithm · DBKNN algorithm

1 Introduction

Electronic commerce is a web site application that's used for selling and purchasing products and online services over the internet and permits customers, partners, and workers to accomplish a variety of their needs and their services. It creates new opportunities for performing profitable activities online [1]. Data mining is the process of analyzing data from different perspectives and summarizing it into useful information. Data mining consists of extract, transform, and load transaction data onto the data warehouse system, Store and manage the data in a multidimensional database system, provide data access to business analysts and information technology professionals, Analyze the data by application software, present the data in a useful format, such as a graph or table. Data mining involves the anomaly detection, association rule learning, classification, regression, summarization, and clustering [2]. Clustering

A. Alfaries et al. (Eds.): ICC 2019, CCIS 1098, pp. 214–227, 2019.
https://doi.org/10.1007/978-3-030-36368-0_18

divides a dataset into different groups. The objects in a dataset are grouped or clustered based on the principle that objects in one cluster have high similarity to one another but are very dissimilar to objects in other clusters. In clustering data objects have no class label. That means when we start clustering, we do not know what the resulted clusters will be, or by which attribute the data will be clustered. For that reason, clustering is also called unsupervised learning [3]. Classification is also known as supervised learning that is the process of finding a set of models or functions that describe and distinguish data classes or concepts where the models derived based on a set of training data. Classification is used to find a model that described classes and concepts [4]. The organization of the paper is as the follows: introduction, related work, proposed model framework for online shopping agency, EMLMT algorithm, proposed model framework for real dataset "easy cash company dataset", DBKNN algorithm, evaluation criteria, result and discussion for online shopping agency dataset, result and discussion for a real dataset, conclusions and future work.

2 Related Works

As presented in [5], a novel method is used for combining clustering with classification algorithms due to improving classification accuracy. The experimental results and analysis show that classification algorithm accuracy can be improved by applying classification techniques after clustering algorithms. As presented in [6], some benefits and some challenges in data mining inside of e-commerce websites are presented in this paper. There are some benefits for e-commerce companies that used data mining algorithms on their websites such as analyzing purchase behavior for a customer, forecasting the new sales and allow these companies to make merchandise planning. On the other hand, there are some challenges such as the transformation of data, data mining scalability and spider identification. As shown in [7], a comparative study of some classification algorithms is presented in this paper which applied to the online shopping agency dataset. The decision table classifier shows in the experimental result as the greater algorithm which can be applied on the online shopping agency to provide the best implementation of a powerful model that will allow a customer to determine their needs from products which produced by e-commerce websites. As presented in [8], a comparative study of some clustering algorithms is presented in this paper by using weka tool. The conclusion of this paper after analyzing the results of testing the clustering algorithms shows that the accuracy of the k-mean algorithm is greater than the hierarchical clustering algorithm and the quality clusters are produced by using the k-mean algorithm when using a large dataset. Data mining inside of e-Commerce is used to make better decision making for a new idea or a new integrated technology. Data mining create a way for decision-makers to be able to make their decision more effective for the improvement of their business [6]. Weka is software written in Java and contains several GUI such as Explorer, Experimenter, Knowledge Flow and Simple CLI. Weka has used data mining tools for comparing between clustering and classification techniques [9]. The aim of this paper firstly is proving that when applying clustering-based classification algorithms to an online shopping agency dataset will give the best results compared to a recent research paper [7] which applied classification algorithms only to the same dataset. Secondly, another aim is improving the result of classification techniques accuracy that applied on a real dataset of easy cash company by applying clustering-based classification algorithms on it.

3 Proposed Model Architecture for Online Shopping Agency Dataset

As presented in Fig. 1, the study framework is applied on an online shopping agency dataset, starting with entering the dataset into a data pre-processing phase to prepare and enhance the model inputs. Following the data preprocessing phase, the data clustering step is mentioned which is necessary to allocate related objects into the same cluster. After the clustering step, the classification step is mentioned which is necessary to help customers to find their desired products in e-commerce website. Then the performance accuracy is calculated by using the confusion matrix and some evaluation criteria. To this end, a selection process for the best hybrid technique which is the EMLMT technique.

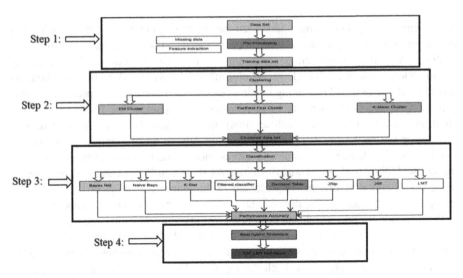

Fig. 1. Proposed model architecture for pre-tested dataset

3.1 Data Description

The comparative study between some classification algorithms that was presented in [7] is applied on online shopping agency dataset to allow this enterprise identifying the best suitable classifier algorithm to this dataset which was the decision table classifier. In this paper clustering-based classification algorithms are applied on the same dataset to improve the performance and accuracy of the results.

3.2   Data Pre-processing

The actual data collected usually have the features that incomplete, redundancy and ambiguity. So as to mine the knowledge additional effectively, pre-processing the data collected is essential. Preprocessing can provide accurate, concise data for data mining. Data preprocessing, contains data cleaning, user identification, user session identification, access path supplement and transaction identification [10].

3.3   Clustering Analysis Process

The main objective of using clustering algorithms is to allocate related or similar objects into groups called clusters [11]. This paper discussed briefly the clustering algorithms that are applied on online shop agency dataset. In this process three clustering algorithms are applied on the selected data. These techniques are expectation maximization (EM) clustering algorithm [12], farthest first clustering algorithm [13], and K-mean clustering algorithm [14].

3.4   Classification Analysis Process

The main difference between classification and clustering is that classification is a supervised mechanism while clustering is an unsupervised mechanism. In classification, the class label is known in advance, while clustering does not assume any knowledge of clusters. This paper discussed briefly the classification algorithms which are applied on online shop agency dataset. Eight classifiers are used on the clustered data to determine the best classifier based on its accuracy. These classifiers are Bayesian networks [15], Naive Bayes algorithm [16], K* classifier algorithm [17], filtered classifier algorithm [18], decision tree (DT) classifier [16], Jrip classifier [18], J48 classifier [19], and logistic model tree (LMT) classifier [18, 20].

4   EMLMT Algorithm

Expectation Maximization Logistic Model Tree (EMLMT) algorithm is a hybrid model that combines the expectation maximization cluster algorithm and the logistic model tree classifier algorithm. As presented in [7], the authors proved that decision table algorithm is the best classifier that must be applied to pretested dataset "online shop agency" to help customer to find their desired products in e-commerce website. This paper proves that EMLMT algorithm gives better performance than decision table classifier algorithm.

Pseudocode of EMLMT algorithm:
Input: Pre-tested dataset
Output: EMLMT Tree
Steps:
1. Expectation step;
      For each point x,
            For each cluster i,
                  Calculate the probability that x belongs to the cluster i;
2. Maximization step;
      For each cluster i,
      Re-estimate the initial parameters to maximize likelihood of the points
3. Repeat the expectation step and maximization step until the parameters converge.
4. Final clustered data.
5. LMT (clustered data)
                        root = new Node ()
                        alpha = getCARTAlpha(clustered data)
                  root.buildTree(clustered data, null)
                  root.CARTprune(alpha)
6. buildTree (clustered data, initialLinearModels)
            numIterations=crossValidateIterations   (clustered   data,
      initialLinearModels)
            initLogitBoost (initialLinearModels)
                  linearModels = copyOf(initialLinearModels)
                  for i = 1...numIterations
            logitBoostIteration(linearModels, clustered data)
                  split = findSplit (clustered data)
                  localExamples = split.splitExamples(clustered data)
            sons = new Nodes[split.numSubsets()]
                  for s = 1...sons.length
            sons.buildTree(localExamples[s], nodeModels)
7. crossValidateIterations (clustered data,initialLinearModels)
            for fold = 1...5   initLogitBoost(initialLinearModels) //split into
      training/test set
                  train = trainCV(fold)
                        test = testCV(fold)
                        linearModels = copyOf(initialLinearModels)
                  for i = 1...200
                  logitBoostIteration(linearModels,train)
            logErrors[i] += error(test)
            numIterations = findBestIteration(logErrors)
                  return numIterations

5 Proposed Model Architecture for Easy Cash Company Dataset

As presented in Fig. 2, which illustrates the study framework for a new real dataset, starting with data pre-processing required to prepare and enhance the model inputs. Following the data preprocessing, the data clustering step is mentioned which is necessary to allocate related objects into the same cluster. After the clustering step, the classification step is mentioned which is necessary to help customers to find their desired products in e-commerce website. Then we calculate performance accuracy by using the confusion matrix and some evaluation criteria. Finally, choosing the best hybrid technique which is the DBIBK technique.

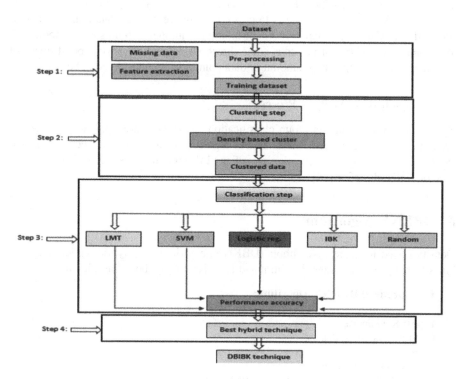

Fig. 2. Proposed model architecture for new real dataset

5.1 Data Description

In this paper, classification algorithms are applied after applying some clustering algorithms on the real dataset to improve the performance and accuracy of the results of classification. The dataset contains some attributes as follows: ProductID, Name, ProductCategory, SellStartDate, SellEndDate, ModifiedDate, ListPrice, and AgeGroup.

5.2   Data Preprocessing

The actual data collected generally have the features that incomplete, redundancy and ambiguity. In order to mine the knowledge more effectively, pre-processing the data collected is essential. Preprocessing can provide accurate, concise data for data mining. Data preprocessing, includes data cleaning, user identification, user sessions identification, access path supplement and transaction identification [10].

5.3   Clustering Analysis Process

In this stage, a density-based clustering technique is used on the easy cash company new data set. In this technique, clusters are defined as cluster that is separated from other on the basis of varying densities. Thus, a cluster of certain density is surrounded by points with low density. The basic idea is to check if there are enough data points in neighborhood of any point to satisfy criteria of minimum number of points in neighborhood. This minimum number of points is some threshold defined by us. If a point does not have more than that threshold amount of data point it is not considered to be in clusters.

5.4   Classification Analysis Process

Based on the new dataset, four classification algorithms are applied to view the accuracy of the clustered data. These algorithms are support vector machine (SVM) [21, 22], logistic regression classifier [23], random forests classifier [24], and IBK or KNN classifier [24].

6   DBKNN Algorithm

Density Based K-Nearest Neighbors (DBKNN) algorithm is a hybrid model that combines Density Based cluster algorithm and K-Nearest Neighbors classifier algorithm.

Pseudocode of DBKNN Algorithm:

Input: Real dataset
Output: Classified dataset
Steps:
1.   Select any arbitrary point p.
2.   Find all direct reachable points from that point.
3.   If p is border point, no point is directly reachable from p, thus select next point in dataset.
4.   If point is core point it yields a cluster.
5.   Continue this for all point in data points in our real dataset.
6.   For each point in clustered real dataset:
     a. find the Euclidean distance to all training data point.
     b. store the Euclidean distances in a list and sort it.
     c. choose the first k points.
     d. assign a class to the test point based on the majority of classes present in the chosen points.
7.   End

7 Evaluation Criteria

There are some terms such as true positive (TP) and false positive (FP) that used in classification tasks to compare the results of the tested classifier with trusted external judgments. The true positive and false positive refer to whether that prediction agrees to the external judgment, occasionally it is called the observation. Let P positive instances and N negative instances for some condition. Then, true positive rate (TPR) and false positive rate (FPR) are calculated as presented in Eqs. (1) and (2):

$$\text{True positive rate (TPR)} = \text{TP}/\text{P} = \frac{\textbf{TP}}{\textbf{(TP+FN)}} \tag{1}$$

$$\text{False positive rate (FPR)} = \text{FP}/\text{N} = \frac{\textbf{FP}}{\textbf{(FP+TN)}} \tag{2}$$

Where, true positive (TP) means that the label on the selected dataset is predicted correctly while false positive (FP) means that the label on the selected dataset is predicted falsely. Precision and recall are calculated as presented in Eqs. (3) and (4):

$$\text{Precision} = \frac{\textbf{TP}}{\textbf{(TP+FP)}} \tag{3}$$

$$\text{Recall} = \frac{\text{TP}}{\text{(TP+FN)}} \tag{4}$$

F-measure: is a measure that merges precision and recall is the consistent mean of precision and recall, the F-measure or F-score is calculated as presented in Eq. (5):

$$\text{F-measure} = 2(\text{Precision} \times \text{Recall})/(\text{Precision} + \text{Recall}) \tag{5}$$

Confusion Matrix is also called error matrix or contingency table is a specific table that permits visualization of the performance measure of an algorithm, typically a supervised learning one. Each field of the matrix represents the instances in a predicted class, whereas each tuple represents the instances in an actual class. In Eq. (6) we calculate the classifiers accuracy, which is the percentage of predictions that are correct. In Eq. (7) we calculate the mean absolute error, it is the prediction probability of the correct class, divided by the actual probability of the class and N is the number of classes.

$$\text{Classifiers accuracy} = \frac{(\text{TP} + \text{TN})}{(\text{TP} + \text{TN} + \text{FP} + \text{FN})} \tag{6}$$

$$\text{Classifiers Error Rate} = \frac{(\text{FP} + \text{FN})}{(\text{TP} + \text{TN} + \text{FP} + \text{FN})} \tag{7}$$

Receiver Operating Characteristic (ROC) is also known as a relative operating characteristic curve, because it is a comparison of two operating characteristics (TPR and FPR) as the criterion changes [25].

8 Experimental Results for Online Shopping Agency Dataset

The performance and accuracy of the implemented model can be improved by applying clustering-based classification algorithms on online shopping agency dataset.

8.1 Performance Parameters of Classifier Algorithms

The experimental results that were presented in [7] showed that the classification processes are achieved without applying clustering-based classification algorithms. As presented in Fig. 3, the decision table classifier achieved 87.1% for true positive rate (TP rate), 7.8% for false positive rate (FP rate), 88.3% for precision, 87.1% for recall, 87.2% for F-measure, and 95.5% for ROC area. The second-best results presented in [7] were achieved by filtered classifier algorithm that showed 86.8% for true positive rate (TP rate), 7.9% for false positive rate (FP rate), 87.8% for precision, 86.8% for recall, 87.2% for F-measure, and 95.2% for ROC area. Whereas the third best results were achieved by J48 algorithm that shows 86.1% for true positive rate (TP rate), 8.6% for false positive rate (FP rate), 86.2% for precision, 86.1% for recall, 85.9% for F-measure, and 88% for ROC area.

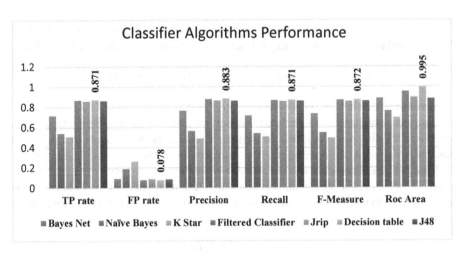

Fig. 3. Performance parameters of classifier algorithms [7]

8.2 Classification Accuracy vs. Clustering-Based Classification Techniques Accuracy

As presented in Fig. 4, the highest new correct of classifier accuracy after applying clustering-based classification techniques achieved 100% by EMLMT algorithm and the lowest new incorrect accuracy achieved 0.0% by EMLMT algorithm. While the decision table (DT) classifier that was presented in [7] achieved the highest correct of the classifier accuracy after applying only classification processes a rate of 87.13% and the lowest incorrect accuracy achieved 12.87%.

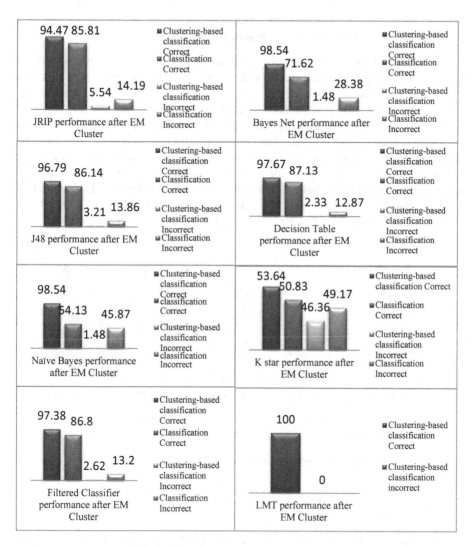

Fig. 4. Classifiers accuracy after EM cluster

9   Experimental Results for Easy Cash Company Dataset

As presented in our paper [26], the performance and accuracy of the implemented model can be improved by applying clustering-based classification algorithms on real dataset of easy cash company.

9.1   Performance Parameters of Classifier Algorithms

The experimental results showed that the classification processes are achieved without applying clustering-based classification algorithms on real dataset. As presented in Fig. 5, the best classifier IBK (KNN) classifier achieved 99.3% for true positive rate (TP rate), 0.7% for false positive rate (FP rate), 99.3% for precision, 99.3% for recall, 99.3% for F-measure, and 100% for ROC area. The second-best results were achieved by Random Forest classifier algorithm that showed 99.2% for true positive rate (TP rate), 0.8% for false positive rate (FP rate), 99.2% for precision, 99.2% for recall, 99.2% for F-measure, and 100% for ROC area. Whereas the third best results were achieved by Logistic algorithm that shows 99.1% for true positive rate (TP rate), 0.01% for false positive rate (FP rate), 99.1% for precision, 99.1% for recall, 99.1% for F-measure, and 100% for ROC area respectively.

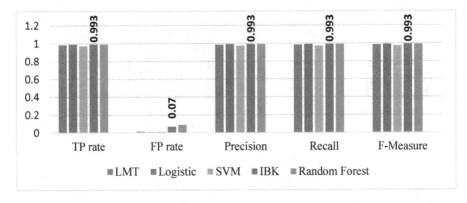

Fig. 5. Performance parameters of classifier algorithms

9.2   Classification Accuracy vs. Clustering-Based Classification Techniques Accuracy

As presented in Fig. 6, the highest new correct of classifier accuracy after applying clustering-based classification technique achieved a rate of 100% by Logistic classifier, IBK classifier, SVM classifier, and Random Forest classifier while the lowest new incorrect of classifier accuracy after applying density-based cluster achieved 0% rate by IBK classifier, Logistic classifier, SVM classifier, and Random Forest classifier.

While the IBK classifier achieved the highest correct of the classifier accuracy after applying only classification processes on the real dataset was equal to 100% and the lowest incorrect of classifier accuracy achieves 0% by IBK Classifier.

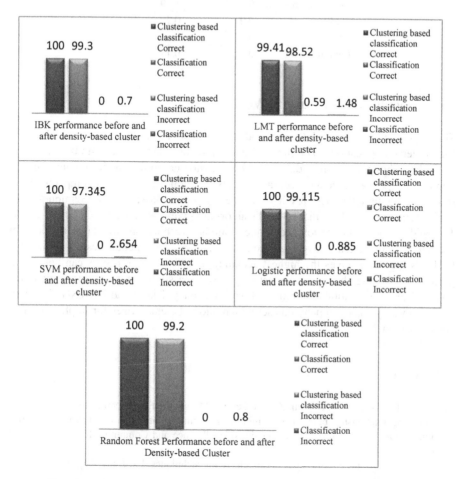

Fig. 6. Performance classifier accuracy before/after density based clustering

9.3   Execution Time for the Real Dataset

As presented in Table 1, after applying density-based cluster, the best classifier time was recorded with IBK and Random Forest with an execution time of 0 and 0.02 s respectively while the latest classifier is LMT classifier that achieved a total time of 0.25 s. But after applying only classification operations, also the IBK classifier was the fastest classifier with a total time of 0 s while the latest classifier is Logistic classifier that achieved a total time of 1.39 s.

Table 1. Execution time before/after clustering process

Classifier algorithm	Density-based	Only classifier
LMT	0.25	0.88
Logistic regression	0.1	1.39
SVM	0.03	0.22
IBK	0	0
Random forest	0.02	0.17

10 Conclusion and Future Works

This paper explains two architecture models to conduct enhance classification of data in E-commerce applications. The first architecture model illustrates the study framework for online shopping agency dataset to help customer finding their products and to improve the performance and accuracy of classification techniques. A comparative test is applied to find the best result of clustering-based classification techniques. The experimental results show that EMLMT algorithm gives the highest accuracy of 100%. To validate the classification techniques, another architecture model is applied for another dataset called "easy cash company". The experimental results show that DBKNN algorithm gives the highest accuracy of 100%. These results can help companies in selecting the optimal clustering-based classification algorithm which was EMLMT algorithm suitable to online shopping agency dataset and DBKNN algorithm suitable to easy cash company dataset which allow the enterprises for implementing a powerful model.

References

1. Rao, T.K., Khan, S.A., Begum, Z., Divakar, C.: Mining the E-commerce cloud: a survey on emerging relationship between web mining, E-commerce and cloud computing. In: IEEE International Conference on Computational Intelligence and Computing Research, pp. 1–4 (2013)
2. Mann, A.K., Kaur, N.: Survey paper on clustering techniques. Int. J. Sci. Eng. Technol. Res. **2**(4), 803–806 (2013)
3. Witten, I.H., Frank, E., Hall, M.A., Pal, C.J.: Data mining: practical machine learning tools and techniques (2016)
4. Han, J., Pei, J., Kamber, M.: Data Mining: Concepts and Techniques. Elsevier, Amsterdam (2011)
5. Alapati, Y.K., Sindhu, K.: Combining clustering with classification: a technique to improve classification accuracy. Int. J. Comput. Sci. Eng. **5**(06), 336–338 (2016)
6. Ismail, M., Ibrahim, M.M., Sanusi, Z.M., Nat, M.: Data mining in electronic commerce: benefits and challenges. Int. J. Commun. Netw. Syst. Sci. **8**, 501–509 (2015)
7. Ahmeda, R.A., Shehaba, M.E., Morsya, S., Mekawie, N.: Performance study of classification algorithms for consumer online shopping attitudes and behavior using data mining. In: International Conference on Communication Systems and Network Technologies, pp. 1344–1349 (2015)

8. Chaudhari, B., Parikh, M.: A comparative study of clustering algorithms using WEKA tools. Int. J. Appl. Innov. Eng. Manage. (IJAIEM) **1**(2), 154–158 (2012)

9. Sharma, N., Bajpai, A., Litoriya, R.: Comparison the various clustering algorithms of WEKA tools. Int. J. Emerg. Technol. Adv. Eng. **2**(5), 73–80 (2012)

10. Lingras, P.: Rough set clustering for web mining. In: IEEE International Conference on Computational Intelligence, pp. 1039–1044 (2002)

11. Gunasekara, R.P., Wijegunasekara, M.C., Dias, N.G.: Comparison of major clustering algorithms using WEKA tool. In: IEEE International Conference on Advances in ICT for Emerging Regions, pp. 272–273 (2014)

12. Abbas, O.A.: Comparisons between data clustering algorithms. Int. Arab J. Inf. Technol. **5**(3), 320–325 (2008)

13. Revathi, S., Nalini, D.T.: Performance comparison of various clustering algorithm. Int. J. Adv. Res. Comput. Sci. Softw. Eng. **3**(2), 67–72 (2013)

14. Elavarasi, S.A., Akilandeswari, J., Sathiyabhama, B.: A survey on partition clustering algorithms. Int. J. Enterp. Comput. Bus. Syst. **1**(1), 1–4 (2011)

15. Bayat, S., Cuggia, M., Rossille, D., Kessler, M., Frimat, L.: Comparison of Bayesian network and decision tree methods for predicting access to the renal transplant waiting list (2009)

16. Vaghela, C., Bhatt, N., Mistry, D.: A survey on various classification techniques for clinical decision support system. Int. J. Comput. Appl. **116**(23), 14–17 (2015)

17. Wiharto, W., Kusnanto, H., Herianto, H.: Intelligence system for diagnosis level of coronary heart disease with K-star algorithm. Healthc. Inform. Res. **22**(1), 30–38 (2016)

18. Dan, L., Lihua, L., Zhaoxin, Z.: Research of text categorization on WEKA. In: IEEE International Conference on Intelligent System Design and Engineering Applications, pp. 1123–1131 (2013)

19. Sharma, A.K., Sahni, S.: A comparative study of classification algorithms for spam email data analysis. Int. J. Comput. Sci. Eng. **3**(5), 1890–1895 (2011)

20. Landwehr, N., Hall, M., Frank, E.: Logistic model trees. J. Mach. Learn. **59**(1–2), 161–205 (2005)

21. Nizar, A., Dong, Z., Wang, Y.: Power utility nontechnical loss analysis with extreme learning machine method. IEEE Trans. Power Syst. **23**(3), 946–955 (2008)

22. Wu, X., et al.: Top 10 algorithms in data mining. Knowl. Inf. Syst. J. **14**(1), 1–37 (2008)

23. Meenakshi, M., Geetika, G.: Survey on classification methods using WEKA. Int. J. Comput. Appl. **86**(18), 16–19 (2014)

24. Chetty, G., White, M., Akther, F.: Smart phone based data mining for human activity recognition. Procedia Comput. Sci. **46**, 1181–1187 (2015)

25. Ragab, A.H., Noaman, A.Y., Al-Ghamdi, A.S., Madbouly, A.I.: A comparative analysis of classification algorithms for students college enrollment approval using data mining. In: Proceedings of the Workshop on Interaction Design in Educational Environments, pp. 1–8. ACM (2014)

26. Mostafa, A.M., Maher, M., Hassan, M.M.: Enhancing clustering-based classification algorithms in E-commerce applications. J. Theor. Appl. Inf. Technol. **96**(18), 6095–6105 (2018)

Performance Dashboards
for Project Management

Samiha Brahimi$^{(\boxtimes)}$ ⓘ, Aseel Aljulaud ⓘ, Anwar Alsaiah ⓘ,
Norah AlGuraibi ⓘ, Mariam Alrubei ⓘ, and Haneen Aljamaan ⓘ

Department of Computer Information Systems,
College of Computer Science and Information Technology,
Imam Abdulrahman Bin Faisal University,
P.O. Box 1982, Dammam, Saudi Arabia
sbrahimi@uod.edu.sa

Abstract. In order to improve the quality of decisions, companies are trying to find solutions for better supervision during the progress of the projects. Dolf Technologies is a business located in Saudi Arabia with their headquarters in Khobar. The company has several challenges concerning project management. These challenges are influencing the quality and the punctuality of the delivered tasks. One effective way to deal with such a problem is to monitor all these tasks in an effective way. This paper reports on the case of employing performance dashboards by DOLF Technologies. The suggested solution consists of two dashboards, one is destined to operational control level employees and the second is dedicated to strategic level management. Both dashboards are designed using Tableau software connected to online excel sheet where the company data is stored. The first solution is the operational dashboard displays the progress of each task in each subproject, colored by if the task is on time or overdue. Moreover, working hours left compared with the deadline. As well as, the overall progress of each subproject displayed by how much it is finished in percentage out of 100. The second solution is the managerial dashboard an abstraction of the operational dashboard. It shows vertical progress bars; each visualizes the frequency of delays in tasks that each sub-project has. In addition, pie charts show the percentage of completed tasks for each subproject. The dashboards have been deployed and the initial feedback is positive.

Keywords: Project management · Decision support · Dashboard

1 Introduction

Dolf Technologies is a Saudi based company established in 2006 [1], with their headquarters in Khobar. It provides E-learning solutions to satisfy technology needs of educational institutions and corporations around Saudi Arabia and the Gulf region. Their solutions are built based on several challenges the customers usually encounter; related to either their training, education or the improvement of workforce performance.

Hence, in Dolf Technologies, the efforts are focused on assisting the clients to accomplish their E-learning goals and make a difference in the overall growth of either

© Springer Nature Switzerland AG 2019
A. Alfaries et al. (Eds.): ICC 2019, CCIS 1098, pp. 228–240, 2019.
https://doi.org/10.1007/978-3-030-36368-0_19

the employees or the students in educational institutions; all while keeping in mind the scalability and customizability of the solutions. However, the company has several decision making challenges of its own, among which some are to the project management. In fact, the number of projects run simultaneously implies monitoring difficulties and hence delays in tasks and projects delivery. Besides, this influences the quality of the delivered tasks as decision are made under pressure when deadlines are not met. As per [2], this may as well result in cost escalations, and other foreseen and unforeseen business problems. A business activity monitoring dashboard is suggested to permit both operational and strategic level control to follow-up with the progress of the projects, subprojects and tasks in Dolf Technologies. Figure 1 shows the structure of the company and the problem as well as the suggested solution. The rest of the paper is organized as follows: Sect. 2 presents the literature review and the related work, Sect. 3 discuss the research methodology. Each step of the methodology is explained in a separate Sects. 4, 5, 6 and 7 for intelligence phase, design phase, choice phase and implementation phase respectively. Finally, Sect. 8 concludes the paper.

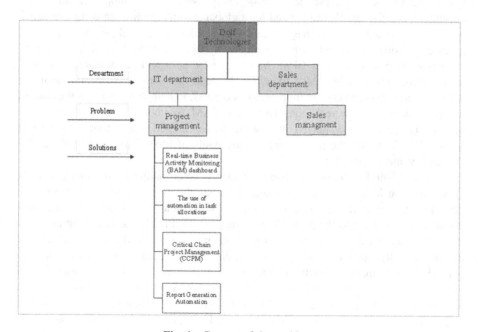

Fig. 1. Context of the problem

2 Literature Review

One of the solutions that were provided for similar problems is automated in task allocation. Usually, when projects are complex, they require a lot of labor work and time. Thus, the company in some cases might exceed the specified deadline; especially when the tasks are not properly structured. Automating some tasks ensures that they are identical in their format, which can also prevent human error, providing better project management. CruiseControl is a free open source tool that helps the team members in the project to implement some tasks that will not delay the project and will run on their specified schedule. One of the tasks is alerting the team members about any changes that occurred in the code and by whom. This allows the entire team, including the project manager to be informed immediately to check the code and fix any problems that might occur beforehand. Also, automation of unit tests ensures that the project will not encounter any delays when the testing phase starts, and it can generate reports of any critical failure. This tool provides the option of choosing a specific time slot in order for the tasks to run as planned. Using CruiseControl allows the project manager to control the progress of the project and minimize the delays that could happen [4].

Another solution is the use of real-time Business Activity Monitoring (BAM) dashboards; which helps in monitoring the activities and the compliance to the schedules and budget in real time. The use of such dashboards can help project managers monitor the overall performance in all its aspects. Also, it enables them to monitor each task to see how well it performs in real-time and respond to any changes that occur to each of these tasks immediately. Monthly of Supply (MoS) BAM dashboard, is a live dashboard created for a global automotive Korean company which was facing problems with managing their global sales offices and plants. It uses two types of performance monitoring measurements, which are: MoS as KPI and equipment management process as BPM. MoS was used as a KPI to measure the performance of the current state of MoS to help in the decision-making process. Furthermore, they used equipment management process as a BPM, to help them monitor the state of the equipment used in real-time. The MoS BAM dashboard was split into three monitoring categories displayed by region, these categories are: minute-by-minute MoS value shown on the map of the world, levels of MoS value, and levels of the current inventory value [3].

Critical Chain Project Management (CCPM) is based on the Theory of Constraints (ToC) that considers a system as manageable when the most important constraint that gets in the way of achieving the project's goals has been identified and improved, until it's no longer a threat to the project's deadlines [4]. CCPM's most important aspect is the idea of activity duration estimation while keeping an eye on the constraints related to each activity such as resources, uncertainty, task duration overestimation, and unneeded safety margins. Furthermore, CCPM emphasizes the project's resources to provide the best project scheduling in order to reduce or minimize project delays; as well as provide more transparency of how the project is performing. Boeing, world's largest aerospace company, uses CCPM as an advanced methodology to manage their projects. Boeing admits that resource competition and uncertainty are unavoidable, resulting in their use of CCPM to limit the amount of work in progress by avoiding multitasking, prioritizing tasks, preventing task duration overestimation, and monitoring the remaining duration of critical tasks and the consumption of project-level buffers, and shift resources from non-critical tasks to critical ones [5].

Another solution is Report Generation Automation, which is the process of scheduling a report to automatically refresh and be delivered to specific places at a specific regular interval. Report automation eliminates the need to manually generate reports, reducing the possibility of errors and saving the team time to work on their project. Automating reports, daily or weekly, is done by scheduling them to be generated and sent directly to the manager. Where then, the manager will receive the customized reports that fit his need by automatically generating all data from any system, application, web, or internal database. Radiant Info Systems Ltd. uses report generation automation by applying the JReport tool to produce detailed, interactive reports and charts for planning on a daily, hourly or minute-by-minute basis. The available JReport pages are displayed immediately to the project manager; while the rest is processed in the background [6].

3 Research Methodology

According to the definition of Simon's Model for decision-making [7] (see Fig. 2). The process of making a decision is a sequence of distinct stages. The first phase is the intelligence phase where a problem or opportunity is identified. According to Simon's model, a problem is a situation that is not according to the rules or standards. While an opportunity is looking for a more promising solution to the current situation. In that sense the case study at hand represents a non-solved problem as tasks are not delivered on time and with lower quality. In the intelligence phase, a clear understanding of the problem/opportunity is established. Reality is evaluated to determine the need for making a decision. After that, the problem is formulated in terms of variables representing the different sub-problems and related decisions. The next step of Simon's model involves designing the model that is used to provide the solution. Here, the suggested dashboards are designed and built starting from the variables identified in the intelligence phase. The third step of Simon's model is Choice. At this stage, it is shown how users can make decision based on the suggested dashboards. Finally, implementation phase reports on the use of the dashboards by the business employees and how decisions are now made easily and effectively.

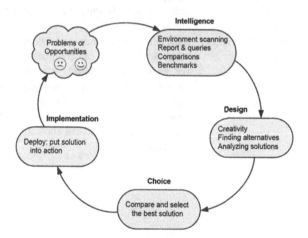

Fig. 2. Decision making process (adopted from [7])

4 Intelligence Phase

In this phase, information was collected about the management issues faced by the employees in Dolf Technologies. These problem are represented in the form of a typical decision making model i.e. decision variables, result variables and uncontrolled variables. Table 1 summarizes the intelligence phase.

Table 1. Problem model

Problem model		
Model components	Variables	Description
Decision variable	X1: Deadline of tasks for subproject 1. X2: Deadline of tasks for subproject 2. X3: Deadline of tasks for subproject 3.	The project manager will monitor the progress of the tasks, and based on the current delays, s/he will decide to extend the deadlines.
	X1: Human Resources for sub-project 1. X2: Human Resources for sub-project 2. X3: Human Resources for sub-project 3.	The project manager will monitor the progress of projects based on the performance of team members and find out which team is delaying the progress of the project by the frequency of delays to decide whether there's a shortage of team members.
Result variable	Y1: delivery time Y2: Quality	Result variable defines the quality of the solution or the alternative. That is, if given value of the decision variable is selected if it results to a good value of the result variable.
Uncontrollable variable	Customer cooperation	Some tasks require the reply of the customer; the ideal situation is where the customer is cooperating on time.
	Cultural differences	The cultural differences and different backgrounds of the team members can complicate the collaboration of the team, hence, affect the progress of the project.
Intermediate variable	Employee productivity	Reaching a high level of employee productivity is needed for the projects to be delivered on time and with high quality. Hence, employees productivity can identify the good/bad alternative as it influences the result variable.

Then, data have been collected from the company regarding their projects. The dataset is a simple excel progress sheet the members of the project share online. The dimensions of the subprojects are:

- **Phase**: The different stages of the projects, each with multiple tasks.
- **Courses**: A column representing the courses names, which are demonstrating the subprojects.
- **Task**: Different tasks names separated by phases.
- **[1-n]**: The weeks for the project where each week is a column the team can fill with "X" if they finished a part of the task in that week, eventually the number of Xs is expected to be equal to the number of required weeks.
- **Completed**: The weeks completed so far which is calculated by the sum of the filled cells of the weeks.
- **Required**: The weeks required to finish a task.

The dataset has been enhanced, there are fields that have been added in order to implement the solutions. The fields are as specified below:

- **%done of the task**: Percentage of the of progress of each task which is the completed weeks divided by the required weeks.
- **Deadline**: The date where this task must be done in order to decide if the task is overdue.
- **Today**: A cell that calculates today's date.
- **Scale**: The percentage (100%).
- **Overdue**: A cell that calculates today's date and the deadline, if the day has surpassed the deadline and the task is not completed (completed weeks are not equal to the required weeks) then it is an overdue task (True).
- **Sum**: The total number of %done tasks.
- **%Total Done**: A cell that calculates the percentage of **total done** tasks divided by the number of all the tasks.
- **Project team**: A column that summarizes the project teams that are working on each project, each with different members divided among the different project phases.

5 Design Phase

Dolf PMRD consists of two dashboards, an operational dashboard and a more abstract managerial dashboard; both created using Tableau. The operational dashboard mostly visualizes information in a per-task manner; where it has a horizontal task progress bars section and a task deadline section, both showing the progress of each task, and the color for each task indicates how much it has left to the deadline. If the color is red, it means that the tasks are overdue and need deadline extension. However, if the color of the tasks is green, it means that the tasks still have time before its deadline or are done within the deadline. These two sections are repeated to show the visualizations for each sub project. This dashboard also includes an overall project progress bar, shown separately for each sub-project, indicating the percentage work done for each one.

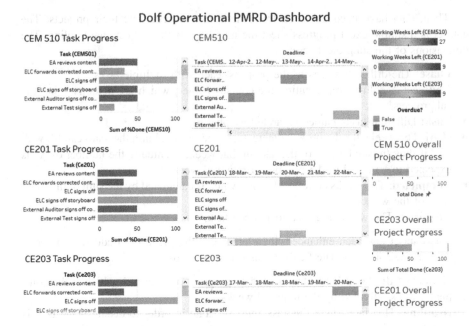

Fig. 3. Dolf operational dashboard

Using this dashboard, operational manager will be able to view tasks for each sub-project, and the weeks left on each task. If a task is delayed, by viewing the remaining weeks needed to finish working on each task and decide to increase it; assuming that the required weeks of the tasks do not increase the subproject's deadline. By changing the deadlines earlier, it can help in steering the project back on track and allows it to finish on time (Fig. 3).

The managerial dashboard on the other hand, is an abstraction of the operational dashboard; it will be used to discover the delays in the projects held by different team members. It shows vertical progress bars; each visualizes the frequency of delays in tasks that each sub-project has. Furthermore, the pie chart on the left, shows the percentage of completed tasks for each sub-project in a different colored slice.

Using this dashboard will help the manager to decide which task is delaying the phase, so they can decide what action needs to be taken in terms of assigning extra team members, developing certain skills, or acquiring more resources for the task to be finished on time (Fig. 4).

Dolf Managerial PMRD Dashboard

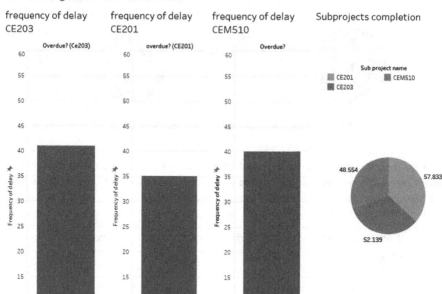

Fig. 4. Dolf managerial dashboard

6 Choice Phase

During the choice phase, an alternative (solution to the problem) rather than another can be selected by the user based on the criteria of the choice. The latter in the case study in hand are represented by the result variables. For instance, a manager set the list of required human resources in a way that maximizes the quality of the output. Similarly, the deadlines are specified in way that ensures the are going to be met with decreasing the quality. This is achieved through the effective monitoring both dashboards are offering.

7 Implementation

The dashboard has been deployed on Windows computers using Tableau 2019.1 trial version. After about ten days of the deployment, a survey was sent in order to get their feedback on the dashboard. Due to the small number of answers, the results varied and are as the follows:

Starting with the employee's demographics, majority of the employees who answered the survey were young adults ranging from 20–35, who mostly worked in the company for less than a year; while the rest range from 36–51 years old and worked in the company for more than 6 years (Fig. 5).

Fig. 5. Screenshots of analysis for questions 1 and 2

After that, the employees were asked about if they were satisfied with the previous project management method; half of the employees answered that they were satisfied with the previous method, while the other half were not (Fig. 6).

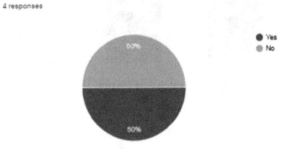

Fig. 6. Screenshots of analysis for question 3

Afterwards, they were asked to rate their agreement to the following questions:

- "After using the new dashboard, I rarely miss a deadline or delay of a task I have", half of them strongly agreed to it; while the other half disagreed (Fig. 7).

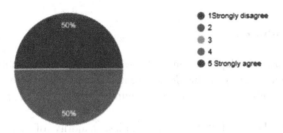

Fig. 7. Screenshots of analysis for question 4

- "After using the dashboard, I am able to organize my tasks with the others better", 50% of the employees strongly agreed, while 25% were neural and the other 25% were strongly disagreed (Fig. 8).

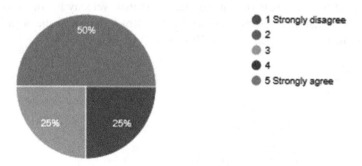

Fig. 8. Screenshots of analysis for question 5

- "After using the dashboard, I am able to efficiently manage my schedule to finish all task within the deadline", 25% of the company's employees strongly agreed and 50% agreed; while 25% disagree with that statement (Fig. 9).

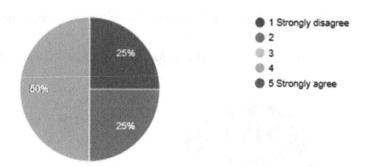

Fig. 9. Screenshots of analysis for question 6

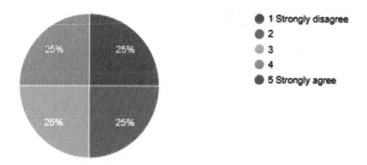

Fig. 10. Screenshots of analysis for question 7

- "The overall performance of the project management has been improved?". 25% of the employees disagreed, 25% were neural, 25% agreed, and the other 25% strongly agreed with the previous statement (Fig. 10).
- "My tasks velocity has increased approximately:", the employees rated the increase as, 50% of the them believe that they increased their velocity by 70%–100%, and 25% believe that their velocity has increased by 40%–60%; while the other 25% has believe their velocity increased by 10%–30% (Fig. 11).

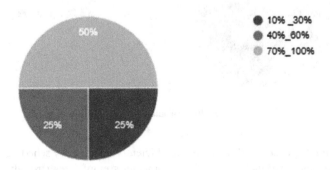

Fig. 11. Screenshots of analysis for question 8

Then, when they were asked for their opinions on the following yes/no questions, they all gave the same answers; which were yes.

- "Do you see yourself using this dashboard for the next 5 years?" (Fig. 12)

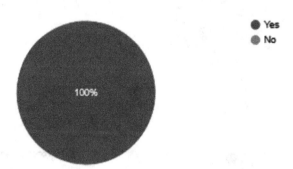

Fig. 12. Screenshots of analysis for question 9

- "Would you recommend this solution to other companies?" (Fig. 13)

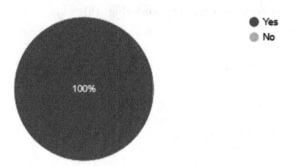

Fig. 13. Screenshots of analysis for question 10

- "Was the dashboard easy to understand?" (Fig. 14)

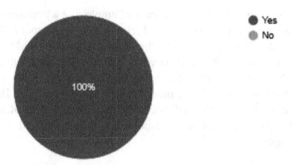

Fig. 14. Screenshots of analysis for question 11

- "Did the dashboard include all the needed information that would help you increase the efficiency of your tasks?" (Fig. 15)

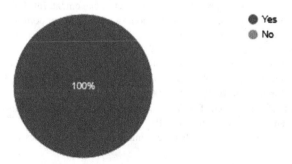

Fig. 15. Screenshots of analysis for question 12

Lastly, their answers on the question "How did these solutions compare to your expectations?" were positive saying that it met their expectations, was user friendly, helpful, and a great aid to manage their work (Fig. 16).

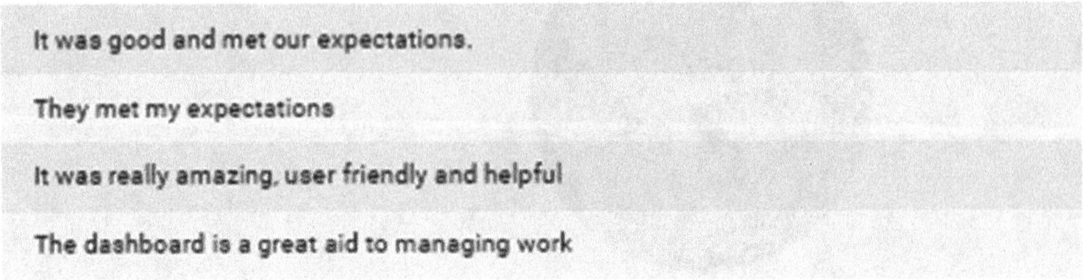

It was good and met our expectations.

They met my expectations

It was really amazing, user friendly and helpful

The dashboard is a great aid to managing work

Fig. 16. Screenshots of analysis for question 14

8   Conclusion

In conclusion, this paper has reported the case of employing a performance monitoring dashboard for project management in Dolf Technologies. The paper followed a typical decision making methodology to explain the different stages of building and utilizing the dashboards. As part of this, a deployment survey has been launched to collect feedback about the dashboard from the employers. In general, it has been concluded that most of the feedback of the implemented dashboard was positive. However, due to the short period during which the feedback is collected, the number of responses is not high. In fact, it is expected that more responses will be generated by the final submission of this paper.

References

1. https://linkedin.com/company/dolf-technologies. Accessed: 20 Feb 2019
2. Altahtooh, U.A.: Time error in project management: a case study in Yanbu, Saudi Arabia. Bus. Manag. Stud. **2**(1), 58–64 (2016)
3. Khaled, E.E., Gunes, K.A.: Applied software project management. Int. J. Proj. Manag. (2004)
4. Kang, J.G., Han, K.H.: A business activity monitoring system supporting real-time business performance management. In: Proceedings - 3rd International Conference on Convergence and Hybrid Information Technology, ICCIT 2008 (2008)
5. Rezaie, K., Manouchehrabadi, B., Shirkouhi, S.N.: Duration estimation, a new approach in critical chain scheduling. In: Proceedings - 2009 3rd Asia International Conference on Modelling and Simulation, AMS 2009 (2009)
6. Reporting Software Designed for Your Applications. https://www.jinfonet.com/product/reporting-software/. Accessed: 16 Jun 2019
7. Sharda, R., Delen, D., Turban, E.: Business intelligence and analytics business intelligence and analytics:

Neural Iris Signature Recognition (NISR)

Ali Mehdi[1], Safaa Ahmad[2], Rawand Abu Roza[2],
Mohammed Alawairdhi[3], and Mousa Al-Akhras[2,3(✉)]

[1] Department of Computer Science, University of London, London, UK
[2] King Abdullah II School of Information Technology,
The University of Jordan, Amman, Jordan
mousa.akhras@ju.edu.jo
[3] College of Computing and Informatics, Saudi Electronic University, Riyadh,
Kingdom of Saudi Arabia
{malawairdhi,m.akhras}@seu.edu.sa

Abstract. The security and the proper identification of individuals are vital requirements for many different applications. Biometric systems in general provide automatic recognition and identification of individuals taking advantage of the unique features of every individual. Iris recognition has a great advantage over other biometric recognition techniques, due to its huge variability of patterns among individuals. Consequently, Iris recognition tasks, even on a large database like the Chinese Academy of Sciences' Institute of Automation (CASIA) can be searched without finding a false match. The objective of this research is to create an iris recognition system with high accuracy. This is achieved by utilizing Daugman algorithm and other techniques.

Keywords: Iris · Pattern recognition · Daugman · Canny operator · Hough transform algorithm

1 Introduction

Biometric systems provide automatic recognition and identification of individuals taking advantage of the unique characteristics or features possessed by every person. Different biometric systems have been built using various techniques that include fingerprints, facial recognition, voice recognition, hand geometry, handwriting, the retina and the iris as presented in this research. Eye's iris is the colored portion of the eye. Iris region is located between the pupil and the white sclera as shown in Fig. 1. In the first processing stage of this research, an image file of a human eye is read and displayed on a display screen. Then the image of the iris is extracted from the rest of the eye region. In order to perform this extraction accurately, the pupil, the iris and the eyelids need to be identified.

In the second processing stage, the features of the iris pattern are calculated using Daugman algorithm. This well-known algorithm was chosen for iris recognition as it provides high accuracy [1]. An iris template is obtained from the proposed system and is tested against templates stored in the database until either: (1) a match is found; thus, the person is identified, or (2) a match is not found; thus, the person is declared unidentifiable.

© Springer Nature Switzerland AG 2019
A. Alfaries et al. (Eds.): ICC 2019, CCIS 1098, pp. 241–251, 2019.
https://doi.org/10.1007/978-3-030-36368-0_20

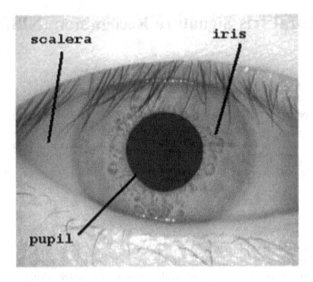

Fig. 1. The human eye

The rest of this paper is organized as follows. Section 2 presents the related work. Section 3 describes the proposed system while Sect. 4 details the methodology for Iris recognition. The matching methodology is described in Sect. 5 while conclusions are presented in Sect. 6.

2   Related Work

Cruz et al. used Daugman algorithm on Raspberry Pi, to develop an Iris Recognition device with the aim of enabling more applications for iris recognition [1]. Their research applied some image processing techniques to process the image before passing it to the application to enable system adaptation to the limitations of Raspberry Pi. Their system rejected registered actors more than accepting impostors due to the hardware limitations. This was achieved based on the tests implementation, the False Acceptance Rate (FAR) and False Rejection Rate (FRR).

Singh et al. [2] described some techniques to create an Iris Recognition System. They utilized a fusion mechanism, which is a combination of Circular Hough Transform and Canny Edge Detection. The purpose of this combination was to detect iris boundaries in digital images of the eyes. They also applied Haar wavelet to extract iris patterns as feature vectors. Finally, Hamming Distance operator was implemented to compare the quantized vectors to determine whether the two irises are similar.

The paper presented by Jan et al. [3] presented an iris localization algorithm that includes: (1) suppressing specular reflections, (2) localizing the boundaries of pupil and iris circles in two stages, and (3) regularizing the boundaries of iris circle by applying radial gradients and active contours. The authors claim that their work accepts off-axis eye images, glasses, contact lenses, non-uniform lighting, specular reflections, eye-lashes, eyelids occlusions as well as hair.

In a recent research conducted by Gaxiola et al. [4], a modular deep neural network architecture was applied for recognizing individuals by their iris patterns. This architecture consists of three modules, each one works with a deep neural network. Their algorithm works with an iris database. Pre-processing techniques extract the area of interest allowing the removal of the noise surrounding the iris. The pre-processed iris images are used as inputs to the modular deep neural network, while the output is the identified individual.

3   System Description

The proposed system contains iris recognition, an enrollment interface and a repository system. The image of a person eye is either added to the system or checked to see whether the person can use the system. If the person is enrolled for the first time, the image will be sent to the iris recognition system to save the iris to the templates database and the personal account information is saved to the repository system. In the event of checking the validity of the person, the image is pre-processed so that the iris features are extracted and compared with the stored templates in the templates database to find a match; if there is a match, the repository system will open the client's account as illustrated in Fig. 2. Table 1 describes the components of the proposed system.

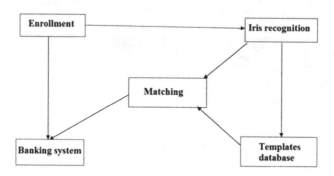

Fig. 2. System's Description

Table 1. The components of the proposed system.

Component	Description
Enrollment	• This sub system allows existing clients to sign in/new clients to sign up
Iris recognition	• This sub system makes a pattern template for the iris by localizing the iris region, normalizing and extracting the iris features
Matching	• This sub system attempts to make a match between the new pattern and the patterns stored in the templates database
Repository system	• This sub system provides clients with the possibility to reading/writing images from/to their account. Repository database is connected to the templates database
Templates database	• This database contains the client number with two images for each client (2 templates and 2 masks)

4   Methodology of Iris Recognition

To automate the recognition of iris patterns, three main tasks need to be performed: (1) identify the location of the iris in an image. (2) convert iris information into a template that can be calculated such as a biometric template. (3) the data must be stored in order to load and compare these conversions. The three tasks are illustrated in Fig. 3.

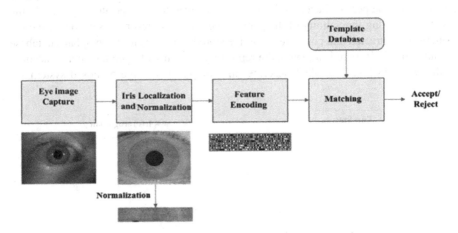

Fig. 3. Iris Recognition system

4.1   Eye Capture

The eyes database (CASIA-IrisV4) [5] is used as shown in Fig. 4. This version of the database, which is an extension of CASIA-IrisV3, contains six subsets. CASIA-IrisV4 contains the three subsets from CASIA-IrisV3 that are CASIA-Iris-Interval, CASIA-Iris-Lamp, and CASIA-Iris-Twins, as well as three other subsets which are CASIA-Iris-Distance, CASIA-Iris-Thousand, and CASIA-Iris-Syn [5]. CASIA-IrisV4 includes

54,607 iris images in total that are combination of more than 1,800 actual subjects and 1,000 virtual subjects. Iris images in the database consist of 8-bit gray-level files in JPEG format, collected under near infrared illumination.

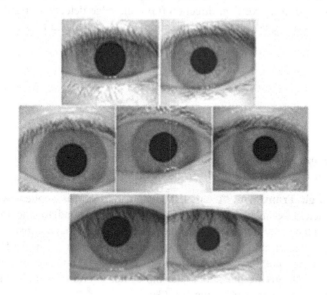

Fig. 4. Samples from the CASIA database

4.2   Iris Localization

In order to locate the iris and the eyelids, a Hough transform algorithm is used on the eye's edge map, which is extracted using the Canny edge detection algorithm from the original eye image. Hough transform algorithm can be implemented in order to spot the parameters of simple geometric objects such as lines and circles present in an image. The localization stages are illustrated in Fig. 5.

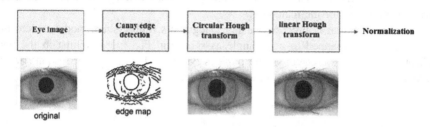

Fig. 5. Localization stages

Canny Edge Detection. To make optimal edge detection of circles and lines, canny edge detection is utilized. Any edge in an image can point in any direction, the Canny algorithm implements four different filters in order to locate the horizontal, the vertical and the diagonal edges in the blurred image [6]. For the first derivative in the horizontal direction (Gy) and in the vertical direction (Gx), the edge detection operator returns a value. Then the edge gradient and the direction can be calculated by Eqs. (1) and (2), respectively:

$$G = \sqrt{G_x^2 + G_y^2} \tag{1}$$

$$\theta = tan^{-1} \frac{G_y}{G_x} \tag{2}$$

The edge map is resulted by calculating the first derivatives of intensity values in an eye image and then set a threshold for the result.

Circular Hough Transform. A Circular Hough transform is applied twice, first to find the iris/sclera boundary from the whole eye, and second to find the pupil/iris boundary from the iris region. For each edge point, Circular Hough transform will draw a circle using different radii in the Hough space. The highest point in the Hough space resembles the radius and the center coordinates of the circle that is best defined by the edge points [7]. By giving the radius and the center coordinates, drawing the circle becomes fairly straight forward using Eq. (3):

$$x_c^2 + y_c^2 - r^2 = 0 \tag{3}$$

Linear Hough Transform. In the Linear Hough transform, vertical edge map is used to detect the eyelid. The algorithm works by drawing a line on the edge at the intersection point with the iris circle.

4.3 Normalization

In this stage the iris is transformed into a fixed dimensional image, so that all the irises have the same size for the matching.

The normalization is processed using Daugman's rubber sheet model, where the circular region is mapped to a rectangle as shown in Fig. 6 [8]. Whilst in the normalization process, the center of the pupil is considered as a reference point; meanwhile, the radial vectors circle through the iris region.

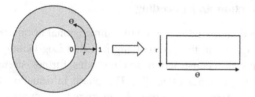

Fig. 6. Daugman's rubber sheet model [8]

The homogenous rubber sheet model developed by Daugman algorithm, re-maps each point within the iris region to a pair of polar coordinates (r, θ) such that r is in the interval [0, 1] and θ is the angle [0, 2π].

The re-mapping conducted on the iris region from (x, y) cartesian coordinates to the normalized non-concentric polar representation is modeled as:

$$I(x(r,\theta), y(r,\theta)) \rightarrow I(r,\theta) \tag{4}$$

With

$$x(r,\theta) = (1-r)x_p(\theta) + rx_l(\theta) \tag{5}$$

$$y(r,\theta) = (1-r)y_p(\theta) + ry_l(\theta) \tag{6}$$

Where I(x, y) is the image of the iris region, (x, y) are the actual Cartesian coordinates, (r, θ) are the corresponding normalized polar coordinates, and xp, yp and xl, yl are the coordinates of the pupil and iris boundaries along the θ direction. The result of the normalization process is shown in Fig. 7.

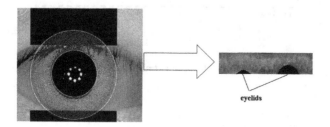

Fig. 7. Normalization process

4.4   Feature Extraction and Encoding

Feature extraction is done by reducing the two-dimensional normalized iris pattern into a one-dimensional signal and then convolving it with a Log-Gabor wavelet transform, which enables identical reconstruction and provides further strength to the mathematical properties of the Gabor filters [9]. The phase information that is resulted for both the real and the imaginary responses is quantized, generating a bitwise template using Daugman algorithm.

The angular and the radial resolutions are adjusted to be 240 and 20 pixels, respectively. There are two bits that are used to represent the quantized phase information for each pixel. Finally, the total size of the iris template is 9600 bits as illustrated in Fig. 8.

The features extracted from the iris are stored into a database for future use when a person needs to be identified. Each person has two images (2 templates and 2 masks). Sample results are presented in Fig. 9.

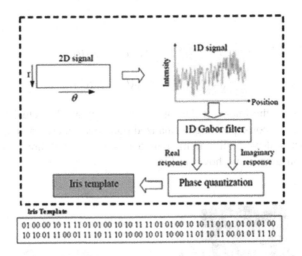

Fig. 8. Feature extraction stages

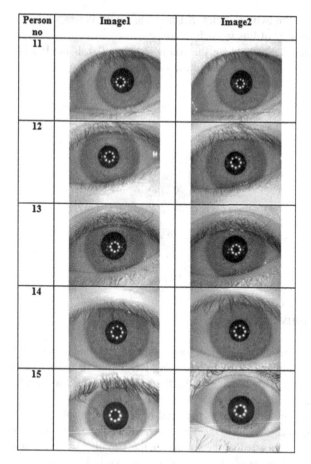

Fig. 9. Eye images of the persons used in the template database

5   Matching Methodology

Comparison between the two irises is done using Hamming Distance (HD) which measures the number of disagreeing bits between two binary patterns [10].

The local binary pattern operator is an image operator that performs a transformation process on the image into an array or image of integer labels describing certain parts of the image. These labels are then used for further image analysis represented by matching.

The methodology compares the use of the iris code data and the noisy mask bits, the adjusted form of the HD is denoted by:

$$HD = \frac{1}{N - \sum_{k=1}^{N} Xn_k(OR)Yn_k} \sum_{j=1}^{N} X_j(XOR)Y_j(AND)Xn_j'(AND)Yn_j' \qquad (7)$$

Xj and Yj are the two iris codes, Xn_j and Yn_j are the corresponding noisy mask bits and N is the number of bits in each template.

The verification threshold for the HD is less than 0.4. If the HD is more than 0.4, then there is no matching between these two irises.

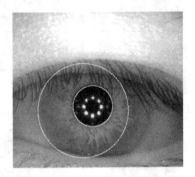

Fig. 10. Wrong localization

6 Conclusions

The objective of this research is to create a system that functions as an iris recognition tool utilizing Daugman algorithm and other techniques in order to produce a system with high accuracy. This is achieved by the successful use of localization process and the matching methodology.

Over one hundred eye images are used in our experiments. Since the localization depends on the image quality, the percentage of successful localization is 91%. The common error encountered is the failure of the Circular Hough transform wrapping around the circumference of the iris image as shown in Fig. 10.

References

1. Cruz, F., et al.: Iris recognition using Daugman algorithm on Raspberry Pi. In: 2016 IEEE Region 10 Conference (TENCON), pp. 2126–2129. Singapore (2016)
2. Singh, N., Gandhi, D., Singh, K.: Iris recognition system using a canny edge detection and a circular hough transform. Int. J. Adv. Eng. Tech. 2(2), 221–228 (2011)
3. Jan, F., Usman, I., Agha, S.: Iris localization in frontal eye images for less constrained iris recognition systems. Elsevier J. Dig. Sig. Proc. 22(6), 971–986 (2012)
4. Gaxiola, F., Melin, P., Valdez, F., Castro, J.R.: Person recognition with modular deep neural network using the Iris biometric measure. In: Castillo, O., Melin, P., Kacprzyk, J. (eds.) Fuzzy Logic Augmentation of Neural and Optimization Algorithms: Theoretical Aspects and Real Applications. SCI, vol. 749, pp. 69–80. Springer, Cham (2018). https://doi.org/10.1007/978-3-319-71008-2_6
5. Center for Biometrics and Security Research. http://www.cbsr.ia.ac.cn/china/Iris%20Data bases%20CH.asp. Accessed 29 May 2019

6. Fu, F., Wang, C., Li, Y., Fan, H.: An improved adaptive edge detection algorithm based on Canny. In: the Sixth International Conference on Optical and Photonic Engineering (icOPEN 2018), Shanghai, China (2018)

7. Okokpujie, K., Noma-Osaghae, E., John, S., Ajulibe, A.: An Improved Iris segmentation technique using circular hough transform. In: Kim, K.J., Kim, H., Baek, N. (eds.) ICITS 2017. LNEE, vol. 450, pp. 203–211. Springer, Singapore (2018). https://doi.org/10.1007/978-981-10-6454-8_26

8. Johar, T., Kaushik, P.: Iris segmentation and normalization using Daugman's rubber sheet model. Int. J. Sci. Tech. Adv. 1(1), 11–14 (2015)

9. Fischer, S., Šroubek, F., Perrinet, L., Redondo, R., Cristóbal, G.: Self-invertible 2D log-gabor wavelets. Int. J. Comput. Vis. 75(2), 231–246 (2007)

10. Riley, R., Graham, J., Baldwin, R., Fisher, A.: Register Hamming distance from side channels. In: Proceedings of SPIE Cyber Sensing, May (2018)

Healthcare Information System Assessment Case Study Riyadh's Hospitals-KSA

Muna Elsadig[1,2(✉)], Dua' A. Nassar[1(✉)],
and Leila Jamel Menzli[1,3(✉)]

[1] Information Systems Department, College of Computer and Information
Sciences, Princess Nourah Bint Abdulrahman University, Riyadh, Saudi Arabia
{Memohamedahmed, Danassar, lmjamel}@pnu.edu.sa
[2] College of Computer Science and Mathematics, University of Bahri,
Khartoum, Sudan
[3] Laboratory RIADI-GDL, ENSI, University of Manouba, Manouba, Tunisia

Abstract. The assessment and evaluation of information system's quality is vital and necessary. Health information system (HIS) is broadly spread and usage. Nowadays, HIS is attaining reputation importance and a boundless potential for developing countries. HIS has espoused by diversities healthcare providers to convey a qualified patient safety, patient healthcare services, efficient and effectiveness patient care, minimum medical faults, and patient satisfaction by gaining access to truthful information at anytime and anywhere. In KSA, many hospitals adopted HIS so it is becoming essential to evaluate the quality of these systems. This work implements Delone & McLean (D&M) quality model to evaluate the quality of HIS systems in Riyadh in order to sustain the quality of patient care and improve it if required. Delone & McLean quality model is the most validated and popular model used to qualify the factors of success of HIS system. The main objective is to assess the HIS placed in KSA hospitals, which leads to higher quality for patient healthcare. This study emphases on six interrelated measurements of IS success criteria that have been specified by the model. These measurement criteria are information quality, system quality, user satisfaction, services quality, use and net benefits. According to D&M model, these factors interrelated and has positively effect to each other.c In this study, a questionnaire is disseminated to all possible stakeholders of HIS in four hospitals in Riyadh. The analysis of the results gathered from the questionnaire is conducted to validate the success of HIS and to recover the HIS Quality in KSA Hospital.

Keywords: Health information system · Information system quality models · Delone & McLean model

1 Introduction

Recently, Health care providers are oriented to use Health information systems, which become essential applications to demonstrate basic services for health informatics platforms. It provides services that increase the qualified, effectiveness and efficiency of patient's health care delivery by guaranteeing that the information generated is of a high quality. Varieties of factors can affect the total quality of HIS such as information

© Springer Nature Switzerland AG 2019
A. Alfaries et al. (Eds.): ICC 2019, CCIS 1098, pp. 252–262, 2019.
https://doi.org/10.1007/978-3-030-36368-0_21

quality, system quality, user satisfaction, services quality...etc. Several models have been constructed to evaluate the success and the quality of information systems such as Delone & McLean quality model [1], Technology Acceptance Model (TAM) Davis's model [2], and ISO Quality model [3]. These models measure varieties of factors. The embracing and acceptance of Healthcare information system need to be reinforced by confirmation the success quality of these systems. Delone & McLean quality model is the furthermost validated and popular model used to measure the factor of success of HIS. In KSA mainly the capital Riyadh government's hospitals and private hospitals adopted HIS. In This paper an analysis will be conducted to improve the HIS Quality in KSA Hospitals by focusing on six interrelated dimensions of IS success that have been specified by the Delone and Mclean model.

The introduction section of this paper presents IS, HIS quality models and their significance. A background about information system Quality models is then detailed. Section three deliberates and describes the research methodology using Delone and Mclean model in details. Finally, the results obtained are analyzed, discussed and conclusion is inferred.

2   Background

During the last three decades, many Quality models are introduced. In 1989, Davis proposed Technology acceptance model (TAM) in his doctorate thesis. The TAM model established on theory of reasoned action (TRA) that has been used to clarify individual's acceptance behavior [2, 4]. User's behavior is the key factors in IS that TAM model based on the perceived ease of use factors and the perceived usefulness factor. The TAM used to study the Technology acceptance model, which has been used to investigate the individual technology acceptance behavior in diversities of information systems.

In 1991, International Standards organization generated ISO/IEC 9126:1991 model for Software system and engineering system Products quality, which was established to support the systems quality needs. It distinguished six quality characteristics and described system and software product evaluation process model. The International Standard organization revised ISO/IEC 9126-1: in 2001, and incorporates the same software quality characteristics with some amendments [5]. In 2011, The Canadian Standards Association (CSA) and The Standards Council of Canada (SCC) introduced the ISO model for engineering Systems and software Quality Requirements and Evaluation i.e. (SQuaRE) System and software quality models. The SQuaRE are series of International Standards (ISO/IEC 25000 to ISO/IEC 25099) which consists of characteristics and sub characteristics, for computer system quality, and software product quality [6, 7]. Both ISO (the International Organization for Standardization) and IEC (the International Electro technical Commission) form the specialized system for worldwide standardization are responsible for generating the ISO/IEC205010 [8]. The model is applicable to both computer systems and software products and is composed of eight characteristics. Those characteristics defined by this model are relevant to all software products and computer systems. The characteristics and sub characteristics provide consistent terminology for specifying, measuring and evaluating system and software product quality. The eight quality characteristics are: functional stability, performance efficiency, compatibility, usability, reliability, security, maintainability, portability. These eight characteristics are independent of users and context.

In 1992, the D&M model has been developed, which has a different viewpoint from TAM model. Researchers (Delone and Mclean) tried to bring perception and arrangement to the "dependent variable" – information systems success factors - in IS Quality research. The D&M IS Success Model, was based on theoretical and empirical IS researches conducted by a number of researchers on the period between1970 to1980. The D&M model has been applied and validated diverse IS [1, 9, 10].

Later in 2003, DeLone and McLean reexamined their own model and prepared minor modifications to it by adding new factor which create a new dimension [9, 11]. Moreover, In 2102 D&M have introduced an integrated success model that integrated (TAM) and D&M updated model [12]. Subsequently, ten dimensions were anticipated for measuring information system success.

The measurement of IS success and its effectiveness are critical to recognize of the significance and efficiency of IS management actions and IS investments. Different researches used the different models to measure the HIS quality [13–18]. Most of them used the updated model of Delone and Maclean, which works on measuring the success of IS. They found the model of Delone & Maclean is a good one, which can be used to make precise assessment and evaluation for HIS. [14, 15, 17–19]. Some studies adopted Delone and Maclean model to assess and evaluate the Electronic Health Record (EHR) in developing and developed countries such the studies conducted on the Ethiopian HIS [14] and the public Korean hospitals [17]. Petter and Fruhling also applied Delone and Maclean to assess emergency information system [18]. The main objective of this research is to apply the updated D&M model to study the quality of HIS system in Riyadh hospitals' in KSA, which aims to:

- Measure the success factors of the HIS in Riyadh, KSA.
- Assess and validate the Quality of HIS in Riyadh, KSA.

3   Research Methodolgy

In this work, we use the updated Delone and Mclean [14] to evaluate four Riyadh's hospitals King Abodullah hospital, King Fahad Medical City, King Abdulaziz medical City and one private hospital. The model specified six major interrelated concepts of information systems success factors, which are the quality dimensions (system, information, and service quality), the two dimensions affect the system use and user satisfaction and finally for last quality dimension, The Net user satisfaction. The most important in the correlation is the hypotheses that all the factors affect positively as mentioned below in the model. The structure of the model concepts and their incentive are detailed in [1, 13, 15]. The model dimensions are explained as follows:

- System quality: which is used to measure the attributes of the HIS.
- Service quality: which aims to measure the term of the quality of the services support extracted by HIS's developer.
- Information quality: which aims to measure the value of Health information and the health information system characteristics provided by HIS, i.e. accuracy, reliability,

and trustworthiness, which help to study operationalized information quality in terms of the correctness, usefulness and timeliness of the information generated by the hospital information system in use.

- Intention to use: this is concerned by evaluating the way HIS is used.
- User satisfaction: it is one of the most important measures of systems success and is usually measured by overall HIS user satisfaction.
- Net benefits: this is a consideration of the most important measures of HIS success, and it constitutes the extent to which an HIS contributes to the success of various stakeholders, whether positive or negative.

To assess the success factors HIS system, HIS system must be tested and assumed against the hypotheses proposed by Delone and Maclean success Model.

The construction and interrelationship between the criteria to be measure are shown in Fig. 1.

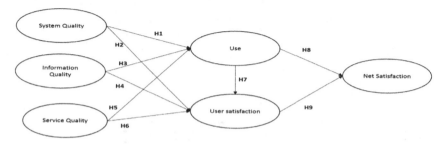

Fig. 1. Updated Delone and McLean model (2003) [9] and Research hypothesis.

The following hypotheses were assumed and tested:

H1: HIS quality will positively affect use.
H2: HIS quality will positively affect user satisfaction.
H3: Health Information quality will positively affect use.
H4: Health Information quality will positively affect user satisfaction.
H5: Service quality will positively affect use.
H6: Service quality will positively affect user satisfaction.
H7: HIS Use will positively affect user satisfaction.
H8: HIS Use will positively affect perceived net benefit.
H9: User satisfaction will positively affect perceived net benefit.

4 Result and Discussion

For effective and statistics results, a survey has been conducted and distributed to all HIS stakeholders in four Riyadh hospitals mentioned in Sect. 3. Both online and paper-based questionnaires (Appendix A) are distributed to about 578 HIS stakeholders, including doctors, nurses, receptionist, patients. The total number of retained responses is about 210.

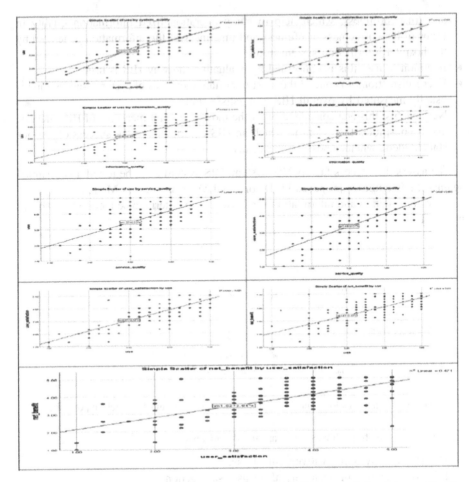

Fig. 2. The correlations' r-values scatter show the positive linear correlation between Quality factors as stated in H1-H9

The questionnaire includes 24 questions which have been divided into six sections based according to the six quality dimensions of IS success measures as mentioned in Sect. 3. The first one is related to "system quality" and it contains four questions. The second section is "information quality", and it has four questions. The third section is "service quality" and it has four questions as well. The fourth section is "Use" that contains four questions. The fifth section, which refers to "user satisfaction", and it contains three questions. The last section is related to net benefit and is evaluated through five questions.

In this questionnaire, a Five Likert scale is used. i.e. strongly agree, Agree, Neutral, Disagree and Totally disagree (Appendix A).

To analyze the gathered data the Statistical Package for Social Science (SPSS) is used to calculate the correlation coefficient and the regression value in order to check whether the hypotheses H1 to H9 are approved or no. The correlation between criteria are graphically represented Fig. 2. Each graphs show the linear positive correlation between the criteria as H1 to H9 stated. These results are obtained, and discussed in work done by the authors in [20].

Figure 2. shows the strong positive correlation between two dimensions according to the hypothesis. The analysis in this study is to calculate the correlation r- value that should range from −1 as a perfect negative correlation to 1 as perfect positive correlation due to the rule of thumbs from Akoglu [21].

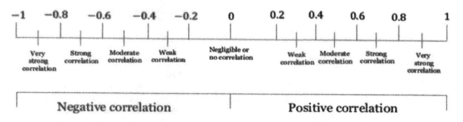

Fig. 3. Pearson's correlation coefficient interpretation [21]

The interpretation of the correlation coefficient is analyzed using the Pearson's correlation coefficient as explained in Fig. 3. The obtained results of r-value are shown in Table 1. The results show that the health information system in Riyadh hospital is with high quality as the success of the factors conferring from Delone and Maclean quality model has positive effect.

This inference is obtained using the regression values for all hypothesis with 0000 and all the correlation coefficients are >0.5. This means that the strength of the relationship is strong in most relationships. The observed relationship strength between dimensions show significance to others. The less correlation factor was the service quality with the use dimension 0.640 which means that some improvement is needed.

Table 1. The r-value for H1 - H9

Hypotheses	r-value	Result assessment
H1	0.697	System quality has a positive effect on use is true
H2	0.752	System quality has a positive effect on user satisfaction is true
H3	0.714	Information quality has positive effect on use is true
H4	0.737	Information quality has positive effect on user satisfactions true
H5	0.640	services quality has positive effect on use is true
H6	0.682	Services quality has positive effect on user satisfactions true
H7	0.830	Use will positively affect user satisfaction
H8	0.702	Use will positively affect perceived net benefit
H9	0.686	User satisfaction will positively affect perceived net benefit

While the high positive value is 0.83, which means that there is high positive effect between the use and user satisfaction. All correlation coefficient less than 0.7 need to be improved to reach the higher positive effects [20].

Further testing is carried out by evaluating each criteria and its sub criteria. All the 24 sub criteria in the survey are tested and evaluated by calculating the mean values and standard deviation values. The obtained values are represented in Fig. 4. All the mean values of the sub criteria are above the assumed average value which 2.5. The mean values from "3 to 4" indicate the need for more improvement to achieve the optimal performance.

Table 2 shows the overall mean value calculated for each criteria. The results show that they are above the average.

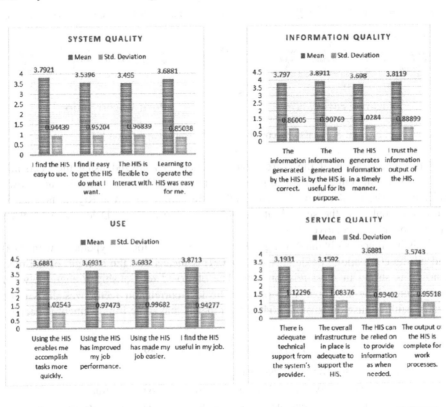

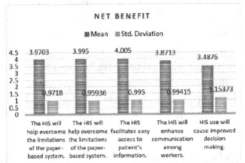

Fig. 4. The representation of the ean value and standard deviation of the 6 criteria and 24 sub – criteria

The highest achieved success factor is the net benefits, which is about 3.8469 out of 5. However, the lowest 3.4487 out of 5 is related to service quality. According to these values HIS in Riyadh hospitals - KSA need to pay more attention to the service quality and to search for improvements solutions.

Table 2. The assessment of the overall mean value for the quality criteria

Criterion	The overall mean value	Result assessments
System Quality	3.6287	Greater than 2.5 the System Quality achieved is above the average
Information Quality	3.7995	Greater than 2.5 the Information Quality achieved is above the average
Service Quality	3.4487	Greater than 2.5 the Service Quality achieved is above the average
Use	3.7339	Greater than 2.5 the Use achieved is above the average
User satisfaction	3.6518	Greater than 2.5 the user Satisfaction achieved is above the average
Net Benefits	3.8469	Greater than 2.5 the Net benefits achieved is above the average

5 Conclusion and Future Work

In KSA, HIS provides many services to improve the effectiveness and efficiency of patient care delivery. The required patient care can be achieved by ensuring the high quality of generated information and health care process. The adoption of Healthcare information system need to be supported by validating the success of the quality's criteria of these systems. The quality and success factors of HIS in KSA were measured by using the updated Delone and Maclean Model. The conducted case study, through four hospitals in the Riyadh city, shows significant results and recommendations. In fact, the obtained results show that all six quality criteria are connected and has a positive linear correlation i.e. all the correlation factors for all criteria are high and greater than 0.5, where the min is 0.64 for "services quality has positive effect on use". Meanwhile, the max is 0. 83 for "Use will positively affect user satisfaction". These results show that the quality of HIS is high. The "Service quality" and "Use" Criteria need additional improvements to capture uppermost of health care performance in KSA. All mean values of the overall criteria and sub criteria are above the average value, which is 2.5.

As conclusion, since four hospital in Riyadh successfully implement and adopted HIS with high quality, a unified HIS can be used and implemented in all hospitals in KSA with high quality. for future work, a new quality model can be introduce by adding new quality criteria or integrating ISO model with updated D&M model to assess the quality of Health Care Information system.

Acknowledgments. This research was funded by the Deanship of Scientific Research at Princess Nourah bint Abdulrahman University through the Fast-track Research Funding Program.

Appendix a

QUESTIONNAIRE ABOUT HEALTHCARE INFORMAION SYSTEM (HIS):

	Strongly agree	Agree	Neutral	Disagree	Strongly disagree
I find the HIS easy to use.					
I find it easy to get the HIS do what I want.					
The HIS is flexible to interact with.					
Learning to operate the HIS was easy for me.					
The information generated by the HIS is correct.					
The information generated by the HIS is useful for its purpose.					
The HIS generates information in a timely manner.					
I trust the information output of the HIS.					
There is adequate technical support from the system's provider.					
The overall infrastructure in place is adequate to support the HIS.					
The HIS can be relied on to provide information as when needed.					
The output of the HIS is complete for work processes.					
Using the HIS enables me accomplish tasks more quickly.					
Using the HIS has improved my job performance.					
Using the HIS has made my job easier.					
I find the HIS useful in my job.					
I am satisfied with the functions of the HIS.					
The HIS has eased work processes.					
I am generally satisfied using the HIS.					
The HIS will help overcome the limitations of the paper-based system.					
Using the HIS will cause an improvement in patient care delivery.					
The HIS facilitates easy access to patient's information.					
The HIS will enhance communication among workers.					
HIS use will cause improved decision making.					

References

1. DeLone, W.H., McLean, E.R.: Information systems success: the quest for the dependent variable. Inslilulc of Management Stienees. Inf. Res. **3**(1), 60–95 (1992)
2. Fred, D., Perceived, D.: Usefulness, perceived ease of use, and user acceptance of information technology. MIS Q. **13**, 319–340 (1989)
3. Abran, A., Al-Qutaish, R.E.: ISO 9126: analysis of quality models and measures. Software Metrics and Software Metrology, Chap. 10, pp. 205–228. Wiley-IEEE Computer Society, New York, September 2010
4. Venkatesh, V., Morris, M.G., Davis, G.B., Davis, F.D.: User Acceptance of Information Technology: Toward a Unified View. MIS Q. **27**(3), 425–478 (2003)
5. Azuma, M.: SQuaRE: the next generation of the ISO/IEC 9126 and 14598 international standards series on software product quality. In: ESCOM (European Software Control and Metrics Conference), April 2001
6. ISO: ISO/IEC 25010: Systems and software engineering – Systems and software Quality Requirements and Evaluation (SQuaRE) – System and software quality models 4 (2011)
7. Estdale, J.: App Stores & ISO/IEC 25000: Product Certification at Last? In: Phalp, K., et al. (eds.) SQM XXIV: Systems Quality: Trends and Practices, pp. 37–48. Southampton Solent University (2016)
8. ISO/IEC 25010:2011. Systems and software engineering Systems and software, Quality Requirements and Evaluation (SQuaRE) – System and software quality models. Iso.org. https://www.iso.org/standard/35733.html, Accessed 24 Oct 2018
9. Delone, W.H., McLean, E.R.: The DeLone and McLean model of information systems success: a ten-year update. Manag. Inf. Syst. **19**(4), 9–30 (2003)
10. Seddon, P.B.: A respecification and extension of the DeLone and McLean model of IS success'. Inf. Syst. Res. **8**(3), 240–253 (1997)
11. Urbach, N., Muller, B.: Information systems theory: explaining and predicting our digital society. In: Dwivedi, Y.K., Wade, M.R., Schneberger, S.L., New York, vol. 1, Chap. 1 pp. 1–18. Springer, New York (2012). https://doi.org/10.1007/978-1-4419-6108-2
12. Zaied, A.H.: An integrated success model for evaluating information system in public sectors. Emerging Trends Comput. Inf. Sci. **3**(6), 814–825 (2012)
13. Baraka, H.A., El-Gamily, I.H.: Assessing call centers' success: a validation of the DeLone and McLean model for information system. Egyptian Inf. **2**(14), 99–108 (2013)
14. Tilahun, B., Fritz, F.: Modeling antecedents of electronic medical record system implementation success in low resource setting hospitals. MC Med. Inf. Dec. Making (2015). 1186/s12911-015-0192-0
15. Ojo, A.L., Popoola, S.O.: Some correlates of electronic health information management system success in Nigerian teaching hospitals. Biomed. Inform. Insights **7**(7), 1–9 (2015)
16. Chatterjee, S., Chakraborty, S., Sarker, S., Lau, F.Y.: Examining the success factors for mobile work in healthcare: a deductive study. Dec. Support Syst. **46**(3), 620–633 (2009)
17. Cho, K.W., Bae, S.K., Ryu, J.H., Kim, K.N., An, C.H., Chae, Y.M.: Performance evaluation of public hospital information systems by the information system success model. Healthc Inform. Res. **21**(1), 43–48 (2015)
18. Petter, S., Fruhling, A.: Evaluating the success of an emergency response medical information system. Int. J. Med. Inf. **7**(80), 480–489 (2011)
19. Bossen, C., Jensen, L.G., Udsen, F.W.: Review Evaluation of a comprehensive EHR based on the DeLone and McLean model for IS success: approach, results, and success factors. Int. J. Med. Inform. **82**(10), 940–953 (2013)

20. Esadig, M., Nassar, D.A.: Evaluation of healthcare information system using Delone and McLean Quality model, case study KSA. Int. J. Adv. Trends Comput. Sci. Eng. (2019)
21. Akoglu, H.: User's guide to correlation coefficients. Turkish J. Emergency Med. **18**(3), 91–93 (2018)

Network and IoT

OpenCache: Distributed SDN/NFV Based in-Network Caching as a Service

Shiyam Alalmaei[1]([✉]), Matthew Broadbent[2]([✉]), Nicholas Race[2]([✉]),
and Samia Chelloug[1]([✉])

[1] Information Technology Department, College of Computer and Information
Sciences, Princess Nourah bint AbdulRahman University,
Riyadh, Kingdom of Saudi Arabia
{smalalmaei, Sachelloug}@pnu.edu.sa
[2] School of Computing and Communications,
Lancaster University, Lancaster, UK
{m.broadbent, n.race}@lancaster.ac.uk

Abstract. In-network content caching allows content to be located towards the edge of the network, closer to users. This approach addresses the challenge of exponentially increasing video traffic. We consider OpenCache: an open-source, highly configurable, efficient and transparent in-network caching that leverages Software Defined Networking (SDN) to benefit last mile environments. However, due to its reliance on a centralised OpenCache controller and SDN controller, it suffers from three issues: scalability, reliability and high availability. In this work, we build on and extend the capabilities of OpenCache as a caching solution by leveraging Network Functions Virtualisation (NFV) and using a distributed SDN controller. We discuss the architectural design and technology decisions for the caching platform distribution including the functional components and highlight the role of virtualising, orchestrating and managing the key processes of caching content and control functions. Our target is to design an open-source, distributed in-network caching platform that is highly available, reliable and with automated elasticity to enable serving the increasing VoD traffic quickly and efficiently.

Keywords: Video-on-demand (VoD) · Software Defined Networking (SDN) · Network Functions Virtualisation (NFV) · Open Network Operating System (ONOS) · Open Source MANO (OSM) · Distributed in-network caching · Opencache

1 Introduction

Internet video traffic is predicted to increase to 82% of all consumer Internet traffic by 2021 [1]. End users expect the best possible quality in the video streaming experience. At the same time, high definition (HD) video streaming will continue to move to Ultra HD and 3D. Trying to meet the growing demand for Video on Demand (VoD) service, where individuals can retrieve previously recorded content at a time after it was initially broadcast or made available, and the increasing popularity of HD content, adds a huge burden on the underlying network infrastructure, it has to

© Springer Nature Switzerland AG 2019
A. Alfaries et al. (Eds.): ICC 2019, CCIS 1098, pp. 265–277, 2019.
https://doi.org/10.1007/978-3-030-36368-0_22

provision delivery throughput in the order of tens of Mbps for just one stream. Currently, VoD requests are handled individually, using a unicast content delivery paradigm. This means naively ignoring the duplicate independent flow requests for the same content from different users at different times. Hence, a very large amount of identical contents is delivered on the same network segments repeatedly [2].

In order to address this problem, in-network caching service came up, which caches the contents locally in the edge networks very close to the end-users. In-network caching has been proved to be an efficient solution to improve the efficiency of network utilisation and the data retrieval performance.

The new paradigms of Software Defined Networks (SDN) [3] and Network Functions Virtualisation (NFV) [4] have recently redefined the vision of designing, deploying and managing networking services. Combined together, they provide network managers with a complete, programmatic and flexible control of a dynamic view of the network. These paradigms are discussed in Sect. 2. Telecommunications providers and over-the-top (OTT) content providers have taken a great interest in leveraging on these technologies. In this context, this paper builds on and extends the OpenCache capabilities [2, 5] as a distributed SDN/NFV based in-network caching as a service (CaaS), focusing on the emerging capabilities of distributed SDN and the support of NFV. Our target is to design and implement a distributed in-network caching platform that is highly available, reliable and automatically elastic.

The remainder of the paper is organised as follows. Section 2 presents the background necessary to extend OpenCache as a distributed SDN/NFV based caching solution, whilst related work is presented in Sect. 3. Section 4 introduces design objectives, whereas the distributed OpenCache proposed architecture is described in Sect. 5. Features of the proposed architecture are described in Sect. 6, and finally, Sect. 7 concludes the paper and future work.

2   Background Information

2.1   Software Defined Networking

Software Defined Networking (SDN) is a very promising networking paradigm that facilitates decoupling the control plane in a network from the data plane and provides logical centralisation of network control, management and programmability. External applications (*i.e.* OpenCache) are provided centralised network perspective and status, and the means to programmatically manage and control the forwarding devices functionalities through the SDN controller based on the application profile and user demands quickly and cohesively.

Distributed Software Defined Networking. The standard centralised approach for SDN is based on a single controller managing all forwarding devices. However, this leads to a single point of failure and poses severe limitations to network scalability and reliability. Moreover, it may get over-loaded with large number of devices to handle, which disrupts the network functionality. Finally, in geographically large networks, forwarding devices can be physically very far from the controller. This induces large latency in flow modifications due to the propagation delays.

Distributed SDN controllers overcome all of the above limitations [6]. Multiple instances of the controller manage the whole network jointly. The network is divided into different sub-domains, each is under the control of one controller instance. Distribution of the control functionality increases scalability and improves the reliability of the control plane. Furthermore, large networks that suffer from the big distance between the controller and the network devices can be handled, because the device control is distributed and can be balanced among the controllers, thus improving the controller reactivity.

Consistency Mechanisms for Distributed SDN. The main challenge of distributed SDN controllers is to guarantee a logical centralised global view of the network state. The same global network view must be known at each controller to make correct decisions. This behaviour should be transparent to the application layer, and requires keeping all the shared data structures synchronised through some consistency mechanisms. Some of the main consistency mechanisms that have a direct application in SDN networks are *eventual consistency* and *strong consistency* [6]. Eventual consistency provides a weak form of consistency. This implies that for some time, some controllers may read values different from the actual updated ones; but eventually after some time, all the controllers will have the updated values. In return, this mechanism is employed for superior read/write performance and high availability. On the other hand, strong consistency mechanism ensures that when a controller updates some data, then no other controller is allowed to read this specific data until it gets updated at all (or most of) the other controllers. This implies that each controller reads always the most updated version of a data. This mechanism is employed in systems that prioritise consistency over high availability.

Design Choices for Distributed SDN. There are two main design choices for distributed SDN controllers, namely, hierarchical and flat models [6]. Each model distributes the network information among controllers differently. In hierarchical model, one (or some) controllers in the cluster have the whole up-to-date global network state. This model has hierarchical controls that run from top to bottom among controllers. The bottom of the hierarchy contains local controllers that maintain the switches in each sub-domain and keep only their respective local network state. Meanwhile, the top of the hierarchy contains the root controllers that manage the coordination between local controllers. Therefore, local controllers must first query network information from the root controllers before they can execute any inter-domain operation. From the coordination perspective, the number of root controllers should be kept minimal; hence, this model tends to be more consistent since fewer controllers maintain the global network state. However, this also means that fewer backup controllers are available to take over the failed controller. Additionally, SDN controllers in this model are divided into two roles (root and local) with different capabilities. Due to this difference, the local controller may not be able to take over the root controller and vice versa.

On the other hand, in the flat model, all of the controllers in the cluster are peers and have the same privileges and maintain the whole global network state. All of them can contact and notify each other directly to construct the global network state. Therefore, the flat model is easier to maintain. It has a robust failover mechanism; any controller in the cluster can simply take over a failed controller because they are all peers. Finally, it ensures fast access to the global topology stored at each controller. However, a main issue of this model is the overhead of the all-to-all communications between controllers to share the global state.

The survey in [6] compares between hierarchical and flat models. The hierarchical model is more scalable and efficient due to maintaining and synchronising the global network state between root controllers only. However, flat model provides a straight forward failover mechanism and robustness due to the similar roles of the controllers and direct communication between them. Additionally, high performance systems can benefit from the flat model, since a global network view is stored locally at each controller.

Two most popular distributed SDN controllers are Open Network Operating System (ONOS) [7] and OpenDaylight [8]. ONOS is principally designed for telecommunications companies, service providers and carrier networks. It is designed to support hybrid networks with a focus on scalability, high availability and performance. On the other hand, OpenDaylight is primarily designed for datacenters with the capability to support many southbound interfaces that are facing the data plane devices to bring legacy network and next generation network together.

Open Networking Operating System (ONOS). Open Networking Operating System (ONOS), is a distributed SDN controller that adopts the flat model to achieve a logically centralised SDN controller through a replicated state machine model. ONOS allows achieving high throughput, low latency, scalability, fault-tolerance and high availability. Each ONOS controller in the cluster is responsible of managing the switches under its sub-domain, and updating their state on the distributed data stores. For reliability reasons, each switch can connect to multiple ONOS controllers, but only one will be its master, whereas, the other controllers are standby. The master controller has full control over the switch it masters in terms of read/write capabilities on the switch forwarding tables. However, the standby controllers only have read capabilities on the switches connected to them and could become the new master of the switch in case the main master has failed.

Applications on top of ONOS, can view the whole network topology and may read/update the network view to decide on forwarding policies. We mention that there are many releases for ONOS. Each one of them provides some new features.

Distributed Stores and Consistency Protocols in ONOS. The distributed data stores implement the distributed databases in ONOS. The main ones are the following:

Mastership store which keeps the mapping between each switch to its master controller and it is managed by a strongly consistent protocol, using RAFT consensus algorithm [9], A RAFT implementation requires a cluster of nodes (*i.e.* controllers) each having a database (*i.e.* mastership data store) which is replicated in all nodes. There has to be a leader of the cluster for coordinating the consistency between the nodes, which is responsible for receiving update requests from all the nodes and then relaying database updates to the other nodes. Once the majority of the follower nodes have acknowledged the update, this is actually committed. In the case of network partitions, only the side with the majority of the nodes will be able to update the database, hence avoiding conflicting updates in two different network partitions. In ONOS, for scalability issues, multiple instances of RAFT algorithm run simultaneously. This implies that the data stores are actually partitioned (sharded) into different parts, each of them managed by a different RAFT instance.

The other main distributed data store is the *Network topology store*, which describes the network topology in terms of switches, links and hosts. It is managed in an eventually consistent protocol called anti-entropy, which is based on a simple gossip algorithm in which each controller picks at random another controller in the cluster at fixed intervals (usually 3–5 s), and then sends a message to compare their respective topology views. If a controller is aware of newer information that the other controller does not have yet, then they exchange that information to update their stores. This ensures that all the controllers achieve consensus on the network topology, according to an eventually consistent model. This approach quickly detects and synchronises a controller that has a slightly drifted state. Moreover, it quickly synchronises a new controller that joins the cluster with the rest.

2.2 Network Functions Virtualisation

Network Functions Virtualisation (NFV) is fundamentally changing how network services are deployed and managed by providing flexibility, agile service delivery, auto-scalability and optimal resource usage. These services are provided over the same common infrastructure. The European Telecommunications Standards Institute (ETSI) has defined a framework for Network Functions Virtualisation and Management and Orchestration Architectures (MANO) [10]. These open-source architectures are broadly defined to allow development, extension and testing in proprietary ways. Section 5 explains how OpenCache is mapped to this framework.

The ETSI MANO functional blocks are explained below:

- *VNF:* is a functional block representing the Virtualised Network Function implemented on commodity hardware.
- *Operation/Business Support System (OSS/BSS):* includes collection of operation and business applications for operators and service providers that are used to provision and operate their network services. This block is not tightly integrated into the NFV architectural framework but is expected to work in coordination with it.
- *VNF Manager (VNFM):* configures and manages single or multiple VNFs' lifecycle (*i.e.* instantiate, update, query, scale up/down, terminate) on its domain. It is responsible for Fault, Configuration, Accounting, Performance and Security Management (FCAPS) for the virtual part of the VNF.
- *Network Functions Virtualisation Infrastructure (NFVI):* consists of both virtual and physical hardware (*e.g.* compute, storage, and networking) and software (*e.g.* hypervisors) components. Together they provide the infrastructure VNF resources.
- *Virtualised Infrastructure Manager (VIM):* controls and manages the NFVI resources that are usually within one operator's infrastructure domain. There may be multiple VIMs in an NFV architecture.
- *Element Management (EM):* is not part of the MANO, however it has an important role to play. It is responsible for VNFs (FCAPS). The EM collaborates with the VNFM to perform those functions. EM is responsible for the FCAPS for the functional part of the VNF opposed to VNFM, which also manages the FCAPS of the VNF but only for the virtual part (*e.g.* reporting an issue with spinning up a VNF).

- *Network Function Virtualisation Orchestrator (NFVO):* has two primary goals; the first goal is to manage and coordinate NFVI resources across multiple VIMs. The second goal is to manage and coordinate the lifecycle of network services (*i.e.* create, update, query, delete) across multiple VNFMs. NFVO achieves its first goal by a sub component called resource orchestrator (RO), which is responsible of the coordination, authorisation, allocation and de-allocation of NFVI resources by communicating with the VIMs through their north bound APIs. To achieve the second goal of the NFVO, it uses a sub component called the Network Service Orchestrator (NSO), which creates end-to-end service between different VNFs that may be managed by possibly different VNFMs and coordinates groups of VNF instances that jointly realise more complex network functions (also called VNF Forwarding Graphs).

Authors in [11] compare between several NFV MANO projects. However, OSM [12], is an open source NFV MANO platform that is considered as the reference implementation for the NFV MANO since it is hosted by ETSI and aligned with its information models to meet the requirements of production NFV.

3   Related Work

OTT content providers (e.g. Youtube) rely on Content Delivery Networks (CDN) for content delivery, which provide a series of large number of cache server mirrors with global coverage, in order to push content to the edges of the Internet to ensure low latency. However, CDNs do not reduce the bandwidth utilisation on edge networks, as multiple duplicate flows of the same request will be created and traverse the external link to reach to the CDN. Recent reports [1] show that 77% of all Internet video traffic will cross CDNs by 2021, compared to 67% in 2016; this traffic can be reduced by deploying in-network caching. Therefore, OTT providers have started to deploy and remotely manage edge caching servers in telecommunication operators' networks [13]. Indeed, deploying in-network caching service that is more flexible, configurable and located closer to the end-users, would complement CDNs and truly benefit edge networks by reducing the external bandwidth and the load from the CDNs, and increasing the QoS for the end-users.

OpenCache [2, 5] is an open-source, highly configurable, efficient and transparent in-network HTTP caching service that leverages SDN technology, and supports the ETSI NFV MANO framework. It aims to improve the VoD distribution efficiency, network utilisation and increase the Quality of Experience (QoE) for the end-user, by caching video assets as close to the end-user as possible. OpenCache has three entities namely, OpenCache Controller (OCC), OpenCache Node (OCN) and a key-value store. Network operators and service providers can program the desired caching behaviour on the OCC which communicates with the SDN controller and OCNs via a JSON-RPC interface. OCC instructs the SDN controller to add the matching redirecting rules for the cacheable content in the flow tables of the switches to redirect the user's packets appropriately to the closest OCN. OCN caches video content, so when it receives a request for accessing the cached video from a user, it delivers the video content to the user directly if there is a cache-hit; otherwise, the OCN requests the video from the original VoD server. The key-value store acts as a database, which records the metadata and caching state of user requests and video content. As a result of caching the contents very close to the user, the following benefits arise: the external link usage gets reduced 100%; it helps also in reducing the load from the VoD content provider and all transient networks along the path to the end-user. Additionally, end-users can experience higher QoE [2].

The in-network SDN based solutions presented in [2, 5, 14–16] lack for scalability, high availability, reliability and elasticity of the caching control plane due to relying on a centralised cache controller that would not be able to scale with the increasing VoD requests. It is a single point of failure that would disrupt the caching service if it fails and negatively reflect on the service availability. The work in [15], additionally doesn't leverage the NFV capabilities.

4   Design Objectives

Our objective is to extend the current OpenCache design [2, 5] to overcome the limitations mentioned above. We will present a distributed in-network caching architecture with multiple OCCs that are physically distributed but logically centralised by leveraging distributed SDN controllers to achieve high availability, elasticity and reliability even under heavy VoD requests. Moreover, this architecture is associated with NFV MANO platform, where caching functions become software applications (VNFs) leading to flexibility and agile service delivery. We choose ONOS as the distributed SDN controller because it is designed to provide high performance, high availability, reliability and scalability. These features are important to meet the exponentially growing VoD requests. On the other hand, we choose OSM as the NFV MANO because it is hosted by ETSI and considered as the reference implementation for the NFV MANO that meets the requirements of production NFV. Therefore, we expect that the proposed architecture provides support for high availability, reliability, elasticity and automation of end-to-end cache service delivery.

5   Distributed OpenCache Proposed Architecture

Considering the aforementioned objectives described above, first, we will describe how OpenCache is associated with the NFV MANO framework. Then, we will present the distributed OpenCache architecture.

Figure 1 identifies how the functional components of the ETSI NFV framework are adapted for OpenCache as detailed as follows.

OpenCache main functional blocks are represented as VNFs, which are the Virtual OpenCache Controller (vOCC), Virtual OpenCache Node (vOCN), Virtual Backup Store and Virtual Load Balancer. VOCC has the main role in the functional lifecycle management and orchestration of the vOCNs because it has all of the required details of the caching process. It is responsible for controlling, querying, dynamically configuring and automatically scaling up/down the vOCNs. However, vOCC delegates the heavy lifting of creation and deletion of the VNFs to the VNFM. The aforementioned VNFs constitute a VNF forwarding graph that is created, coordinated and managed by the NFVO based on the network operator policies. It manages the lifecycle of the NFVI corresponding resources (possibly across multiple VIMs). Then the VNFM instantiates the services with respect to the policies that define the VNF graph.

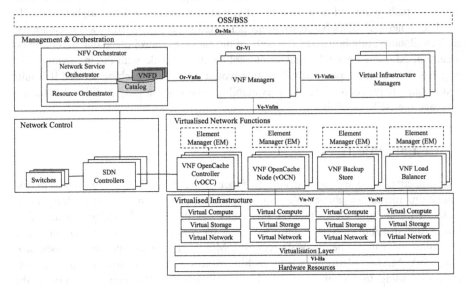

Fig. 1. OpenCache mapped to ETSI NFV framework

The proposed distributed OpenCache architecture that leverages SDN/NFV and constituent layers are illustrated in Fig. 2.

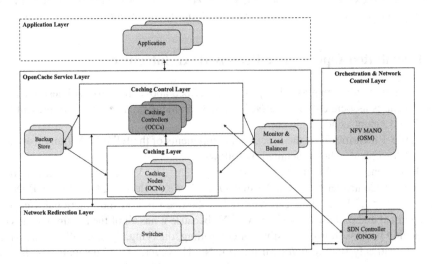

Fig. 2. OpenCache architecture

The top of this architecture is the application layer. It is responsible for defining the behaviour of the caches. This is where third-party developers will interact with the whole deployment through the controller API. This ensures a separation between OpenCache functionality and the cache behaviour.

Then there is the orchestration and network control layer that is responsible for orchestrating the service and network redirection layers, and manages the underlying network. It includes the NFV MANO (*i.e.* OSM) and the SDN controllers (*i.e.* ONOS).

Below the application layer, is the service layer; this is where the core functionality of OpenCache lies. It contains two sub layers namely, *caching control layer* and *caching layer*. The caching control layer consists of multiple physically distributed but logically centralised controllers. It is responsible for the behaviour of all of its connected caching nodes. Furthermore, the caching controllers interact with the NFV MANO and SDN controllers, in order to provide flexible resource allocation and network forwarding. On the other hand, the caching layer typically consists of a number of caching services, running across multiple distributed cache nodes, which directly serve content in response to user requests. Caching node can host multiple services simultaneously, each of which is responsible for delivering a unique set of content to the client. OpenCache controllers and nodes can run on dedicated physical resources, or virtualised ones that are managed by the aforementioned NFV MANO.

Elasticity of services and resource consumption is critical. Therefore, there is a monitoring and load balancing entity for the caching control and the caching layer. This entity is responsible for monitoring the services and resources periodically and taking actions based on some thresholds and criteria in order to scale them up/down. If the monitoring and load balancing entity needs to add or remove resources, then it communicates with the MANO.

Reliability is a key feature too, so there is a backup server that is used by the caching control layer and the caching layer. The backup server stores the whole caching meta-data, state and topology, it periodically refreshes them so that any needed information could be restored back from this backup server. This server also needs to be backed up for more reliability. It provides additional reliability besides the reliability and failover mechanisms provided by ONOS.

The final and lowest layer is the network redirection layer. It redirects user requests for content towards the suitable caching nodes instead of the original VoD server. This is managed and modified by the SDN controller.

To achieve our proposed objectives mentioned in Sect. 4, OCCs and OCNs rely on the distributed SDN controller ONOS. They are implemented as ONOS applications to leverage its capabilities offered as follows:

- Mapping between OCCs and OCNs is based on the mastership mapping between ONOS controllers and the switches that connect these OCNs as illustrated in Fig. 3. Each switch is controlled by a single master ONOS controller and can be connected to other standby controllers that can takeover if the master fails. Figure 3, illustrates a scenario of 3 ONOS controllers that have OCC running on top, and there are 4 switches connected to these controllers. The solid line depicts that a switch is mastered by the connected controller, whereas the dashed line depicts that a switch is connected to standby controllers. OCC is an ONOS application that is aware of the switches mastered by the hosting ONOS controller. Therefore, it controls the OCNs connected to these switches. According to the scenario in Fig. 3., OCC (A) controls OCN 1, 2 and 3. OCC (B) controls OCN 4 and OCC (C) controls OCN 5. When the mastership relation changes either due to failover mechanism or load balancing, this reflects on the mapping between the OCC and OCNs as shown in Fig. 4. In this scenario, OCC (A) fails, so switch 1 and switch 2 fall back to the corresponding standby controllers, which will be their new masters.

- Fault-tolerance is one of the main features of ONOS. Once an ONOS controller failure is detected, then a new backup controller is selected which has a running OpenCache application to resume the work of the failed one.
- Accessing the global network state locally which is built by ONOS.
- Distributed primitives for managing distributed state are offered for ONOS application developers which enable creating different instances to manage their application state. They provide high availability, scalability and durability by offering strong and eventual consistencies.

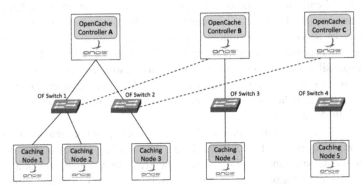

Fig. 3. Mapping OCCs to OCNs depends on masterships between ONOS controllers and switches

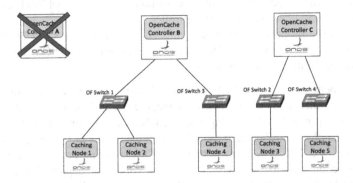

Fig. 4. Mastership changes due to ONOS controller failure or load balancing is reflected on the mapping between OCCs and OCNs

- Leveraging the clustering capability that enables defining and grouping multiple ONOS instances in a cluster which are aware of the others and can communicate with them directly. Additionally, when an application is activated in one instance, this reflects on all other instances in the cluster automatically. This gives a great benefit of separating the caching control layer and the caching layer into two separate clusters, each with its own functionalities.

6 Features of the Proposed System

The synchronisation in this distributed architecture is achieved by sharing two types of data representations, namely, caching view and caching control state.

Caching view is a representation that depicts essential information about the existing OCCs, OCNs, mapping between them and a list of the services stored at each OCN. This information is important to be correct and consistent between all OCCs because it will be exposed to third-party application layer on top of them. So, it should be strongly consisted between OCCs to give these applications more freedom to connect to any OCC.

On the other hand, *Caching control state* is a detailed representation that contains all of the information related to caching control such as the user requests, responses, notifications, connected OCNs, contents … etc. This caching control state is different at each OCC based on its sub-domain. The caching control state is eventually consistent between the OCC and its backups and uses the anti-entropy protocol for synchronisation. Likewise, OCNs need to synchronise their own caching states that contain all of the caching nodes related details.

The distributed architecture would have the following features:

6.1 Reliability

The flat model has an advantage in terms of robust failover mechanism because all OCCs have the same role and privileges, so any OCC in the cluster can simply take over a failed peer. Each OCC maintains its own caching control state based on its connections to OCNs. It has to periodically share its caching control state with its backup before the failure actually happens. In order to reduce the resource consumption (*i.e.* bandwidth, compute and storage), a single backup controller at least would be selected to share the caching state with. However, the degree of reliability (number of backup controllers) that share the caching state can be tuned based on the available resources. If ONOS did not fall back to the intended and expected backup controller(s) when a failure happens, this means that the new selected backup controller doesn't have a copy of the caching state of the failed controller, and it needs to retrieve this information from the dedicated backup server. Therefore, each controller sends a copy of its caching state to its backup controllers and another copy to the backup server too. This is shared in an eventually consistent fashion with anti-entropy synchronisation. Similarly, OCNs share their caching states with their backups. However, the backup nodes selection priority is based on the closeness to the node itself. OCNs also share the actual cached content.

6.2 Automated Elasticity

A monitoring and load balancing service is responsible for monitoring all of the OCCs without involving a man in the middle. It takes actions of load balancing if some thresholds (*i.e.* CPU, requests throughput) have been exceeded which indicate overloaded resource consumption. Load balancer will migrate caching nodes afterwards. If all backup controllers cannot handle the overload, then the load balancer needs to ask the VNFM to add a new vOCC to the caching control layer. The new controller synchronises with other controllers by getting a copy of the global caching view and the caching control state of the nodes that will be migrated to it from the backup server. Additionally, monitoring and load balancing service is responsible for scaling down the control plane. So, when the controllers are underutilised, then it asks the VNFM to remove some controllers to reduce resource consumption. Similarly, caching nodes have the same elasticity feature but with the consideration of the original cache placement.

6.3 High Availability

The flat model redundancy offered by ONOS and the backup servers provide reliability and robustness that reduces the service disruption time in case of failures. Moreover, the load balancer collaborates with the VNFM to balance the load between the available resources and add/remove them as necessary to try avoiding service disruption due to overloaded resources. All of this lead to a highly available service. Additionally, since all OCCs are peers, then applications have the freedom to connect to any OCC.

7 Conclusion and Future Work

In this work, we proposed a distributed SDN/NFV based in-network content caching architecture as an extension to OpenCache, to overcome the main issues that it suffers from: scalability, reliability and high availability. We discussed the architectural design and technology decisions that we made for the caching platform distribution and functional components. We highlighted the role of the distributed SDN and NFV in virtualising, orchestrating and managing the key processes and control functions. Further, we presented the features of our platform design. The proposed platform is an open-source, distributed in-network caching that is expected to be highly available, reliable and with automated elasticity to enable serving the increasing VoD traffic quickly and efficiently. This work is still in the initial stages and under development, so in our future work, we plan to analyse the performance and measure the gains of the distributed platform opposed to the original non-distributed OpenCache. Several features would be examined and different QoE metrics would be evaluated. For example, the scalability of the distributed architecture would be measured by the increase in the VoD requests throughput. Whereas the effect of the failover mechanism would be measured by the response latency and buffer occupancy at the client side. Additionally, the placement of the OCCs and OCNs could be examined to measure its impact on the response latency and bitrate.

References

1. CISCO VNI: Cisco Visual Networking Index: Forecast and Methodology, 2016–2021. Technical report (2017)
2. Georgopoulos, P., Broadbent, M., Plattner, B., Race, N.: Cache as a service: leveraging SDN to efficiently and transparently support video-on-demand on the last mile. In: 23rd International Conference on Computer Communication and Networks, pp. 1–9 (2014)
3. Kreutz, D., Ramos, F.M.V., Veríssimo, P.E., Rothenberg, C.E., Azodolmolky, S., Uhlig, S.: Software-defined networking: a comprehensive survey. Proc. IEEE **103**(1), 14–76 (2015)
4. Mijumbi, R., Serrat, J., Gorricho, J.-L., Bouten, N., Turck, F., De Boutaba, R.: Network function virtualization: state-of-the-art and research challenges. IEEE Commun. Surv. Tutor. **18**(1), 236–262 (2016)
5. Broadbent, M., King, D., Baildon, S., Georgalas, N., Race, N.: Opencache: a software-defined content caching platform. In: Proceedings of the 1st IEEE Conference on Network Softwarization, pp. 1–5 (2015)
6. Oktian, Y.E., Lee, S., Lee, H., Lam, J.: Distributed SDN controller system: a survey on design choice. Comput. Netw. **121**, 100–111 (2017)
7. ON.LAB: ONOS. https://onosproject.org/
8. Linux Foundation: OpenDaylight. https://www.opendaylight.org/
9. Ongaro, D., Ousterhout, J.: In search of an understandable consensus algorithm. In: USENIX Annual Technical Conference, pp. 305–320 (2014)
10. ETSI Industry Specification Group (ISG) NFV: ETSI GS NFV 002 V1.1.1: Network Functions Virtualisation (NFV), Architectural Framework. Technical report (2013). https://www.etsi.org/deliver/etsi_gs/NFV/001_099/002/01.01.01_60/gs_NFV002v010101p.pdf
11. De Sousa, N.F.S., Perez, D.A.L., Rosa, R.V., Santos, M.A., Rothenberg, C.E.: Network service orchestration: a survey. Comput. Commun. **142–143**, 69–94 (2019)
12. ETSI: Open Source MANO. https://osm.etsi.org/
13. Limbach, F.: Cooperative service provisioning with OTT players – an explorative analysis of telecommunication business models. In: 25th European Regional ITS Conference Brussels, Belgium (2014)
14. Liu, Y., Point, J.C., Katsaros, K.V., Glykantzis, V., Siddiqui, M.S., Escalona, E.: SDN/NFV based caching solution for future mobile network (5G). In: European Conference on Networks and Communications (2017)
15. Chiang, W.-K., Li, T.-Y.: An extended SDN-based in-network caching service for video on demand. In: International Computer Symposium (2016)
16. Trajano, A.F.R., Fernandez, M.P.: ContentSDN: a content-based transparent proxy architecture in software-defined networking. In: IEEE 30th International Conference on Advanced Information Networking and Applications (2016)

Comparative Study of the Internet of Things Recommender System

Halima Bouazza[✉], Laallam Fatima Zohra, and Bachir Said

Faculté des nouvelles technologies de l'information, et de la communication,
Laboratoire de l'Intelligence Artificielle et les Technologies de l'Information,
Université Kasdi Merbah Ouargla, Ouargla 30 000, Algeria
bouazza.halima@gmail.com, laallamfz@gmail.com,
saidbachir@gmail.com

Abstract. The Internet of things is a technological revolution which brings the virtual and physical world into the same ecosystem. Hence, the growing proliferation of data, objects and services provided by many IoT objects and platforms which has contributed to the problem of information overload. Thus, it makes difficulties to discover and offer products and services that may be in the interest of users.

Suggesting suitable items, things and services to IoT users based the data generated from objects owned by those users is discussed in many papers, the purpose of this paper is to illustrate how recommendations can be applied in the IoT area, taking into account the characteristics of the domain and proposing new recommendation approach for the IoT domain. In this context, we also provide a review of some remarkable existing works in the recommendation technologies in IoT.

Keywords: IoT · Recommender system · Collaborative filtering · Content based filtering · Knowledge based filtering · Ontology

1 Introduction

Nowadays the notion internet encompasses not only the computer and their peripherals but it made up also by every surrounding object such us daily life object (refrigerator, television, thermostat, air conditioner and so on) and wearable things (bracelet, clothes, glasses and so forth).

These objects also called things collaborate in order to achieve a common goal, which is enhancing our lives in diverse aspect like domestic, healthcare, transportation, logistic…etc. furthermore it offers a high quality of service. The emerging Internet of Things (IoT) bridges the gap between the physical and the digital worlds which leads to grow the proliferation of services, objects and data, thus enables a deeper understanding of user preferences and behaviors

Putting human beings at the center of information systems, personal and ambient sensors, communicative tools, mobile and ubiquitous computing devices, offers unprecedented opportunities for deeper insights, more meaningful and faster [1]. Rich interactions and relations between users and things gives the opportunity to Research in

© Springer Nature Switzerland AG 2019
A. Alfaries et al. (Eds.): ICC 2019, CCIS 1098, pp. 278–285, 2019.
https://doi.org/10.1007/978-3-030-36368-0_23

Human Computer Interaction (HCI) and Knowledge Discovery in Databases and Data Mining (KDD) to develop methods which help users identifying, extracting, visualizing and understanding useful information from these huge masses of high-dimensional data and often weakly structured and/or non-standardized [2]. At this point appears the necessity of decision support tools which is most commonly known as recommender systems. Therefore, developing efficient and effective recommendation approaches to better meet the interests of users and must encounter unprecedented difficulties in finding an ideal service from the large number of services, where recommender systems (RSs) are software systems that analyzes information about items, users, and interactions between them in order to recommend the most appropriate items to users by predicting their interest in a particular item [3]. RSs have proved their effectiveness in different areas, especially in the e-commerce domains. However, they have not achieved their maturity in the IoT field yet.

The aim of this paper is to give a review about how Recommender Systems are applied in IoT area and to propose new approaches for system recommendation for the IoT domain. In this context, we also provide an overview of existing approaches of recommendation technologies in IoT. The next section describes a background about IoT, Recommender system and the characteristic and requirement of the IoT recommender system. The related works are portrayed in the Sect. 3. Further in Sect. 4 we discuss the available works and our proposed approach. Finally, the last section concludes our paper.

2 Background

2.1 Internet of Things

The Internet of Things (IoT) is an innovative paradigm that is rapidly gaining momentum in the current wireless telecommunication scenario [4]. The fundamental idea of this concept is the ubiquitous presence surrounding us with a set of things or different objects - such as Radio Frequency Identification (RFID) tags, sensors, actuators, smart phones, and so forth. - Which, through unique addressing schemes, are likely to interact with each other and cooperate with their neighbors to achieve common objectives. Figure 1 depicts the element of the IoT ecosystem.

The Internet of Things (IoT) is someway a leading step to a smart world with ubiquitous computing and networking. It proposes to make different tasks manageable for users, such as easy monitoring of various events surrounding us. With ubiquitous computing, computing will be implanted wherever and programmed to act automatically with autonomous triggering.

Indeed, the central power of the IoT idea is the high impact on various aspects of daily life and behavior of potential users. From a private user, the most apparent effects of the IoT will be evident in both working and domestic areas. In this context, assisted living, domestics, e-health, improved learning are simply some examples of possible application scenarios in which the IoT paradigm will play a leading role soon. Thus, from the aspect of business users, the most obvious consequences will be equally

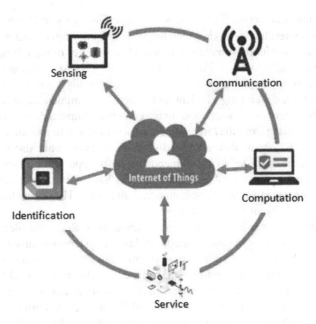

Fig. 1. The IoT elements

apparent in fields like automation and industrial manufacturing, logistics, business/process management, intelligent transport of people and goods [5].

Furthermore, the interconnected device networks can result a big number of intelligent and autonomous applications and services bringing significant personal, professional, and economic gains. In addition, IoT allow the suggestion of suitable items, things and services to IoT users based the data generated from objects.

2.2 Recommender System Background

The emerging Internet of things (IoT) accelerates the growth of data available on the Internet, which inhibits the power of traditional research paradigms of digging the information from massive and deep resources to cope with the needs of end users. To benefit from the connectivity and valuable data generated by these objects from intelligent spaces and building automation solutions and services, intelligence mechanisms are needed to suggest or recommend suitable items to IoT users based on this available data.

Recommender systems are, as clarified in the introduction, "software tools and techniques providing suggestions for items to be of use to a user" [6]. Recommender systems are commonly categorized into four categories based on the approach they use to arrive at the recommendations: content-based approaches, collaborative filtering, knowledge based and hybrid techniques.

(1) Content-based approaches use the knowledge about items existing in a system to display items that are similar to those previously rated by a user [6]. The recommendation process is essentially to match the attributes of the user profile against the attributes of the content of item. The result is a relevance judgement that represents the user's level of interest in this item [7].

(2) Collaborative filtering techniques: These systems depend on the interactions between users and items in the system. Generally, collaborative filtering algorithms rely on similarity between users that have interacting with the system with similar ways by rating the same items implicitly or explicitly. Thus, Items that are relevant to these users are also expected to be relevant to the active user and are included in the list of recommendations [8].

(3) Knowledge based recommender system: This category of recommender system depends on the knowledge engineering [9]. Knowledge engineering is a contentious issue in this approach in which are achieved using certain techniques i.e. The representation of knowledge is an integral part of the expertise engineering. Hence, knowledge engineering plays the vital role in knowledge-based technique, such as ontology, to represent all the knowledge required in the system [10].

(4) Hybrid recommendation [11]: in order to identify more accurate recommendation, the idea of merging basic recommendation approaches is relevant in such a way that one benefits to compensate the shortcoming of the other.

2.3 Recommender System in IoT Characteristic and Requirement

Despite the fact the success of the RSs in variety fields, The IoT has special characteristics that add more complexity and more challenges to the IoT recommender system.

- Heterogeneity: IoT deploys large number of different kinds of things and implement wide diversity of various wireless technologies and communication protocols.
- IoT recommender system has the ability to categorize the end-users more accurately in which real-time communication provisions data analysis and conversation among applications and services.
- Scalability: Due to the wide geographical distribution and the large number of IoT objects, scalability is a critical issue that must be applied in IoT systems.
- Mobility allows the organization of objects by changing structure. Thus, IoT systems must support reliable services provider between moving objects.

The above features make certain applications suffer from certain gaps and may become incapable of performing effective tasks in the IoT. Similarly, the recommender system faces new challenges and they are much more complex than traditional recommender systems for many reasons:

- Highly dynamic: The dynamic nature of things calls for models that can quickly adapt to the ever-changing status of things and always display the most up-to-date recommendation results.
- Correlation between objects: RS must have the ability to investigate heterogeneous relationships among different objects and services, which adds involvedness to RS.

These relationships will necessitate whole analysis and identification to produce precise recommendation results.

- contextual information or Spatiotemporal correlation, such as time and place. Nevertheless, the heterogeneous nature of spatiotemporal data is a major challenge for the recommendation.

3 Related Works

IoT recommendation systems still in their infancy nevertheless there are many remarkable works in this field in which IoT is exploited as source of information, media of propagation or both. Furthermore, IoT recommender system suggest items such as food, Objects or IoT services.

Recommendation of suitable objects to perform the needed task has been investigated in [12] wherever the main contributions are: (i) emphasizing on things recommendation as well as analyze the correlation between objects, which has considerable influence on the preferences of users and the human decision-making process. (ii) Furthermore, the correlation among things correlations can be revealed and exploited for helping user-thing usage pattern prediction. Particularly, authors have developed a hyper graph-based approach to devise things implicit correlations in a query-rank style, in which composite relationships in user thing interactions can be exposed at highest without needless information damage. At last (iii) they have proposed a successive technique based on the Monte Carlo method to continuously monitor the state of availability of physical objects, and incorporates this dynamic characteristic of physical objects in the proposed framework to improve the results of recommendations.

Authors of [13] present the idea of building a digital inventory based on gathered data from the installed application on the smart devices whereas the installed apps are also an opened door to gather information about customer needs and interests to automatically perform a digital inventory for each consumer. Recommender systems may use these inventories for collaborative filtering and/or to offer products and services related to consumers in a non-intrusive manner.

Indeed, the recommendation in the era of healthcare using IoT prove its effectiveness, since authors of [14] proposed type-2 fuzzy logic and fuzzy ontology–based decision-making knowledge to automate the total procedures of foods and drugs recommendation for IoT-healthcare systems. This proposed system encompasses two layers: a security layer and a type-2 fuzzy ontology–based decision-making knowledge layer. The security layer avoids unauthorized access to a smart refrigerator and medical devices, and examines the true condition of the accurate patient before the recommendation of foods and medicines. The type-2 fuzzy ontology–based semantic knowledge layer extracts the patient danger feature values via wearable sensors, controls the patient's health condition using type-2 fuzzy logic, retrieves medicine and food information from the fuzzy ontology, and then recommends treatment for a smart medicine box and foods for a smart refrigerator, according to the patient's condition.

In the similar context, in [15] authors have introduced ProTrip, a health-centered tourism recommendation system based on hybrid filtering mechanisms as well as intelligent recommendation models. ProTrip is built upon an ontology-based framework which semantically exploits health and nutrition information and manipulates a hybrid filtering mechanism proposed by Blanco-Fernández et al. [16], which is a combination of the three basic filtering types, i.e. collaborative filtering, content-based filtering, and knowledge-based filtering. The nutrition and health-oriented profile are used to enhance the fulfillment and to represent the data recovered in order to meet the user's necessities. User information are crucial in the health and nutrition field when certain climatic conditions and certain foods are reserved for users because of their health problems [17].

In order to visualize right information at the right time, in the right place, in the right way, to the right person according to his context of use, preferences, goals, profile and the used devices. [1] proposes a solution based on a multilevel recommendation system (RS) based on a set of services allowed to recommend related information based on the user's profile and context of use, and to generate an iterative process which contains users in the decision-making actions enthusiastic to clarify data and choice their ultimate visualization and the collaboration way to implement. Additionally. It is essential to consider the human being not only as an individual in IoT system but also as a member in the social communities of interest [18]. Therefore, the idea exploited in [1] is to integrate the recommender system of services with social analysis and crowdsourcing, and interpretations which leads to new significant use and presentation of data rely on the exploitation of the information from social network.

In the same context, integrating cognitive reasoning into Social IoT in order to recommend daily tasks in smart homes have been discussed in [19] where authors have used the cognitive reasoning to combine objective and subjective aspects of the context to characterize user situations. This reasoning mechanism has been applied into a task-based intelligent recommender system to be adapted to user situational objectives, which are detected through calendars, preferences, daily habits as well as smart home features and conditions. Whilst the IoT service recommendation presented in [20] is summarized in followed points: the first is presenting a scalable method to calculate the predicted values, where a node estimates its own predictions rather than depending on a central system. (ii) the second is using an algorithm for measuring the influence of one node on another, using a combination of trust and similarity between them, which is resistant to Collaborative Filtering data sparsity problems.

Moreover, Recommendation of IoT services and things to users is investigated in the paper [3] where authors have examined and evaluated recommendation algorithms in the IoT by censoriously compare the fulfillment of various algorithms. For the correlation between objects, users and services, Mashal et al. have proposed a graph-based model for IoT systems wherever the system is modeled by a tripartite graph with hyper-edges among users, objects, and services then they conduct experimentation in which they analyze and discover correlations between performances of different algorithms. They also display that the graph-based recommendation algorithm can be used to mature the efficiency of the recommender system for the IoT. In addition, they show that some algorithms work reasonably well and produce high quality results (Table 1).

Table 1. Comparaison between works

Works	Contextual data	Correlation between objects	Correlation between users	Trust	Recommender type
[1]	Yes	No	Yes	No	Collaborative filtering
[3]	No	No	No	No	Knowledge Based Recommender
[12]	Yes	Yes	Yes	Between users	Collaborative filtering
[13]	No	No	No	No	Content based
[14]	Yes	No	No	Yes	Knowledge Based Recommender
[15]	Yes	No	No	No	Hybrid
[19]	Yes	Yes	No	Between objects	Knowledge Based Recommender
[20]	No	Yes	Yes	Objects and users	Collaborative filtering

4 Discussion

Previous IoT recommender system based on the objects which owned by users themselves. This leads to an inefficient exploitation of IoT available data generated by various objects. In fact, an optimal recommendation of services can be achieved with the help of Social IoT (SIoT) by using data generated by various IoT applications.

Where the SIoT is the resulted paradigm by merging the IoT with the social networks in order to build a profile of objects based on IoT data that can be exchanged with SIoT network to be accessible to other IoT services intelligently. In addition, SIoT gives a dynamic nature to the devices, organizations and social structures involved in IoT to improve the intelligent availability of data where nodes form social relationships between them similar to that of a social network. In addition, the aforementioned works suffers due to surroundings problems. The problem of cold start is the best example of a problem of circumstances, where new members, such as clients or things, are involved in the recommendation framework [21]. Hybrid recommender system may solve the cold start problem by consolidating multiple filtering techniques in order to create a recommendation framework which predicts the rating in an elementary way.

5 Conclusion

Indeed, IoT create the bridge between the physical and the digital worlds which makes a huge availability of data. This latter should be extracted and analyzed in order to suggest suitable items to IoT users based the data generated by those objects. In this paper is we have illustrated how recommendations can be applied in IoT scenario by clarifying the characteristics of the IoT domain and the challenges of IoT recommender system, taking into account the contextual data and after discussing the different available works in the IoT era we proposed new recommendation approach using the social IoT.

References

1. Valtolina, S., Mesiti, M.: Barricelli BR User-Centered Recommendation Services in Internet of Things Era
2. Szalay, A.S.: Science in an exponential world, pp. 21–23 (2020). https://doi.org/10.1038/440413a
3. Mashal, I., Alsaryrah, O., Chung, T.: Algorithms in internet of things. J. Ambient Intell. Humaniz. Comput. (2016). https://doi.org/10.1007/s12652-016-0357-4
4. Atzori, L., Iera, A., Morabito, G.: The Internet of Things: a survey. Comput. Networks **54**, 2787–2805 (2010). https://doi.org/10.1016/j.comnet.2010.05.010
5. Atzori, L., Iera, A., Morabito, G., Nitti, M.: The social internet of things (SIoT) - When social networks meet the internet of things: Concept, architecture and network characterization. Comput. Networks **56**, 3594–3608 (2012). https://doi.org/10.1016/j.comnet.2012.07.010
6. Ricci, F., Rokach, L., Shapira, B.: Introduction to Recommender Systems Handbook
7. Lops, P., De Gemmis, M., Semeraro, G.: Content-based Recommender Systems: State of the Art and Trends (2011)
8. Sarwar, B., Karypis, G., Konstan, J., et al.: Item-Based Collaborative Filtering Recommendation
9. Lu, J.: A Personalized e-Learning Material Recommender System, pp. 374–379 (2007)
10. Journal, A., Sciences, A. Ontological Approach in Knowledge Based Recommender System to Develop the Quality of E-learning System Ontological Approach in Knowledge Based Recommender System to Develop the Quality of E-learning System (2012)
11. Burke, R.: Hybrid Recommender Systems: Survey and Experiments, pp. 1–29
12. Yao, L.: Things of Interest Recommendation by Leveraging Heterogeneous Relations in the Internet of Things of Interest Recommendation by Leveraging Heterogeneous (2016). https://doi.org/10.1145/2837024
13. Frey, R.M., Xu, R., Ilic, A., Car, S.: A Novel Recommender System in IoT, pp. 4–6 (2015)
14. Ali, F., Islam, S.M.R., Kwak, D., et al.: Type-2 Fuzzy Ontology – aided Recommendation Systems for IoT – based Healthcare Type-2 fuzzy ontology – aided recommendation systems for IoT – based healthcare. Comput. Commun. 0–1 (2018). https://doi.org/10.1016/j.comcom.2017.10.005
15. Vijayakumar, R.L.V., Chilamkurti, N.: An ontology-driven personalized food recommendation in IoT-based healthcare system. J. Supercomput. (2018). https://doi.org/10.1007/s11227-018-2331-8
16. Blanco-Fernández, Y., López-Nores, M., Pazos-Arias, J.J., García-Duque, J.: An improvement for semantics-based recommender systems grounded on attaching temporal information to ontologies and user profiles. Eng. Appl. Artif. Intell. **24**, 1385–1397 (2011). https://doi.org/10.1016/j.engappai.2011.02.020
17. Al-Nazer, A., Helmy, T., Al-Mulhem, M.: User's profile ontology-based semantic framework for personalized food and nutrition recommendation. Procedia Comput. Sci. **32**, 101–108 (2014)
18. Fischer, G.: Communities of Interest: Learning through the Interaction of Multiple Knowledge Systems, pp. 1–13
19. Hussein, D., Han, S.N., Lee, G.M., et al.: Social Cloud-based Cognitive Reasoning for Task-oriented Recommendation in the Social Internet of Things
20. Nizamkari NS (2020) for Service Selection in IOT. 1–5
21. Chikhaoui, B., Chiazzaro, M., Wang, S.: An improved hybrid recommender system by combining predictions. In: Proceedings - 25th IEEE International Conference on Advanced Information Networking and Applications Workshops, WAINA 2011, pp. 644–649 (2011)

High DC-Gain Two-Stage OTA Using Positive Feedback and Split-Length Transistor Techniques

Jamel Nebhen[1(✉)], Mohamed Masmoudi[2],
Wenceslas Rahajandraibe[3], and Khalifa Aguir[3]

[1] College of Computer Engineering and Sciences,
Prince Sattam Bin Abdulaziz University, P.O. Box 151,
Alkharj 11942, Saudi Arabia
j.nebhen@psau.edu.sa
[2] National Engineering School of Sfax, BP. 1173-3038 Sfax, Tunisia
Mohamed.masmoudi@enis.tn
[3] Aix Marseille University, CNRS, IM2NP UMR 7334, 13451 Marseille, France
{wenceslas.rahajandraibe,khalifa.aguir}@im2np.fr

Abstract. A fully differential and split-length transistors (SLT) CMOS two-stage operational transconductance amplifier (OTA) is presented. The proposed amplifier is designed in a CMOS 65 nm process with a 1.2 V supply voltage. The main advantage of this proposed amplifier is the use of both positive feedback technique and the split-length transistors to enhance its DC-gain without affecting the stability, unity-gain bandwidth (UGBW), output voltage swing and power dissipation of the conventional two-stage amplifier. The DC-gain is increased by about 40 dB. The two-stage OTA has been successfully verified and a comprehensive analysis has been provided for common mode gain, differential-mode gain, power supply rejection ratio, input-referred noise and the effect of using SLT on DC-gain sensitivity. The proposed two-stage OTA is used in a flip-around sample-and-hold amplifier (SHA) circuit. A total harmonic distortion of about 0.0018% is obtained for the output spectrum of the SHA circuit.

Keywords: Two-stage OTA · CMOS split transistor · DC-gain · UGBW · Noise · FOM

1 Introduction

The operational transconductance amplifier (OTA) is an essential basic building block in the modern analog and mixed-signal system [1–4]. Various applications require high-gain and high bandwidth as well as high speed amplifiers that can drive capacitive load under low supply voltage. Among these applications, there is the bandgap voltage references, the sample-and-hold amplifier (SHA), the high-resolution analog-to-digital converters and digital-to-analog converters [5–7]. The supply voltage of the traditional amplifiers continues to scale down. Therefore, the classic cascade topologies are no longer suitable for achieving high DC-gain because they decrease the voltage swings. Thus, it is very difficult to design a complementary metal-oxide-semiconductor

© Springer Nature Switzerland AG 2019
A. Alfaries et al. (Eds.): ICC 2019, CCIS 1098, pp. 286–302, 2019.
https://doi.org/10.1007/978-3-030-36368-0_24

(CMOS) amplifier combining at the same time high DC-gain and high unity-gain bandwidth (UGBW). This is a special and handicap problem in low-voltage systems. To increase the DC-gain, a practical solution is to cascode transistors with long channel and biasing these devices at low current levels. On the other hand, to obtain high UGBW, a practical solution is to design a single-stage amplifier with short channel transistors and biasing these devices at high current levels.

In order to improve the DC-gain of amplifier circuit, several techniques have been proposed [8–11]. Cascoding circuit, like the folded-cascode and telescopic amplifier, is a well-known technique to enhance the DC-gain [8]. The main drawback of this technique is the limitation of its output voltage swing. On the other hand, two-stage amplifier is a very suitable circuit to provide a high DC-gain and large output swing. The main drawback of this method is its poor stability. Therefore, the circuit can quickly become unstable if it does not compensate properly [9]. Another method to enhance the DC-gain of amplifier is the gain-boosting technique. The main drawback of this technique is the increase of both power dissipation and layout area owing to use of auxiliary amplifiers [10, 11].

If the amplifier circuit is designed in low-voltage process, the method of bulk-driven may be used to enhance its DC-gain [12–14]. However, in CMOS technologies, the main drawback of a bulk-driven MOS transistor is that its bulk-source transconductance is smaller compared to its gate-source transconductance and insufficient in some systems [15]. Furthermore, bulk-driven method generates some problems such as degradation of the amplifier's phase margin due to the effect of non-dominant poles caused by the added current mirrors [16]. Therefore, the UGBW is smaller considering the same current.

To enhance the gain of the amplifier circuit, positive feedback technique proves to be a good candidate. Because of scaled technologies, the intrinsic gain of MOS transistor is importantly degraded. To avoid this problem, some systems use the positive feedback to increase the DC-gain. For example, in [17, 18], the DC-gain is increased by about 18.5 dB due to a method based on a positive feedback. However, the drawback of this technique is the significant increase of the chip area. In [19, 20], the DC-gain is increased however, the UGBW is decreased. A folded-cascode amplifier with positive feedback is proposed to increase DC-gain [21]. However, the drawback of this method is the high sensitivity of the circuit towards process variations. The circuit of two-stage amplifier with the method of hybrid-cascode compensation is shown in Fig. 1 [22]. The first stage is a folded cascade amplifier and the second stage is a common-source amplifier. The amplifier developed in this paper uses the technique of positive feedback and the technique of split-length transistor (SLT) to increase the output resistance of the second stage. Therefore, the DC-gain is increased without changing neither the UGBW, nor power dissipation, nor stability and nor output swing. In addition, the reduction of the sensitivity of DC-gain towards process variation can be done by the technique of SLT.

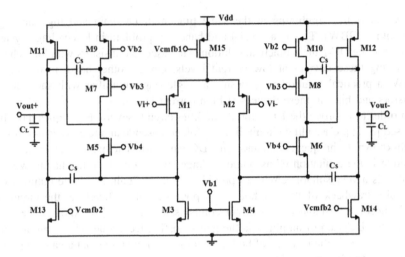

Fig. 1. Circuit of the conventional two-stage OTA using the technique of the hybrid-cacode compensation [22].

This paper describes the design of a proposed two-stage OTA using a positive feedback technique and split-length transistor to enhance the DC-gain. It is organized as follows. First, the description of the proposed SLT technique is given in Sect. 2. Then, a theoretical analysis of the proposed circuit is given in Sect. 3. After, simulation results and comparison are presented in Sect. 4. Finally, the paper is concluded in Sect. 5.

2 Split-Length MOS Transistor Analysis

Despite a regular MOSFET and a split-length MOS transistor have the same geometrical structure; however, the second transistor has a better transconductance and output resistance than the first one. If the regular metal-oxide silicon field-effect transistor (MOSFET) is used to enhance the gain, then it requires a long channel. Else, if the same regular MOSFET is used to increase the speed, then it requires a short channel. The split-length MOS transistor has a major asset compared to the regular MOSFET. With the same channel length, the split-length MOS transistor will increase the gain without affecting the speed.

The small signal model of a split-length MOS transistor is shown in Fig. 2 [23, 24]. Transistors M1 and M2 are tied together. Moreover, they have the same width W and their lengths are L_1 and L_2 respectively. The common-gate voltage V_g of split-length MOS transistor specify the operating regions of transistors M1 and M2. To identify the operating region of a transistor, we compare its V_g with its threshold voltage V_{th}. In this case, if V_g is greater than V_{th} of both M1 and M2, then M1 operates in linear region and M2 operates in saturation region. In addition, V_{th} of drain transistor M2 decreases because of the bulk bias. Therefore, the drain-source voltage V_{ds} of source transistor M1 increase. As a result, the operating region of M1 moves from linear inversion region to the edge of saturation or moderate inversion region.

Equation (1) describes the output resistance of split-length MOS transistor with bulk bias R_{out} and Eq. (2) describes its output resistance with positive feedback R_{outp}. If $g_{mbr2} > 1$, then R_{outp} is a negative value. In addition, the split-length MOS transistor input transconductance g_m is depicted in Eq. (3).

$$R_{out} = r_1 + r_2 + (g_{m2} + g_{mb})r_1r_2 \simeq (g_{m2} + g_{mb})r_1r_2 \tag{1}$$

$$R_{outp} = \frac{r_1 + r_2 + (g_{m2} + g_{mb})r_1r_2}{1 - g_{mb}r_2} \tag{2}$$

$$g_m = \frac{g_{m1}r_1 + g_{m2}r_2 + g_{m1}(g_{m2} + g_{mb})r_1r_2}{r_1 + r_2 + (g_{m2} + g_{mb})r_1r_2} \simeq g_{m1} \tag{3}$$

First, simulations of parameter g_m of n-channel split-length MOS transistor are carried out for different gate and bulk voltages of M2. Then, simulations of its parameter R_{out} are also performed. Results are shown in Fig. 3a and b. Looking at the characteristics of Fig. 3a, we can conclude that a higher value of transconductance g_m can be achieved if the channel length L_1 has a short value. Moreover, the total effective transconductance g_m decrease if the length L_1 increase. Similarly, for the p-channel split-length MOS transistor, its small-signal parameters are extracted to design the proposed two-stage OTA.

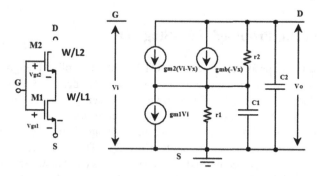

Fig. 2. Split-length MOS transistor with the small-signal equivalent model.

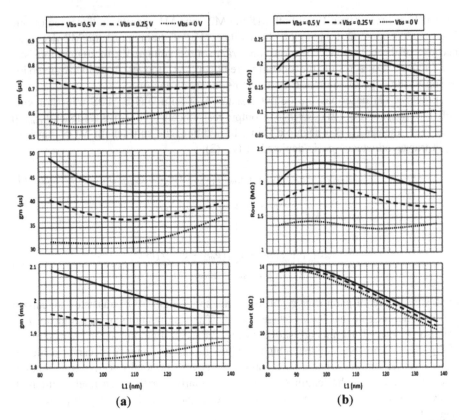

Fig. 3. Simulation results of the split-length MOS transistor: (a) Transconductance of SLT (W = 10 μm and L = 0.13 μm); (b) Output resistance of SLT

3   Design of the Proposed Two-Stage OTA

Figure 4 shown the proposed two-stage OTA with all splitted-length transistors. A folded cascade amplifier and a common-source amplifier depict respectively the first and the second stage of the OTA. To improve the frequency response of the proposed circuit, we use the technique of hybrid-cascode compensation to obtain simple and accurate poles and zeros relations [22]. All the n-channel and p-channel MOSFET transistors of the two-stage OTA are splitted [25–28]. The proposed two-stage OTA includes two current mirrors composed by transistors sets (M18a, M18b, M19a, M19b) and (M16a, M16b, M17a, M17b). To enhance the DC-gain of the OTA circuit without any change in the UGBW, the idea is to create a positive feedback loop. In this case, the output signal $Vout+$ is applied to the drain of transistor M16a and the output signal $Vout-$ to the drain of transistor M19a.

The current mirror small-signal analysis is realized at the output terminal $Vout+$. The output resistance R_{CS} can be written as

$$R_{CS} = \frac{1}{X+Y-Z} \tag{4}$$

With $X = g_{m18a}/(1 + g_{m18a}R_{18b})$, $Y = 1/(g_{m16a}r_{ds16a}R_{16b} + r_{ds16a} + R_{16b})$ and $Z = g_{m16a}/(1 + g_{m16a}R_{16b})$. Where g_{m16a} and g_{m18a} are the transconductance of transistors M16a and M18a, R_{16b} and R_{18b} are the channel resistance of transistors M16b and M18b is in triode region. Therefore, the DC-gain of the two-stage OTA is written as

$$A_d = g_{m1a}R_{out1}g_{m11a}R_{out2} \tag{5}$$

$$R_{out1} = g_{m7a}r_{ds7a}r_{ds9a} \parallel [g_{m5a}r_{ds5a}(r_{ds1a} \parallel r_{ds3a})] \tag{6}$$

$$R_{out2} = \frac{1}{g_{ds11a} + g_{ds13a} + G_{CS}} \tag{7}$$

Where g_m denotes the trans-conductance of transistors, R_{out1} denotes the output resistance of the first stage and R_{out2} denotes the output resistance of the second stage, r_{ds} denotes the drain-source resistor, $G_{CS} = 1/R_{CS}$ and $g_{ds} = 1/r_{ds}$. If we choose the denominator of Eq. (7) in the vicinity of zero with $g_{ds11a} + g_{ds13a} + G_{CS} > 0$, then we can drastically increase the differential voltage gain A_d.

After performing the analysis of the common-mode gain, we perform the analysis of the current mirror output resistance R'_{CS} that can be written as

$$R'_{CS} = \frac{1}{X+Y+Z} \tag{8}$$

With $X = g_{m18a}/(1 + g_{m18a}R_{18b})$, $Y = 1/(g_{m16a}r_{ds16a}R_{16b} + r_{ds16a} + R_{16b})$ and $Z = g_{m16a}/(1 + g_{m16a}R_{16b})$. Therefore, from Eq. (8), the second stage's output resistance can be written as

$$R'_{out2} = \frac{1}{g_{ds11a} + g_{ds13a} + G'_{CS}} \tag{9}$$

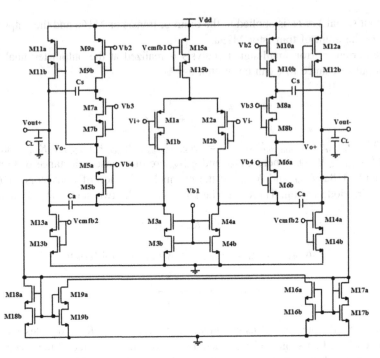

Fig. 4. Proposed two-stage OTA using the all split-length MOS transistors and the positive feedback techniques.

Where $G'_{CS} = 1/R'_{CS}$. From Eqs. (8) and (9), it is clear that R'_{out2} is fewer than R_{out2}. Therefore, this feature is very effective to reduce the common mode gain A_{cm} that can be written as

$$A_{CM} = \frac{g_{m1a}R_{out1}}{1 + 2g_{m1a}r_{ds15a}} g_{m11a}R'_{out2} \tag{10}$$

A small variation of power supply voltage directly affects the signal on output nodes. We perform a PSRR analysis to evaluate this degradation and to view how well the proposed two-stage OTA can reject ripples coming from its input power supply at various frequencies. The PSRR can be written as

$$PSRR = \frac{-A_d}{\left(\frac{g_{m15a}}{2} + g_{m9a}\right)R_{out1}g_{m11a}R'_{out2}} \tag{11}$$

Therefore, from Eq. (11), increasing the differential-mode gain A_d and decreasing the R'_{out2} can improve the PSRR of the proposed two-stage OTA.

The noise source of the proposed two-stage OTA originate from flicker noise and thermal noise components. For low frequency and for typical bias conditions and device geometries, the flicker noise component is usually larger than the thermal noise component. The total noise of a MOSFET from the Gray and Meyer noise model is given as [30]

$$\frac{\overline{v_n^2}}{\Delta f} = \frac{K_n}{C_{OX}WLf} + \frac{8KT}{3g_m} \tag{12}$$

Where K_n denotes the flicker noise coefficient, g_m denotes the transconductance parameter of the MOSFET device, C_{OX} denotes the gate oxide capacitance per unit area, W denotes the channel width, L denotes the channel length, f denotes the frequency and Δf denotes the bandwidth. Noise analysis of the proposed two-stage OTA can be written as

$$\frac{\overline{v_{eq}^2}}{\Delta f} \approx 2\left[\overline{v_{n1a}^2} + \overline{v_{n3a}^2}\left(\frac{g_{m3a}}{g_{m1a}}\right)^2 + \overline{v_{n13a}^2}\left(\frac{g_{m13a}}{g_{m1a}}\right)^2\right] \tag{13}$$

Substituting Eqs. (12) into (13), the total input-referred noise of the proposed two-stage OTA can be written as

$$\begin{aligned}
\frac{\overline{v_{eq}^2}}{\Delta f} &\approx \frac{8KT}{3g_{m1a}}\left(1 + \left(\frac{g_{m3a}}{g_{m1a}}\right)^2 + \left(\frac{g_{m13a}}{g_{m1a}}\right)^2\right) + \frac{K_p}{C_{OX}L_{1a}W_{1a}f} \\
&+ \frac{K_n}{C_{OX}L_{3a}W_{3a}f}\frac{g_{m3a}^2}{g_{m1a}^2} + \frac{K_p}{C_{OX}L_{13a}W_{13a}f}\frac{g_{m13a}^2}{g_{m1a}^2}
\end{aligned} \tag{14}$$

The transfer function of the conventional two-stage OTA can be written as [22]

$$A_v(s) = \frac{A_0\left(1 + \left(\frac{s}{w_{z_1}}\right)\right)\left(1 + \left(\frac{s}{w_{z_2}}\right)\right)\left(1 + \left(\frac{s}{w_{z_3}}\right)\right)}{\left(1 + \left(\frac{s}{w_{p_1}}\right)\right)\left(1 + \left(\frac{s}{w_{p_2}}\right)\right)\left(1 + \left(\frac{s}{w_{p_3}}\right)\right)\left(1 + \left(\frac{s}{w_{p_4}}\right)\right)} \tag{15}$$

Where A_0 denotes the DC-gain of the OTA. Therefore, from Eq. (15), the dominant pole can be written as follow

$$w_{p1} = \frac{1}{g_{m11a}(C_a + C_s)R_{02}R_B} \tag{16}$$

In the small-signal model of the proposed two-stage OTA, shown in Fig. 5, the technique of using a positive feedback changes its frequency response. Thus, the output resistance of the second stage was changed by this feedback.

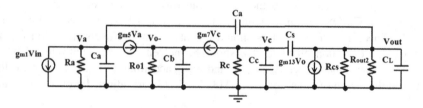

Fig. 5. Small-signal equivalent circuit of the proposed two-stage OTA.

According to the positive feedback, the dominant pole of the proposed two-stage OTA becomes

$$w_{p1.prop} = \frac{1}{g_{m11a}(C_a + C_s)R_{out2}R_B}$$ (17)

In the conventional two-stage OTA, only the dominant pole location depends on the output resistance of the second stage [22]. Therefore, the location of other poles and zeros does not affect by the positive feedback. In fact, from Eq. (17), the dominant pole can be decreased while remain unchanged other poles and zeros. Thus, the pole of splitted transistor is performed without any variation of the UGBW of the proposed two-stage OTA. As a result, this is a very important characteristic of split-length transistor used in the proposed circuit.

The DC-gain of op-amp is directly affected by a minor change in the transconductance g_m of the components producing negative resistance [29]. Moreover, a large variation in the op-amp DC-gain will be resulting. However, an interesting solution to alleviate this problem is to use the tail resistor. For more explanation, if the component g_m without the tail resistor has a small offset of ($\Delta g_m/g_m$), then the same component gm using the tail resistor has a new offset, which can be written as

$$\frac{\Delta g_{m,new}}{g_m} = \frac{\left(\frac{(g_m + \Delta g_m)}{1 + (g_m + \Delta g_m)R}\right) - \left(\frac{g_m}{1 + g_mR}\right)}{\left(\frac{g_m}{1 + g_mR}\right)}$$

$$= \frac{1}{1 + (g_m + \Delta g_m)R} \times \frac{\Delta g_m}{g_m},$$ (18)

Therefore, it is clear that from Eq. (18) the offset of component g_m was reduced by a factor of $1/[1 + (g_m + \Delta g_m)R]$ due to the use of the tail resistor. Furthermore, a negative resistance is created at the output of the second stage by using the technique of split-length transistor. Transistors (M16b, M17b, M18b, M19b) are in triode region. As a result, their channel resistance depicts an embedded tail resistor. Thus, the split-length transistor allows to decrease the sensitivity towards process variation.

4   Simulation Results and Comparison

To verify the accuracy of the obtained relations, the proposed and conventional two-stage OTA are designed in a CMOS 65 nm technology with a 1.2 V supply voltage as shown in Fig. 6. Table 1 shows the size of transistors, passive components and bias voltages. In a CMOS 65 nm technology, V_{ds-sat} of transistor is between 50 mV and 100 mV. Therefore, the transistors should operate in strong inversion region [8]. In addition, this condition alleviates the short-channel effects [8]. Input-referred noise depends on transconductance g_{m1a}, g_{m3a} and g_{m13a} according to Eq. (14). Thus, if the width and the length of transistors M1a, M3a and M13a are adjusted properly, then the input-referred noise can be reduced. For *Ca* and *Cs* capacitors, their values are chosen to ensure a tradeoff between the stability and speed.

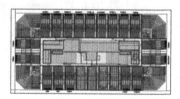

Fig. 6. Layout of the two-stage OTA with the CMFB circuit in 65 nm CMOS process with an area of 120 μm × 160 μm.

To cancel the first zero by the second pole of the proposed two-stage OTA, *Ca* and *Cs* capacitors are given equal values. In order to increase the transconductance g_m value, transistors (M5a, M6a, M7a, M8a, M11a, M12a) should be fixed with a proper size. Therefore, their non-dominant poles are moved far enough from the unity-gain bandwidth. Transistors (M3a, M4a, M9a, M10a, M13a, M14a, M15a) are connected as a current source. Each transistor should satisfy the $V_{ds\text{-}sat}$ condition mentioned before. Therefore, the voltage V_{eff} of transistor M15a is chosen as small as possible, nearly about 50 mV, because if V_{eff} has a great value, then it limits the two-stage OTA input-common mode range. To improve the gain and reduce the flicker noise and DC-offset, input transistors must have a great length *L*. In addition, dimensions of split-length transistors are chosen in the objective to increase the differential voltage gain A_d of the proposed two-stage OTA. Figure 7 shows the open-loop frequency responses of the proposed and the conventional two-stage OTA. From the result of the schematic level simulation, it is clear that the DC-gain is improved by about 40 dB for the proposed circuit. Both conventional and proposed two-stage OTA have the same UGBW of 600 MHz and the same phase margin of 70°. In the same way, the conventional and

Table 1. Transistors and other elements parameters for proposed and conventional two-stage OTA.

Device	(W/L)	Parameter	Value
M1, M1a, M1b, M2, M2a, M2b	60 μm/0.13 μm	C_a	1 pF
M3, M3a, M3b, M4, M4a, M4b	45 μm/0.13 μm	C_S	1 pF
M5, M5a, M5b, M6, M6a, M6b	18 μm/0.13 μm	C_L	1 pF
M7, M7a, M7b, M8, M8a, M8b	60 μm/0.13 μm	V_{b1}	0.55 V
M9, M9a, M9b, M10, M10a, M10b	60 μm/0.13 μm	V_{b2}	1.1 V
M11, M11a, M11b, M12, M12a, M12b	60 μm/0.13 μm	V_{b3}	0.65 V
M13, M13a, M13b, M14, M14a, M14b	60 μm/0.13 μm	V_{b4}	0.9 V
M15, M15a, M15b	45 μm/0.13 μm		
M16a, M16b, M19a, M19b	3 μm/0.13 μm		
M17a, M17b, M18a, M18b	2 μm/0.13 μm		

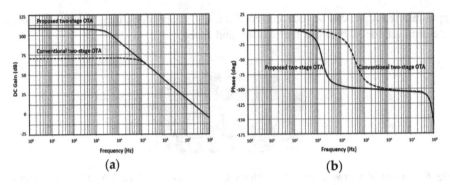

Fig. 7. Proposed and conventional two-stage OTA open-loop responses: (a) DC-gain; (b) Phase margin.

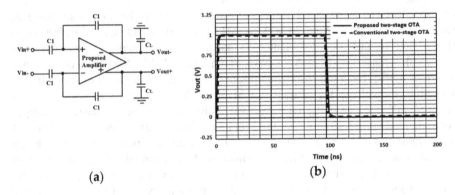

Fig. 8. Unity-gain capacitive buffer two-stage OTA large signal step responses: (a) Unity-gain capacitive buffer circuit; (b) Large signal step response of the two-stage OTA

proposed circuit are used as a capacitive buffer with a unity gain. The capacitive buffer, shown in Fig. 8a, drive a 1pF total capacitive load ($C1$ = 2 pF, $C2$ = 2 pF) [29]. To measure the slew rate of the circuits, a 1 V_{pp} and 5 MHz square wave signal was applied. The results are shown in Fig. 8b. In the same condition, both conventional and proposed two-stage OTA have the 1% settling time measurement of about 3.2 ns. Therefore, the proposed circuit is not suitable to drive a resistive load. The analysis of DC-gain, differential output swing, power dissipation, phase margin, slew rate, UGBW, input-referred noise, power supply rejection ratio (PSRR) and common mode rejection ratio (CMRR) are carried out for both conventional and proposed two-stage OTA. Table 2 evaluate the comparative simulation results in three process and temperature corners as TT for Typical-Typical, FF for Fast-Fast and SS for Slew-Slew. From Table 2, all specifications of conventional and proposed circuit are remained unchanged excepting DC-gain, PSRR and CMRR. We perform the analysis of the PSRR and CMRR for both circuits by including an input offset at TT (27 °C) corner. The simulation results are shown in Fig. 10. In the same conditions, the proposed two-stage OTA has better PSRR and CMRR than the conventional two-stage OTA.

Table 2. Performances and specifications of proposed and conventional two-stage OTA.

Device	Conventional two-stage OTA			Proposed two-stage OTA		
	TT(27 °C)	FF(−40 °C)	SS(90 °C)	TT(27 °C)	FF(−40 °C)	SS(90 °C)
Technology	65 nm	65 nm	65 nm	65 nm	65 nm	65 nm
Supply (V)	1.2	1.2	1.2	1.2	1.2	1.2
DC-gain (dB)	74	68	78	110	95	102
Input-referred noise (nV/$\sqrt{\text{Hz}}$)	14	13	14	7	8	7
UGBW (MHz)	390	490	320	600	710	540
Phase margin (deg)	71	70	71	71	70	70
Power diss. (mW)	6	9	5.6	5.5	8	4.5
Slew rate (V/µs)	860	1028	755	880	1050	750
CMRR (dB)	108	116	128	125	128	145
PSRR (dB)	80	75	110	109	101	116

The flip-around SHA samples from a 2 MHz input frequency and $A_{in,diff} = 0.4$ Vpp amplitude sinusoidal input signal. Fast Fourier transform (FFT) analysis of the SHA using 256 points is performed and output result is shown in Fig. 9b. Consequently, the total harmonic distortion is easily calculated and it is about 0.0018%. We should know that the conventional and proposed circuit have the same THD. For a case study, the proposed two-stage OTA is used in an 80 MS/s flip-around sample-and-hold amplifier (SHA) [30] (Fig. 9a). To evaluate the effect of both process and mismatch variations on the proposed two-stage OTA, Monte Carlo (MC) simulations are performed. Thus, a 1200-run simulations are carried out. The MC histogram of the proposed circuit is shown in Fig. 11a, b, c and the results are summarized in Table 3.

The results reveals that if the process and mismatch variations are taken into account, then the specifications of the proposed two-stage OTA are not significantly changed. To evaluate the proper operation of the proposed circuit, Table 4 shows a comparison between its post-layout simulation results with some circuit's methods existing in the state of the art. The layout area of the proposed circuit is smaller compared with almost existing methods. In addition, the DC-gain of the proposed circuit is 110 dB, which is the highest one. It is at least 14 dB more than the other sited solutions.

A very important parameter to evaluate the well function of the proposed two-stage OTA is its input-referred noise. The proposed two-stage OTA exhibits the lowest input-referred noise compared to other circuits. From Fig. 11d, the input-referred noise of the proposed two-stage OTA is about 7 nV/$\sqrt{\text{Hz}}$.

Table 3. Monte Carlo and input-referred noise analysis of the proposed two-stage OTA.

Specifications	Mean value	Standard deviation
DC-gain (dB)	110	6.7
Input-referred noise @ 1 kHz (nV/$\sqrt{\text{Hz}}$)	7	1.1
Phase margin (deg)	70	0.2
UGBW (MHz)	600	2

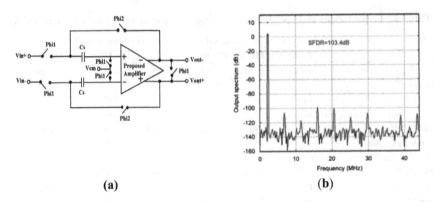

(a)   **(b)**

Fig. 9. FFT and flip-around of the SHA output circuit: (a) Flip-around SHA [30]; (b) FFT response of the SHA circuit.

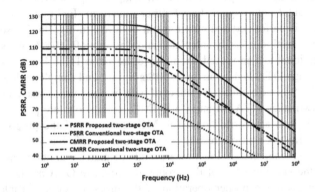

Fig. 10. PSRR and CMRR responses of the proposed and conventional two-stage OTA.

In order to achieve a comparison of the other performance parameters, we use the commonly two figures of merit FOM_S referring to the small signal and FOM_L referring to the large signal behavior, which they can be written as [31–33]

$$FOM_S = \frac{UGBW \cdot C_L}{I_T} \tag{19}$$

$$FOM_L = \frac{SR \cdot C_L}{I_T} \tag{20}$$

These figures of merit show a trade-off between speed performances and total bias current I_T for a given load C_L. Therefore, the higher the value of these figures of merit, the better is the two-stage OTA performance. Therefore, Table 4 shows a good value of both FOM_S and FOM_L achieved by the proposed two-stage OTA.

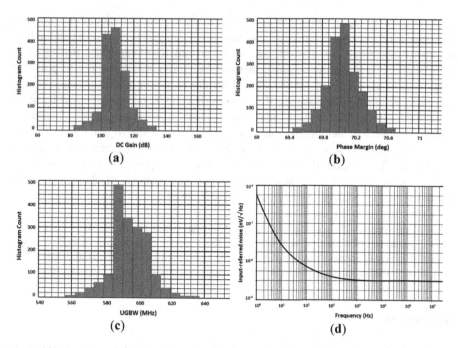

Fig. 11. Histogram of Monte Carlo simulations and input-referred noise response of the proposed two-stage OTA: (a) DC-gain; (b) Phase margin; (c) UGBW; (d) Input-referred noise.

Table 4. Proposed two-stage OTA performances comparison with the state of the art.

	This work[a]	[13]	[14]	[18][b]	[19][a]	[27][b]	[31]	[34]
Technology	65 nm	180 nm	130 nm	180 nm	180 nm	0.5 μm	0.6 μm	0.18 μm
Supply voltage (V)	1.2	1	0.25	0.9	1.8	3	3	1.2
DC-gain (dB)	110	64	60	67	74	82	83	96
Input-referred noise @ 1 kHz (nV/√Hz)	7	–	–	33	160	–	–	160
UGBW (MHz)	600	2	0.002	278	368	12	19.5	374
Phase margin (deg)	70	45	53	62	60	85	56	59
Power dissipation (mW)	2.5	0.13	$18\ 10^{-6}$	1.7	7.9	1.2	1.44	7.9
Slew rate (V/μs)	880	0.7	$7\ 10^{-4}$	0.7	190	10	13.8	826
FOM_S (MHz.pF/mA)	286	15	417	293	85	300	608	86
FOM_L (V.pF/mA)	365	5	146	200	190	250	431	192
CL (pF)	1	1	15	2	1	30	15	1

[a]Post-layout simulation; [b]Schematic level simulation.

5 Conclusion

This paper introduces a new fully differential split-length all transistors two-stage OTA designed in a CMOS 65 nm process with a 1.2 V supply voltage. To increase the DC-gain, the proposed circuit uses the positive feedback technique and the split-length all

MOS transistor at the same time. In order to evaluate the well function of the proposed two-stage OTA, firstly, a comprehensive theoretical analysis is carried out and helpful parametric equations are derived. Secondly, several simulations are performed to evaluate effectiveness of the proposed method. As a result, simulation results prove the advantages of the proposed method. Due to the use of the positive feedback technique and the split-length all transistors, the differential voltage gain is increased by about 40 dB. This differential voltage gain improvement is achieved without increasing power consumption and neither changing stability nor UGBW nor output voltage swing. The proposed two-stage OTA is used in an 80 MS/s SHA circuit. Therefore, it achieves a THD of about 0.0018%. Finally, the noise response of the proposed two-stage OTA is very well. It exhibits a low input-referred noise of about 7 nV/$\sqrt{\text{Hz}}$ within the frequency range from 10 Hz to 1 kHz frequency.

Acknowledgements. This project was supported by the Deanship of Scientific Research at Prince Sattam Bin Abdulaziz University under the research project 2019/01/11709. It was conducted jointly in cooperation with Aix-Marseille University, IM2NP laboratory UMR-CNRS 7334, France, during the academic year 2018-2019.

References

1. Zhao, X., Fang, H., Ling, T., et al.: Low-voltage process-insensitive frequency compensation method for two-stage OTA with enhanced DC gain. AEU-Int. J. Electron. Commun. **69**, 685–690 (2015)
2. Neag, M., Oneț, N., Kovács, I., et al.: Comparative analysis of simulation based methods for deriving the phase- and gain-margins of feedback circuits with op-amps. IEEE Trans. Circ. Syst. II. Exp. Briefs **62**, 625–634 (2015)
3. Zuo, L., Islam, S.K.: Low-voltage bulk-driven operational amplifier with improved transconductance. IEEE Trans. Circ. Syst. I. Regul. Pap. **60**, 2084–2091 (2013)
4. Esparza-Alfaro, F., Pennisi, S., Palumbo, G., et al.: Low-power class-AB CMOS voltage feedback current operational amplifier with tunable gain and bandwidth. IEEE Trans. Circ. Syst. II. Exp. Briefs **61**, 574–578 (2014)
5. Cho, Y.K., Park, B.H.: Single op-amp second-order loop filter for continuous-time delta–sigma modulators. Electron. Lett. **51**, 619–621 (2015)
6. He, L., Zhu, G., Long, F., et al.: A multibit delta–sigma modulator with double noise-shaped segmentation. IEEE Trans. Circ. Syst. II. Exp. Briefs **62**, 241–245 (2015)
7. Sahoo, B.D., Inamdar, A.: Thermal-noise-canceling switched-capacitor circuit. IEEE Trans. Circ. Syst. II. Exp. Briefs **63**, 628–632 (2016)
8. Johns, D., Martin, K.: Analog Integrated Circuit Design. Wiley, Hoboken (1997)
9. Asloni, M., Hadidi, K., Khoei, A.: Design of a new folded cascode Op-Amp using positive feedback and bulk amplification. IEICE Trans. Electron. **90**, 1253–1257 (2007)
10. Gulati, K., Lee, H.S.: A high-swing CMOS telescopic operational amplifier. IEEE J. Solid-State Circ. **33**, 2010–2019 (1998)
11. Bult, K., Geelen, G.J.G.M.: A fast-settling CMOS op-amp for SC circuits with 90-dB DC gain. IEEE J. Solid-State Circ. **25**, 1379–1384 (1990)

12. Kulej, T., Khateb, F.: Bulk-driven adaptively biased OTA in 0.18 μm CMOS. Electron Lett. **51**, 458–460 (2015)
13. Raikos, G., Vlassis, S.: Low-voltage bulk-driven input stage with improved transconductance. Int. J. Circ. Theory Appl. **39**, 327–339 (2011)
14. Ferreira, L.H.C., Sonkusale, S.R.: A 60-dB gain OTA operating at 0.25-V power supply in 130-nm digital CMOS process. IEEE Trans. Circ. Syst. I. Regul. Pap. **61**, 1609–1617 (2014)
15. Razavi, B.: Design of Analog CMOS Integrated Circuits. McGraw-Hill, New York (2001)
16. Akbari, M., Hashemipour, O.: Enhancing transconductance of ultra-lowpower two-stage folded cascode OTA. Electron. Lett. **50**, 1514–1516 (2014)
17. Khameh, H., Shamsi, H.: On the design of a low-voltage twostage OTA using bulk-driven and positive feedback techniques. Int. J. Electron. **99**, 1309–1315 (2012)
18. Khameh, H., Mirzaie, H., Shamsi, H.: A new two-stage op-amp using hybrid cascode compensation, bulk-driven, and positive feedback techniques. In: 8th IEEE International NEWCAS Conference on (NEWCAS), pp. 109–112 (2010)
19. Pude, M., Mukund, P.R., Burleson, J.: Positive feedback for gain enhancement in sub-100 nm multi-GHz CMOS amplifier design. Int. J. Circ. Theory Appl. **43**, 111–124 (2013)
20. Tran, P.T., Hess, H.L., Noren, K.V., et al.: Gain-enhancement differential amplifier using positive feedback. In: IEEE 55th International Midwest Symposium on Circuits and Systems (MWSCAS), pp. 718–721 (2012)
21. Farahmand, S., Shamsi, H.: Positive feedback technique for DC-gain enhancement of folded cascode op-amps. In: IEEE 10th International New Circuits and Systems Conference (NEWCAS), pp. 261–264 (2012)
22. Yavari, M.: Hybrid cascode compensation for two-stage CMOS op-amps. IEICE Trans. Electron. **88**, 1161–1165 (2005)
23. Cunha, A.I.A., Schneider, M.C., Galup-Montoro, C.: An MOS transistor model for analog circuit design. IEEE J. Solid-State Circ. **33**, 1510–1519 (1998)
24. Ferreira, L.H.C., Pimenta, T.C.: Extraction of MOS parameters from BSIM3v3 model using minimum square method for quick manual design. Proc. IEE Circ. Dev. Syst. **153**, 153–158 (2006)
25. Ferreira, L.H.C., Pimenta, T.C., Moreno, R.L.: An ultra-low-voltage ultralow-power CMOS miller OTA with rail-to-rail input/output swing. IEEE Trans. Circ. Syst. II. Exp. Briefs **54**, 843–847 (2007)
26. Ning, N., Yang, F., Zhiling, S., et al.: A low-sensitivity negative resistance load fully differential OTA under low voltage 40 nm CMOS logic process. Chin. Sci. Pap. **688**, 1–7 (2012)
27. Saxena, V., Baker, R.J.: Indirect compensation techniques for three-stage fully-differential op-amps. 53rd IEEE International Midwest Symposium on Circuits and Systems (MWSCAS), pp. 588–591 (2010)
28. Furth, P.M., Thota, N.R., Nammi, V.H., et al.: Low dropout (LDO) voltage regulator design using split-length compensation. In: IEEE 55th International Midwest Symposium on Circuits and Systems (MWSCAS), pp. 1088–1091 (2012)
29. Assaad, R.S., Silva-Martinez, J.: Enhancing general performance of folded cascode amplifier by recycling current. Electron. Lett. **43**, 1–2 (2007)
30. Gray, P.R., Meyer, R.G.: Analysis and Design of Analog İntegrated Circuits. Wiley, Hoboken (2001)
31. Ho, K.P., Chan, C.F., Choy, C.S., et al.: Reversed nested Miller compensation with voltage buffer and nulling resistor. IEEE J. Solid-State Circ. **38**, 1735–1738 (2003)

32. Grasso, A.D., Palumbo, G., Pennisi, S.: Advances in reversed nested miller compensation. IEEE Trans. Circ. Syst. I. Regul. Pap. **54**, 1459–1470 (2007)
33. Grasso, A.D., Palumbo, G., Pennisi, S.: Three-stage CMOS OTA for large capacitive loads with efficient frequency compensation scheme. IEEE Trans. Circ. Syst. II. Exp. Briefs **53**, 1044–1048 (2006)
34. Anisheh, S.M., Shamsi, H., Mirhassani, M.: Positive feedback technique and split-length transistors for DC-gain enhancement of two-stage op-amp. IET Circ. Dev. Syst. **11**, 605–612 (2017)

Automated Detection for Student Cheating During Written Exams: An Updated Algorithm Supported by Biometric of Intent

Fatimah A. Alrubaish[✉], Ghadah A. Humaid, Rasha M. Alamri,
and Mariam A. Elhussain

Department of Computer Information Systems, College of Computer Science
and Information Technology, Imam Abdulrahman Bin Faisal University, P.O.
Box 1982, Dammam, Saudi Arabia
{2150000689, 2150011140,
2150004064, maelhussein}@iau.edu.sa

Abstract. This research proposes an upgrade to existing algorithms to build a model that detects cheating intent. The algorithm is supported by a composition of technologies and devices that includes a thermal detector attached with a surveillance camera and enhanced with an eye tracking system. Basically, when students intend to cheat, their body will emit a certain range of heat due to the interaction of the human's body and their feelings. The emitted heat will trigger the camera to focus and detect the students' face, next it will detect their eyes and start analyzing their movement and then determine whether a student has the intention to cheat or not. Eventually, applying this model would be very helpful in detecting the cheating intentions of the students, and the use of it is not limited to the educational environments only it could be applied on other areas with minor adjustment.

Keywords: Biometrics · Eye tracking · Eye movement · Cheating

1 Introduction

Measuring and statistically analyzing the unique physiological or behavioral humans' characteristics is the definition of Biometric Technology [1]. The main purpose of using these technologies is to access control, identification, or identify people who are under surveillance. There are two types of biometrics, behavioral and physiological [2]. Behavioral biometrics are the unique ways of which people are acting. They include the recognition of walking gait, typing patterns and speech. While the physiological biometrics relates to the specific characteristics, dimensions, and measurements of the human's body. They include fingerprint, retinal scan, iris scan, hand geometry, vascular patterns, and finally the facial recognition which is one of the major concerns of this research [3]. Using one or a combination of these biometric technologies, will allow and assist in detecting a variety of humans' intentions including students' cheating intention in exams. According to Webster's New World Dictionary "cheat" is defined as "the act of deceiving or swindling" [4]. In educational environment, it refers to breach of academic integrity. As a general perspective, students usually tend to cheat in

A. Alfaries et al. (Eds.): ICC 2019, CCIS 1098, pp. 303–311, 2019.
https://doi.org/10.1007/978-3-030-36368-0_25

exams when they could not answer, face difficulties or uncertainty in answering a question. When students start planning to cheat, they will experience a verity of emotions including worry, tension, fear or maybe anger [5]. Our bodies interact with our emotions and this interaction occurs in a variety of ways. In the cheating case, the body temperature will rise, and it will start emitting a range of heat out of it. This will make the student detectable when using surveillance cameras attached with a thermal detector. Also, in written exams, when students intended to cheat, they will start looking around to decide which paper they will cheat from. This is also detectable by focusing on their eyes and applying an eye tracking technique. Since using one technology or technique to detect the cheating intentions of students may reveal with misleading and inaccurate results. This research aims to construct a model that detects the cheating intentions of students during conducting the written exams. The model is designed to figure out the students' bodily emotions and facial expressions, specifically the eye movements. It is composed of a surveillance camera attached with a thermal detector and an eye movement tracker. The technologies to be used include a surveillance camera, which is one of the most common technologies used in the corporeal security, and a thermal detector that is attached to it. The thermal detector is a well-known device used to detect any heat comes from any object whether it's a live creature or a material. In addition, the eye-tracking technology that can be applied using a variety of techniques and the one will be used in this model, is the detection of the student's eye's pupil. After applying a differentiation of gray color shades through the camera that will further allow the tracking of the eye movements according to its deviation from its center, this can be done by distinguishing between the dark shade (pupil) and the bright shade (white area in the eye) [6]. The research is organized as follows: Sect. 2 discusses and reviews the relevant literature. Sections 3 and 4 describes the research methodology along with the proposed model of this research and illustrate the way of how it will work to detect the cheating intention of the students. Finally, Sect. 6 represents the conclusion.

2 Literature Review

Recently, biometrics becomes a reliable method for authorization and authentication. The biometric process generally divided into different stages depending on the biometrics application: enrollment and comparison. The enrollment stage is where subjects are registered in a biometric database. The system scans pre-defined user's biometric characteristics for the first time and produce a raw digital image or record which is then used to create a stored template. When the user get authenticated, the biometric system captures their biometrics data and compare it with a stored template. The biometric systems have been enhanced and upgraded to be multi-modal instead of unimodal. The biometric systems are classified into two types, unimodal biometric systems, and multi-modal biometric systems which called consent biometrics. The unimodal biometric systems are used only for one type of biometrics, it could be physical or behavioral. For example, using only fingerprint or hand signature as a stand-alone way of authentication. On the other hand, the multi-modal biometric systems use two or more types of biometrics, depending on the purpose of their usage. As suggested in [5], the user authentication systems can use multi-modal biometrics to figure out the intention of users when they get authenticated.

In another work [7], An Automated Biometric of Intent Identification System (ABoIIS) is identified to find a potential threat in highly secured facilities through scanning the invisible intention of the passengers. The proposed system is based on the discrete emotion theory and face expression analysis technique, in order to identify the bad intention from the elementary points in the face that defined as the Action Unit (AU). These AUs considered as the alphabet of the emotional language, since they have been produced by decomposing the face into 45 points. Also, it is proposed to implement the system with the following principles: the emotional language of thought, machine learning, and real-time performance. Through combining these principles, the proposed system will analyze the face expressions based on the extracted action units. Then, classify these AU to six basic emotions joy, sadness, anger, disgust, fear, and surprise, in order to acquire an accurate and real-time result.

Furthermore, the use of eye movements as a biometric in human authentication, is proposed by [8] to assist in getting an accurate result after conducting measurements on twelve participants' eye movements. The eye movements data has measured the dynamics of pupil sizes, gaze velocity and infrared reflections of the eyes' distances. The integration of eye movements-based identification with general video-based biometric systems shows that the perfection of biometrics requires uniqueness, universal, permanent over time, easy to measure, cheap in costs, and have high user acceptance. Hence, the use of only one type of biometric doesn't meet all these requirements. As mentioned earlier, the biometric authentication tasks are divided into two types the identification and verification tasks. The identification is compared to the unknown biometric sample into the database in the identification stage. On the other hand, the verification tasks consist of verifying whether the provider of the biometric sample is the one who is claims to be. So, that makes the idea of using the physical biometrics from a security perspective and specially to detect the intention of cheating by eye movements as a biometric.

Cheating in exams is widespread instrument between students around the world regardless of the huge development that have been conducted so far. One of widely application of biometric is using it to authorize student and detect cheating in e-exams. There are three types of exams, traditional exams, online exams and distance exams (D-exams). Study in 2017 focused on the cheating in third type, D-exams. There are two methods have been proposed to detect the cheating in exams, authentication and online proctor. The model has been developed based on the authentication method. The authentication includes using two types of biometrics, the fingerprint, and the eye tracking. The Exam management system manages this proposed method. This system utilized to detect any status of cheating in D-exam by using the fingerprint reader for continuous student authentication and the eye tracker for the observation of the student through the D-exam session [9].

On the other hand, Authors in [10] conducted a research on traditional exams type that proposed an approach to figure out the bodily emotions and facial expressions of students in education environments among the exams' conduction. The proposed model uses a hidden surveillance camera and an embedded thermal imaging detector attached to it. The camera is located at a suitable place in the examination halls to identify the students who have the intention to cheat through the abnormal heat that is emitted from their bodies due to the emotions they feel. This model is developed based on the facial expressions analysis and emotions recognition that are retrieved, in form of images from the surveillance system. The data will not be collected until the camera detect a specified range of heat from the student body. Then, the surveillance camera will focus on the student face and record a video to analyze the facial points in order to compare them with the standard pattern that has been generated and used as a main reference for comparison of the facial key points after comparing the images with the pattern. Next, at the classification stage, the SVM (Support Vector Machine) classifier will be applied to distinguish the various expressions. Finally, the intention of cheating will be either confirmed or discarded.

Authors in [6], proposed an intelligent alarm system based on visual eye tracking algorithm to detect cheating in exam halls. The algorithm detects the human subject from the environment followed by the face and eye detection. The process starts by tracking and analyzing the eye's movement to determine whether the student cheating or not, and if the student recognized as a cheater, the system will generate an alarm message to the instructor that shows that someone is cheating in the exam. Furthermore, the eye detection in this algorithm has been presented as an efficient and effective mechanism The detection of the pupil movement will be achieved through segmenting the eye portion into different gray levels, where each level of the gray color will be classified for a specific black and white portion from the eye. Also, the pixel intensity and edges information of the student's eye will be analyzed from low-resolution images.

3   Research Methodology

The proposed research is our contribution to have biometric of Intent detection model that is expected to enhance real-time detection of cheating intent. The methodology that will be formulated based on surveillance cameras with thermal imaging detector technique that is proposed from [10] and eye movement tracking and analysis technique that is proposed from [6].

The proposed system from [10] use surveillance cameras with thermal imaging to detect any cheating attempt from any student in the exam halls. Figure 1 presents the flow of the system which will focus on the student based on their body temperature and evaluate the facial expression from frames that has been taken from captured video then store it in the database. This will be enhanced in the proposed model by providing a real-time eye movement tracking analysis in order to have an instant and faster result since it will focus on the eye movement and analysis instead of evaluating the entire facial expression.

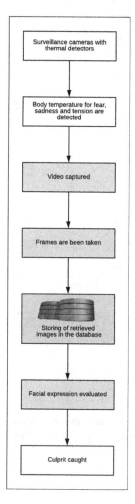

Fig. 1. Flow diagram for the reviewed system. (Modified after Niveditha P.R. *et al.*: Recognition and evaluation of facial expression and emotion of students using surveillance cameras with thermal detectors. IJSCAI. 2014; 2:1)

The proposed model from [6] is based on an intelligent visual eye tracking algorithm, as shown in Fig. 2. The main phase of this algorithm focuses on detecting the frontal view of the human from the video that has been captured from the scene and processes it as frames, in order to detect the face and then followed by eyes detection which will lead to the eye movement analysis and detection. The human detection in the proposed model will be enhanced with two verification techniques, which are the body temperature and the facial expression which won't require captured video since it will provide instant and a real-time result.

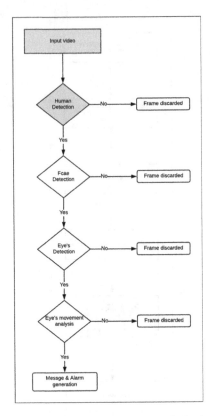

Fig. 2. Flow diagram for the reviewed model. (Modified after Javed and Aslam: An intelligent alarm based visual eye tracking algorithm for cheating free examination system. IJISA. 2013; 10, 86–92)

4 Proposed Model

The proposed model is designed to be used in the educational environment. It strives to assist in detecting the students who have the intention to cheat while conducting the written exams, in an accurate and an efficient manner. The Fig. 3 below illustrate the flow of the proposed model. The model will use surveillance camera embedded with a thermal detector that constructed to monitor the body temperature and compare it with a specified heat range. The proposed model is divided into 5 stages, that demonstrates the algorithm used to classify whether the student has any cheating intentions while conducting the written exam.

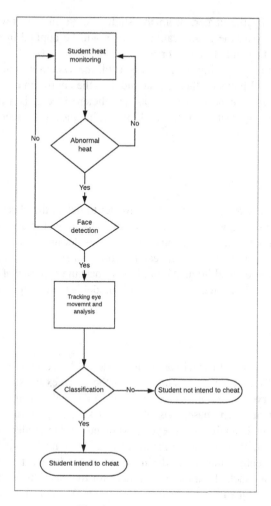

Fig. 3. Proposed model

In addition, it will also assist the instructor in detecting and preventing these mal-attempts. The surveillance camera is located in a suitable hidden place at the hall to monitor the students' and detect their emotions through the heat emitted from their bodies. The initial step will be triggered when any abnormal body heat emits from any object placed in the mentoring region through the camera. If the object's temperature overcome the specified heat range, which is defined to be between 104 °C–107 °C [10]. The next step, the camera will focus on the object to detect its face, in order to identify if the object is human or not. Once, the human face detected successfully the eyes will be detected, in order to start the eye tracking analysis process through the segmentation of eyes colors technique. This technique segments the eye into portions based on different grey levels colors, each level represents the specific portion of the eye [6]. The model will analyze the pupil movements depending on the colored segments detected by the camera from the student's eye in the previous step. After completing the analysis, the classification process will be applied in order to classify whether the student intends to cheat or not.

Furthermore, if any cheating intention detected, the system will alert the instructor in charge, so they will focus on the student and take the appropriate action towards the situation. This modal can be considered as an efficient mechanism for detecting the cheating intentions since it is using multiple techniques to detect and verify the cheating intentions.

5   Limitation

The study focuses on proposing an updated model to detect the cheating intentions of students while conducting written exams. However, the model is designed to detect the abnormal heat emitted from the students' bodies, considering the standard human temperature. Furthermore, the processes of heat detection and eye movement tracking will be for one student at a time. In addition, it is hard to estimate the accuracy of the classifier and the time of detection of the algorithm unless the model is being implemented.

6   Conclusion

In conclusion, the proposed model has been developed based on two existing models. The first model [10], that recognize and evaluate the facial expression and emotions of students using a surveillance camera attached with a thermal detector. The other model [6], is an intelligent alarm based visual eye tracking algorithm for cheating free examination system. It analyzes the eye movements of the student from a captured video. The proposed model is an enhancement of both models, it provides instant detection of the cheating intentions during conducting the written exams. It uses a surveillance camera attached with a thermal detector to detect the bodily emotions and an eye-tracking technique to track the eye movements. These techniques were selected carefully and each one of them is used as a standalone verification or identification technique, and by combining them in one model we will ensure that the results will be as accurate as possible. The implementation of this model has been left for future work due to the lack of time and resources.

References

1. Search Security TechTarget "Biometrics". https://searchsecurity.techtarget.com/definition/biometrics
2. Ngugi, B., Kamis, A., Tremaine, M.: Intention to use biometric systems. e-Service J. J. Electr. Serv. Public Private Sect. 7(3), 20–46 (2011). https://doi.org/10.2979/eservicej.7.3.20
3. Seyal, A.H., Turner, R.: A study of executives' use of biometrics: an application of theory of planned behaviour. Behav. Inf. Technol. 32(12), 1242–1256 (2013). https://doi.org/10.1080/0144929X.2012.659217

4. Merriam Webster "Cheat". http://www.merriam-webster.com/dictionary/cheat
5. Gilady, E., Lindskog, D., Aghili, S.: Intent biometrics: an enhanced form of multimodal biometric systems. In: Conference Proceedings, pp. 847–851. IEEE (2014). https://doi.org/10.1109/waina.2014.133
6. Javed, A., Aslam, Z.: An intelligent alarm based visual eye tracking algorithm for cheating free examination system. Int. J. Intell. Syst. Appl. 5(10), 86–92 (2013). https://doi.org/10.5815/ijisa.2013.10.11
7. Chamieh, J., Al Hamar, J., Al-Mohannadi, H., Al Hamar, M., Al-Mutlaq, A., Musa, A.: Biometric of intent: a new approach identifying potential threat in highly secured facilities. In: Conference Proceedings, pp. 193–197. IEEE (2018). https://doi.org/10.1109/w-ficloud.2018.00037
8. Bednarik, R., Kinnunen, T., Mihaila, A., Fränti, P.: Eye-movements as a biometric. In: Joensuu, Kalviainen, H., et al. (eds.) SCIA 2005. LNCS, vol. 3540, pp. 780–789. Springer, Heidelberg (2005). https://doi.org/10.1007/11499145_79
9. Bawarith, R., Basuhail, D.A., Fattouh, D.A., Gamalel-Din, P.D.S.: E-exam cheating detection system. Int. J. Adv. Comput. Sci. Appl. (IJACSA) 8(4), 6 (2017)
10. Niveditha, P.R., Subhashini, R., Divya, G.: Recognition and evaluation of facial expression and emotion of students using surveillance cameras with thermal detectors (2014). Accessed 25 May 2019. https://pdfs.semanticscholar.org/a0b1/d32177cab04d96020e64b01c578203cb0fdc.pdf

Integration of Internet of Things and Social Network

Social IoT General Review

Halima Bouazza[✉], Laallam Fatima Zohra[✉], and Bachir Said[✉]

Faculté des nouvelles technologies de l'information Et de la communication,
Laboratoire de l'Intelligence Artificielle et les Technologies de l'Information,
Université Kasdi Merbah Ouargla, 30 000 Ouargla, Algeria
bouazza.halima@gmail.com, laallamfz@gmail.com,
saidbachir@gmail.com

Abstract. Recently, the concept of the Internet as a set of connected computer peripherals is changed into a set of surrounding elements related to human living space, such as household appliances, machinery, transportation, storage of enterprises and property and so forth which is known as the internet of things IoT.

Social Network and IoT are both among the most promising paradigms, merging these technologies lead to a wide range of intelligent services and application.

A new paradigm known as the Social Internet of Things (SIoT) has been introduced and proposes the integration of social networking concepts in Internet of Things.

In this paper, we intend to examine the approaches used to exploit the concepts of social networking via the Internet of things, the technologies behind them, the proposed architecture, the contribution of SIoT compared to the IoT, the classification of some related works rely on the contribution mentioned above and, research challenges and open issues.

Keywords: Internet of Things · Social Network · Social Internet of Things · Ubiquitous computing

1 Introduction

The Internet of Things (IoT) is a new paradigm which integrates not only the traditional computer but also many kinds of things or objects around us, those objects are managed by a large number of technologies. Additionally, over unique addressing schemes and standard communication protocols, objects can communicate with each other and interact with their neighbors in order to reach common goals.

Currently, Social networks and IoT are the most attractive technologies, Social networks are formed of nodes of people, and the edges between these nodes represent their relationships. Social Network (SN) services are essentially promoted as a huge network of people where the relationships between those are shaped and described.

© Springer Nature Switzerland AG 2019
A. Alfaries et al. (Eds.): ICC 2019, CCIS 1098, pp. 312–324, 2019.
https://doi.org/10.1007/978-3-030-36368-0_26

Lately the idea of merging the "Internet of Things" and the "Social Networks" worlds is feasible, or even desirable. Things can not only be a component of traditional networks, they can also be a part of a SN of smart connected things that lead to an effective management of relationships by mimic human being behavior, a scalable and efficient service discovery and composition, as well as trustworthiness management [1].

For this reason, the three worlds of Internet, IoT and SN are combined to bring the physical real world into the virtual world. The resulting paradigm, called Social Internet of Things (SIoT), has the potential to support new applications and networking services for IoT in more efficient and effective methods [2], this is due to the increasing of awareness, Hence, SIoT paradigm would carry various desirable implications into a future world populated by intelligent objects permeating the daily life of human beings.

The remainder of this paper is organized as follows, Sect. 2 displays a background about the internet of things and social networks, Sect. 3 presents a general review of Social IoT; its architecture, key improvement, … and so forth, Sect. 4 is devoted for presenting some related works and its classification according to their domain of contribution and in Sect. 5 we present the main challenges and open issues of the SIoT, Finally, we finish this paper by a conclusion.

2 Background

2.1 Internet of Things

The Internet of Things (IoT) is an innovative paradigm that is rapidly gaining momentum in the current wireless telecommunication scenario. The fundamental idea of this concept is the ubiquitous presence surrounding us with a set of things or different objects - such as Radio Frequency Identification (RFID) tags, sensors, actuators, smart phones, and so forth. - Which, through unique addressing schemes, are likely to interact with each other and cooperate with their neighbors to achieve common objectives.

The Internet of Things (IoT) is someway a leading step to a smart world with ubiquitous computing and networking. It proposes to make different tasks manageable for users and give other tasks, such as easy monitoring of various events surrounding us. With ubiquitous computing, computing will be implanted wherever and pro-grammed to act automatically with autonomous triggering; it will be omnipresent.

Indeed, the central power of the IoT idea is the high impact on various aspects of daily life and behavior of potential users. From a private user, the most apparent effects of the IoT will be evident in both working and domestic areas. In this context, assisted living, domestics, e-health, improved learning are simply some examples of possible application scenarios in which the IoT paradigm will play a leading role soon. Thus, from the aspect of business users, the most obvious consequences will be equally apparent in fields like automation and industrial manufacturing, logistics, business/process management, intelligent transport of people and goods [1].

The principle objective of IoT is to allow us to uniquely identify, signify, access and manage things at anytime and anywhere by using the internet. The interconnected device networks can result in a big number of intelligent and autonomous applications and services bringing significant personal, professional, and economic gains (Fig. 1).

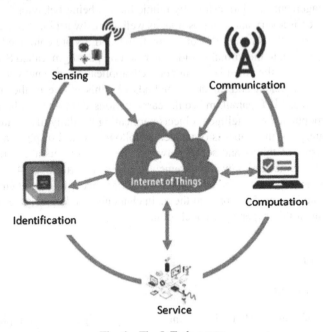

Fig. 1. The IoT elements

2.2 IoT Communication Models and the Problem Related to

From the analysis of the potential communication model of IoT we can summarize:

Thing-To-Thing Communication Model: This model represents that two devices or more can connect directly and communicate to each other without any intermediate application server, this model usually used in applications such as smart home, which use a small packet of data to communicate to each other.

Thing-To-Cloud: In this model, IoT devices connects directly to the cloud Internet service as an application service provider for data exchange and traffic control messages, nevertheless, the interoperability challenges emerge when we use things with different technologies.

Thing-To-Gateway: The IoT devices connect each other through an intermediate gateway application layer as a channel to access the cloud service.

Back-End Data Sharing Model: This model is an extension of the Single Thing-To-Cloud thus authorized third parties can accessed to objects and sensors to export and analyze data from the Cloud (Fig. 2).

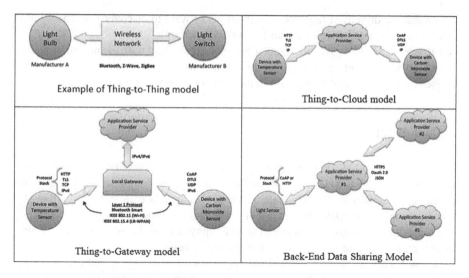

Fig. 2. The 4 models of communication of IoT

Scientist predict that there will be around 50 billions of connected objects by 2020, In addition, The IoT has broader overall scope than conventional host communications, Thus, whatever the application scale, small (smart home) or large (smart city, factory) scalability is an absolute need for the IoT. That can guarantee a seamless communication with objects and people. Each one of those objects might provide functionalities as a service, an efficient service discovery requests a good identification of suitable service, and furthermore, users want to know the available services and the information about their objects.

More than that, objects in IoT establish relationships with "things" that can provide needed services when they come in contact, the malfunction of devices can carry out discriminatory attacks, so it is crucial to assess the trustworthiness of service providers and the performance of the application to satisfy the service requester and maximize application performance.

Besides, IoT encompass a huge number of objects, hence each object has to deal with an enormous number of access and receive a huge number of queries, furthermore the relationships established among those objects have to be managed efficiently by the IoT platform.

2.3   The Social Network (SN) and Its Features

Social network; A social networking sites are an online platform that allow users to create a public profile and interact with other users i.e. SN allow people (1) to build a public or semi-public profile, (2) describe the relationships between People (3) view and browse their list of connections. The nodes in SN refer to individuals and the edges between the nodes describe the relationships between the people. Moreover, the SNs are characterized by the following characteristics:

- Community driven: In fact, social network users want to discover new friends also reconnect their old friends whom lost any contact with.
- Interactive: The SN gives the users a big space to interact with events, news and so forth so we can get and react with the latest news.
- User based: users update the information on social network on real time.

3 Social IoT

Nowadays, SN and IoT are both among the most promising paradigms, merging these technologies lead to a wide range of intelligent services and applications to deal with the many challenges that individuals and organizations face in their daily lives by allowing people to be related to anyone, anywhere, at any time. While IoT studies [2, 3] have typically mentioned communication to the physical world by detecting or acting through many different devices to be the biggest novelty.

A new paradigm called Social IoT (SIoT) which refers to a set of embedded objects connected via internet through unique addressing schemes, considering humans related data such as profiles, preferences, habits i.e.: Social IoT is used for context awareness through engaging users and users' profile in order to provide user-oriented services and recommendations. For this purpose, there are two considerations: (1) increasing sociality (or connectivity) and (2) enhancing pervasiveness (or availability) [4] (Fig. 3).

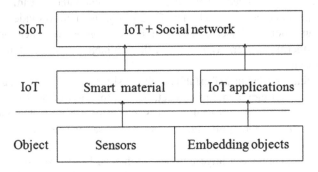

Fig. 3. Combination of social network and IoT

3.1 Key Improvement of SIoT

The actual implementation of the seamless integration between social and IoT worlds brings the main characteristics of social network to the IoT; here we summarized the main improvement expectant of SIoT:

Interactivity: The pairing between humans and things in IoT can take place in two forms: (1) human- to-human, or (2) machine-to-machine interaction, and it can be achieved using the normal physical interaction in case of humans or various computer networks in case of things. Authors in [4] claim that implementing human-to-machine cooperation is essential to achieve the completed vision of SIoT. The SIoT extend the notion of SN from people to the objects so the interactivity is one of the advantages of SIoT that has a positive influence overall system.

Collaboration and Sharing Information: This perspective appears to be the most critical one in order to realize a full convergence of both the social and IoT worlds because the collaboration and sharing information occur between human, between things and between human and things. Considering social values, SIoT ultimately enables humans and things to act as producers or consumers [5].

Handled-Data: It is also very important to consider the kind of data acquisition and handling techniques required to be considered in pervasive environments. Authors in [4] categorize data acquisition techniques into two categories: (1) proactive data recovery that is usually uses crawling techniques, learning algorithms, or various data analysis algorithms and (2) reactive data acquisition which habitually operates in a real-time way using various data mining and query techniques.

3.2   SIoT Architecture

- The SIoT system contain server, gateway and object, these components are distributed to three main layers [8], Sensing layer, Network layer and Application layer [1]. The architecture of each object may vary depending on the model of communication discussed in Sect. 2.2.
- **SIoT server:** the server is situated in the application layer also it encompasses three sub-layers, The Base layer is *The Handling data layer* which consists of database for storing and managing data with their descriptors, ontology databases, semantic engines and communications. *The Resource management Sub-layer* comprises tools which implement the key functionality of the SIoT system such as ID management, profiling and relationships management. *The Interfaces sub-layer* is devoted to ensure the best way of communication between objects, humans, and services.
- **The object:** the sub-layers, which the objects consists of, may mainly vary rely on their nature, we have 2 kind of objects; dummy objects (sensors) and smart objects (smart phone)

In simple scenario, the dummy object' role is just sending the sensing data to another equipment (gateway) in this case the object encompasses just the lowest layer which is the sensing layer. Otherwise, the smart object may contain the three sub-layers, Sensing, Network and Application. This latter encompasses the SIoT application as well as the social agent and the service management agent, which are presented in Fig. 4.

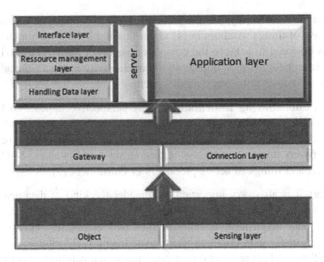

Fig. 4. Architecture for the SIoT ecosystem [1]

The social agent is dedicated to communicate with SIoT servers to update profiles, friendships, discover and request social network services, it also implemented to allow objects to communicate to each other when they are close geographically.

The Service management agent is responsible for interfacing with humans that can control the object behavior of the object when communicating within their social network.

- **The Gateway** made up only of the Network layer to ensure the connection between the SIoT server and objects.

3.3 The Contribution of SIoT Comparing to the IoT

Relationships Management: Things on the Social IoT can mimic the human being behavior on Social Networks, in addition from the analysis of possible service and application typologies, built on the envisaged Social Internet of Things. Authors in [4] propose the followed classifications of the defined relationships:

Parental Object Relationship (POR): established among objects produced by the same production batch, that is to say, generally homogeneous objects from the same manufacturer and in the same period. Furthermore, objects can establish a *Co-location object relationship* (C-LOR), this type of relationships defined among objects (either homogeneous or heterogeneous) worked always in the same place (as in the case of sensors, actuators, and augmented things used in the same environment such as a smart home or a smart city) this relationships can also be established sporadically between vehicle and smart objects when they meet in the same space, also the objects can mimic the relationships between workmates in *Co-work object relationship* (C-WOR) this latter established whenever the objects cooperate to produce a common IoT application (as in the case of objects coming into contact to be used together and cooperate for applications such as emergency response, telemedicine, and so forth.

Heterogeneous objects, which belong to the same owner (mobile phones, music players, game consoles, etc.), can establish a relationships named *Ownership object relationship* (OOR). The last relationships defined in [4] is the *Social object relationship* (SOR) which established when objects come into contact, sporadically or continuously, because their owners come in touch with each other during their lives (e.g., devices and sensors belonging to friends, classmates, travel companions, colleagues) (Fig. 5).

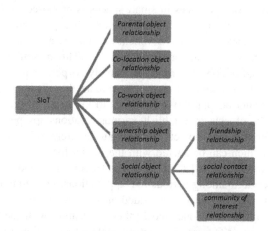

Fig. 5. Type of relationships between object on SIoT

Scalability: SIoT structure can be shaped as necessary to ensure the seamless of the network. Hence, the scalability is guaranteed as on human social network. Further, every node capable to create social relationships with other things.

Service Discovery: based on the scalable system each object can look for the requisite service by exploiting the information about its relationships to guarantee an efficient search for the desired services and objects in the same way humans find for knowledge in SN.

Trustworthiness: fulfilling the trust management consist of: collect the required information in order to make a trust relationship decision, evaluate the criteria of choosing the trust relationship, verify and readdress the existed relationships, Moreover, ensure the dynamic change of trust relationships [6]. A level of reliability can be established to take advantages of the degree of interaction between things that are friends.

4 Related Works

In order to improve the performance of service discovery of resources, the [7] have proposed a new resource discovery mechanism founded on the similarity of preference and motion patterns (RDPMs). In the first place, they abstracted the predilections of the nodes from their profile table and their resources, as well as the motion model of their trajectories using the clustering method AGNES. Then, they generated the cosine similarity of the node's preferences and motion model to construct a sub- community in a three-dimensional Cartesian coordinate system. Forming the virtual global communities using the similarity found among the sub-communities, ultimately to improve the search performance for the resources. Finally, they designed a resource discovery algorithm that can dynamically adjust the search radius to balance performance and communication costs.

In [8], a new framework of services based on a cognitive reasoning approach for the discovery of dynamic SIoT services in smart spaces is proposed. In other words, it is proposed to reason about the users' situational needs, their preferences and other social aspects as well as the surrounding environment to generate a list of services adapted to the situation, corresponding to the needs of the users. This reasoning approach is then implemented as a proof of concept prototype, namely Airport Dynamic Social, within a smart airport. Finally, an empirical study to evaluate the efficiency of the reasoning approach shows a better adaptability of services to the needs of the situation.

The SIoT allows objects to establish various relationships people-to-things and things-to- things. Furthermore, objects belonging to different IoT applications can build their own profiles, which can be shared with the Social IoT. Based on the established relationships and objects profile [9] have provided a concept of exploiting the SIoT for recommendation services among various IoT applications. For more understanding the concept of recommendation, authors provided an illustration application scenario.

Here in [10] Authors went one step further by dealing with the highly heterogeneous environment of IoT from the current state of evolution of the novel SIoT paradigm solved scalability issues. First, they analyzed two features of IoT heterogeneity: (1) object types and formations as well as socialization problems and (2) communication protocols for interoperability. Then, to support seamless service discovery, they presented the on-site service discovery architecture in the heterogeneous IoT environment, consisting of four main functional schemas: discovery region determination, on-site agent selection, query based on the location and management of roaming.

In SIoT, it is very important to define appropriate rules for objects to select good friends, as these affect the performance of the services developed over this social network. The [11] addressed this problem by analyzing the possible strategies for the benefit of the overall navigability of the network. Based on the properties of the local network, Authors proposed five heuristics, which also likely have an impact on the overall structure of the network. Then they conducted in-depth experiments to analyze performance in terms of giant components, average degree of connectivity, local aggregation, and average path length.

Unexpectedly, they found that minimizing local clustering in the network provided the best results in terms of average path length. In addition, they performed further analysis to understand the potential causes, which were related to the number of hubs in the network.

The importance of trust management appears in the case where the owners carry their IoT devices when they move from a friendly environment (e.g., a social club) to an unfriendly environment (e.g., a neighborhood one does not go often). The aim in [12] is improving the security and enhance the performance of social IoT applications more particularly in dynamically changing environments. Authors intend to design and validate an adaptive trust management protocol that can dynamically fit trust design parameter settings responding to environmental changing conditions to afford accurate trust assessment and to maximize application performance. They focused on trust protocol design that can deal with malicious nodes. The proposed protocol had desirable trust convergence, accuracy, and resiliency properties. Further such protocol has to take into consideration the dynamic changing of social relationships among the "owners" of devices in IoT systems in spite of the presence of misconduct of nodes which disrupt the functionality of a social IoT system.

Objects in Social IoT create social relationships autonomously in order to find the trusted objects, which can provide the needed service. The main contributions in [13] is definition of two models for trustworthiness management based on the solutions proposed for P2P and social networks. In the subjective model, which is closer to the social scenario, each node calculates the trustworthiness of its friends based on its own experience and the opinions of friends in common with the potential service provider. In the objective model, obtained from the P2P scenario, the information on each node is distributed and stored using a Distributed Hash Table (DHT) structure so that any node can use the same information.

- Assessment of the benefits of trustworthiness management in IoT, which illustrates how it can efficiently isolate almost all misbehaving nodes in the network at the expense of increased network traffic caused by the exchange of feedback.

Classification of Works According to the Domain of Contribution

In the Subsect. 3.3, we discuss the contribution of SIoT comparing to IoT then we review the majority of work in the area of SIoT environments. In this section, we provide a classification of those related work based on the domain of their contribution in Table 1.

Table 1. Classification of related works based on SIoT contribution

Related work	Relationships management	Scalability	Service discovery	Trustworthiness
[7]			✓	
[9]	✓		✓	
[11]	✓			
[8]			✓	
[10]		✓		
[12]				✓
[13]				✓

5 Challenges and Open Research Issues

Integrating IoT and SN is not a spur of the moment but this technology still an immature. With the aim of making a mature SIoT paradigm, there are still many challenges that must be faced prior to the worldwide deployment of this technology:

Interoperability and Standardization: Due of the heterogeneous nature of IoT things, including the different information processing and communication skills, as well as the characteristics and data, relationships and capabilities of the SN user, the system must be able to Manage this variety of data types, ensuring interoperability between all Components, the most widespread method to achieve the interoperability by using the ontology this latter is a technique of specification and conceptualization of a set of objects and the relationships among them well formulated.

Power and Energy Management: Objects that participate in the SIoT generally move around and are not bound to unlimited power. Therefore, users, who use portable devices that usually, work with batteries. Therefore, energy saving is a conditioning factor in the plan and operation of SOI, and effective energy management should be implemented at all levels, M2M device communications to interface design.

Interactions and Interfaces: The SIoT base will focus on providing users with a high-level experience that can consume and produce data and services from objects and other users. Therefore, the human- centered interface should present a user-friendly way to interact with objects and users. The way users and devices interact with each other is always an open challenge. Some approaches such as [9] and [14] propose a set of possible interactions between the different elements, but most are focused on specific applications. A global set of interactions must be defined, as well as methods for managing these interactions, for example, users can obtain data from their own devices, Authors in [9] propose that SIoT constructs an object profile based on IoT application data that can be exchanged with the SIoT network to be accessible to other IoT applications, in this way, SIoT recommends applications and information to its users.

Semantics and Context Management: The SIoT aims to provide functionality in several situations and a set of devices can be used for several purposes simultaneously. Thus, the ability to properly manage the current context not only improves the performance of the system, but also makes it more usable by providing unequivocal access and interpretation of data. A semantic management context can be made as (1) first analyze existing definitions for each of the terms (2) and from this conclude a definition of the whole term [15] Semantic approaches based on RDF (Resource Description Format) and OWL (Ontology Web Language) can be extended to include descriptors for SIoT users and device characteristics, which facilitates interoperability across all components [4].

Data mining and Emotional Artificial Intelligence: Humans contact their personal device more than their family members; more and more smart devices will be able to aware the emotions and moods of their owner rely on certain data and facts. Further, Emotional AI allows daily life objects to detect, analyze, process and react based on the emotional states and moods of humans. In addition, Emotional AI can lead to high quality of experience i.e. stockholders may base their decision on the emotional reactions rather than the rational ones.

6 Conclusion

In this paper we introduced how the convergence of the Internet of Things (IoT) technologies with the social networking concepts has led to a new paradigm named the Social Internet of Things (SIoT), then we presented a general review of Social IoT; its architecture, key improvement and the contribution of this paradigm comparing to IoT, and for more clarification of the SIoT we have given some related works and its classification according to their domain of contribution next we defined research challenges and open issues which have to be accomplished to obtain a mature technologies.

References

1. Atzori, L., Iera, A., Morabito, G., Nitti, M.: The Social Internet of Things (SIoT) - when social networks meet the Internet of Things: concept, architecture and network characterization. Comput. Netw. **56**, 3594–3608 (2012)
2. Atzori, L., Iera, A., Morabito, G.: SIoT: giving a social structure to the Internet of Things. IEEE Commun. Lett. **15**, 1193–1195 (2011)
3. ITU: The Internet of Things. Itu Internet Rep 2005, no. 212 (2005)
4. Ortiz, A.M., Hussein, D., Park, S., Han, S.N., Crespi, N.: The cluster between Internet of Things and social networks: review and research challenges. IEEE Internet Things J. **1**, 206–215 (2014)
5. Guinard, D.: A web of things application architecture - integrating the real-world into the web. Ph.D. th, ETH Zurich, no. 220 (2011). http://webofthings.org/dom/thesis.pdf
6. Grandison, T., Sloman, M.: A survey of trust in internet applications. IEEE Commun. Surv. Tutor. **3**(4), 2–16 (2000)
7. Li, Z., Chen, R., Liu, L., Min, G.: Dynamic resource discovery based on preference and movement pattern similarity for large-scale social Internet-of-Things. IEEE Internet Things J. **4662**, 1 (2015). http://ieeexplore.ieee.org/lpdocs/epic03/wrapper.htm?arnumber=7140727
8. Hussein, D., Han, S.N., Lee, G.M., Crespi, N., Bertin, E.: Towards a dynamic discovery of smart services in the social Internet of Things. Comput. Electr. Eng. **58**, 429–443 (2017)
9. Saleem, Y., Crespi, N., Rehmani, M.H., Copeland, R., Hussein, D., Bertin, E.: Exploitation of social IoT for recommendation services. In: 2016 IEEE 3rd World Forum Internet Things, WF-IoT 2016, pp. 359–364 (2017)
10. Park, S., Hussein, D., Crespi, N.: On-site service discovery along user roaming over Internet of Things. In: 2015 IEEE International Conference on Consumer Electronics, ICCE 2015, pp. 194–195 (2015)
11. Nitti, M., Atzori, L., Cvijikj, I.P.: Friendship selection in the social Internet of Things: challenges and possible strategies. IEEE Internet Things J. **2**, 240–247 (2015)
12. Chen, I.R., Guo, J., Bao, F.: Trust management for SOA-based IoT and its application to service composition. IEEE Trans. Serv. Comput. **9**, 482–495 (2016)

13. Nitti, M., Girau, R., Atzori, L.: Trustworthiness management in the social Internet of Things. IEEE Trans. Knowl. Data Eng. **26**, 1253–1266 (2014)
14. Beltran, V., Ortiz, A.M., Hussein, D., Crespi, N.: A semantic service creation platform for Social IoT. In: 2014 IEEE World Forum Internet Things, WF-IoT 2014, pp. 283–286 (2014)
15. Jacoby, M., Antonić, A., Kreiner, K., Łapacz, R., Pielorz, J.: Semantic interoperability as key to IoT platform federation. In: Podnar Žarko, I., Broering, A., Soursos, S., Serrano, M. (eds.) InterOSS-IoT 2016. LNCS, vol. 10218, pp. 3–19. Springer, Cham (2017). https://doi.org/10.1007/978-3-319-56877-5_1

Enhanced Priority-Based Routing Protocol (EPRP) for Inter-vehicular Communication

Amaliya Princy Mohan and Maher Elshakankiri[✉]

Department of Computer Science, University of Regina, Regina, Canada
{ams011,Maher.Elshakankiri}@uregina.ca

Abstract. Recently, Vehicle-to-Vehicle communication has become an important research area as it provides connectivity for vehicles to improve the universal efficiency and safety of the transportation systems. Even with many routing protocols being proposed for Inter-Vehicular communication (IVC), there are still some remaining issues for advanced research work as the nodes in the vehicular communication are highly mobile and unstable. Thus, the proposed work uses existing VANETsim simulator for broadcast routing to deliver high priority messages at the application layer using a way-point mobility model which considers practical vehicular environment including road intersections and traffic lights. The existing routing protocol is improved using a way-point mobility model and we compare the linear mobility model of existing routing protocol with a way-point mobility model. Also, in the implemented work, all vehicles in the proposed simulation take an alternate path in the event of any emergency.

Keywords: IVC · Priority-based Routing Protocol (PRP) · Way-point · Stable · Safety · VANETsim

1 Introduction

Vehicular communication requires cooperation between vehicles and Road Side Units (RSU) to distribute each other with information such as safety warning messages and traffic information. There are two types of vehicular communication: Intra-Vehicle Communication takes place within a vehicle. Whereas, Inter-Vehicle Communication concerns about the communication that happens between vehicles or vehicles and sensor nodes placed in and around various locations besides the roadside units. Dedicated Short Range Communication (DSRC) provides an opportunity to assist communication between vehicle-to-vehicle and vehicle-to-roadside equipment. The new DSRC standard assigns 75 MHz of bandwidth in the 5.9 GHz band for the second generation DSRC. DSRC, which is an accompaniment for cellular technology provides higher data rates with minimal latency rate in the communication link. Currently, the IEEE task group is working on the IEEE 802.11p standard of DSRC to ensure stability for both the PHY and MAC layer [1].

The DSRC spectrum consists of six service channels of 10 MHz each and one control channel of 10 MHz for vehicular communication. Channel 178 is reserved for the control channel, and each OBU observes this control channel for broadcasting and

© Springer Nature Switzerland AG 2019
A. Alfaries et al. (Eds.): ICC 2019, CCIS 1098, pp. 325–337, 2019.
https://doi.org/10.1007/978-3-030-36368-0_27

receiving safety messages. Since the bandwidth is limited, the FCC recommends transmitting messages within 200 μs to deliver high priority messages in a short span of time. DSRC communication uses IEEE 802.11 standard for the MAC layer. DSRC uses the Enhanced Distributed Coordination (EDCF) of 802.11e to deliver high priority messages in the vehicular communication [1]. This function allocates access category (AC) queues for every channel on each vehicle. It has provided two priority queues for public safety application and non-public safety application.

The applications of DSRC are grouped into the succeeding four classes: Vehicle-to-Vehicle, Vehicle-to/from-Infrastructure, Vehicle-to-Home and Routing Based applications [2]. The Vehicle-to-Vehicle application comprises pre-crash warning, lane change warning and emergency braking of forwarding vehicle. Whereas, Vehicle-to/from Infrastructure application includes traffic signal violation warning, intersection collision warning, curve speed warning and road condition warning. These applications are categorized by a governmental agency as public safety application. The application messages of DSRC may be either periodic or event-driven. In this proposed work, we will work on the routing protocol for Vehicle-to-Vehicle and Vehicle-to/from-Infrastructure application.

Using vehicle-to-vehicle (V2V) communication, any vehicle can determine the position of another vehicle up to few meters away. The vehicles interact with each other through Emergency Warning Messages (EWM) system to anticipate and react during an emergency. Most applications in the vehicular system depend on the location information of other vehicular nodes. The security challenges involved in V2V communications are verifying the authentication of users and the reliability of transmitted messages due to the increased mobility of vehicles acting as nodes.

The utmost important components for inter-vehicle communication are On-Board Unit (OBU) and a Road-Side Unit (RSU). All vehicles are supplied with an OBU and an Omni-directional antenna. An OBU acts as a transceiver to perform the computational operations within a vehicle. The Omni-directional antenna is used by the OBU to access the wireless channel for transmitting messages between vehicles and RSU. The RSUs are static devices located along the roadside and has a transceiver, antenna, sensors and processors. This introduces a challenge of collecting and storing these large amounts of traffic-related data in some server. When a vehicle is involved in an accident, it transmits an emergency warning message to other vehicles to avoid further accidents [5].

In the proposed system, both RSU and vehicles periodically broadcast for a specific interval of time about the road condition and vehicular state to other vehicles within their communication range [6]. The information transmitted by every vehicle is anonymous and does not include any identification number with them. A sophisticated security system has to be used to ensure that all information exchanged between vehicles is authentic and trustable.

The proposed work is structured as follows: Sect. 2 describes the motivation and related work. The implementation of the proposed work and its results are discussed in Sect. 3. Section 4 introduces the simulation results. Section 5 provides the conclusion and future work of this proposed work.

2   Motivation and Related Work

Routing is the challenging task in Inter-Vehicle Communication as the nodes are highly mobile and unstable [2]. This causes the frequent disconnections in vehicular communication and produces a rapidly changing network topology. There are two types of routing protocol available for vehicular ad-hoc networks: topology-based routing and location-based routing. The topology-based routing performs packet transmission using information about the network link. On the other side, location-based protocol transfers packet based on nodes geographic position [11]. They are further partitioned into proactive and reactive algorithms [12]. Inter-Vehicular Communication informs about accidents, traffic signals and road conditions before the drivers using warning messages. When an accident or road blockage occurs in the highway, the forwarding vehicle informs about this emergency event to the neighboring vehicles using high priority warning message to avoid a further collision on the highway [3].

Chakkaphong et al. propose a reliability-based priority routing protocol to allocate different quality of services (QoS) for different types of messages [7]. The proposed routing protocol uses a contention window mechanism to transmit the packets on a valid channel. It uses implicit acknowledgment and retransmission approach to attain high reliability and maximum message broadcasted distance. This system categorizes safety messages with three level of urgencies: very urgent, urgent and general messages. The proposed algorithm calculates the priority value for each broadcasted message using an exponential function as the message priority decreases with an increase in the dissemination distance. The contention window size for the MAC layer is calculated using the priority value (P) and dissemination distance (d). Thus, higher priority messages with smaller contention window size are delivered before other message types.

A reliable and stable routing protocol has been proposed by Sivakumar et al. to transmit data packets from source to destination vehicles [8]. This work introduces the Reliability Index (RI) as a routing metric to measure the accuracy of the communication link between two nodes. The best path between source and destination is chosen based on the Reliability Index value. They have calculated the index value using vehicles speed, position and direction. The proposed routing protocol consists of two phases: Route Formation phase and Route Maintenance phase. The Route Formation phase uses Route Request and Route Reply control messages to establish the routes between source and destination. The best stable routes are determined based on the calculated Reliability Index value using the STABLE_ROUTE function. In case of any link failure, the Route Maintenance phase is used to identify the next possible best to reduce the delay in finding routes between source and destination.

Moumena et al. propose the route-finding algorithm to establish the shortest-time route between source and destination based on the available road condition. The major ingredients of this protocol are Zone of Relevance (ZOR) and Geocasting protocol. Each vehicle in the DSRC communication identifies its own set of vehicles within a certain geographic area, which is known as Zone of Relevance [9]. This protocol uses Zone Route Request and Zone Route Reply approach to discover various possible routes between source and destination and the shortest-time path problem is solved using the Dijkstra's algorithm. The proposed work uses flooding technique with Zone Route Request and does not consider any change in the network topology as the vehicles move from one Zone of Relevance to another Zone of Relevance.

Hequn et al. investigate the performance of various Geocasting routing protocols to learn about the environmental effects on these protocols. The proposed work used a region based Geocasting routing simulator and generated a traditional traffic environment to determine the impacting factors on these protocols [10]. In most of the scenarios, DRG which uses a distance-based backoff algorithm to determine relay nodes and controls flooding by not sending beacon messages to the neighboring vehicles showed better Packet Delivery Ratio and lowest Packet Delivery Time. The performance analysis study by Amirhossein et al. reveals that when MANET based routing protocols are applied to vehicular ad-hoc networks, their performance decreases as the velocity and density of the vehicle increases [7]. This study shows that substantial improvements are required as we apply reactive and proactive routing protocols on the vehicular ad-hoc networks.

The proposed Enhanced Priority-based Routing Protocol (EPRP) for broadcasting warning messages is implemented at the application layer. VANETsim simulator is used to compare with existing Priority-based Routing Protocol (PRP) [7]. The key challenges in delivering the broadcast messages are: no retransmission for failed broadcast transmission, no max-level recovery on broadcast frames, hidden terminal problem, increase in collision rate for an increase in sender's distance and multi-hop broadcasts. In this work, we compare way-point mobility model with linear mobility model of existing routing protocol in terms of throughput, packet delivery ratio, delay and dissemination distance.

3   Implementation of Proposed Work

3.1   Priority-Based Routing Protocol (PRP)

Priority-based Routing Protocol (PRP) is based on broadcast communication. One of the main factors to be considered in mobile nodes is choosing the best mobility model for the routing protocol. The proposed work is implemented using the way-point mobility model rather than the linear mobility model as discussed in the existing work.

The way-point mobility model is widely used in simulations due to its simplicity and allow vehicles to move independently to their chosen destination with a selected speed. This feature of the way-point mobility model allows the vehicles with multiple optional routes to reach their destination and considers the practical vehicular environment, which includes road intersections, too. Whereas, the linear mobility model permits the vehicles to reach their destination by following a linear path. The vehicles do not take an alternate path in case of any blocking event as they have no optional routes available. The existing routing protocol did not discuss taking an alternate best path in case of damaged road conditions to avoid further crash among vehicles, and no performance metrics have been evaluated. We have modified the existing VANETsim simulator based on our requirement by assigning message priorities to each broadcasted message and adopted way point mobility model to evaluate performance metrics. In the proposed work, the time out value of the simulator is also modified to enable retransmission process.

We assume that all vehicles have the potential to learn about their location using Global Positioning Systems (GPS). They also have sensors to detect for any abnormality on their vehicles. The proposed system uses a priority-based routing protocol for broadcasting emergency messages between vehicles and an RSU. In case of an emergency, the affected vehicle broadcasts the emergency warning in the form of high priority message to the nearest Road-Side Unit. RSU analyzed the transmitted message and based on the analyzed result; the RSU produces an alert message to the nearer vehicles to avoid a collision and take alternate routes. RSUs are placed in various regions like schools, hospitals, animal crossroads, traffic signals and road intersection areas to produce warning messages to vehicles moving towards that area to slow down their speed.

In our simulation, the communication area is partitioned into various regions, and vehicles in each region broadcast about its speed, position and direction to all nearer vehicles in that region. Each message forwarded by the vehicles and RSUs are assigned with a priority value [4] which is calculated based on the existing Priority Index value in Eq. (1).

$$I = ke^{(-0.05*d)} \tag{1}$$

Where I is priority index, k is priority coefficient and d is the dissemination distance from a location where an event has occurred. We use decreasing exponential function to indicate that the priority of a message decreases with an increase in the dissemination distance. We assign k values like 10, 5 and 2 based on the urgency level of the broadcasted message. Priority value P is calculated based on the value of index value I, as with P = 1 for I greater than or equal to 5; P = 2 for I greater than or equal to 2.5 and less than 5; P = 3 for I less than 2.5.

The value P = 1; is assigned to highest priority messages with their indexes greater than or equal to 5. With the indexes value between 2.5 and 5, the priority value P for the messages is 2. The lowest priority value P = 3 is assigned to general messages. The implicit acknowledgment mechanism is implemented by retransmitting the same message by other nodes to the sender. This guarantees the sender that the preceding transmission is successful. We have set the timeout value for all messages, and the sender must receive the acknowledgment within that time. In case, if the sender does not receive an acknowledgment, then the sender considers it as a failed transmission and retransmits the higher priority message again. The sender tries to retransmit for three attempts after which the message will be dropped.

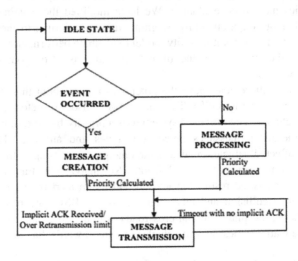

Fig. 1. State diagram of existing Priority-based Routing Protocol (PRP)

The state diagram for Priority-based routing protocol is shown in Fig. 1. Initially, all vehicles are in an idle state. In case, any event has occurred or receives a message from neighboring vehicles; the vehicle changes from an idle state to message creation or message processing state. At the message creation state, the vehicles determine the priority value for any message and then claims for transmission. Whereas, at the message processing state, the priority value of the received message is examined. If the priority value is 1, then that message is broadcasted first to all vehicles within their communication range. The proposed system stops broadcasting when an implicit acknowledgment is received, or the maximum limit for retransmission is met. Each message is fully distributed by using repetitive transmission mechanism. The proposed system offers a solution for failed broadcast transmission; one of the key challenges in distributing broadcast messages.

3.2   Performance Metrics

The following performance metrics are evaluated to understand the behavior of Priority-based Routing Protocol (PRP).

- Throughput: Throughput is the number of packets that are passing through the channel for a given unit of time. This performance metric shows the total number of packets that have been successfully delivered from source vehicle to destination vehicle, and it can be improved with increasing vehicle density. It is measured in Kilobytes per second (Kbps).
  Throughput = Number of bytes received from source to destination/Observed Duration.
- Packet Delivery Ratio: Packet delivery ratio is defined as the ratio of the number of the delivered data packet to the destination. This illustrates the level of delivered data to the destination. Packet delivery ratio is given by the formula.
  Packet Delivery Ratio = Number of packets received/Number of packets generated or sent.
- Delay: Delay is defined as an amount of time taken by the transmitting vehicles to deliver a packet from source to destination. Delays are caused due to various reasons including distance, congestion, error recovery mechanism and the time taken by receiving vehicles to process the transferred data.

4   Simulation Results

To evaluate the performance of the Enhanced PRP, we implement the proposed work using VANETsim simulator which uses way-point mobility model. The VANETsim simulator is developed in Java and provides an interface to import maps from the OpenStreetMap project. Thus, it supports the simulation of traffic on real road network. We can individually simulate each vehicle, and they make decisions on their own to make the simulation as realistic as possible. The simulator also provides a graphical user interface along with a powerful editing tool. This tool facilitates the creation and modification of maps as well as scenarios. The editor tool provides an option to load the map in .xml or.osm format.

VANETsim simulator consists of four tabs: simulate, edit, reporting and about. The simulate tab is used for loading the saved map and scenarios file to construct a VANET environment. Also, this tab provides the facility to start and pause our simulation along with displaying various information about a vehicle. Whereas, the edit tab of the simulator affords a converter function to transform the map in.osm format to.xml. Even this tab provides an option to load and save the newly created map and scenario files in. xml format. The reporting tab reveals the statistics for simulation that has been performed. The default parameter values for the simulation are shown in Table 1.

Table 1. Default parameter values for simulation

Parameters	Default values
Scenario area	$1,000 \times 1,000 \text{ m}^2$
Vehicle's position	Random
Mobility model	Way-point
Time interval between vehicles	3 s
Vehicle's speed	Uniformly distributed (80, 100 km/hr)
Communication range	250 cm
Total number of vehicles	10–50 vehicles
Priority of messages	Very urgent
Packet type	UDP
Packet size	500 bytes
Time out period	2500 ms
Simulation time	500 s
Number of simulation runs	20 times

The proposed system uses the way-point mobility model to create a real-time traffic environment by allowing users to add traffic lights, RSUs, vehicles, streets and events. In the way-point mobility model, each source vehicle begins by pausing for a fixed number of seconds and travels towards the destination. In our simulation environment, we are using "The University of Regina" map in.xml format. The total number of vehicles is varied from 10 to 50 vehicles for each simulation. The simulator divides the loaded map into various regions, and vehicles are deployed at each region to create real-time traffic. All the vehicles move with the same speed of 100 km/h. While creating a scenario, the time interval between each vehicle is entered to maintain distances among vehicles.

The simulator uses four different vehicle types: cars, trucks, police and aggressive. Each vehicle type differs by size and speed. For our simulation, we use all vehicle types and add a block event at few places. When a vehicle detects this block in front of it, then the vehicle broadcasts a high priority warning messages to all nearby vehicles to reduce their speed and to take alternate routes to avoid collisions. When a block event is detected, the proposed system assigns P = 1 for penalty messages, P = 2 for all messages from RSUs and P = 3 for all other message types. Figure 2 shows the simulation scenario of the existing routing protocol using linear mobility model. Figure 3 shows the real-time simulation after loading the "University of Regina" map and adding the required vehicles, RSUs, traffic lights and blocks for our proposed work.

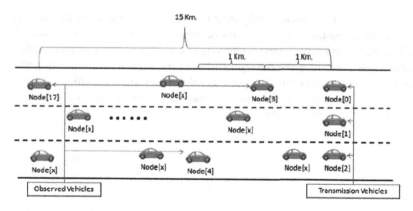

Fig. 2. Simulation scenario of linear mobility model in existing PRP

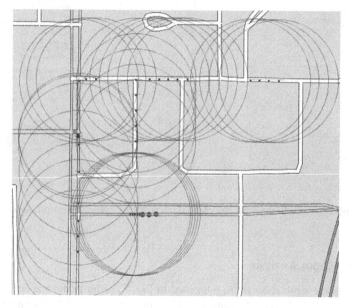

Fig. 3. Simulation scenario of way-point mobility model in enhanced PRP

During the addition of vehicles, the simulator uses a two-way point model to place a starting and finishing point for our transmission. The time interval among vehicles has been specified in seconds to avoid collision between vehicles. From Fig. 3, we can see that when a forwarding vehicle detects any block or damaged road in front of them, they create the highest priority warning message (Unique message). Then, they broadcast these emergency messages to all nearer vehicles and RSUs. When a neighboring vehicle receives this warning message, they use a sort function to arrange the received messages in ascending order based on their priority value (P) and then broadcasts very urgent message before all other received messages. By using this procedure, the nearer vehicles apply their braking system and takes the next shortest path to avoid a pile-up. The sender gets acknowledged by receiving the same broadcasted message within the timeout interval. The vehicle at the last mile of the communication path also receives the higher priority message to take different path to the destination. The simulator displays various information such as vehicle id, travel distance, current speed, number of priority messages transmitted and travel time for the marked vehicle as shown in Fig. 4.

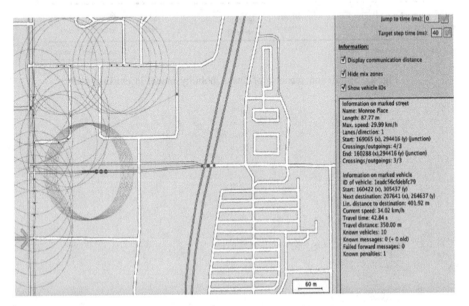

Fig. 4. Simulation result showing vehicles taking alternate route and information on marked vehicle

4.1 Throughput Analysis

According to the simulation result presented in Fig. 5, better performance is shown by the implemented Enhanced Priority-based Routing Protocol (EPRP) under different scenarios. We can see from the graph that the way-point mobility model shows better throughput compared to linear mobility model. The reason behind this is there is an alternate path available for way-point mobility model to reach their destination in the event of accident or road blocks. The effective throughput of the way-Point mobility model is achieved in respect to data being broadcasted to all vehicles at the end of the communication path and due to minimization of packet loss.

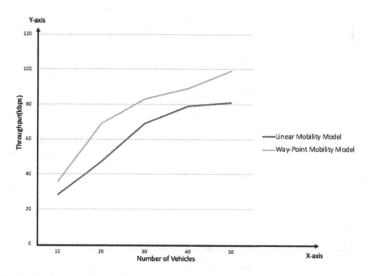

Fig. 5. Throughput graph of Enhanced Priority-based Routing Protocol (EPRP)

4.2 Packet Delivery Ratio (PDR) Analysis

As can be clearly seen in Fig. 6, the packet delivery ratio is very much better for Way-Point mobility model when the number of vehicles has been increased in the simulation environment. The reason for the better packet delivery ratio is that a greater number of vehicles are connected in the roadways and available for communication to deliver packets to all nearby vehicles with lesser congestion. Whereas in the Linear Mobility model in the event of an emergency, the vehicles do not choose the next available alternate path and this results in greater data traffic congestion. This makes the existing protocol less reliable to transmit high priority messages to destined vehicles.

4.3 Delay Analysis

From Fig. 7, the delay ratio is much less for the simulation environment with a greater number of vehicles compared to the one in which few vehicles are available for delivering packets. The delay ratio for 50 nodes is found as 13.4%, and for 10 nodes the value is found as 41% for Way-Point mobility model. This is obtained by setting a timeout value for retransmission of broadcasted messages until an implicit acknowledge received by the sender. The priority assigned broadcasted message reaches the sender within the timeout interval as an implicit acknowledgment. The retransmission limit is set to three, same as the existing PRP algorithm after which the broadcasted message gets dropped. This, in turn, increases the throughput and reduces the delay of the implemented protocol at the application layer.

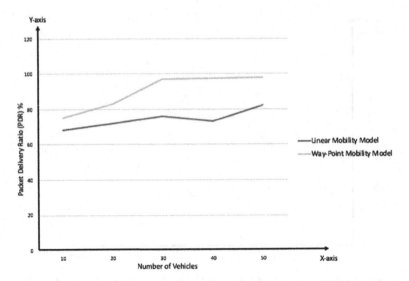

Fig. 6. Packet Delivery Ratio (PDR) graph of Enhanced Priority-based Routing Protocol (EPRP)

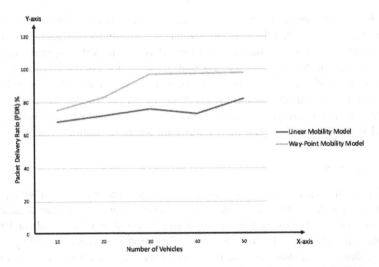

Fig. 7. Delay graph of Enhanced Priority-based Routing Protocol (EPRP)

5   Conclusion

We have proposed the implementation for Enhanced Priority-based Routing Protocol (EPRP) using way-point mobility model at the application layer. Also, the proposed work evaluates and compares the performance metrics for the implemented routing protocol using way-point mobility model and linear mobility model. The proposed work provides a QoS mechanism for message prioritization and counts data dissemination at last mile of the communication path. The simulation results exhibit that the highest priority messages are broadcasted first, and the vehicles take an alternate path in case of emergency. A significant improvement with reference to the network's throughput and packet delivery ratio is attained using implicit acknowledgement and retransmission technique.

In the future, we plan to implement the unicast, multicast, geocast and anycast routing using the same simulation scenario. As per the literature survey, a reliable and stable routing protocol appears to be a better solution to transmit data packets between source and destination using Reliability Index (RI) value. This protocol uses a reliability index which is updated as the vehicles move from one region to another region. Thus, this prediction-based routing considers the unstable nature of vehicles and offers a next best alternate routing path in the event of an emergency condition. The shortest routes between the vehicular nodes are roughly determined using vehicles speed and deterministic motion patterns. We can also employ cryptography techniques in this project to secure and verify the authenticity of the transmitted message.

References

1. Peng, H., Liang, L., Shen, X., Li, G.Y.: Vehicular communications: a network layer perspective. In: arXiv.org. Cornell University, New York (2017)
2. Dua, A., Kumar, N., Bawa, S.: A systematic review on routing protocol for vehicular ad hoc networks. Veh. Commun. 1(1), 33–52 (2014)
3. Brendha, R., Prakash, S.J.: A survey on routing protocols for vehicular ad hoc networks. In: 4th IEEE International Conference on Advanced Computing and Communication Systems, India (2017)
4. Tarapiah, S., Aziz, K., Atalla, S.: Analysis the performance of vehicles ad hoc network. In: 4th Information Systems International Conference, Indonesia (2017)
5. Zhou, H., Xu, S., Ren, D., Zhang, H.: Analysis of event-driven warning message propagation in vehicular ad hoc networks. Ad Hoc Netw. 55, 87–96 (2017)
6. Ren, M., Khoukhi, L., Labiod, H., Zhang, J., Veque, V.: A mobility-based scheme for dynamic clustering in vehicular ad-hoc networks (VANETs). Veh. Commun. 9, 233–241 (2017)
7. Suthaputchakun, C., Sun, Z.: Priority based routing protocol with reliability enhancement in vehicular ad hoc network. In: IEEE International Conference on Communications and Information Technology, Hammamet, Tunisia (2012)
8. Sivakumar, T., Manoharan, R., Kuppusamy, K.S.: A stable routing protocol for vehicular ad hoc networks. In: IEEE First International Conference on Networks & Soft Computing (2014)
9. Chaqfeh, M., Lakas, A.: Shortest-time route finding application using vehicular communication. In: IEEE WCNC 2014 Track 4 (Services, Applications, and Business) (2014)
10. Zhang, H., Wang, R., Larsson, T.: Simulation of region-based geocast routing protocols. In: IEEE International Conference on Connected Vehicles and Expo (ICCVE) (2014)
11. Liu, J., Wan, J., Qiao, Y.: A survey on position-based routing for vehicular ad hoc networks. Telecommun. Syst. 62(1), 15–30 (2016)
12. Singh, S., Agrawal, S.: VANET routing protocols: issues and challenges. In: IEEE Recent Advances in Engineering and Computational Sciences (RAECS), India (2014)

Author Index

Abbas, Safia I-43
Abd Latiff, Muhammad Shafie I-132
Abdelouhab, Fawzia Zohra II-201
Abdul Jalil, Masita I-99
Abel, Jürgen II-3
Abul Seoud, Rania Ahmed Abdel Azeem
  I-85
Abutile, Sarah II-126
Aguir, Khalifa II-286
Ahmad, Safaa II-241
AL Mansour, Hanan I-260
Alabdan, Rana II-144
Al-Akhras, Mousa II-241
Alalmaei, Shiyam II-265
Alamri, Rasha M. II-303
Alamro, Rawan I-317
Alanazi, Amal II-126
Alaskar, Lama I-301
Alawadh, Mohammed II-52
Alawadh, Monerah II-52
Alawairdhi, Mohammed II-241
Albrikan, Alanoud II-126
Aldossari, Amjad I-15
Alduailij, Mai I-301
Aleidi, Sumaya I-162
Alenazi, Azhar I-15
Alenazi, Tahani I-15
Algahtani, Ghada I-15
AlGarni, Abeer I-183, I-236
AlGuraibi, Norah II-228
Alhalawani, Sawsan I-148
AlHalawani, Sawsan I-170
Alhamdan, Ayah II-93
Alhamdan, Hanadi I-290
Alharbi, Lujain I-69
Alharthi, Haifa II-126
Alhenaki, Dana I-148
Aljamaan, Haneen II-228
Aljeaid, Dania I-69
Aljedaie, Alanoud M. I-57
Aljres, Rawan II-126
Aljulaud, Aseel II-228

Alkabkabi, Amal I-203
Alkhawaldeh, Abdullah A. K. I-119
Almuhajri, Mrouj I-275
Almuhana, Aljawharah M. I-57
Almutairi, Suad I-245
Alnabet, Nuha I-148
Alnanih, Reem II-40
Alrajebah, Nora I-162
Al-Rasheed, Amal I-211, I-317
Alrashidi, Bedour F. I-57
Alrobai, Amani I-224
Alrubaia, Reem II-126
Alrubaish, Fatimah A. II-303
Alrubei, Mariam II-228
Alsaiah, Anwar II-228
Alshaya, Sara I-211
Alsolai, Hadeel II-60
Alsuhaibani, Dalia I-162
Al-turaiki, Israa II-52
Altuwaijri, Sara II-93
Alzahrani, Hanaa II-40
Alzaid, Wafa I-15
Aoul, Nabil Tabet II-103
Atmani, Baghdad I-111, II-81, II-103,
  II-115, II-201

Bakali, Assia II-174
Bakara, Zuriana Abu II-30
Bashir, Mohammed Bakri I-132, II-71
Batouche, Mohamed II-161
Benamina, Mohamed I-111, II-81, II-115
Benbelkacem, Sofia I-111, II-81, II-115
Benfriha, Hichem II-103
Benhacine, Fatima Zohra II-81, II-201
Bezbradica, Marija I-245
Bouazza, Halima II-278, II-312
Boufama, Boubakeur II-161
Boughaci, Dalila I-3, I-119
Boughaci, Omar I-3
Brahimi, Samiha II-228
Broadbent, Matthew II-265
Broumi, Said II-174

Chelloug, Samia   II-265
Crane, Martin   I-301

Douah, Ali   II-103

Elamsy, Tarik   II-161
Elhussain, Mariam A.   II-303
ElMannai, Hela   I-183, I-236
Elsadig, Muna   II-252
Elsaid, Mayada   II-93
Elsaid, Shaimaa Ahmed   I-15, II-126
Elshakankiri, Maher   II-325

Hamdi, Monia   I-183, I-236
Hassan, M. M.   II-214
Humaid, Ghadah A.   II-303

Ismail, Suryani   I-99

Jilani, Musfira   I-224, I-290
John, Maya   I-193

Kenkar, Zubaydh   I-170
Khemliche, Belarbi   II-103
Kurdi, Heba   I-162

Lathamaheswari, Malayalan   II-174
Lundy, Michele   I-260

Maeeny, Samerah   I-15
Maher, Mohamed   II-214
Makram, Ibram   I-85
Mansoul, Abdelhak   I-111, II-115
Masmoudi, Mohamed   II-286
McCarren, Andrew   I-211, I-317
Mehdi, Ali   II-241
Menzli, Leila Jamel   II-252
Mohamad, Mumtazimah   I-99

Mohammad, Omer K. Jasim   I-43
Mohan, Amaliya Princy   II-325
Mohd, Fatihah   I-99
Mohemada, Rosmayati   II-30
Mostafa, Ayman Mohamed   II-185, II-214

Nagarajan, Deivanayagampillai   II-174
Nassar, Dua' A.   II-252
Nasser, Abanoub   I-85
Nebhen, Jamel   II-286
Noora, Noor Maizura Mohamad   I-99, II-30

Race, Nicholas   II-265
Rahajandraibe, Wenceslas   II-286
Rahim, Mohd Shafry Mohd   II-16
Roper, Marc   II-60
Roza, Rawand Abu   II-241

Said, Bachir   II-278, II-312
Salami, Fati Oiza   II-16
Shaheen, Sara M.   I-148
Shaiba, Hadil   I-193, I-245
Smarandache, Florentin   II-174
Suen, Ching   I-275
Suliman, Yusra Mohamed   II-71

Taileb, Mounira   I-203
Talea, Mohamed   II-174
Tallab, Shahad   II-52

Vidanagea, Kaneeka   II-30

Walke, Ashay   I-8

Yahya, Wan Fatin Fatihah   I-99
Yousif, Adil   I-132, II-71

Zohra, Laallam Fatima   II-278, II-312

Printed in the United States
By Bookmasters